Palestinian Politics after the Oslo Accords

Palestinian Politics after the Oslo Accords

Resuming Arab Palestine

NATHAN J. BROWN

University of California Press

BERKELEY   LOS ANGELES   LONDON

Portions of Chapter 3 previously appeared in *The Middle East Journal.*

University of California Press
Berkeley and Los Angeles, California
University of California Press, Ltd.
London, England
© 2003 by the Regents of the University of California

Library of Congress Cataloging-in-Publication Data
Brown, Nathan J.
  Palestinian politics after the Oslo accords : resuming Arab Palestine /
Nathan J. Brown.
    p.   cm.
  Includes bibliographical references and index.
  ISBN 0–520–23762–5
  1. National state.   2. Palestinian Arabs—Politics and government—
1993–   3. Palestinian National Authority.   I. Title.
JC311 .B766   2003
956.95'3054—dc21   2002154933

Manufactured in the United States of America

12   11   10   09   08   07   06   05   04   03
10   9   8   7   6   5   4   3   2   1

to Ariel and Eran

Contents

Preface

My professional interest in the topic of this book began in 1996 when I first read that the newly emerging Palestinian Authority was drafting a constitution. At the time, I was writing a book on Arab constitutional development, and the Palestinian experiment offered an opportunity to understand the process of constitution writing as it was occurring. I was able to follow the debates and the various drafts as they emerged, speak to some of the participants in the drafting process, and compare the Palestinian experience with that of other Arab societies. As my interest in the topic broadened, I began to see parallels between emerging patterns of Palestinian institutional development and those I had seen elsewhere in the Arab world (where my previous research had focused on Egypt and the Arab states of the Gulf).

I also became convinced that describing the Palestinian experience with an eye to both the domestic and the broader Arab perspective—rather than understanding Palestinian politics primarily through the prism of the conflict with Israel—would have several benefits. The approach would be fresh; it would more accurately capture the project of those involved in building Palestinian institutions as they themselves saw it; and it would produce far more germane comparisons than the implicit and explicit comparisons with Israel and the Zionist movement so much more common in English-language writings on the topic.

However, my personal interest in the topic of this books is so different from—and often the mirror opposite of—my professional interest that I avoided writing on the topic for a considerable time. First, my personal interest dates back far before 1996; indeed, I have been interested virtually all of my adult life. Second, as with many Americans, my initial fascination with politics in the Middle East grew out of an interest in the Arab-Israeli conflict (which my scholarly orientation suggested should not be overemphasized). Third, I have a strong hope (and conviction) that some version of Palestinian and Jewish nationalist aspirations can simultaneously be met. Some of the more enthusiastic advocates of both nationalist causes find this hope naïve; in the heated atmosphere of the conflict, many see such naïveté as hostility. This will undoubtedly lead some to conclude that I treat Palestinian politics with too much respect and empathy; others will feel that I display too little or that I gloss over the true obstacles to Palestinian national progress.

Aware that anyone who dares to write on the topic of Palestinian politics can make many people astonishingly angry, I simply eschewed any scholarly research on the subject for a long time. More generally, the problem was not that I did not care about Palestinian politics but that I cared too much; I was also convinced that offering a scholarly analysis in a volatile field would add little to highly polemicized debates.

In 1996, I began to change my mind for three reasons. First, the Oslo Accords greatly changed the atmosphere. They did not, of course, resolve the Arab-Israeli conflict, but they sufficiently confused matters that some of the more tired polemical positions began to disintegrate. I was therefore convinced that there was room for less partisan scholarship. And the prospect of directly observing processes that I had studied historically elsewhere in the Arab world was intellectually exciting. Finally—and ultimately most critically—I was interested (along with all members of my family) in living for a period in Israel. Given my past work in Arab societies, that made Palestinian politics the logical topic of my inquiry.

In 1999 and 2000, I conducted most of the research on which this book is based. I was supported partly by a Fulbright grant that involved teaching at Ben-Gurion University in Israel. In retrospect it seems odd that I was able to conduct research on Palestinian politics while affiliated with an Israeli university, but at the time no Palestinian or Israeli displayed the slightest discomfort with the arrangement. I owe thanks to the Fulbright program, to its administrators in Israel (at the United States Israel Educational Foundation, USIEF), and personally to several individuals who assisted me: Renee Taft, Joel Migdal, Harry Harding, and Jill Crystal in the United States; Shimon Arbel and Judy Stavsky at USIEF; and David Newman and Yoram Meital at Ben-Gurion University. My colleagues and students at Ben-Gurion University were warm and welcoming and deserve thanks as well. In addition to support from the Fulbright grant, I also received funding for this research for the United States Institute of Peace. Steve Riskin, April Hall, and Judy Barsalou at the institute have been supportive both bureaucratically and intellectually.

After returning from the region, I spent the 2000–01 academic year as a scholar in residence at the Middle East Institute. There I was able to write most of this manuscript and exchange views with its very hospitable staff. David Mack and Tamara Wittes are especially worthy of mention in this regard.

Of course, the conclusions in this book are my own, and the responsibility for its contents lies with me rather than with USIEF, the United States Institute of Peace, or the Middle East Institute.

I have been assisted in this research by some quite able student assistants. Kevin Kreutner, Maha Juweied, and Jessica Lieberman all helped me at George Washington University. At Ben-Gurion University, Muhammad al-'Atawneh arranged many meetings on the West Bank and proved a convivial and erudite companion at many of my interviews and a good friend since. His own scholarly interest focuses on Saudi Arabia, but he proved quite able in helping me a little closer to home.

I owe a debt to a large number of people for supplying critical information for this book. Among them are Ron Sheiko, Lauren Ross, David Meale, Alfred Khoury, Muhammad Shadid, Amy Hawthorne, Margaret Zacknoen, Maher Hashweh, Maria Traficanti, Chris George, 'Atiya Abu al-Murr, and 'Umar Abu al-Humus. Mustafa al-Mar'i responded with both accuracy and good cheer to a cascade of e-mail inquiries about the fine points of Palestinian law. All the individuals listed in the interview section of the bibliography deserve thanks as well; for all its problems, Palestinian society is very welcoming to foreign researchers with endless questions.

Partly because I began working on Palestinian politics with little previous background, I have prevailed on a large number of friends, colleagues, and acquaintances to read my work. In no particular order, I would like to thank Ibrahim Abu Lughod, Fouad Moughrabi, Nubar Hovsepian, David Matz, Agustin Velloso, Falk Pingel, Asem Khalil, Lewis Roth, Noam Shelef, Lara Friedman, Elie Podeh, Kathleen Christison, Philip Mattar, Khalil Mahshi, Walter Reich, Keith Schultz, Sheila Carapico, George Bisharat, Unni Kjus Aahlin, David Schenker, Sam Kaplan, and Ellen Kelly. In addition, I was able to present some of my research (and collect valuable comments) at conferences and events organized by the American Embassy in Tel Aviv in Gaza (arranged by Jihad al-Wazir and Julie Connor), the Hubert Humphrey Institute for Social Research at Ben-Gurion University, the Middle East Institute in Washington, and the Adam Institute in Jerusalem. At the University of California Press, Lynne Withey, Kate Warne, and Elisabeth Magnus helped turn the manuscript into a book in a timely and helpful manner.

My wife's own expertise in the subject matter of this book has improved its content; her editing skills have improved its presentation. And her interest in living in Israel meant that this book was no burden on my family obligations. Indeed, partly for that reason, I have dedicated the book to our children, Ariel and Eran. I would not have bothered to write it without them. I do not mean to say that I wrote it for them to read, though they are interested enough in its subject matter. But their own interest in living overseas for a year made it possible to write. Their easy integration into Israeli society as well as their easy understanding of—and interest in—their father's activities (much of which were conducted in Palestinian society) made it possible for me to conduct this research without neglecting my duties as a parent. As a father and as a scholar, I could never ask for more.

1 Resuming Arab Palestine

> The Palestinian state has existed since the days of the British
> Mandate.
>> YASIR 'ARAFAT to Bill Clinton at Camp David, Maryland,
>> July 2000, quoted in Akram Haniyya, "Camp David Papers"

> This is not the Palestine we dreamed of.
>> Professor at Bir Zayt University, 1999

In June 1999, an independent task force on Palestinian governance announced its final report in a press conference in Gaza. Sponsored by Henry
Seigman of the American Council on Foreign Relations and chaired by
Michel Rocard, the former French prime minister, the task force com-
manded the respectful attention of senior Palestinian officials. Yet the report
consisted of page after page of criticism of the operation of Palestinian political institutions and recommendations for sounder practices—couched in
diplomatic terms, to be sure, but amounting to a powerful indictment of current Palestinian practice. While the task force report was timed to coincide
with the end of the five-year transitional period established under the Oslo
Accords, the authors insisted that Palestinian political reform could take
place outside the context of relations with Israel: "Without prejudging the
outcome of negotiations between the PLO and Israel, this report recom-
mends reforms that are within the present powers of the Palestinian
Authority to implement even under adverse circumstances."[1]

While stung by the sheer number of criticisms and overwhelmed by the
number of recommendations, the senior Palestinian leadership was forced to
react. In August 1999, Palestinian President Yasir 'Arafat signed a decree
establishing a committee to "follow up" on the "Rocard and Seigman"
report, determine the "procedural measures needed for strengthening the
Palestinian institutions," and "present them to the Cabinet of Ministers for
approval."[2] The committee proceeded extremely slowly, though the Palestinian National Authority (PNA) continued to feel international pressure
over the report, with the recommendations raised at international conferences between the PNA and donor states.[3] The PNA submitted a position
paper in November 1999, lauding the task force report for providing a

"valuable opportunity" and detailing the planned work of the committee.[4] Two months later the committee seemed to score its first (and only) significant achievement when President 'Arafat signed a decree establishing a new economic council charged with ensuring that all PNA revenues entered the public treasury—a critical reform that outside donors had pressed for and a major recommendation of the task force report.[5] The first fruits of the reform came later in the year when the PNA reported frankly on its finances to a donor meeting in Lisbon, claiming that tax revenues were now flowing directly to the treasury as promised, and promising to end the practice of diverting public revenues to public companies without any accountability or oversight by the bodies responsible for public finance.[6]

Donors reciprocated by commending the PNA and offering assistance in other areas designed for reform, such as rule of law. Yet while intense scrutiny and constant pressure by donors led to some fiscal reform, the bulk of the task force recommendations resulted in no action whatsoever— leading the minister of public works to complain in February 2000 that the committee charged with reform had accomplished nothing.[7] And any further progress toward adopting the other recommendations in the report was effectively suspended by the eruption of the second *intifada* in September 2000: international donors scrambled along with the PNA to meet daily needs of the population; public finances were devastated; and some Palestinian institutions all but ceased functioning. In such a context, the ambitious reform agenda of the task force report seemed initially to have become completely irrelevant. Only in 2002 did the issue of reform again move to the center of domestic and international attention.

The story of the "Rocard report" or "Council on Foreign Relations report" (as it was widely known) at first glance appears to be simple: international donors, alarmed at corruption and inefficiency in the PNA, pressured for a series of reforms. They received some limited response in fiscal affairs but were stymied in any broader effort to reform an authoritarian system. Any progress made remained hostage to the broader context of Palestinian-Israeli relations and ultimately fell victim to the reversion to violence scarcely more than a year after the report was issued. Such an understanding renders Palestinian political reform a quixotic enterprise.

Yet a little digging into the domestic context of reform efforts enables us to develop an alternative perspective on the report, seeing it as part of a contest among Palestinians over the proper course for politics in their emerging state. The report carries the name of Michel Rocard and the Council on Foreign Relations, but its principal authors were Khalil Shikaki and Yazid Sayigh, Palestinian academics (one based in Palestine, the other in Britain).

They drew, to be sure, on international expertise on some matters, but they borrowed far more liberally from political debates among Palestinian intellectuals and political activists. When they turned outside the Palestinian context, they looked not only to the reports of the World Bank and the International Monetary Fund but also to the political experience of neighboring Arab states. Indeed, many Arab neighbors might have recognized their own governments' practices in the pages of the report, which could have been applied with fairly minor changes to most countries in the region.

Seen in this context, the report's primary contribution was to codify numerous issues, complaints, and proposals that had been raised in various Palestinian debates—most particularly in stormy sessions of the Palestinian Legislative Council (PLC). Numerous workshops and public meetings had been held, statements had been issued, and books had been published since the founding of the PNA in 1994 on the need for reforming Palestinian institutions and practices. The international sponsorship of the task force report was not irrelevant: it provided some teeth, some information (especially on economic policy and fiscal practices), and even some language. Yet the main contribution of the international sponsorship was to provide an external audience for a series of domestic Palestinian debates. The report's authors did not take their domestic audience by surprise, though some of their interests only puzzled international readers. For instance, their concentration on the proper relationship between the PNA and the Palestinian Liberation Organization (PLO), a frequent topic of Palestinian political discussion, appears arcane to many international observers. The report's insistence on the adoption of clear constitutional principles strikes many in the external audience as noble but legalistic and even naïve. Domestically, however, it has emerged as a constant refrain in internal Palestinian critiques of the record of the PNA. Indeed, those familiar with the process of drafting the report suggest that it was the international members of the task force who insisted on relaxing some of the demanding and critical tone of the report and acknowledging that the PNA was operating in a difficult international setting. The Palestinian participants remained less forgiving of their own officials and regarded the frequent reference to international conditions as an easy excuse for failure. For many Palestinians the realities of limited sovereignty and continued Israeli occupation hardly justified ignoring the need for viable public institutions and proper official practices; indeed, by demanding that PNA performance improve, the Palestinian authors regarded themselves as aiding rather than undermining the nationalist cause.

Their efforts were not always kindly received. The Palestinians who con tributed to the report seemed to be lending ammunition to international critics. Yet in less guarded or charged moments, leading Palestinian officials could sound similar themes. In May 1999, for instance (only a month before the release of the task force report), Information Minister Yasir 'Abd Rabbu reflected on the five years of PNA governance in an interview with a Palestinian daily. The mistakes he cited—the failure to develop Palestinian institutions and the need for greater concentration on fiscal reform, constitutionality, separation of powers, and functioning courts and legal institutions—could have served as an executive summary of the task force report. A high official in the Palestinian Preventive Security force admitted that the problem of the security services came from lack of oversight and legal framework: "The problem is that every apparatus thinks of and determines its jurisdiction in the manner it deems appropriate since there are no particular legislation or clear regulations in this regard. So there is a clash."[8] And in May 2002, three years after the report was issued, many of its themes were picked up by leading Palestinian officials anxious to assert that the PNA could reform itself.

Thus, the issues raised by the task force report had been debated by Palestinians nearly since the beginning of the PNA and hardly died when most of the report's recommendations were smothered by committees and subcommittees. Two years before the task force issued its report, the Palestinian General Control Institute had investigated financial and administrative practices in the PNA's new ministries. It reported its findings to the PLC, which was sufficiently shocked that it began its own investigation. Many of the abuses uncovered seem minor in comparison with regional practices—personal use of ministry cars, unaccounted international long distance calls, padded expense accounts. A few were more significant, such as use of border controls to divert business to relatives of senior officials. Far more remarkable than the corruption was the thorough public airing of specific charges, virtually unprecedented in Arab politics. The report prompted the PLC to call for dismissing the Palestinian cabinet, leading to a yearlong confrontation with President 'Arafat (see Chapter 4).

The struggle between the president and the PLC over corruption did make a few international headlines, but most similar contests have taken place in front of domestic audiences only. (Indeed, a World Bank study actually revealed levels of corruption that were low by the standards of other developing countries and regions—though the finding did little to undermine the PNA's sullied reputation on the issue.)[9] Palestinian chambers of commerce, most of which never elected new boards during the period of Israeli rule from 1967 to 1994, have attempted to revive themselves but have been discouraged by President 'Arafat from holding new elections. Palestinian teachers have launched two bitter wildcat strikes not only aimed at the conservative fiscal policies of the PNA but also demanding new forms of unionization and representation. A group of younger journalists bolted from the PLO-sponsored syndicate and were on the verge of forming a new, independent body—leading to a bitter generational conflict carried out in full public view—when the outbreak of the second intifada disrupted their efforts. Judges have combated the Ministry of Justice and each other over the best way to organize Palestinian judicial and legal affairs. Education ministry officials and Palestinian educators have engaged in a less heated but protracted debate over how to design a new curriculum and how Palestinian schoolchildren should be taught.

Understanding Palestinian politics in such areas solely as a creature of the conflict with Israel not only does a disservice to those involved in working for change but also risks seriously miscasting the issues. To be sure, no area of Palestinian politics can completely escape the external context for long. But that context at best conditions without determining outcomes. Other underlying patterns exist, and this book is an effort to understand and explain those patterns.

Palestinians are engaged in a series of contests and debates over what kind of Palestine they wish to build. What are the prospects for accountable governance, for democracy in any of its social and political senses, and for the rule of law? What do these things mean in a Palestinian context? What is the likely shape of Palestinian politics in the future?

The central theme of this book is that the struggle over defining Palestine concerns not how Palestinian politics should begin but over how it should be resumed: for Palestinians, the creation of the PNA was an act not of creation but of resumption. Palestine is understood—rightly or wrongly—not as a wholly new creation but as something built on a Palestinian past and present; it is shaped not simply by its relations with Israel but also by its history and its links with its Arab counterparts. Political struggles within the PNA concern how to resume Arab Palestine.

RESUMING ARAB PALESTINE

Much of Palestinian politics since the signing of the Oslo Accords has consisted of a struggle over how to build a Palestinian polity as detached as possible from the context of the struggle with Israel. For all of those involved in this struggle, the emerging Palestinian polity is not something wholly new; Palestine is seen as having a long and continuous history—punctuated, to be sure, by international and existential conflict but not wholly defined by that conflict. And Palestine as a political and social entity is seen not simply in the context of its own history but also in an Arab context.

Yet resuming Arab Palestine can be accomplished in many different ways. Palestinian politics since the signing of the Oslo Accords has concerned three very different, often conflicting, senses of *resumption:* resuming Palestine as a political entity, resuming Palestine's Arab identity, and resuming normal politics. Each of these views is based on a different vision of Palestine's past and its present—visions that are not necessarily contradictory, though they suggest different strategies for the future. All are based on politically informed readings of history, as are all nationalist narratives. Yet while they might therefore be seen as tendentious, they involve more than a simplistic insistence on the timelessness of the Palestinian nation (though, as we shall see when considering the educational curriculum, such a nationalist reading of history has appeared in the PNA). All accept the existence of a distinct Palestinian nation, its membership in the broader Arab nation, and the legitimacy of the nationalist struggle.

Resuming Palestine as a Political Entity

According to the first sense of *resumption,* the project of the nascent Palestinian state is not to repudiate Palestinian history but to complete it. In this view, Palestine was created as a distinct political entity under the British mandate, when it built its own institutions, laws, and practices. There are, to be sure, many different ways to view the mandate period: for the Zionist movement at the time, the mandate was a period of building Jewish institutions, initially with the support but eventually in spite of the British authorities. To view mandate institutions as the basis for an Arab state of Palestine seems anachronistic. Indeed, from a Palestinian standpoint, the policies of the British mandate were doubly flawed. First, they were enacted by British authorities hardly accountable to the Palestinian population in any way. Second, the mandate carried with it a British commitment to assist the establishment of a Jewish national home in Palestine, a development Palestinian leaders have always regarded as inimical to their own interests.

Despite its fatal flaws from a Palestinian perspective, however, the British mandate still saw the establishment of schools, courts, and other institutions. The period of the mandate also witnessed the crystallization of Palestinian national identity, which had begun in the late Ottoman period.[10] The task of the Palestinian national movement is—according to this view— to assert Palestinian control over these institutions so that they can develop according to Palestinian, rather than British or Zionist, needs.

Seen this way, the Palestinian defeat in 1948 radically reconfigured the political situation, but it did not erase all mandatory-era institutions and practices. When Transjordan annexed the West Bank (creating the country of Jordan), it assumed control over Palestinian political institutions in the area, giving them an Arab flavor but not a specifically Palestinian one. Egypt allowed greater expression for Palestinian nationalist sentiments under its administration of the Gaza Strip, though in many ways Egyptian control was less liberal than Jordanian. Both adopted rather than erased most mandatory-era institutions.

A new set of political institutions was created in exile, most of which were coordinated, if not dominated, by the PLO after its establishment in 1964. In 1967, the West Bank and Gaza fell under Israeli control. While Israeli occupation policies often greatly constricted the opportunities for Palestinian institutions to operate, they also allowed the West Bank and Gaza to develop increasingly autonomously of Jordan and Egypt (Jordanian connections to West Bank institutions were far less easily broken than Egyptian, however; in some areas they continue even today). Most West Bank and Gazan institutions gravitated toward the PLO; in the mid-1980s the PLO returned the favor by working to support Palestinian institutions in the West Bank and Gaza.

The Oslo Accords, negotiated between 1993 and 1995, can be read as if they construct a new entity, the Palestinian Authority, to administer Palestinians in the West Bank and Gaza through an interim period during which permanent arrangements are negotiated. Yet Palestinians involved in negotiating the accords, and in subsequently building the PNA, never regarded the negotiations as the source of Palestinian institution building or legitimacy. Many saw those agreements as important steps in obtaining Israeli and international recognition but did not see them as constituting Palestinian politics. Nor did they wish the content of the agreements to shape Palestinian political development any more than necessary. The PNA showed little interest in fostering ties with Israel and Israeli institutions beyond what was necessary to make the economy and the Oslo Accords function, sometimes in a minimal way. Some provisions (such as a joint legal committee empowered to review Palestinian legislation) were allowed to wither away, neglected because of their implied limitations on Palestinian freedom of action.

What legitimacy the PNA claimed domestically came from its derivation from the PLO. The task of the PNA was therefore not to build new institutions from the beginning—indeed, the predicament for Palestinian politics was that there were so many diverse and overlapping institutions. Instead, the task was to knit together a disparate set of institutions that had grown up in different settings. West Bank and Gazan law had developed in different directions, but both were equally Palestinian. The PLO had even developed some of its own legal tradition in exile. Professional associations and labor unions had emerged but were generally divided according to location (West Bank, Gaza, and exile). A network of schools educated Palestinians in the West Bank and Gaza, but the curriculum in Gaza was copied from Egypt, while West Bank schools still followed Jordan.

Whether writing a constitution, a new law, or a textbook, PNA officials could claim a history of Palestinian (or, at a minimum, Arab) antecedents on which to draw. Those seeking to build security forces or professional associations had antecedent organizations as well—in the West Bank, Gaza, or the PLO (or all three). Those antecedents rarely gave full expression to Palestinian national identity and current needs, but they could serve as the starting point for future development. And those antecedents—especially those associated with the PLO—were treated with respect by those responsible for developing Palestinian institutions.

Palestine, in this project, has been seen not as an abstract dream but as a real—though interrupted—national and political entity. Palestinian political institutions have been portrayed as having authentic antecedents that need only be revived or redirected toward nationalist ends. This is, to be sure, a very retrospective reading of history, one that imposes a nationalist narrative on a very complicated past. According to this vision, Palestinians are merely assuming control over a set of institutions with a continuous history. These institutions constitute expressions of Palestine's Arab nature. To be sure, they need to be developed, unified, and updated; they also need to be freed from the limitations placed upon them by exile and three decades of Israeli occupation.

Resuming Palestine's Arab Identity

Since signing the first Oslo Accord in 1993, the Palestinian leadership has sought to ground institutional development, not in the agreements with Israel, but instead in the much older process of state building in the Arab world. Where Palestinian antecedents were insufficient or needed to be updated, PNA officials tended to turn to the examples set by Arab countries, especially Jordan and Egypt. The project of the PNA was therefore not simply to resume development of Palestinian institutions but to ensure full Palestinian participation in the Arab world. To some extent, West Bankers tended to look to Jordan while Gazans looked to Egypt. Broader international models were also generally considered (in anything from law to education), but Arab models generally seemed most familiar and fit most comfortably. The structure of the PNA's ministries, the language of its laws, the uniforms of its security forces, the prose of its newspapers, and the structuring of its curriculum had their counterparts elsewhere in the Arab world. Anyone familiar with Arab political and social practices would find much familiar under PNA rule.

The emphasis on the Arab dimension should not be overstated: Palestinian nationalists (at least from the mid-1960s onward) focused on developing an identity partly distinct from a broader Arab national identity. And Palestinians were aware, of course, of the uniqueness of some aspects of their political experience. Many were also conscious that authoritarian political forms common in the Arab world were being imported into Palestinian political practice along with other aspects of Arab political practice. Even those critical of such measures, however, often spoke in terms of presenting different possibilities for Arab politics, of showing positive examples to other Arab states. For them, there was some reason for hope that Palestinian politics could be Arab politics with a difference. The PNA was attempting to assert its rule over a population that had not accommodated itself to earlier political authorities and over a society that had learned to organize its own affairs without (indeed, in spite of) the authority of the Israeli occupation. This would lead Palestinian politics to evolve in a less authoritarian manner than the Arab norm.

The parallels with the broader Arab experience were often far deeper than many Palestinians realized. Most Arab states experienced forms of colonialism that, however intrusive, never extinguished local initiative and precolonial practices; few colonial powers succeeded in eliminating (or even tried to eliminate) all indigenous participation in politics and policy making. And few Arab states received independence completely and unambiguously; instead, it came out of a protracted and indeterminate process. The PNA—which found itself working around, confronting, avoiding, and outmaneuvering Israel and some Oslo provisions—was building a state in a way that Syrians looking to the 1940s or Egyptians looking to the 1920s and 1930s might find quite familiar.

Writings on Palestinian society and politics often include an explicit or implicit comparison with the Zionist movement and Israel.[11] Such a comparison is understandable, but it risks missing much of the context in which Palestinian national efforts are occurring. A comparison between Palestinians and the rest of the Arab world is often far more appropriate for two reasons. First, it captures far better the way that Palestinians themselves envision their task. For most Palestinian officials, the point is not to emulate Israel but to preserve an identity and set of institutions that are both Palestinian and Arab. Rashid Khalidi has written:

> For Palestinians the contrast could not be greater: they have yet to achieve self-determination, independence, or statehood; they are only now painfully integrating their feeble parastate, which grew up in exile, into an administration with the limited powers the Israelis allow them; they have an economy in a shambles after three decades of occupation and several years of *intifada* (which probably had as devastating an impact on the Palestinian economy as did the 1936–39 revolt); they control virtually no resources and have no real allies in the world. The Palestinians, of course, do have one asset in spite of everything: a powerful sense of national identity, which we have seen they were able to develop and maintain in spite of extraordinary vicissitudes.
>
> Palestinian identity, however, is not now and never has been defined solely by the conflict with Zionism and Israel.[12]

Second, a comparison with other Arab countries reveals strong similarities in both form and content. The emerging (or reemerging) Palestinian political, legal, and educational systems will be readily recognizable to Kuwaitis, Algerians, or Egyptians as variations of their own.

Resuming Normal Politics

There was a third and very different sense in which Palestinian politics under the PNA was marked by resumption: for many Palestinians (especially, but not exclusively, for those outside official PNA positions), the establishment of an autonomous authority provided a signal to resume normal political life, emerging after the decades-long dominance of the politics of national liberation. No longer were nationalist concerns and demands for unity to determine all aspects of Palestinian politics.

This attitude was not motivated by the conviction that the Oslo Accords had solved the conflict with Israel. Indeed, many of those advocating resumption of normal life opposed the accords or (more often) felt powerless to affect the outcome of Palestinian-Israeli negotiations. But the failure to resolve nationalist issues was not to hamstring development of Palestinian life in many areas. Indeed, for some it became almost a nationalist imperative to build institutions removed as much as possible from the Oslo Accords and the limitations on Palestinian sovereignty that they implied.

The most internationally visible manifestations of this attitude came in documents like the Rocard task force report (which insisted that serious political reform did not have to wait for the outcome of Palestinian-Israeli negotiations) and in the reports of human rights organizations (which showed little willingness to allow the prevailing security situation to explain persistent PNA human violations). Senior PNA officials, many of whom had a background in high leadership positions in the PLO, often treated such demands as virtually treasonous when they were aimed primarily at an international audience. Most noteworthy in this regard was the *bayan al-ʿashrin* or Statement of Twenty, signed in 1999 by a group of Palestinian intellectuals, political leaders, and dissidents, denouncing the PNA in unusually harsh terms as following "a systematic methodology of corruption, humiliation and abuse against the people."[13] The release of the statement to foreign press agencies, its publication in Syria, and its naming of President ʿArafat provoked a strong reaction and the arrest of most of the signatories not enjoying parliamentary immunity. The PLC, a frequent forum for airing allegations of corruption, refused to back the petition, issuing a statement condemning "the incitement against the name of the symbol of the Palestinian revolution, Abu ʿAmmar, the elected president of Palestine and the PLO and the PNA and the Palestinian people."[14]

Such highly visible controversies—and the ferocious responses they sometimes provoked—often obscured a far more steady and widespread series of efforts to render Palestine a normal political entity. Some leaders of professional associations strove to serve their members better by concentrating on pension funds and licensing rather than political statements. Chambers of commerce sought to educate members about commercial law and marketing rather than serving as rallying points for resistance to Israel. Lower-level labor activists sought to oust those who had achieved positions of leadership when unions were primarily aimed at organizing Palestinians against the Israeli occupation. The PLC insisted on reviewing the PNA budget and obtaining a complete accounting of all expenditures instead of allowing the president a free hand to dispose of Palestinian funds according to national or revolutionary needs. Educators sought to develop a sense of participant citizenship through the school system and develop a national identity based on imagining an unproblematic Palestine, similar to all other states.

The senior Palestinian leadership—schooled in PLO and exile politics and concentrating on nationalist goals—generally exhibited little sympathy with this approach, but those working to construct a normal Palestine were to be found in many areas of Palestinian society: nongovernmental organizations (NGOs), professional associations, the legal community, and the PLC. Their accomplishments were real but often hostage to the same Palestinian-Israeli relationship that they were trying to escape or ignore.

THE NATURE OF THE EMERGING PALESTINIAN STATE

Palestinian political life is characterized by overlapping institutions, confused chains of command, and a multiplicity of authorities. Indeed, Palestinians frequently complain, with considerable justification, that this situation is more than a historical accident; it is a strategy by the leadership to maximize maneuverability. The complicated and ambiguous set of institutions is not simply a political strategy, however; it is also a product of the Palestinian political experience over the past several decades. Since the signing of the Oslo Accords in 1993, a whole new set of structures has been created, mandating that an account of current Palestinian politics begin with a brief overview of the structures and features of the emerging Palestinian state. While the central theme of this book is to ground our understanding of Palestinian politics primarily in a Palestinian and broader Arab context, we cannot forget that the Oslo Accords, interpreted elastically by all sides, have provided important constraints (and some opportunities) for Palestinian institutional development.

While there were some Palestinian efforts to establish a state after the termination of the British mandate over Palestine in 1948, those efforts proved abortive. A provisional All Palestine Government had been established, and that body managed to convene a Palestinian National Council (PNC), which met in Gaza in 1948. But the combination of military defeat and inter-Arab rivalries effectively robbed these attempts of any effectiveness. In 1964, an entirely new PNC met in Jerusalem; acting with Egyptian and Arab support, it established a new body, the PLO. In the wake of the 1967 war, the PLO gained legitimacy in Palestinian eyes, especially after a new generation of political activists, led by Yasir 'Arafat, assumed control over the organization. By 1974, the PLO was declared by the Arab League as the "sole legitimate representative of the Palestinian people." In 1988, the PNC, meeting in Algiers, declared the existence of an independent Palestinian state. Lacking control of any territory, the declaration had limited effect, though the PLO did take on increased trappings of statehood. The PLO continues to be recognized by virtually all Palestinian political groups as the body that represents all Palestinians throughout the world.

The Oslo Accords, negotiated between 1993 and 1995 between Israel and the PLO, were signed by Yasir 'Arafat for the PLO. The first agreement, the September 1993 Declaration of Principles, referred to the establishment of a Palestinian Interim Self-Government Authority and to a synonymous Palestinian Council. Subsequent agreements introduced the term *Palestinian Authority*. Palestinian political terminology departs slightly but significantly from that of the Oslo Accords—the term used in official documents for the body is the *Palestinian National Authority* (PNA). (The council referred to in the documents does exist but styles itself the PLC, part of the PNA (indeed, its legislative branch) but not synonymous with it.

Despite this history, the PNA presents itself to Palestinians not as a body created by bilateral agreements but as an authority deputized by the PLO to administer those areas of the West Bank and Gaza controlled by Palestinians, pending the formal declaration of a Palestinian state by the PLO. (The 1988 declaration is still in effect for Palestinians; a subsequent declaration would merge the PNA and the state of Palestine into a single body, perhaps absorbing the PLO as well.)

Yet if the PNA's leaders worked to ground their state in the PLO and popular legitimacy, they could still not escape most of the provisions of the Oslo Accords and the consequent limitations on sovereignty. Those accords provided for progressive (though vaguely defined) Israeli redeployment in the West Bank and Gaza. Even the ambiguous provisions of the accords have not been fully implemented, leaving the PNA with effective control over all Palestinian towns in the West Bank and Gaza, though Israel still controls the entrances to those towns (and, in the case of Hebron, a significant enclave within the city itself) as well as all of Jerusalem. In 2002, Israel reoccupied parts of many Palestinian cities for sustained periods. The PNA also administers most areas of civilian life (such as education) for Palestinians in the West Bank and Gaza, even those who live under Israeli security control (indeed, the PNA does effectively operate in some areas of Jerusalem).

Yet while the PNA has been able to assume control of most governmental institutions (such as schools and courts) and establish some new ones (such as security forces), it has been limited in many respects. The territorial limitations on Palestinian authority are the most visible and, during times of political conflict, the most debilitating. (They allow Israel to close off all access to—and even occupy at will—Palestinian areas and limit travel among various towns, sometimes—in the case of Gaza—for years.) Not only land but also critical water resources remain under Israeli control. There are other, less visible but perhaps equally significant limitations as well. Palestinian economic and fiscal policy is extremely sharply constrained by the Oslo Accords (especially the 1994 Paris Protocol on economic relations). Perhaps most critically for a would-be state, the PLO agreed to have rates of taxation fixed by Israel, and indeed, much of the tax collection apparatus remains in Israeli hands.[15] The results were not entirely negative prior to 2000, because they resulted in a far healthier fiscal situation for the PNA than would otherwise have been the case, but they still resulted in restrictions on decision making that PNA leaders found noxious on both nationalist and policy grounds. With the outbreak of the intifada, the dependence on Israeli tax collection became far more than annoying: Israel suspended transfer payments, plunging the PNA deeply into deficit and transforming it into a supplicant (chiefly with Arab and European states), pleading for operating funds on a continuous basis.

Despite such limitations, the PNA immediately began operating as if it were a state. It established a series of ministries, an ideological apparatus (with its own broadcasting), and a body of legislation. If a Palestinian wished to travel from Gaza to Ramallah, it was still impossible to ignore the limitations on statehood. However, if a Palestinian went to school, to court, or to apply for a business license, the PNA appeared to be a virtual state. And Palestinians began to complain about the PNA not only because of the ways in which its actions were limited but also because of the way in which it acted: the PNA could be oppressive and corrupt in ways unconnected with the Oslo Accords. To be sure, relations with Israel sometimes maximized such behavior (especially in suppressing Islamist movements), but many Palestinians worried that the patterns set by the PNA augured ill for full statehood, and they redoubled their efforts to foster the development of structures and practices suitable for normal political life.

TAKING PALESTINE SERIOUSLY

Indeed, it might be said that if there is any problem with the perspective adopted in this book, it is that it minimizes the flaws and limitations in Palestinian state-building efforts; in a word, it takes Palestine as a state in the making too seriously. The PNA is so constricted in its actions, according to many of its critics, that it should be viewed as a thinly veiled continuation of the Israeli occupation. A more charitable view—adopted by many senior Palestinian leaders—holds that the realities of the occupation are such that the nationalist issue must remain paramount for all Palestinians. To concentrate on domestic issues is to risk dividing the nation at a time when it faces its most fateful choices. The demands of national unity are such that issues of governance, democracy, and corruption should not be raised too forcefully. Seen from such perspectives, a book placing domestic politics at the center would be premature, politically naïve, or an apology for an unjust peace. These alternative views—that the internal focus is unwarranted— have their own sharp political edge, of course, either hostile to or supportive of the current Palestinian leadership.[16]

Yet here a comparison with the history of other Arab countries is instructive: the Palestinian experience with institution building fits previous patterns in the Arab world more closely than such critics might suspect. With a few exceptions, most Arab states emerged slowly from imperial rule, with external powers ceding authority only gradually and sometimes after protracted struggle. Arab political patterns and institutions did not emerge suddenly with independence but carried over from the preindependence period. In other words, recent Palestinian history seems more than vaguely familiar when viewed in Arab perspective.

Indeed, many political institutions in the Arab world today—including courts, militaries, schools, and constitutions—were created in a period of contested sovereignty, immediately before, during, or shortly after imperial rule. If all political institutions founded under such conditions were dismissed as easily as some have dismissed PNA institutional development, then students of Arab politics would be left with little to understand.

A few examples can illustrate the point. In Egypt, a new court structure was begun in the late nineteenth century at a time of heavy foreign political and economic pressure and to some extent was negotiated with European powers. Reform continued after the British occupation of 1882. Lebanon's current constitution is an amended version of the document first adopted under the French mandate. Many Arab states wrote their legal codes while under colonial rule. Most current Arab school systems were similarly founded under European control. The structures and institutions that resulted in all these instances were not simply products of European imperialism (though their development was heavily conditioned by European control).

The Palestinian case also resembles its Arab counterparts in the protracted and contested achievement of statehood. Egypt may provide the best parallel. Like Israel in the West Bank and Gaza, Great Britain never annexed Egypt even as its presence became increasingly intrusive. Some measure of Egyptian role in governance never ceased throughout the British occupation. When Britain decided to withdraw from Egypt—partly in response to a popular uprising in 1919—it subjected its 1922 acceptance of Egyptian independence to four reservations (involving the Suez Canal, foreigners, foreign and security policy, and the Sudan). Full British acceptance of Egyptian sovereignty took over a decade to negotiate, and British troops remained in the country until the 1950s. The French acceptance of Syrian and Lebanese independence was less drawn out, but it was equally complicated (with the French government negotiating a treaty with both countries, the French parliament rejecting it, and Vichy forces fighting Free French forces for control of the territory in World War II).

Egyptians, Syrians, Lebanese, and citizens of other Arab countries did not suddenly enter their own history upon formal independence; their efforts to build their own institutions were not solely (or even primarily, even under imperial rule) a product of the independence struggle. And imperial powers often shaped institutional development in a negative way: local populations found ways to operate that minimized or undermined imperial authority.

The Palestinian experience with attempting to build autonomous institutions under fairly constricting international circumstances sometimes displays not only general parallels with previous Arab experiences but also very specific similarities in issues and sequences. Like the Oslo Accords, the unilateral British declaration of Egyptian independence of 1922 allowed considerable Egyptian autonomy in internal governance and administration but still provided for continued British influence on legal and security matters. British troops remained in Egypt, controlling critical locations, and intervened in domestic politics (in fairly heavy-handed fashion, including the use of force, though not as extensively as Israel did in the second intifada). And Egyptians reacted to the British role in many of the same ways that the Palestinians now react to continued Israeli presence in Palestinian political life: striving to build institutions that avoided, circumvented, or minimized the British role.

In short, most Arab states were built in circumstances not all that far removed from the Palestinian experience except in time (and arguably degree). External control and influence certainly affected the development of Arab political institutions, but it did not narrowly determine that effort, nor is the study of Arab politics—either before or since imperial control—tantamount to an apology for imperialism. Much Palestinian political energy since 1993 has been expended on making Israel less relevant to Palestinian lives; the many failures and limited successes of such efforts in many areas should not obscure their existence or the real changes that they have brought about. The emerging state of Palestine is following its Arab predecessors in establishing political practices and institutions in a difficult and contested international setting. This book will not ignore that setting, but it seeks to place Palestinians at the center of their own history and politics.

Five areas of emerging Palestinian practices and institutions will receive detailed attention. The first three areas involve the basic structures of politics: the legal framework, the constitution (in theory and in practice), and the legislative process. Chapter 2, on the legal framework, focuses on the struggle to resume Palestinian legal development after the creation of the PNA. Chapter 3 turns attention to the contest over defining the basic constitutional framework for the PNA and the prospective state. Chapter 4 focuses on the PLC, the first legislative body with exclusively Palestinian membership.

The next two chapters turn to broader social areas. Chapter 5 focuses on state-society relations and associational life under the PNA, examining NGOs and professional associations. Chapter 6 concerns education and controversies surrounding the attempt to write a Palestinian national curriculum.

In tracing the course of Palestinian political life in all these arenas, references will be made to broader efforts at understanding the rule of law, democracy, and state-society relations. Recent scholarship in political science (and some older scholarship) enriches our understanding and provides us useful tools for understanding Palestinian politics. This book is not, however, an attempt to construct or even test such theoretical ideas in any formal fashion. The approach is far more eclectic and is aimed not at building theory but at understanding Palestinian politics.

2 The Legal Framework

Disputing in, over, and outside Courts

As far as we are concerned, we are a Palestinian state.
'ARIJ AL-'AWDA, Department of Legal Affairs,
Ramallah Governorate, in personal interview,
March 2000

The PNA moved immediately in the legal realm to reaffirm its continuity with the past and resume the construction of a legal framework along lines similar to those in neighboring Arab countries. Its strong (though not unlimited) success in this effort has now brought Palestinians to face a new set of choices about the role of law in Palestinian society and governance.

The argument presented in this chapter stands in partial contrast to most writings on Palestinian legal developments since 1993. Only those constrained by diplomatic concerns have withheld the sharpest of judgments. For most observers, Palestinian officials inherited an impossible situation and made it worse.

THE HISTORICAL AND POLITICAL CONTEXT OF EFFORTS TO DEVELOP PALESTINIAN LAW

The impossible situation was created, it is often claimed, by the strange welter of laws inherited from the various authorities claiming legislative power in Palestine during this century: the Ottoman Empire, the British mandate, the Egyptian administration of Gaza, the Jordanian annexation of the West Bank, and the Israeli military occupation (and its civil administration). It is not simply claimed that the result is a mongrel because of the very different legal traditions combined. Palestinian law, according to this view, is not one mongrel but two: since 1948, Gaza and the West Bank developed in different directions. One observer claims: "Unifying two distinct legal systems is a challenge Palestinians face with few precedents to draw on; no decolonized country has had to undertake quite such a task in the legal sector before."[1] After 1967 the Palestinian legal system began to atrophy: Israeli military courts steadily encroached on the jurisdiction of the Palestinian courts, and the military government starved them of resources.[2] A United Nations–sponsored report summed up the situation: "In essence, the Palestinian Authority inherited a system which was decades old, and burdened with an incompatible mix of different legal systems. Compounding the problem were the decades of neglect of the aging physical infrastructure, lacking the most basic equipment."[3]

The PNA is often held to have made this confusing situation worse by avoiding any clear indication of what law it would enforce. Instead, the PNA has issued confusing signals and mixed various legislative enactments from the past without clear consistency. New legislative enactments are issued without clear bases. Perhaps most ominous, in some areas the PNA seems to operate outside any legal framework whatsoever: security services, for instance, arrest citizens without any clear authority to do so and ignore orders from courts and resolutions from the PLC calling for release of those extralegally detained.

Critics of the PNA do not hold it solely responsible for undermining whatever legal framework survived occupation: Palestinian agreements with Israel and intense international pressure are often held responsible for pushing Palestinian leaders completely outside the law. A state security court was quickly erected to try those accused of violence against Israeli targets. The court shocked many by holding trials immediately after an arrest, often in the middle of the night, and without any clear procedures or safeguards. Despite such behavior, U.S. Vice President Al Gore greeted the creation of the court as a positive step in a widely noted statement in 1995.[4] Four years later, an exasperated Palestinian Justice Minister Farih Abu Mudayn exclaimed, "When the High Court releases someone, the Israelis and Americans immediately start talking of the revolving door; that we are letting terrorists out. We are between the Israeli hammer and the anvil of the law."[5]

There is little reason to deny that the PNA inherited a complicated legal structure and operated it under international pressure. But the argument presented in this chapter places greater stress on continuity, development, and domestic politics, thus departing from past writings on Palestinian law. While the contrast is strong, there is no absolute contradiction. Indeed, a quick overview of the standard portrait emerging from these other writings reveals that they are not inaccurate by any means, though they sometimes contain exaggeration or overlook critical developments.

First, the claim that the PNA faced an impossibly confused legal situation overstates the incompatibility among the various legal traditions informing Palestinian law. The Palestinian situation was indeed confused but not unusually so: societies trying to integrate *shari'a*-based law with positive law have faced far more vexatious issues, as have those where various pre-colonial methods for settling disputes survived. In particular, the distinction between Gaza and West Bank law is overdrawn: provisions and terminology often varied, but both reflected a strong measure of Egyptian (and civil law) influence on a British mandatory basis.[6] The difference between the two systems may have been comparable to that between England and Scotland or Louisiana and Alabama. As will be seen, the conflict between West Bank and Gaza law was far more political (as each legal community clung to its preferred terminology and practice) than intellectual or doctrinal.

Second, the claim that the PNA failed to clarify the legal situation is similarly exaggerated. While the constitutional framework remained deliberately ambiguous, in most areas the PNA has clearly indicated the applicable law. Its approach to doing so—selecting provisions from the laws of Jordan, Gaza, the British mandate, and Israeli military orders—has indeed been eclectic and often authoritarian and illiberal, but it has been clear. And while it is true that the PNA has disregarded any law whatsoever in cases connected with security (and some other issues as well), it has also begun to lay the legal framework for its authoritarian practices, along patterns followed elsewhere in the Arab world. If there is anything unusual about the Palestinian case in contrast with its Arab neighbors, it is that the PNA has not developed authoritarian legal tools more quickly, preferring extralegal procedures for the present.

Third, the charge that the agreements with Israel and international pressure explain the pervasiveness of extralegal actions is true, but to a lesser extent and in a different way than is usually claimed. Legal development in the PNA has been designed to maximize Palestinian legal autonomy. The PNA has moved completely outside any legal framework on some matters, but it has more often been motivated by a desire to work around the restrictions in the Oslo Accords than to implement them. At other times, it has acted extralegally for its own reasons, unrelated to international pressure.

In short, the sharp criticisms of PNA legal practice, though they do have some basis, do not undermine the themes of this book. Two aspects of PNA legal development will receive extended attention: courts and the framework of laws. In both areas, the PNA's legal efforts have aimed at resumption in the first two senses used in this book. First, continuity with Palestine's Arab past has served as a fundamental legal vision informing current efforts. Second, the PNA has actively worked to rely on the legal experience and practices of other Arab systems in developing its legal framework. Resumption in the third sense—resuming normal political life—has left far stronger intellectual than institutional traces. Members of the PNA's otherwise fractured legal community advocate such an effort, and, while their work has had significant effects, their success is both modest and double-edged.

To understand how the PNA's legal efforts aim at resumption, especially in the first two senses used in this book, our attention will turn first to the court system. An examination of the framework of Palestinian law will follow.

PALESTINIAN COURTS: RESUMPTION, DEVELOPMENT, AND MARGINALIZATION

Courts in the Arab world have proved to be extremely enduring structures. A few Arab court systems have disappeared or had their work absorbed into other systems (such as Egypt's mixed courts, shari'a courts in Kuwait and Egypt, and joint British-Arab courts in the Arab states of the Gulf), but most have proven far less mortal than their creators. New regimes may remold their structures and jurisdiction or supplement them with new judicial bodies, but they very rarely eliminate them.

Palestinian courts are no exception to this pattern.[7] Despite the extremely tumultuous nature of Palestinian politics in the twentieth century, the courts showed remarkable staying power. The first efforts of the PNA were aimed not at creating new courts but at assuming control over existing ones and restoring levels and areas of jurisdiction that the Israeli occupation had removed.

The current Palestinian system of civil courts had its origins in the late Ottoman period and the British mandate.[8] The remnants of that system were continued under the Egyptian administration of Gaza and the Jordanian government in the West Bank. (The Israeli court system is based on identical Ottoman and British antecedents, leading to some odd parallels in the Israeli and Palestinian judicial structures.) Some changes were introduced (most notably, the West Bank system was fully integrated into the Jordanian). Yet the basic structure remained similar. The Palestinian court system had several levels: single-judge magistrate courts *(mahakim al-sulh)* stood as courts of original jurisdiction for smaller cases; multijudge district courts *(al-mahakim al-markaziyya* or *mahakim al-bidaya)* were the first to hear larger cases. An appeals court *(mahkamat al-isti'naf)* heard cases from both of the lower-level courts. This appeals court could also form a High Court, which adjudicated administrative cases (chiefly those for which a state body was a party). Until 1967, and for the West Bank only, there was an additional tier: the Jordanian *makhamat al-tamyiz* in 'Amman sat as the highest court of appeals. Before 1967, a chief justice *(qadi al-quda)* headed the courts in Gaza; the Jordanian judicial council administered the system on the West Bank. Shari'a courts stood alongside the civil *(nizami)* court system for personal status cases.

While the Israeli military administration treated the West Bank and Gaza as distinct territories, its practices remained fairly similar in both places. The courts continued to operate, but certain matters were removed from their jurisdiction. At first, the most significant matters withdrawn from Palestinian courts were related to Israel (for which Israeli military courts operated); Palestinian courts were expressly forbidden from considering cases against the state of Israel or its employees. As the occupation wore on, more matters were transferred from the Palestinian courts to the military courts. The business of the Palestinian courts steadily diminished, and that of the High Courts was particularly affected. Israel also moved to detach the West Bank court system from the Jordanian, barring appeals to the mahkamat al-tamyiz in 'Amman (and eventually allowing appeals to the Israeli High Court). The West Bank Court of Appeals was moved from Jerusalem to Ramallah. In addition, Israeli lawyers were allowed to practice in the Palestinian courts. An officer of the Israeli military occupation (and after 1981 the civil administration) oversaw the system, assuming those roles formerly filled by the Ministry of Justice, the cabinet, the judicial council or chief justice, and the head of state or governor. Thus, the period saw the subordination and marginalization of Palestinian courts.[9]

Resuming Palestinian Courts

After assuming control over matters of justice in 1994, the PNA stripped away some of the effects of the Israeli occupation in a series of presidential decrees. First, in the second law issued by the PNA (Law 2 of 1994), the High Court in Gaza was given jurisdiction over all territory under the new authority.[10] In one stroke, a seemingly important step toward legal unification was taken. Other judicial bodies, such as specialized courts for municipal affairs and taxation, were reinvigorated by the transfer of responsibilities to PNA institutions; a special court was also established for election disputes.[11] New courts were formed in underserved areas—though this was done on an ad hoc basis simply through presidential orders. Finally, Israeli military orders connected with legal and judicial matters were repealed.[12]

Merely removing the effects of the occupation raised an entire series of new problems, however. First, Law 2 of 1994, even as it established the preeminence of the Gaza High Court, left most issues of judicial structure and legal unification unresolved. Second, these moves set off a protracted contest over who had the authority to appoint judges and organize judicial affairs. Was it the president (assuming the authorities of the British high commissioner and the Israeli and Egyptian military governors), or was his appointment authority a mere formality? Was it the minister of justice who held such authority (acting as the executive branch official with jurisdiction over judicial affairs), forwarding decisions to the president for formal approval? Perhaps the chief justice would be responsible, though his authority outside Gaza remained unclear despite Law 2 of 1994. Finally, Jordanian law called for a judicial council, though no such Palestinian body had been created. A protracted struggle took place, both within the judiciary itself and between the minister of justice (who submitted his resignation over the issue) and the chief justice (two occupants of the position resigned in the course of struggles over authority and jurisdiction).

As time wore on, the problems connected with the resumption of Palestinian judicial structures became increasingly political rather than technical and legal. Legal problems could have been gradually resolved, but some of the political issues grew increasingly formidable over time; outside a few measures, the PNA did not begin even a limited effort to resolve many of the conflicts until 1999.

Judicial Unification

The separate traditions of Gaza and the West Bank, divergent but hardly incompatible, were only slowly and incompletely brought together. The public prosecution system was unified by presidential decision in 1995 by appointment of a single attorney general.[13] This move toward unity actually deepened political divisions when the attorney general applied some Gaza law to the West Bank in a haphazard manner. Further efforts at unification of the judicial structures stalled in disputes over matters as small as the design of case files and slightly different legal terminology.[14] The structural and regional rivalry underlying such arguments led some on the West Bank to complain of a "Gaza occupation."[15] Thus, even as pettier disputes about stationery and vocabulary abated, underlying differences continued, connected to political struggles.[16] Some judges on the West Bank questioned whether the chief justice (based in Gaza) had legal authority over them, citing Jordanian law.[17] Members of the Gaza legal community tended to dominate the top legal positions (such as minister of justice and chief justice), but members of the West Bank legal community regarded their structures and personnel as more advanced.

It was not merely judicial structures that remained separate. New legislation covering both the West Bank and Gaza was produced very slowly. The election of the Palestinian Council slowed the process of legal unification because the new council successfully asserted authority over the legislative process. When the council finally began issuing comprehensive laws on critical areas (such as civil service or the judiciary itself), disputes with the executive branch stalled ratification and implementation (see Chapter 4). And the existence of two legal traditions proved useful on occasion as well: members of the executive branch (most notably the president and the attorney general) could mix and match elements of various laws to suit their purpose, as will be seen in more detail below.

Thus, the oft-cited confusion caused by combining two legal traditions was real but exaggerated: the problem was not so much legal confusion as political rivalry and disagreement. Judicial structures and legal provisions in the two areas were not impossible to harmonize on technical or doctrinal grounds. Further, the goal of unification was accepted by all. Work proceeded quite slowly because of political contests within the judiciary, within the broader legal community, and between branches of the PNA. And in the interim, some authorities were not above exploiting the differences for their own purposes.

Structure and Function of the Judiciary

The dispute over unification was connected to broader and even less tractable struggles over the structure of the judiciary itself. Palestinian courts had never enjoyed independence from whatever executive authority prevailed; at most they had achieved in some periods a reasonable level of autonomy in decision making and professionalism. The professionalism of the courts had declined during the Israeli occupation, and autonomy in many administrative matters had disappeared. Palestinian judges were cut off from their colleagues in the Arab world and received little training on their own; their jurisdiction was steadily diminished by Israel rule; and, during the intifada, Palestinians themselves often opted to avoid the courts. When Israel turned oversight of the courts over to the PNA in 1994, the Palestinian judiciary was diminished and demoralized. The PNA did take several measures to strengthen the courts and clarify responsibilities, but many of these steps appeared haphazard, and some actually aggravated divisions within the judiciary, resulting in bitter disputes that disrupted the functioning of Palestinian courts.

For the first three years after the creation of the PNA, the minister of justice and the chief justice in Gaza battled over control of the judiciary. Effective control over budget and administration of the courts lay initially in the Ministry of Justice, and the chief justice tried to wrest away authority over judicial appointments as well. The minister of justice submitted his resignation over the issue but ultimately emerged victorious when the chief justice was forced to retire in January 1998. The ostensible reason was related to the sudden discovery by the General Personnel Council that he had passed the age of retirement, though, since his eventual successor and several colleagues were older, the explanation lacked credibility. Instead, his independence and willingness to criticize the minister of justice in public were held responsible.[18] Yet the defeat of the chief justice hardly resolved matters. Many within the Palestinian legal community called for replacing him as soon as possible. Others—especially among the West Bank judiciary—opposed filling the position, arguing that it had no status in Jordanian law and that a judicial council should be formed instead.[19]

The struggle left the judiciary badly fractured. Some began to refer to a conflict among judges between the "party of the minister" and the "party of the chief justice." Other divisions soon became apparent. Older judges asserted that many newer judges had been appointed on the basis of political connections and lacked proper qualifications, and West Bank judges charged that the judiciary in Gaza received favored treatment. Broader political considerations arose as well. For instance, the senior judge in the West Bank was relieved of his duties in 1996, shortly after his court ordered the release of some Bir Zayt students detained without trial. If the dismissal was intended to signal judges to avoid politically embarrassing rulings, however, it had no such effect: Palestinian courts continued to order releases in similar cases, though (as will be seen) often with little effect. The post of attorney general remained a continuing source of dispute as well. In Arab legal systems operating on a French model, the *niyaba* or public prosecutor is a structure attached to the judiciary and staffed by officers with full judicial status. It is responsible for investigating crimes and presenting evidence to the court. The attorney general (or *al-na'ib al-'amm*) stands at the apex of the niyaba. In some Arab countries the executive exercises influence over the legal system by domination of the niyaba and appointment of the attorney general, refusing to grant them the same independence as the rest of the judicial apparatus. The first Palestinian attorney general, Khalid al-Qidra, quickly earned a reputation for selective prosecution (failing to investigate the politically powerful while showing great energy in prosecuting those deemed politically annoying, often on quite dubious grounds). He was eventually dismissed amidst unpursued charges of corruption and was replaced by a more respected legal figure who lasted less than a year after clashing with security forces over illegal detentions. These broader political struggles—centering as they did on the respect of the president and security forces for legal institutions—attracted greater international attention than some of the more prosaic but deeper political divisions concerning authority over the legal system in general and the judiciary specifically.

In 1998 and 1999, the battle over the judiciary began to emerge in multiple forums. In 1998 some West Bank judges submitted a petition demanding an improvement in working conditions.[20] The dispute over judicial structure was not contained to petitions and private lobbying but escalated beyond, spilling over into court decisions, the PLC, and executive action. In 1998, Palestinian judges in Ramallah struck down the demotion of one of their colleagues because the action had not been taken by the (nonexistent) Judicial Council stipulated in Jordanian law. The court also used the decision as an opportunity to call for an increase in judicial salaries.[21]

It was in this heated atmosphere that the PLC drafted and finally approved a Law on the Independence of the Judiciary, forwarding it to Yasir ʿArafat for approval in November 1998. The law provided for a Supreme Judicial Council with authority over judicial hiring, transfer, promotion, and discipline; the council would have full administrative and budgetary control over the judiciary as well. Such bodies are common in the Arab world, and the Palestinian law borrowed heavily from Jordanian and Egyptian models. In its structure, the council would give the Palestinian judiciary independence rivaled in the Arab world only by its Egyptian counterpart.[22] The PLC then turned to consideration of a further law governing the organization and operation of the courts, though it found it still could not escape controversy. A leading dissident judge appeared at a PLC session discussing the law and was invited to speak; he used the opportunity to criticize the law and the general situation of the judiciary.[23]

The executive finally responded to these pressures in 1999—though not yet by approving the Law on the Independence of the Judiciary. In May 1999, a new High Court for Ramallah was formed (essentially, the measure allowed the West Bank Court of Appeals the same status as the Gaza court of the same name). In June a new chief justice, Radwan al-Agha, a judge with experience in the Gulf states, was appointed. A new attorney general was also appointed, and the formation of a full Judicial Council was promised. When September 1999 came, however, Yasir ʿArafat instead issued a decision granting the new chief justice all the authority of the Judicial Council in Jordanian law. Some legal figures applauded the move as a step toward decreasing executive control over the judiciary, but others charged that it had no legal basis and was hardly a substitute for approval of the law passed by the PLC. And despite the decision, budgetary and administrative matters remained for the present the responsibility of the Ministry of Justice.[24] On an occasion that a judge was arrested (something that might normally be seen as possible only after consultation with the chief justice or Judicial Council), the judge was released only on personal order from President 'Arafat.[25]

When al-Agha began to use his new authority over appointments by changing some judicial assignments in the West Bank, dissident judges organized a strike against the action. The strike ended without the judges obtaining fulfillment of their demands but seemed to leave the Palestinian leadership at a loss. And the PLC continued to wait in vain for presidential approval of the judicial law it had passed. The PLC even attempted to obtain presidential approval by offering a concession: in 2000, it approved an amended version of the law that removed its own role from the appointment of the attorney general.

'Arafat finally responded in June 2000, again by offering a half-measure. While he still did not approve the law, he did appoint a Supreme Judicial Council on an ad hoc basis, offering it full control over appointments, assignments, and budgetary matters. In an oddly worded decree, 'Arafat seemed to cite as a basis for his authority the law he was refusing to sign.[26] Judge al-Agha claimed that the president had promised to sign the law by the beginning of September at the latest, though no reason was given for the delay.[27] The deadline passed unnoticed. In March 2001, at his speech opening the PLC's sixth year, 'Arafat called al-Agha up to the dais to sit at his right hand and proclaimed that judicial reform—including the unsigned law—was now at the "head of our priorities." He further announced that he and al-Agha would meet and arrange matters "within hours."[28] It was over ten thousand hours before he made good on this pledge. In May 2001, while still stalling on his pledge to sign the judicial law, 'Arafat did sign a series of other laws related to the Palestinian legal and judicial framework (on civil trials, criminal procedure, evidence, and court organization).[29] However, even this step was not announced until one month after it had been taken.

The May 2001 laws actually may have equaled in significance the then-unsigned judicial law, which drew far greater attention. Particularly notable was the Law of Civil Court Organization, which allowed considerable internal administrative and budgetary autonomy to the judiciary.[30] The law provided for the formation of a new level of court, the court of cassation (*mahkamat al-naqd*), above the court of appeals, so that the Palestinian court system would resemble its Jordanian and Egyptian neighbors.[31] (The measure offered an odd compromise in this regard: its name was borrowed from the Egyptian equivalent rather than the Jordanian, but its structure more closely resembled the Jordanian in that the body sat as the High Court for some cases—especially those administrative in nature—and as the supreme appeals court in other cases.) The law explicitly authorized the High Court to cancel regulations, decrees, and administrative decisions from public bodies or professional syndicates (a form of judicial review often more important than the review of the constitutionality of legislation). It allowed the High Court to assume temporarily the jurisdiction of the constitutional court as well, but since the constitution had not been approved and the jurisdiction of a constitutional court was established only in the judicial law that 'Arafat had yet to sign, the significance of the step was not clear.[32] Similarly, the law assigned some oversight role to the Supreme Judicial Council, even though 'Arafat's stalling on the judicial law robbed that body of any clear legal status.

The announcement of the new legislation was coupled with the first public statement by a high official in the Ministry of Justice explaining why 'Arafat had been delaying signing the judicial law: the judiciary itself was divided on the matter, and al-Agha had requested unspecified changes. That law would not be promulgated immediately after all; instead, it would be returned to the PLC for amendment. Yet when those changes were finally submitted, the PLC rejected them (on 15 January 2002).[33] Finally, on 14 May 2002—three and one-half years after the PLC had passed the law— 'Arafat announced his approval as part of an effort to convince domestic and international opinion that he was serious about reform. Remarkably, the announcement that he had signed the law had to be coupled with the additional assurance that he had ordered that "the law be published in the *Official Gazette* so that it will become effective immediately"[34]—an unspoken reference perhaps to the Labor Law, which had taken a year and a half after it was signed to be published (see Chapter 4).

It should be no surprise, given this saga, that the judicial law could not go into effect without additional complications. Al-Agha lobbied publicly for 'Arafat not to have the law published and claimed to have his agreement. This time he made his objection public: sitting judges would have to retire under the law's provisions, and al-Agha wished to allow for exceptions (something advocates of judicial independence resisted on the grounds that judges might strive to curry favor in order to postpone retirement).[35] That effort proved unsuccessful, but another one was not: as soon as the law went into effect (in June 2002), 'Arafat issued a decree allowing the current Supreme Judicial Council to serve for one additional year on a provisional basis. The decree clearly contradicted the text of the law, but its provisional nature and the simultaneous Israeli military campaign delayed opposition, though the PLC continued to press for a properly formed council.

Thus, after protracted conflict lasting eight years, the Palestinian judiciary seemed on the verge of gaining an impressive amount of institutional autonomy.[36] The legal order for judicial structures laid down in 2001 and 2002 had the potential to build the most independent judiciary in modern Arab history. But there was still doubt that members of the legal community could ensure that the system provided by law could go into operation or that they could use it effectively.

Caseload and Efficiency of the Courts

Despite the political and structural conflicts that arose, the assertion of PNA control over Palestinian courts initially led to marked increases in popular demands placed on the system.[37] Much of the business of the courts had dried up during the first intifada, as Palestinians moved to settle disputes through a variety of other mechanisms. The courts, operating under the Israeli civil administration, were viewed with some suspicion, and strong social pressure was brought on some with strong legal claims (such as landlords dealing with tenants in arrears) to take a lenient attitude rather than go to court. Such constraints began to evaporate with the construction of the PNA, with the result that Palestinians turned to the courts in rapidly increasing numbers. According to those involved in the legal system, the number of cases more than tripled.[38] By 2000, it had surpassed two hundred thousand.[39]

Yet the PNA was unable to increase the capacity of the court system to handle the influx of cases. Judicial salaries remained low, making it difficult to attract new judges from the private sector. Palestinians judges working abroad (such as in Jordan or the Gulf) were reluctant to return to face significant cuts in income. The Ministry of Justice struggled hard to fill positions of retiring judges; a significant increase in the judicial corps seemed out of its fiscal reach. Between sixty and seventy judges worked for the PNA. By contrast, Egypt, with a judicial system most participants regard as impossibly overburdened, has over one hundred times as many judges for a population approximately thirty times as large (with perhaps fifty times as many cases).

At least according to one study, however, the results may have been less dire than many believed. With funding from the United States Agency for International Development (USAID), DPK, an American consulting firm, embarked on a project with four courts: Ramallah *bidaya* (court of the first instance), Khan Yunis *markaziyya* (central court, the Gazan equivalent of the West Bank bidaya court), Gaza *sulh* (conciliation court, the lowest level of court), and Jenin sulh. In a study of the existing work of the courts, DPK found that the median case lasted slightly over nine months between initial filing and final disposition. Only 10 percent of the cases lasted over thirty-four months.[40] Unsurprisingly, the two sulh courts, with their load of simpler cases, were swifter.

The DPK study seems at first glance to contradict the frequent claims about the slowness of Palestinian justice. For instance, according to a separate estimate, the Nablus court could issue decisions in only two-thirds of the cases submitted to it each year.[41] More anecdotally, by 2000, most lawyers admitted that it took three to five years before a court could issue a decision and that the backlog would only make delays worse in the future. In fact, the DPK study, while remaining the most thorough conducted, hardly proved that delays were not a mounting problem. First, it considered only those cases that had been resolved; those still before the courts were not counted in its figures. Second, it counted a case as resolved when a court had disposed of it—even if resolution was delayed because a court ruling was not implemented or appealed. And DPK also discovered that only 12 percent of the cases resulted in a regular final ruling after a trial. In 25 percent of the cases, a ruling was issued despite the failure of the defendant to appear. And fully 60 percent of the cases were either dropped (by the defendant or by the judge if the defendant failed to appear) or settled. With so many cases settled out of court, it is clear that many Palestinians may have resorted to the courts not simply as a last resort but as one of a variety of strategies to settle a dispute.[42]

The burdens placed on the courts were aggravated by limited administrative support. Court buildings were generally old and poorly equipped, giving a dreary rather than imposing sense of the law.[43] The low level of support extended far beyond symbolism to the substance of the courts' work. Clerks, process servers, and execution officers were few in number, especially given the increasing number of cases. Ramallah had only one execution officer, for instance (other positions went unfilled because of the low salaries). And court work was often hampered by the complex nature of the Oslo Agreements: execution officers could operate in areas under Israeli security control only by wearing civilian clothes and either coordinating their work with the Israelis or going without their knowledge (thus making a far less official—and imposing—appearance). With the administrative support for the courts overseen by the Ministry of Justice (reputed to be one of the most disorganized Palestinian ministries), it seemed unlikely that any improvements would take place in the short term.

In 1999, matters had reached the point that lawyers in Jenin discovered that their local court had run out of paper to keep records of court sessions.

The national bar association called for a regional three-day strike in protest. Fearful that this would only delay their cases still further, the Jenin lawyers decided to cut the strike short.[44] In November, a similar strike was held in protest of conditions at the Tulkarem court.[45] Lawyers could hope to bring attention to the shortcomings of the courts through such actions, but in the end they had few alternatives.

Practicing Palestinian Law

Indeed, in some ways, the Palestinian legal profession more generally suffered from problems analogous to those of the courts.[46] As with the judiciary, resources available to existing lawyers were sparse, and political difficulties hampered their future development. There were few published references or collections of Palestinian law, and continuing education was virtually nonexistent. The Palestinian legal profession was badly divided, not only between the different legal traditions of the West Bank and Gaza, but also along professional and political lines. Professionally, no Palestinian law school existed prior to the 1990s, meaning that Palestinian lawyers had trained in a wide variety of locations (with Egypt and Jordan being the most popular locations). After finishing a degree, a prospective attorney was required to undergo a two-year apprenticeship with a practicing lawyer in Palestine (though some training in Jordan might also be counted).[47] Yet any more demanding requirements—such as a bar examination—would have required supporting legislation and a functioning bar association. A law was finally in place in 1999, but the matter of the bar association touched off political difficulties—by the time the PNA was created, there was not one organization for Palestinian attorneys but three (one in Gaza; one formed on the West Bank under Jordanian rule that boycotted the courts after 1967; and one formed more recently in the West Bank by lawyers not recognizing the boycott). Knitting these three disparate organizations together required a measure of presidential fiat and careful negotiation (as is examined in more detail in Chapter 5). The result was a Palestinian legal profession with inconsistent entry requirements, poor resources, and little professional organization. By 2002, the nascent Palestinian Bar Association had only begun to address these problems.

Palestinian legal education suffered the opposite problem of the legal profession more generally: rather than developing too slowly, law schools were growing too quickly. In the 1990s, four law schools emerged: al-Azhar in Gaza, al-Quds in Jerusalem, al-Najah in Nablus, and Bir Zayt near Ramallah. The emergence of Palestinian legal education offered the possibility of a more unified legal profession, but most law schools stressed quan tity over quality. As in other Arab countries, law became a subject of study for many who simply could not gain entrance to more prestigious academic fields. (Bir Zayt was an exception, developing a graduate program only for a small, elite group of students). Hundreds of students were admitted without the facilities (in terms of libraries or faculty) to educate them, and law schools suffered from the problems affecting Palestinian universities more generally: shortages of funds, labor discord with staff and frequent strikes, and poor infrastructure (ranging from shortage of classrooms to frequent power outages). Thus, the existing body of Palestinian attorneys faced the prospect of growing considerably, though not necessarily with well-trained lawyers.

An Uncertain Welcome for International Assistance

While the signing of the Oslo Accords had been accompanied by pledges of international assistance, very little of that was directed at the legal sector. What assistance did arrive generally ran into a host of political hurdles, with the result that the effect was marginal outside a very few specific areas.[48]

When the PNA was first established, there was considerable international interest in improving the legal system. The only donor to launch a systematic aid program, however, was the World Bank. Other donors either selected specific projects, often on an ad hoc basis (as in the case of most European states or the United States Information Agency), or decided that the conditions were not right for progress in the legal area (a decision reached by USAID).

The pioneering World Bank Legal Development Project focused on five areas.[49] First, task forces were to be established to develop a unified set of Palestinian law codes. This proved to be the most successful aspect of the project, with Gaza and West Bank legal experts drafting a set of law codes; between 1999 and 2002, a series of comprehensive codes governing criminal, civil, and personal status law were completed for submission to the PLC. Second, the project was to foster alternative dispute resolution. This proved more difficult, though a series of training workshops was held. Part of the problem lay with judicial suspicions about attempts to work around the regular judiciary. In the end, the ambitious scope of the project—including introducing arbitration centers attached to courts—was scaled back, and by 2001 the program ended. Third, the project was to develop judicial education, which it did through cooperation with judicial training academies in other countries and through programs at Bir Zayt University. Much of this task was taken up by a later USAID project. A fourth component was the dissemination of legal information. Much of the effort here focused on the simple but important task of collecting and publishing the applicable body of laws (for instance, in 1999 the project published a collection of laws and executive decisions issued by the PNA). Finally, the project included a component on court administration that was suspended when it ran afoul of the unsettled situation resulting from executive-judicial rivalries.

USAID's initial reluctance in 1996 to involve itself in legal matters was based fundamentally on prevailing political conditions. The rivalry between the West Bank and Gaza legal communities was at its height when USAID first considered involvement, and executive interference (and disrespect) for the judiciary had resulted in several widely publicized incidents, leading American officials to question the political will of the PNA to encourage legal development. In 1998, USAID decided that these problems, while not erased, had been alleviated somewhat and that

> Palestinian law and legal institutions are developing and will continue to develop with or without donor assistance. A comprehensive [Rule of Law] Program will support the ongoing evolution and development of a West Bank and Gaza legal system characterized by the effective, efficient, and equitable administration of justice; accountable governance; and open and free markets. USAID has a significant and historic opportunity.[50]

The USAID project was to focus on judicial training, court administration, alternative dispute resolution, support for a judges' association, and legal education. While the general logic of the project reflected American ideological preferences (such as the emphasis on "open and free markets"), the specific elements reflected some of the concerns of the Palestinian legal community. (The idea of a judges' association, for instance, was based partly on the desire of the Palestinian judiciary to emulate its powerful Egyptian counterpart.) Yet USAID was soon to confront the political obstacles that had earlier caused it some hesitation and hampered the far less hesitant World Bank project. The first year after USAID awarded the primary contract was spent negotiating with various PNA bodies (the judiciary, the Ministry of Justice, and the Ministry of Planning and International Cooperation) for approval; with each of these agencies uncertain of its authority to negotiate, frustrated USAID officials finally decided to proceed on their own. No PNA officials objected, but the timing could not have been worse: the second intifada erupted just as the program got underway. In such an atmosphere, some aspects of the program bogged down (for instance, the Palestinian Bar Association was unable to hold elections, as detailed in Chapter 5). Legal education and model courts proved easier to continue, although the caseload of the courts diminished with restrictions on movement that inhibited both litigants and judges.

Other international donors pursued less comprehensive and generally smaller-scale projects, with the European countries showing a particular interest in human rights. Indeed, a small expenditure here was arguably quite effective—a whole host of Palestinian human rights organizations were kept afloat by infusions of European funding.

Why were international donors reluctant to involve themselves in legal and judicial reform? Why were the efforts that did occur so fraught with delays and difficulties in implementation? International assistance for legal development often encounters such problems, partly because legal systems are so socially and politically embedded and donors unfamiliar with (or unwilling to adapt to) local conditions and legal culture.[51] International efforts to develop Palestinian law certainly betrayed such flaws, but in comparison with earlier programs elsewhere, donors showed flexibility and responsiveness to local conditions. Most of the problems and obstacles lay in a deeper set of political difficulties.

First, international assistance efforts inevitably aggravated existing rivalries among Palestinian institutions and often created some new ones. Donors were uncertain when and how to choose between working with the Ministry of Justice and the Palestinian judiciary; both organizations themselves were often badly divided. Working with one Palestinian university led to criticisms from the others. Those who worked directly with NGOs often fared no better: the various human rights organizations often viewed each other as rivals. The availability of donor funds, however modest by international standards, set potential recipients against each other. The PNA seemed unable to develop its own strategy for seeking donor assistance or identifying clear priorities; a vague plan produced in 1996 proved insufficient to guide either donors or PNA agencies on how to develop legal and judicial institutions further.

Second, international donors had their own set of political constraints. USAID was barred by American law from granting funds directly to the PNA but had to implement its own projects. It also shied away from areas likely to embroil it in political controversy in Washington (such as human rights, an area closely connected with the PNA's suppression of Islamist movements). The World Bank generally makes loans to states and therefore had to construct special mechanisms to allow it to make grants to the PLO (and through it to the PNA). In general, the political constraints faced by donors, combined with the PNA's inability to articulate a strategy, resulted in a situation in which international assistance was "donor rather than demand driven."[52] In other words, donors decided their priorities and favored activities; specific agencies (or NGOs) might persuade donors to design programs in a specific way but were powerless to set general priorities. There were, to be sure, efforts to coordinate efforts not only among donors but also among the various Palestinian parties.

Finally, the peculiar patterns of international assistance often went beyond aggravating rivalries to offending nationalist sensibilities. A report on legal assistance by the UN Special Coordinator published the extent of assistance that went directly to NGOs (the ensuing dispute is covered in more detail in Chapter 5). For some PNA officials—especially the minister of justice—this was doubly offensive: not only was some of the money kept out of their hands, but it was also given to organizations that embarrassed and criticized the government.[53] In January 2000 the minister joined some human rights leaders in a workshop and publicly threatened to refuse foreign funding; he charged that such donors hired their own experts at astronomical fees, thus taking back with one hand what they had given with the other.[54]

In this charged political atmosphere, it was no surprise that international assistance efforts produced only modest results. Donors could claim that they made possible significant legislative drafting as well as extensive documentation of human rights abuses, but the more ambitious plans for legal and judicial reform remained at the beginning stage only.

DEVISING ALTERNATIVES

In many ways, the legal system of the PNA was not good enough for some and was too good for others. It was not good enough in ordinary civil and criminal matters because of its sluggishness, inefficiency, and unreliability. It was too good, however, to serve the immediate political needs of the Palestinian leadership—it could not be used effectively to suppress or harass opposition, hold enemies in indefinite detention, or allow the PNA to address Israeli security concerns. As a result, two sorts of alternatives to the regular courts developed: a set of structures involved in alternative dispute resolution and a set of courts and procedures that allowed the Palestinian leadership to operate completely outside the law when it desired. Both these alternatives sprang up as soon as the PNA was created to meet immediate needs. Far from withering away over time, however, both grew increasingly robust.

Alternative Dispute Resolution, Palestinian Style

Palestinian society is rich in unofficial mechanisms for settling disputes. Conflicts (even those of a criminal nature) have often escalated to involve extended families, and mediated and negotiated solutions have often been common in such cases. During the intifada, a general ethos prevailed that greatly discouraged resort to the court system. First, pursuit of litigation (especially in landlord-tenant cases) was stigmatized as undermining social solidarity. Second, structures emerged during the intifada that mediated or settled disputes without involving the regular court system.[55]

Oddly, the construction of the PNA enhanced and formalized alternatives to the courts, even as the judiciary came under complete Palestinian control. First, a backlog of litigation and disputes clogged some courts, especially as the intifada-era norm of avoiding disputation quickly eroded. This was accentuated by the withdrawal of Israeli military courts from litigation involving areas under Palestinian control. Second, the Palestinian courts were given few resources to meet the increased demand. Yet, as discussed above, the backlog and inefficiency of the courts, though real in some places, may have been exaggerated.

Just as important was a host of new Palestinian structures (police and security forces as well as other bureaucracies) that quickly emerged; few of these wished to turn away those seeking help in their disputes. But rather than viewing such alternative dispute resolution as a temporary, emergency measure, the PNA acted to formalize and support such mechanisms, sometimes even more than it supported the regular court system. In general, three sorts of mechanisms emerged.

First, the police and security forces found themselves besieged with complaints from Palestinians regarding all manner of criminal and civil matters. Such petitioners did not wish to be told to go through regular legal channels, fearful that this would lead to years of litigation with no assured result. Many agencies therefore established "legal departments" to handle such cases, arguing that the courts were not yet ready and that settling disputes would keep the parties from resorting to violence. In short, they claimed to be acting in support of public order. However, the involvement of security forces quickly provoked complaints from those who found their methods inappropriately harsh for dealing with local disputes. In effect, such harsh methods were all that such forces had at their disposal: friendly persuasion, rough treatment, threats of imprisonment, or actual imprisonment were the only tools available to resolve a dispute.

What made the involvement of the security forces in disputes especially noteworthy was that it extended from neighborly disputes to criminal cases. In most Arab countries with a niyaba system for criminal prosecution, police are required to turn over all serious crimes to the public prosecutor for investigation (though sometimes misdemeanors are left to the police). Critics charged that the Palestinian police failed to refer all cases, preferring to exercise discretion as to which public body would handle an alleged offense.[56] The effect could be to erase any distinction between civil and criminal cases: civil disputes resulted in detention in order to convince a recalcitrant party to settle; criminal charges would result in bargaining between perpetrator and victim.[57] Even more remarkable, security forces took on a role in the work of other public bodies, such as tax collection (arresting those in arrears until they paid)—sometimes to the horror of the officials receiving the assistance.[58]

Only after five years did some security forces begin to attempt to extricate themselves from such activities. In 1999, the Preventive Security Forces (the first security force on the ground after the accords and composed primarily of members of the local Palestinian Fatah forces rather than returnees from other Arab countries) proclaimed a "professional and behavioral revolution," involving rationalization, clear delineation of duties and responsibilities, increased training, and dismissal of problematic officers. Part of this professionalization involved withdrawing from duties unrelated to security and referring complainants to the police, the courts, or whatever agency was legally assigned jurisdiction. Other security forces claimed to wish to work in a similar direction, again under the rubric of professionalization. Even after this proclaimed revolution, some problems remained difficult to jettison: the absence of effective Israeli-Palestinian legal channels led many Israelis to contact leading Palestinian security officials directly with problems such as automobile theft. In addition, security forces remained broadly active in areas under mixed Israeli-Palestinian security control (and probably in East Jerusalem), where formal channels were cumbersome or ineffective for political reasons.[59] And the outbreak of the second intifada heightened the prominence of the security forces just as it became difficult for the regular courts to function amid constant closures and restrictions on movement.

The second mechanism developed under the PNA for dispute resolution consisted of legal departments in each governorate. Palestinian governorates present a quasi-military appearance. The governorate in Ramallah, for instance, shares quarters with various security apparatuses in a heavily guarded compound surrounded by high walls and watchtowers. It became a focus of worldwide attention in April 2002 because the complex contained

'Arafat's headquarters and was besieged for weeks by Israeli troops. Despite such surroundings, the legal departments appear more bureaucratic than military, characterized by small offices crowded with employees, petitioners, furniture, and filing cabinets. Like the security forces, the governorate legal departments found themselves engaged in dispute resolution from the beginning of their creation; unlike them, they have confronted the task and formalized procedures as much as possible. They claimed authority under the preexisting arbitration law and also as part of their duty of maintaining public order.

In the Ramallah governorate, a complainant is handed a form to describe the nature of the problem. The governorate then sends a notice to the other party beginning with the words "You are to appear . . ." (though governorate officials insist they are powerless to compel any of the parties to come if they prefer not to). Officials then seek to mediate the dispute (though in particularly complex cases the parties might agree to arbitration rather than mediation). The bulk of work is connected with civil matters (especially land, debts, checks, and wages), though some personal status matters (especially support payments) also arise. Generally the disputants are directly involved themselves without attorneys; indeed, many attorneys prefer to avoid such mediation altogether.[60]

The third form of dispute resolution sponsored by the PNA is referred to as mediation between families and tribes (*'asha'ir*). The contribution of the PNA was not to institute such mediation but to endorse and formalize it.[61] This step was based on the claim that violent disputes can often escalate into feuds and that the families of victims (especially in the case of murder or even accidental death) will not regard a case as settled merely through criminal prosecution. According to such a view, a violent crime is an offense not solely against the society (for which a criminal trial is appropriate) but also against a family; it requires either an apology and monetary compensation or a violent retaliation. Some states in the Arab world (most notably Egypt) have worked to suppress such practices, and they remain confined to rural areas. Others (such as Jordan) have tolerated some aspects of tribal justice without always endorsing it. Still other states (especially some in the Arabian peninsula) have left the matter to shari'a courts, where the law differs from tribal law but will still countenance compensatory payments for wrongful death. The PNA reacted by assigning mediation to volunteer, presidentially appointed public figures. Such mediators saw their job as operating alongside the courts to ensure that tribal justice—as well as state justice—is done, generally through arranging formal reconciliation meetings.[62]

The extensive use and formalization of such methods of resolving disputes provoked strong criticisms, primarily from lawyers and judges who saw it as a poor, even corrupt replacement for functioning courts. In the first place, argued the critics, the involvement of executive branch organs in judicial matters was a clear violation of the principle of separation of powers.[63] Second, the critics charged that the mediators did not stop at offering their services to willing disputants but actively pressured parties to drop litigation already before the courts. Third, Palestinian lawyers and judges regarded the involvement of official organs as based on personal connections and social position and therefore as likely to treat the powerful far better than the weak. Fourth, many criticized the training of the mediators, regarding them as unqualified for such work and unfamiliar with the law. Finally, in the view of lawyers and judges, the application of mediation to criminal matters circumvented legal penalties and personalized justice, transforming it from a state concern into a family matter.[64]

Those involved in dispute resolution rejected these criticisms as failing to account for increasing institutionalization and professionalization. First, since participation was voluntary and results are nonbinding, they could not be said to interfere with the work of the courts. Second, the governorates finally agreed not to accept cases that were already before the courts. And resorting to such agencies did not prevent a disappointed party from filing a suit later on. Finally, the mediators defended their own qualifications—the director of the legal department for the Ramallah governorate possessed a doctorate in law; she later completed a number of workshops in conflict resolution.[65] While these responses did not completely satisfy critics, the general direction in the PNA toward developing and professionalizing alternatives to the courts seemed firmly fixed.

Others, especially international donors, directed a very different set of criticisms at the PNA regarding alternative dispute resolution. For them, the problem was that such mechanisms were too poorly developed, especially for business disputes. It is true that the PNA had allowed alternatives to develop, but these were primarily suitable for very local disputes. To satisfy the critics and avoid charges of imposed solutions and encroachment on judicial work, they relied far more heavily on mediation than arbitration. The outcomes of such efforts were only rarely enforceable in the courts—a feature that might entice local litigants to give such methods a try but was likely to have the opposite effect in business disputes, in which quick and binding decisions are often preferred. (Prevailing Palestinian mediation techniques did not preclude the possibility that the matter would eventually wind up in court anyway, starting over from the beginning.) Larger-scale trade and investment disputes generally relied on different forms of alternative dispute resolution that offered speed and efficiency while still maximizing the ability of the two parties to choose governing rules and procedures. Investors and merchants—especially those more experienced in international dealings—often wished to determine the law to be applied and the arbitral forum; the sole task of the courts became enforcement of the results of contractually stipulated arbitration outcomes. Slow and inexperienced courts operating in Arabic were to be avoided as much as possible, and alternative procedures operated by local officials that offered only nonbinding friendly mediation were a poor substitute. In cases in which an international actor had a contractual dispute with an official body, distrust of local procedures was likely to be particularly strong and nearly impossible to allay.[66]

Even for local business disputes, the alternatives to the courts were not well developed. The official bodies involved in arbitration lacked the specific knowledge of business practices to be seen as appropriate for any case more complicated than a bounced check. In many Arab countries, chambers of commerce offer arbitration and mediation services; they have the added authority that comes from the ability to affect reputation in fairly small business communities. The Palestinian bodies had sometimes played a similar role, but three decades of occupation had atrophied their ability in this regard. It was not that Israel had any objection to the bodies operating in business disputes, but the chambers of commerce had lost vitality and were often unable or unwilling to hold new elections under Israeli rule. Whatever energy they retained was often devoted to political activities (see Chapter 5).[67]

Thus, alternative dispute resolution was controversial but well developed for simpler and more local disputes; it was embryonic at best for commercial and international matters. It should therefore be no surprise that it became an early subject of interest for international donors, anxious to build the institutional infrastructure for a market economy. These efforts achieved some modest successes: projects were designed and funded, and some Palestinian legal officials became convinced of the need for further development of alternative dispute resolution. The most significant success came in 2000, when the PLC passed an arbitration law that offered parties considerable freedom in selecting procedures and mandated court enforcement of arbitral awards. Yet passage of the law was only a first step: it provided the legal framework but none of the institutional support necessary; the effort still confronted the more general array of problems that afflicted international assistance in the legal sector discussed above. Ironically, the arbitration law seemed to bring an end to official interest in developing arbitration more fully, and the World Bank project focusing on alternative dispute resolution began to wither from inattention.

Regularizing Exceptions

Immediately after it began operation, the PNA devised a more terrifying alternative to the regular courts: a State Security Court that handled politically sensitive cases ruthlessly and did so, quite literally, overnight. This was the Supreme State Security Court, established by Presidential Decision 49 of 1995.[68] The decision cited three legal provisions for its authority: an earlier presidential decision affirming the validity of laws and regulations in effect before 1967, the 1962 constitutional system for Gaza (issued by the Egyptians), and the 1946 order on the formation of military courts (issued under the British mandate). The decision named five military officers to serve as judges and three officers to serve as prosecutors.

The Supreme State Security Court quickly provoked widespread criticism. It operated whenever the president referred a case and then acted extremely quickly—within days or even hours. Once having convened, the court would hear a case within a few hours and issue its decision immediately—sometimes in the middle of the night. Acquittals were extremely rare (only two of the fifty individuals charged in the first year of the court's operation were released). It is difficult to conceive of a court that would violate more judicial principles. It offered the accused no procedural safeguards (lawyers could be present but had no time to prepare or call witnesses) and clearly acted according to the president's desires. The Supreme State Security Court abandoned all but a few of the forms of legality, yet its basis in a presidential decision prevented any legal challenge to its authority.[69] In a sense, the court operated for those cases in which a specific and immediate result was necessary.

Why construct such a ruthless and unconvincing parody of a judicial structure? While authoritarian measures in the Arab world are quite common, such systematic violation of judicial standards is actually rare. Arab governments more often devise mechanisms to avoid the courts or write authoritarian laws that they expect the courts to apply. Even when exceptional courts are created for clearly political motives, very few could match the record of the Palestinian State Security Court. Even explicitly political courts (such as "revolutionary tribunals" that have been erected in some Arab countries following a change of regime) or military and security courts generally observe more safeguards and take more than a few hours to finish their work. The Palestinian State Security Court was audacious and brazen even by such standards.

Critics charged that the court was established to meet Israeli demands for the PNA to take action against individuals and groups engaged in violent attacks on Israeli targets. This is partly true, but the record of the court strongly suggests a more subtle additional motivation: the court was probably created not only to meet Palestinian obligations under Oslo but also to deflect them. Eight months after establishing the court, the Palestinians and Israelis finally signed the Interim Agreement ("Oslo II") governing the transitional period. Tucked away in one of the annexes was a Palestinian pledge to transfer those "suspected of, charged with, or convicted of an offense that falls within Israeli criminal jurisdiction." However, "if the individual requested is detained in custody or is serving a prison sentence, the side receiving the request may delay the transfer to the requesting side for the duration of the detention or imprisonment."[70] In other words, the PNA would have to extradite Palestinians whom Israel suspected of crimes unless they were already in detention. Such extradition would be extremely unpopular among Palestinians, making it virtually impossible politically. By acting quickly to try and sentence those involved (or suspected of involvement) in crimes against Israeli targets, the PNA could avoid having to choose between its obligations under the agreement and domestic political pressures, which made extradition unthinkable.[71] In short, the court seemed tailored to diminish a difficult political problem for the PNA: the domestic repercussions of unjust trials would be less than those caused by extradition, and the Israelis and Americans cared less about legal niceties and more that violent opponents of Oslo be incarcerated somewhere. While no Palestinian public official acknowledged this basis for the court's existence (indeed, none would even acknowledge that the complex wording of the Interim Agreement required extradition, and few Palestinians knew of the provision), the nature of cases referred to the court makes this part of its purpose quite clear. Virtually all the initial cases brought to the court involved those whose extradition Israel was likely to demand.[72] And while the court frequently sentenced those it convicted to death, the president rarely gave the required approval for the execution to be carried out (leading to indefinite imprisonment).

Having been created to serve this political goal, however, the court proved too tempting an instrument to ignore. In the court's second year, it moved against a prominent human rights activist and strident critic before global outcry caused the authorities to relent. In highly publicized cases in 1999 and 2000, several Palestinians accused in crimes provoking public outrage were referred to the court. Indeed, such cases finally led to the implementation of the death penalty. In August 1998, two brothers were executed for a conflict between two families that led to a dual murder. The sequence of events—the murder, public outcry, arrest, trial, sentence, and execution—

took only three days. The following February a colonel in one of the security services was executed after being convicted of the rape of a five-year-old boy in a one-hour trial. While the accused protested his innocence, demonstrations following the crime led to enormous public pressures on the authorities to resolve the case. And when the second intifada began, the State Security Court proved an efficient and ruthless device for meting out punishments to suspected collaborators.

While some of its actions met political needs, the Supreme State Security Court also provoked bitter domestic criticism. Lawyers, high officials, human rights activists, and members of the PLC found the court's violation of procedural safeguards noxious and repeatedly pressured the PNA for corrective action. Some—such as the bar association, the PLC, and human rights groups—called for abolition of the court altogether. They used the promulgation of the Law on the Independence of the Judiciary in May 2002 to point to the court's weak legal basis and press for its abolition. Others, such as the minister of justice, claimed that there was need for such a court because of the difficult international and security situation. They acknowledged, however, that the court should be reconstructed on a firmer legal basis, with qualified judges and clear and fair procedures.[73]

Indeed, the PNA moved in the direction of developing the legal basis of the state security court after 1998. One step taken in November 1999 justifiably worried the critics: the court was given a permanent prosecutor, Khalid al-Qidra. Al-Qidra, who had previously served as attorney-general for all of the PNA and then as a judge in the State Security Court, had been held responsible not merely for egregious violations of human rights but also for arresting human rights activists. His appointment maintained the system in the hands of a proven and merciless presidential loyalist.

Other measures, however, helped mollify those who accepted that there had to be some role for security courts. In 1998, President 'Arafat issued a decision assigning supply and price cases to the State Security Court.[74] The step had several effects, most of which only became clear over time. First and most obviously, a new class of crimes was assigned to the security court. It gradually became clear that the court was to deal with cases far more prosaic than suicide bombings: selling expired foodstuffs or violating price controls would now result in a trial in the security court.[75] This seemed harsh, but it was not unusual in the Arab world (in which such offenses are deemed threats to the public safety and order). Yet as harsh at it seemed, the change marked a step toward a firmer legal basis for the court: no longer would the court meet only when summoned by the president on a case-by-case basis; instead a clear category of offenses was assigned to the court. And such cases would be prosecuted not by a special security prosecutor but by the regular niyaba. In short, the widening of the jurisdiction of the court was connected with regularizing its procedures and integrating it with other legal and judicial structures.

A second effect was to bifurcate the State Security Court into two very different structures. The 1995 measure was based on Gaza law and mentioned the "Supreme State Security Court," whereas the 1998 decision was based on West Bank (and thus Jordanian) law and mentioned simply the "State Security Court." The effect was to create two distinct and separate security courts. The first, the Supreme State Security Court, was the same body formed in 1995 to serve presidential wishes in uncomfortable political situations. It continued to deliver its verdicts with its customary ruthless efficiency. The second court more closely resembled the regular courts. It had two stages corresponding to the seriousness of the offense (though no clear appeals procedure existed, except to the president). It dealt chiefly with economic crimes.[76]

Thus, the evolution of the State Security Court brought the Palestinian judicial structure more closely in line with prevailing Arab (and especially Egyptian) practice: a regular judiciary was allowed to develop professionally and reasonably autonomously for most normal cases (even those economic crimes coming under the jurisdiction of "security courts") and a political judiciary stood ready to do the regime's bidding when necessary. The Supreme State Security Court remained even less respectful of legal and judicial norms than its Arab counterparts, but its existence was not allowed to prevent the slow movement of the regular judiciary in a professional direction.

THE LEGAL NARRATIVE OF THE PALESTINIAN LEADERSHIP: RESUMING FROM THE PAST WITHOUT LIMITING THE FUTURE

One leading Palestinian lawyer has sharply criticized the legal vision of the Palestinian leadership as lacking any coherent vision or narrative to guide it.[77] While that may have been the case before the establishment of the PNA, it no longer holds true: the series of legislative enactments issued by the PNA articulate a clear and coherent legal vision—and even the contradictions and ambiguities in the legal order being constructed are very much products of that vision.

The PNA could have positioned itself legally in several different ways. First, it could have recognized its own existence as based in the Oslo

Accords, which spelled out in extreme detail many aspects of its structure and competencies. Second, the PNA could also be viewed as an arm of the PLO or of the state of Palestine, created by the 1988 declaration of independence. Third, the PNA might pose as an entirely new entity, existing in a legal vacuum and occupying the position of the first legitimate authority in the area under its control.

The legal vision of the Palestinian leadership has at times adopted elements of each of these orientations, yet it differs from all of them. The legal enactments of the PNA present a picture of an emerging sovereign body, assuming control over a continuous and preexisting legal entity.[78] Palestinian legal development begins with the creation of a distinctive Palestinian political entity under the British mandate and continued under Jordanian and Egyptian rule. That development was punctuated by Israeli occupation, itself recognized as a source of law, though almost never by name. The creation of the PNA in 1994 simply asserted Palestinian control over subsequent legal development. While sovereignty is not directly asserted, no limitations on sovereignty are recognized. Indeed, Palestinian lawmakers were sometimes quite explicit: they were working under the conditions of the interim period but anticipating full statehood. And such statehood would not erase their efforts; the laws they had written were designed to continue in effect.[79]

The Palestinian leadership thus has a body of law already in place. That law, however, exists not to restrict the leadership but to guide it and offer it possibilities. The creation of the PNA not only brought law under Palestinian control; it also made its operation an emanation of presidential will.

Resumption from the Past

The first decision issued by Yasir 'Arafat as president of the PNA (and indeed the legal document that fixed the name *Palestinian National Authority* instead of *Palestinian Authority*) stated simply that

1. The laws, regulations, and orders in effect before June 5, 1967 remain effective in the Palestinian territories "the West Bank and Gaza Strip" until their unification is completed.

2. The civil [nizami], shari'a, and sectarian courts at all levels will continue in performing their work according to the applicable laws and regulations.

3. The civil and shari'a judges and the members of the public niyaba will continue performing their duties in all parts of their jurisdiction according to the laws.[80]

This order, issued on May 20, 1994—even before 'Arafat moved from Tunis to Gaza—was widely interpreted as an attempt to turn the clock back to 1967, eliminating all the legal changes and military orders effected by the Israeli occupation. Such a step would have been a clear violation of the Oslo Accords (which left Israeli military orders in effect until specifically repealed with the approval of a joint Israeli-Palestinian legal committee). In fact, however, 'Arafat's decision had an entirely different impact: Israeli military orders remained very much in effect, as will be seen below. The decision was an act of affirmation rather than erasure; 'Arafat effectively connected the emerging Palestinian entity to its pre-1967 past. This applied both to the courts that would enforce the law and to the law they would apply. It also asserted the principle that the PNA was now responsible for the law and the courts.

Indeed, other decisions aimed at affirming administrative and bureaucratic continuity in a similar fashion. Decision 2 of 1994, also issued in Tunis, ordered all government workers to remain in their positions and continue their work.[81] And the PNA's first law (as opposed to executive decision or *qarar*) provided for the continuation of village and town government.[82]

Subsequent Palestinian laws, decisions, and decrees generally cite a legislative history where relevant, to give either the background to the text or its legal basis. Generally, mandatory, pre-1967 Jordanian, and Gaza law are cited where relevant. For instance, a 1998 decision changing the fees for transferring land ownership opens explaining that it is issued:

> After an examination of the Law of Land Transfer Number 29 of 1920, effective in the provinces of Gaza, and especially paragraph 16,
>
> The Regulation of Land Transfer of 1939, effective in the provinces of Gaza,
>
> The Law of Fees for Registering Land, Number 26 of 1958, effective in the provinces of the West Bank,
>
> Order 374 of 1955, related to the civil defense tax effective in the provinces of Gaza, and especially section Z of paragraph 1,
>
> Law 5 of 1965, related to the liberation tax effective in the provinces of Gaza,
>
> And Decision 104 of 1997, related to changing the fees of transferring land.[83]

Palestine emerges from such texts not as a sudden invention of the Oslo Accords or a revolutionary creation of the PLO but as an established and continuous legal entity in which legitimate authority now lies in the hands of President Yasir 'Arafat.

The Law That Dare Not Speak Its Name

Despite the pretensions of such texts, Palestinian history has been far from continuous. In particular, the years between 1967 and 1994 saw a steady stream of Israeli military orders. Those orders covered not only security and military matters but also a whole host of criminal and especially civil matters. They had insinuated themselves so thoroughly into Palestinian life that any attempt to abolish them would require great care. The PNA therefore continued to maintain most Israeli military orders, repealing them or replacing them quite slowly. Decision 1 of 1994 had left a widespread public impression that thousands of Israeli military orders had been repealed with a one-page text, and the PNA used delicate wording in subsequent legislative enactments to avoid directly acknowledging that no such step had been taken. Until instructed otherwise, Palestinian courts were still expected by the leadership to enforce Israeli military orders, and they obediently followed executive will. Indirect and obscure wording made clear that legislative drafters were embarrassed by this reality but felt that the alternative was legislative chaos.

The ambiguous status of Israeli military orders was clarified—in the most oblique possible language—at the end of 1994, when Yasir 'Arafat issued by executive fiat a law canceling a list of forty-seven "circulars, orders, decisions, and military instructions."[84] One was required to refer to the attached list to discover that the Israeli military commander had issued all of the canceled orders after the 1967 war. Many dealt with security and legal affairs and affected Gaza only. This left over one thousand military orders implicitly in effect in Gaza and a slightly larger number in the West Bank. In 1995 a further step was taken toward embedding Israeli military orders in Palestinian law when a law was issued transferring to the PNA "all the authorities and competencies provided for in legislative enactments, laws, decrees, circulars, and orders effective in the West Bank and the Gaza Strip before May 19, 1994."[85] Coming nearly a full year after Decision 1, this law authoritatively established that the earlier edict had not erased Israeli military orders by any means.

Maintaining Israeli military orders was a politically embarrassing legal necessity. Entire areas of law (such as that dealing with the value-added tax) simply did not exist in preexisting West Bank and Gaza law. In other areas (most notably insurance), Israeli military orders were regarded as far more appropriate and up-to-date than the pre-1967 laws. Rather than abolish all military orders, the Palestinian leadership established a committee to review them and gradually began to repeal those it found inappropriate.[86] For instance, in 1996 'Arafat repealed the military orders allowing Israeli lawyers to work in Palestinian courts, this time by issuing a decision.[87] An additional ninety-four military orders were repealed in 1998.[88]

The PNA took care in its legislative drafting to avoid referring to the source of military orders, just as most legislative texts were written to avoid any mention of Israel's continuing influence or the limitations on Palestinian sovereignty. The Oslo Accords, which had extensive legal provisions, have never been cited as a source of authority. Even monetary amounts were specified in American dollars or Jordanian dinars; Israeli shekels (the currency most often used in the West Bank and Gaza) were not mentioned. The closest to an acknowledgment of this limitation came in the law of consular fees, which stated that dollars were to be used "until the Palestinian currency is issued."[89] Another formula was to refer to "Jordanian dinars or its equivalent in legally tender currency," a clear but nonspecific reference to the Israeli shekel.[90]

In a similar vein, the president of the PNA was required—in a decree he issued for himself—to swear an oath to God to "be faithful to the homeland, to preserve the constitution and the law, and to preserve the interests of the Palestinian people, the safety of its land, the realization of its security and national aspirations."[91] As with the school curriculum (see Chapter 6), such an oath implied the existence of a sovereign state; the president was requiring himself to defend a constitution that had not been written and territory that had never been defined. A law governing evidence in civil and commercial cases barred use of information connected with "state security" that had not been legally published—ignoring the PNA's status as something less than a state.[92] Similarly, Palestinian legislation occasionally made reference to Jerusalem—such as a law establishing Jerusalem as the permanent seat of the High Court—but allowed, without elaboration or reference to the prevailing political situation, Gaza and Ramallah to serve as temporary alternatives.[93]

Yet the Israeli military orders had so insinuated themselves in Palestinian law that on occasion implicit recognition had to give way to explicit mention. A cabinet decision regarding banking, a decision on compensation of traffic accident victims, and a decision on the authority of the attorney general all referred to Israeli military orders.[94] Even on such occasions, however, the legislative enactment used the most oblique language possible. The decision on banking mentioned only "changes made" in Law 95 of 1966, effective in the West Bank and obscuring the Israeli origin of those changes. The attorney general was offered the use of Israeli military orders with very general wording; he was to exercise the authorities "stipulated in the laws, regulations, instructions, and orders effective in the lands of the Palestinian National Authority."

Mixing and Matching Sources of Authority

For the leadership, then, the legal structure of Palestinian society has been formed over the past century by a variety of political authorities that may have lacked nationalist legitimacy but whose laws remain until changed. What of the development of Palestinian law since the PNA was formed in 1994? Who has the authority to issue legislative texts, and on what basis does that authority lie?

The answer that emerges from a reading of Palestinian legislative texts since 1994 is that the president has several different sources of authority that grant him virtually total discretion in determining which elements of Palestine's diverse legal heritage are to be applied and that his power to issue new legislation is also extremely wide. Legal structures and the body of Palestinian legislation exist to guide but not restrict presidential action.

First, virtually all legislative enactments—laws, decisions, and decrees—issued by Yasir 'Arafat since 1994 cite his authority not merely as president of the PNA but also as president of the Executive Committee of the PLO. The relationship between the two bodies is never made clear, and several Palestinian political activists have expressed frustration at 'Arafat's tendency to shift between his two positions in order to maximize his authority.[95] The PLO, which retains its claim as the sole legitimate representative of the Palestinian people (even while the creation of the PNA has led most PLO institutions to atrophy) would seem to lend its legitimacy to the PNA, and several legislative enactments by the PNA seem to rely on the PLO for authority. For instance, many of the early pieces of PNA legislation cite the approval of the PLO Executive Committee, and several cite PLO laws or regulations. The Palestinian election law—which formed the constitutional basis for many PNA institutions—contains a lengthy passage taken from the 1988 Declaration of Independence to justify the structures it establishes.[96] And PLO law is sometimes directly applied in PNA areas, particularly in the military courts. This reliance on the PLO could prove politically helpful: in 1998, 'Arafat issued a decree to protect "national unity and prevent incitement" during a time of sharp regional tensions over the peace process and American actions in Iraq.[97] The decree provoked severe domestic criticism for its sweeping language, but 'Arafat was able to use the PLO in support of his action—the decree cited the PLO penal code (issued in 1979) and forbid (among other things) "incitement to violate agreements which the PLO has concluded with fraternal or foreign states." The PLO was here used to criminalize calls to abandon Oslo. Yet the PNA could also be used to govern the PLO. Most remarkable in this regard was the provision of the civil service law—passed by the PLC but not submitted to any PLO body—that gave the PNA cabinet authority over grades and salary schedules for PLO cadres.[98]

At other times, PNA legislative drafters eschewed such complicated devices and simply presented the justification for a decision in terms both sweeping and laconic: "the president of the Executive Committee of the Palestinian Liberation Organization, the president of the Palestinian National Authority, by the authorities vested in him, and according to the requirements of the public interest."[99] No specification of the authorities or their source or of the nature of the public interest involved is given. Usage of such phrases would seem to indicate that the president has undefined (and perhaps unlimited) authority. He might wish to explain the background or the specific basis for a particular legislative action but need not do so.

In fact, this legal vision of presidential authority does seem implicit in much PNA legislation, though it is rarely made explicit.[100] The very laws that govern how new laws are to be issued were issued directly by the president. All three legislative enactments that established the basic legal framework for the PNA (Decision 1 of 1994, affirming the continued applicability of the pre-1967 legal framework, Law 4 of 1995 on the legislative process, and Law 5 of 1995, transferring authority to PNA institutions) were issued by 'Arafat without the approval of any body (citing only "the authority vested in him" and "the requirements of the public interest"). And it is precisely these three enactments that are used to justify many subsequent laws, decrees, and decisions. In short, the legal framework for the PNA is, according to these texts, nothing but a product of presidential will and authority. The president gives the law its effectiveness and is therefore unlikely to be governed by it, except insofar as he chooses.

This feature of the PNA legal framework places the oft-cited confusion of Palestinian laws in a very different light. It is true that Palestinian law is now drawn from various historical periods in ways that some observers find incoherent. Yet there is a fundamental consistency underlying the blending of legislative enactments: those that are applied are the ones that the president wishes to have applied. The president affirms the applicability of pre-1967 legislation, determines which post-1967 military orders are still in effect, and issues post-1994 laws, decisions, and decrees. And he does so largely as he sees necessary. Indeed, on one occasion, the PNA executive decided to apply a 1990 Jordanian law. (In the West Bank, the *waqf*, which administers religious endowments and oversees charitable work, operates under the 1990 Jordanian law; in all other instances legislative changes since 1967 in Jordan are not applied in the West Bank. The application of the 1990 law was determined by the waqf minister—a position held by 'Arafat himself since the death of the previous minister.)

It is true that the creation of the PLC effectively ended 'Arafat's monopoly on issuing new legislation. Perhaps anticipating the importance of the creation of the PLC, 'Arafat issued the 1995 election law—which determined the structure of the council and its mandate—only after the PLO's Executive Committee had approved it.[101] Yet the PLC has managed only to share some authority to draft and issue legislation; it has not been able to force the president to become subservient to the law. (See Chapter 4 for more detail.) 'Arafat is now largely unable to issue a law that has not been passed by the PLC, though his ability to issue presidential decrees and decisions is unimpaired. Indeed, the scope of such presidential decrees widened after the construction of the PLC: some matters that had been covered by laws (such as the repeal of Israeli military orders) became, after 1996, the subject of presidential decisions not subject to PLC action. On one occasion, 'Arafat went so far as to issue a decree-law while the PLC was not in session. The decree extended the 1965 Jordanian law of tourism to Gaza.[102] Most parliamentary systems allow for provisional emergency measures to be adopted in the absence of parliament. In this case, however, the nature of emergency in Gaza tourism lay unexplained. The PLC was formally notified of the action when it next met, but there was no indication that the decree-law's effectiveness was provisional unless it gained immediate PLC approval. And the president has refused to accept that he is subject to the law in other ways. Initially, he even contested the right of the PLC to initiate legislation, claiming that it had to come from the cabinet. When PLC adopted a set of standing orders that covered how the executive branch was to be consulted, 'Arafat refused to act in accordance with its provisions.

In the end, the creation of the PLC has not limited the president's authority in any way but one: he now has a partner in the legislative process that is not responsible to him. The change has some significant effects, but, as will be seen below, it may actually undermine the effectiveness of Palestinian law.

ALTERNATIVES FOR RESUMING PALESTINE'S LEGAL DEVELOPMENT

The legal record of the PNA has attracted considerable criticism both internally and externally for its disregard for, even hostility to, legal norms and its willingness to vitiate legal procedures when the interests of high officials or international pressures have demanded it. In fact, the record of the PNA is not what such criticisms have suggested, though it has come close on many occasions. The PNA has worked not to subvert the law but to resume Palestine's legal development. The three senses of *resumption* have led in very different directions and have sometimes directly contradicted each other.

Resuming from Palestine's Past

The PNA was most successful in asserting legal continuity in Palestine's past. It did so, however, in such a way that it left law as a tool of the ruler and subject to his will. In this sense, the position of Yasir 'Arafat fit squarely in the pattern of Palestine's past: the British high commissioner, the Egyptian military governor, and the Israeli military governor all created law but were not governed by it. (Jordanian rule was only slightly less personalistic, with a king loosely constrained by constitutional text.)

The vision pursued by the PNA left law as a tool in the hands of the ruler but allowed him to completely ignore it when he wished. Such a flagrant disregard for legal procedures is actually a departure from the norm in the Arab world, where even the most authoritarian rulers often follow legal niceties in inflicting the harshest and most arbitrary of measures. This is not to argue that the law is always and uniformly enforced in all Arab countries; but blatant and systematic spurning of legal forms is rare. Authoritarian practices are sanctioned by law, and even when the authorities act in ways that are clearly illegal, they mold their actions according to prevailing legal norms.[103] What is therefore remarkable about the PNA is its decision to eschew legal norms and structures altogether on sensitive issues.

Treatment of the media provides a clear example of this pattern. Prior to the election of the PLC, Yasir 'Arafat issued a restrictive press and publications law that was greeted with great suspicion by journalists and human rights activists.[104] They need not have worried—while the law gave the executive many tools to rein in the press, none were used. The PNA has harassed and detained journalists, forced some publications out of business, and given clear instructions to editors on what can and cannot be printed— but all through crude threats rather than the refined tools made available by the law. Radio stations have been closed down on official orders—without mentioning a single legal justification. Journalists have been arrested without charges and then expected to publish advertisements thanking the president when they are released. In short, in restricting the media, the PNA has eschewed the legal tools available to it and acted extralegally.

Such behavior is not episodic but extends to several areas of PNA affairs, operating completely outside any legal framework. State monopolies exist in several sectors (such as cement and gasoline) without any legal framework to guide them. Part of the Palestinian budget has operated completely at presidential discretion, despite the existence of a comprehensive budget law designed to mandate procedures and ensure accountability (see Chapter 4 for more detail). Security services report directly to the president or to the minister of the interior (a position also held by Yasir 'Arafat), refusing to subject themselves to oversight by the PLC or the courts.

Perhaps most indicative of this vision of the extralegal (and essentially sovereign) nature of presidential authority is the PNA's insistence on detaining individuals without charges, even in the face of a release order from a court.[105] Detention without charges is hardly unknown in the Arab world, but generally there are legal mechanisms that allow for (and even limit) such a practice. The PNA is therefore unusual not in the fact of such detentions but in failing on most occasions to give them any legal form whatsoever. Moreover, in its treatment of the courts, the PNA occasionally moves beyond bypassing the law to violating it. Political opponents and members of Hamas or other groups violently opposed to the Oslo Accords have been the chief target of such practices: they are arrested by one of the security services, detained in PNA prisons, and released only upon the order of the president. Over fifty times, lawyers acting on behalf of such detainees have successfully convinced the Palestinian High Court (in either Gaza or Ramallah) that such detentions have no legal basis, only to have the court order ignored. This practice gained international attention in June 2002, when the Palestinian High Court in Gaza ordered the release of the leader of the Popular Front for the Liberation of Palestine, Ahmad Sa'dat. Israel accused Sa'dat of complicity in the assassination of its tourism minister, but the PNA had detained him without charges. Given the absence of any legal basis for his arrest, the court ordered him released—leading to a cabinet statement explaining that the ruling would be ignored.

Security and prison officials involved explain—when they respond at all—that they take their orders from the president, implicitly but clearly arguing that the president's will stands above the law and all legal institutions. When a newly appointed attorney general attempted to force prisons to comply with release orders, he was forced out of his position.[106] Even when members of the security services are held accountable for their actions in court, it is only because the president has permitted it.[107]

After half a decade, the PNA showed signs of moving in the direction of other Arab states by its authoritarian actions and the pattern of the pursuit of what others have described as "rule by law" rather than "rule of law."[108] The judiciary was more unified and autonomous, the security services promised additional professionalization, and the PNA moved tentatively toward greater fiscal regularity and openness. Much of this effort was disrupted by the eruption of the second intifada, and some was reversed. Yet even before September 2000, the PNA's slowness in following Arab legal patterns by continuing to act extralegally and illegally seemed puzzling.

Resuming Palestine as an Arab State

There are influential figures within the PNA who have worked to build a legal system fully on the Arab model. They have argued that extralegal and illegal actions corrupt and weaken Palestinian institutions and prevent the development of healthy political practices. Abandoning use of such actions would not weaken the PNA and its leadership, they have argued, but strengthen and regularize its authority. The judiciary and the minister of justice have generally pursued such a vision, in which Palestinian legal institutions and practices are faithfully observed. In legal and institutional terms, this approach has realized much success, however slowly: new laws have been passed, and new judges have been eventually added. By 2000, Palestinian legal development finally seemed to be genuinely emerging in accordance with this vision. The outbreak of the intifada represented a setback in some important ways. Courts had difficulty functioning under the closure. Some courtrooms and records were destroyed in Israeli raids. New militias and armed groups occasionally directed their fire not simply at Israeli targets but also, quite literally, at suspected collaborators (bypassing the legal system) or even judges, prosecutors, and lawyers.[109] Yet the attempt to resume Palestinian law has continued, as new judges have been appointed, new laws promulgated, and new codes developed.

Perhaps the most persistent institutional actor pursuing such a vision is the Diwan al-fatwa wa-l-tashri' (Bureau for Legal Consultation and Legislation), an autonomous arm of the Ministry of Justice that reports directly to the cabinet. The Diwan dates back to the very beginning of the PNA; its task is to draft and review legislation and provide legal advice to the government and all the ministries and agencies of the PNA. It resembles the Council of State found in Egypt and some Arab countries, lacking only its judicial function. (The Council of State combines legal advice and drafting with adjudication of administrative cases in Egypt; the Palestinian Diwan has clear ambitions to move in that direction). The Diwan was headed from its inception by Ibrahim al-Daghma, a figure of tremendous legal influence; until he was promoted to minister of justice from June to October 2002, he had a modest public profile. (Al-Daghma had earlier briefly acted as minister of justice when Farih Abu Mudayn resigned in a dispute over judicial appointments; he returned to his former position when Abu Mudayn's resignation was forgotten.) The inclination of the Diwan is generally to adopt Egyptian models and legislation where appropriate; the majority of its lawyers are Egyptian trained. And the Diwan claims—not always successfully—tremendous authority. Not only must it review all legislation (and draft much of it), but it also asserts technical authority over legal advisors in all ministries, governorates, and public institutions.[110]

The vision offered by the Diwan is thoroughly legal, though it is not necessarily either liberal or democratic. For the Diwan, official institutions should operate through and according to clear laws and regulations; the source and content of those laws and regulations are of less concern. For instance, al-Daghma argued very strongly for presidential approval of the independence of the judiciary law. He did so not on liberal or democratic grounds but on the grounds of the observation that the laws that an independent judiciary would enforce would be those approved by the president.[111] The Diwan further argued against the authority of the PLC to initiate legislation. The PLC may be democratically elected, but the legislative process had already been laid down in 1995 before the PLC came into being. Law 4 of 1995 provides for a role for the cabinet and the Diwan in initiating and drafting legislation. While it has accommodated itself to working with the PLC, the Diwan's earlier opposition stood not on ideology but only on legislative text. Were a basic law or constitution to be adopted that spelled out a less presidential system, the Diwan would have no objection to adapting to the new procedures.

Why does the PNA continue to operate outside a legal framework in many areas, eschewing the more common (and, from an executive perspective, fairly attractive) alternative of rule by law? Palestinians often point to the particularities of their situation—the PNA is not a sovereign body; it operates under tremendous international pressure; and it is beholden to the Oslo Accords. In such an atmosphere, how can it develop like other states in the region?

In fact, in all these ways, the position of the PNA is far less unusual than is generally recognized. Many Arab states—especially those controlled by the British—achieved independence in a gradual and contested way without developing the selective aversion to legal procedures demonstrated by the current Palestinian leadership. Egypt received independence by unilateral British action, subject to reservations, in 1922. Even when the reservations on Egyptian independence were negotiated away in 1936, the British retained some role in Egyptian politics. Transjordan and Iraq similarly achieved sovereignty only after passing through a British mandate; the mandate ended not in total independence but in a treaty that negotiated the terms of British hegemony. The relationship between the PNA and Israel is not a precise copy of the British mandatory regimes and its successors in such countries, but there is a strong resemblance in the way sovereignty is being achieved through a protracted, negotiated, and fundamentally unequal process.

The resemblance is particularly strong in the legal realm. In Iraq and Egypt, the British devised legal mechanisms to place their position in the country beyond the control of legal institutions and processes. When faced with strong nationalist movements, they found legal ways to pressure the governments in such countries to place the bilateral relationship with Britain outside the political process. In some countries (such as Egypt and the Gulf), the British were very slow to cede legal jurisdiction over foreigners, effectively limiting the reach of the local legal system. And newly independent governments sought not to rebuild the courts and the legal system from the beginning but merely to maintain control over them.

These tactics shaped the development of law, legal systems, and judiciaries in the former British possessions, but they did not lead the governments of those countries to operate outside any legal framework. French decolonization—in Algeria, Morocco, Lebanon, and Syria—often followed a similar grudging and contested pattern, though generally in a more condensed time frame. Arab states leaving direct British and French control followed the path of legalizing authoritarianism, the path that the PNA has pursued quite slowly. The PNA's slowness in legalizing its practices is explained less in international than in domestic politics. The problem is, ironically, that liberal and democratic forces are too strong—or at least too strategically located.

Resuming Normal Politics

The third sense of *resumption*—pursuing a normal (and often liberal) political order—has had the least influence on Palestinian legal development. The problem has not been the weakness of political forces working for the rule of law—they have been very strong in particular areas of Palestinian political life. The pockets of their strength—in the PLC, the human rights movement, and parts of the judicial and legal establishments—have been insufficient in themselves to enforce a liberal vision of the rule of law. But have been able to block many routes for the executive. The PLC has often deferred to presidential wishes in accepting defeat or delay on some pieces of legislation (such as the Basic Law and many aspects of the budget), but it has been unwilling to author authoritarian pieces of legislation. The judiciary has been unable and unwilling to pursue a full constitutional confrontation with the executive, but it has not been able to escape from the pressures of human rights organizations seeking release orders for those extralegally detained.

In the first years of the PNA, there was considerable legal development in the second sense of *resumption*—building a system on the prevailing (and authoritarian) standards of the Arab world. Prior to 1996, laws and decisions were issued—generally solely on the president's authority—establishing the framework for a legalist but authoritarian system. The process of drafting legislation, the repeal of some Israeli military orders (with the maintenance of others), and the organization of the press were all spelled out in law or decision. Other pieces of major legislation—governing NGOs, political parties, and even an early draft of the Basic Law itself—were proceeding along similar lines. All of these laws would have been consistent with rule by law; none would have effectively established the rule of law (if by that term we mean forcing all state institutions to submit to legal rules that are not solely their creation).

In 1996, the PLC was elected. In a process described more fully in Chapter 4, it moved to assert its primacy in the legislative process. It brought about drastic changes in draft legislation (on NGOs and the Basic Law, for instance), pursuing its vision of a liberal and democratic legal order. It attempted to bring democratic accountability to other parts of the political order, even those deemed most sensitive, such as the budget and the security services. This effort may have largely failed, but it left significant effects.

The executive of the PNA ignored, bypassed, or defeated much of the PLC's efforts, but it had lost its exclusive control over Palestinian legislation. Those matters that could now be decreed without resort to the PLC—such as the cancellation of additional Israeli military orders or the jurisdiction and formation of the State Security Court system—were still addressed by presidential decision. Some matters that were properly left for legislation—such as the formation of the Supreme Judicial Council—were also the subject matter of presidential decisions. (The PLC tended to withhold criticisms of such actions as long as they were deemed to be movements in the correct direction.) But many significant matters—such as the structure of the judiciary as a whole, the budget, or the constitutional order itself—were not definitively addressed, often forming the subject of protracted struggles and even stalemate between the PLC and the executive.

Unable to legislate its vision of the proper legal order, the executive of the PNA, and especially the president, often reverted from authoritarian legal means to entirely extralegal and illegal actions. The result has been a legal order that is moving to resemble that of its Arab neighbors, but only very slowly.

3 Constituting and Reconstituting Palestine

> The legal character of the Arab Palestinian people shall be embodied in the state. The state is a symbol of national unity. It shall safeguard respect for the constitution and preserve independence, unity, territorial integrity, and the orderly proceedings of government in adherence with constitutional provisions. The rule of law and justice shall be the basis of governance, the motivation for the work of governing authorities, and the protector of the rights of the people and their democratic values.
>
> Articles 13 and 14, draft Palestinian constitution, February 2001

Those who speak in Palestine's name have declared it to be an independent state twice (1948 and 1988). They have declared their firm intention to do so many more times and declared their fervent wish to do so more times still. On four occasions (1948, 1988, 1996, and 1999) their efforts have actually progressed to the stage of beginning to draft constitutional documents for the new state. Yet Palestine remains without a recognized constitutional framework, and its leadership has exhibited ambivalence about pursuing efforts further.

Constitutions in the Arab world have been written to serve several different purposes.[1] First, they have served as an important marker of sovereignty. Most Arab states issued a new (often first) constitution upon independence from imperial rule. The symbolic importance of a constitution is thus heightened in the Palestinian context, with sovereignty more often proclaimed than realized. One newspaper columnist referred to a constitution as "a birth certificate for the nation."[2] A Palestinian official has likened drafting a constitution to other aspects of state building, including "establishing an airport, airline, telephone code, and broadcasting."[3]

Second, constitutions have been used to serve a more prosaic set of purposes. They organize power and authority, clarify responsibilities and chains of command, and lend legitimacy to political procedures and their outcomes. The legitimacy of Palestinian institutions, their sources of authority, and their relationship with each other have always provoked discussion and debate. Since the Oslo Accords and the establishment of the PNA (which existed alongside the PLO), the authority of various Palestinian bodies and their relationship to each other have grown particularly controversial (and confusing). Palestinians now have the PLC, the PNA presidency, the PLO Executive Committee, the PLO Central Committee, the presidency of the PLO's Executive Committee, and the PNC to represent them. Fairly basic questions (What is the status of PLO Executive Committee members who attend PLC sessions? What happens if the PNA president neither signs nor vetoes a law passed by the PLC? Must a Palestinian prison official must obey an order issued by a Palestinian court?) remain sharply debated and unresolved. Many Palestinians saw a constitution as a necessary tool to decide such issues.

Third, constitutions can do more than define authority; they can also regulate it. Liberal constitutional documents are designed not merely to organize authority but also to guide its exercise in accordance with broader liberal values of individual rights and tolerance as well as democratic values of accountability and popular participation. At times Palestinians seeking to build not merely a sovereign but also a liberal, democratic political order have seen a constitution as a critical instrument in guiding and restraining the state they seek to build.

These purposes are not logically in contradiction, but they lead to different results. And they can sometimes operate in tension with each other. Using a constitution solely to assert sovereignty, for instance, might result in a document that asserted its basis in the popular will (thus making the state deserving of international recognition) while remaining inattentive to ensuring the regular expression of that will in democratic procedures. Indeed, if sovereignty (the first set of purposes) is the goal, writing a constitution that restricts political authority (the third set of purposes) or even governs it in ways that might diminish flexibility (the second set of purposes) might be seen as undesirable. Palestinian constitutional efforts have therefore often operated at cross-purposes, which explains why so many constitutions have been drafted for Palestine without being promulgated. In this sense, there have been four sustained attempts to constitute Palestine. None has culminated in full success. The result is not the absence of a constitutional framework—there is such a framework for Palestine now—but only the absence of a clearly authoritative document that serves any of the three sets of purposes. The Palestinian constitutional tradition that has emerged is therefore self-contradictory. On the one hand, it offers a barely checked presidentialism, based on the absence of clear legal limitations on presidential authority and a constitutional order by default that is highly authoritarian. On the other hand, there is an emerging liberal constitutional tradition that dominates debates about constitutions and inspires many of the drafting efforts—but may be so liberal that it has become unpalatable to the Palestinian leadership.

THE FIRST EFFORT

Palestine became a distinct political entity with the creation of the British mandate in the aftermath of World War I. In other mandates in the Arab world, the British and the French allowed constitutional structures to develop—circumscribed, to be sure, by the ultimate authority of the mandatory power. Those constitutional efforts—in Lebanon, Syria, Iraq, and Transjordan—were based partly on a nascent constitutional tradition (the Ottoman constitution of 1876 had governed all the Arab areas now under mandatory control; the brief Syrian Arab Kingdom had also drafted its own constitution before it was suppressed by the French in 1920). And in all cases, the constitutions survived the mandate. In Lebanon and Jordan, the constitution currently in force is an amended version of the constitution adopted under the mandate.

Palestinian leaders sought to follow a similar path. Some Palestinian political leaders had themselves participated in Ottoman constitutional structures as well as the abortive Syrian state; all were also very much aware of constitutional and broader political developments in neighboring Arab lands. Yet any effort to develop Palestinian constitutional structures—even under the rubric of the British mandate—ran afoul of the fundamental conundrum of mandatory-era politics. Britain had received a mandate from the League of Nations to govern Palestine and develop it for self-rule. But the mandate also incorporated the text of the Balfour Declaration, Britain's 1917 statement of support for the creation of a Jewish "national home" in Palestine. Both these conditions were fairly vague, but they proved impossible to reconcile. Self-rule entailed development of representative and constitutional structures; a Jewish national home meant at a minimum the possibility of substantial Jewish immigration to Palestine. Any step toward empowering the Palestinian majority would endanger the continuation of Jewish immigration. The proposals offered by the British to allow for some kind of representative assembly and the development of constitutional institutions therefore fell short of the minimal requirements articulated by the Palestinian leadership. Attempts by Palestinian leaders to establish their own structures often foundered on internal disagreements and, especially after the revolt of 1936, British hostility.

The end of the mandate therefore left at best a mixed constitutional legacy to Palestinians: the development of constitutionalist aspirations alongside the reality of unchecked autocracy. On the one hand, any Palestinian political platform included demands for self-government, majority rule, and the development of constitutional institutions. In that sense, the mandate heightened the importance of constitutional issues for the Palestinian national movement. On the other hand, the structures developed by the mandate offered barely disguised authoritarianism: the legal framework had been developed not only to impose mandatory rule on a hostile population (by the time of the end of the mandate, both the Palestinian and Zionist leaderships regarded the mandatory authority as unfriendly) but also to allow the British high commissioner virtually unchecked authority. Those legal mechanisms have not withered: British emergency regulations are still in use, and a succession of authorities—Egyptian, Israeli, and Palestinian—have effectively assumed the position formerly occupied by the high commissioner.

In the aftermath of World War II, as the British mandate collapsed, Palestinian leaders moved to construct an independent state with Arab assistance.[4] The Palestinian leadership had been decimated by the 1936 revolt and the consequent British actions; many leaders were in exile, and efforts to build a unified structure for the leadership had collapsed. In 1946, the newly formed Arab League assumed responsibility for designating a revived leadership organization, the Supreme Arab Organization (Al-hay'a al-'arabiyya al-'ulya, often referred to in English as the High Arab Executive or Arab High Committee; an earlier body by this name had existed under the mandate). Relying on contributions from Arab states, the organization brought together various leaders and organizations and began to establish a rudimentary apparatus for pursuing diplomatic and state-building goals. The British and the United Nations both acknowledged the organization, and the organization developed its own proposal to develop a democratic and constitutional state to succeed the mandate. With Jews still in the minority, such a step would have represented a bitter defeat for the Zionist movement. In November 1947 the UN General Assembly opted instead to endorse a plan to partition Palestine into a Jewish and an Arab state.

The Supreme Arab Organization and the Arab League rejected the UN partition resolution, and as the British moved to terminate the mandate unilaterally, it became clear that the conflict between Palestine's Arab and Jewish populations would be resolved by military means. While the Supreme Arab Organization saw the moment as propitious for preparations for statehood, it was held back by the Arab League and found itself marginalized for several reasons. First, the organization had no military force to speak of but relied on loosely organized Palestinian bands and, after the termination of the mandate on 15 May 1948, the support of armies of Arab countries. Second, the Arab League operated by consensus, and King 'Abd Allah of Transjordan became an implacable opponent of the Supreme Arab Organization. 'Abd Allah was far more willing to consider some form of partition and aimed also to unite his kingdom with the Arab sections of Palestine.[5] As long as 'Abd Allah was opposed, it was difficult to garner Arab support for any moves to transform the Supreme Arab Organization into a provisional government or declare a Palestinian state. Third, even the organization's backers in the Arab League (most notably Egypt) retained some suspicions of the organization, fearing that its confrontational attitude and the notoriety of its leader (Amin al-Husayni, who had spent some of the war years in Nazi Germany) might aggravate existing diplomatic and military difficulties. When the first round of Arab-Israeli fighting ended in a cease-fire on 11 June, the Supreme Arab Organization sought Arab League endorsement of moving toward statehood and formation of a national council. It obtained only the formation of a civil administration for those parts of Palestine under Arab control, and that administration answered to the Arab League rather than the organization.

In late September 1948, key Arab states finally moved to support the formation of a provisional government, *Hukumat 'umum filastin* (All Palestine Government), and the convening of a Palestinian National Council, motivated largely by fears that 'Abd Allah would proceed with annexation of sections of Palestine under Transjordanian control and obtain international recognition. Elections to any Palestinian body were impossible in wartime conditions, so prominent individuals and leaders of various Palestinian organizations and groups were invited to join the council in Gaza (under Egyptian control). The individual selected to spearhead the effort and head the provisional government, Ahmad Hilmi, seemed an ideal compromise candidate. He had served various Hashimite rulers, and 'Abd Allah had appointed him military governor of Jerusalem. But Hilmi had also worked for Amin al-Husayni during the mandate period. The newly selected prime minister promptly sent a cable to the United Nations declaring that

> the Arabs of Palestine who are the owners of the country and its indigenous inhabitants and who constitute the great majority of its legal population have solemnly resolved to declare Palestine in its entirety and within its boundaries as established before the termination of the British Mandate an independent state and constituted a government under the name of the All-Palestine Government deriving its authority from a representative council based on democratic principles and aiming

to safeguard the rights of minorities and foreigners, protect the holy places, and guarantee freedom of worship to all communities.[6]

The All Palestine Government's decision to convene a Palestinian National Council in Gaza (with Amin al-Husayni elected Speaker) did not go uncontested even within the Arab arena: it led to 'Abd Allah's summoning of a rival grouping in 'Amman.

On 1 October 1948, the PNC made good on Hilmi's promise and declared "complete independence" in the "entirety" of Palestine "and the establishment of a free, sovereign, and democratic state, in which the citizens enjoy their freedoms and rights." Palestine would march "with its sister Arab states in building Arab glory and serving human civilization."[7] The provisional government sought recognition from other Arab states, control over Palestinian military forces, and financial support from the Arab League. Six Arab states offered immediate recognition, though the rival Palestinian body convening in 'Amman insisted that the provisional government represented only its own members. The PNC issued a provisional constitutional declaration, expressed its confidence in the provisional government, and then went into recess. In its provisional constitution, the council assigned legislative power to itself and called for a constituent assembly to write a permanent document. But beyond suggesting a parliamentary system, this effort gave little indication of the form that Palestinian politics should eventually take and provided only a skeletal framework for governance.

The council's first session was its last. Shortly after the body went into recess, the Egyptian authorities in Gaza brought Amin al-Husayni to Cairo and placed him under house arrest. The All Palestine Government continued operating, preparing a budget and working to secure diplomatic recognition by other Arab states. But the end of Arab-Israeli fighting in 1949 rendered it irrelevant. The West Bank fell under Transjordanian control and was eventually annexed. That left the government controlling only Gaza, but even there Egyptian military administration effectively dominated. Several members of the government accepted Jordanian cabinet positions, indicating that the government no longer even represented itself. Ahmad Hilmi moved the government to Cairo, where it remained a largely forgotten body until his death in 1963.

This first declaration of independence represented an extremely inauspicious beginning for Palestinian statehood. Its effects were extremely limited. Yet it did leave two legacies, however tenuous. First, the Palestinian agitation for democratic government as the mandate ended and its proclamation of fealty to democratic principles in its declaration of independence and provisional constitution amounted to the first authoritative statement of how Palestine was to be governed. To be sure, no democratic structures could be built under the political conditions operating under the mandate or the subsequent war. And the declarations of democratic intentions were made partly for tactical reasons (because Arabs were in the majority) and partly to garner international recognition (from hegemonic democratic states). But the verbal commitment to democratic constitutionalism made in 1948 has been repeated and never repudiated.

Second, the All Palestine Government, however ineffectual, did give way directly to a more lasting structure. Upon Ahmad Hilmi's death in 1963, the Arab League, responding to Egyptian prodding, convened a new body, termed the Palestinian National Council like its 1948 predecessor. That body in turn established the PLO in 1964. In 1988, almost a quarter-century after that step, a subsequent session of the PNC declared independence once again. And it was the organization created by the PNC—the PLO—that signed the Oslo Accords with Israel, establishing the PNA. The link between the structures established in 1948 in Gaza and those established in the West Bank and Gaza in the 1990s is direct, though it is often forgotten.

Palestine's constitutional history after 1949 followed different paths in Gaza and in the West Bank. Both posed problems for subsequent constitutional efforts, though for different reasons. In Gaza, constitutional structures presupposed distinct Palestinian nationality and eventual statehood but effectively continued the autocracy of the mandate. The West Bank came under Jordanian rule, with a more liberal constitutional framework but one predicated on the rejection of Palestinian national identity.

While Egypt did not annex Gaza, it allowed for only a limited measure of Palestinian constitutional development.[8] Initially Egyptian administration in Gaza was purely military, with the Egyptian military governor assuming all the (unlimited) authority of the British high commissioner. In 1955, the Egyptian cabinet issued a Basic Law for Gaza pending the establishment of a Palestinian state. It provided for an administrative governor, appointed by the Egyptian cabinet and serving under the Egyptian Ministry of Defense. The governor would be head of an executive council, joined by the heads of major government departments (none of whom were Palestinian). A Palestinian Legislative Council was also constructed, consisting of members of the executive council as well as some representatives of the Gazan population. The brief document did purport to guarantee a few rights and freedoms, but generally only within boundaries provided by law. A more extended constitutional document was issued in 1962, reaffirming most of the structure and content of the earlier document (with a few minor changes), but including an ideological section in line with the emerging Nasserist brand of Arab nationalism. The Egyptian-promulgated documents, like the mandatory constitutional arrangements, offered little prospect of accountability and only limited (and effectively consultative) popular participation. For that reason they were later rejected by those assigned to draft Palestinian constitutional documents in the 1990s.[9] But the Egyptian documents affirmed the legitimacy of a separate Palestinian entity and introduced Palestinians to Egyptian legal models and traditions.

Jordan provided a very different constitutional model, due partly to the participation of Palestinians in its formation. After occupying the West Bank during the war, the Jordanian regime convened Palestinian bodies to rival the PNC in Gaza. These bodies, meeting first in 'Amman and then in various cities of the West Bank, endorsed the unification of the West Bank with Transjordan. Palestinian suspicions of 'Abd Allah and of Hashemite autocracy led the king to agree to constitutional revision as the price of unification. Yet 'Abd Allah was assassinated before the constitutional revisions could be completed. Operating under a weak king ('Abd Allah's son, Talal, was eventually deposed by the parliament for mental incompetence), the Jordanian parliament approved a series of amendments that greatly liberalized the Jordanian constitution.[10] The introduction of Palestinian deputies to the Jordanian parliament enhanced the standing of those insisting on liberalizing constitutional reforms and moving Jordan in the direction of a constitutional monarchy. But rising Arab nationalism led to a confrontation between an increasingly bold opposition and the king. A failed coup attempt and an increasingly nationalist parliament led King Husayn to have opposition deputies expelled from parliament and parties disbanded. These changes effectively ended the Jordanian constitutionalist experiment in 1957. After that point, the strongly royalist flavor of Jordanian political life, combined with the denial of Palestinian nationality implicit in Jordanian annexation of the West Bank, rendered the Jordanian constitution less attractive as a model for subsequent Palestinian constitutional development.

In 1967, both the West Bank and Gaza came under direct Israeli military rule. The limited forays made in developing constitutional institutions under Egyptian and Jordanian rule came effectively to an end. Israel issued separate proclamations for the West Bank and Gaza, assigning all constitutional authority to the Israeli military governor. After that point, and even after the construction of a "civilian administration" in the 1980s under the military governor, the autocracy of the mandate period returned with full force. And even Israeli interest (especially early in the occupation) in developing some structures for Palestinian institutional development in the West

Bank and Gaza was regarded with extreme suspicion by the Palestinian leadership as an attempt to undercut the PLO and either disguise annexation or establish an Israeli protectorate.

THE SECOND EFFORT: DECLARING A STATE AND LIBERAL PRINCIPLES—AND POSTPONING THEM

In November 1988, the PNC met in Algiers and issued a declaration of independence. The move received tremendous international attention, coming as part of an effort to begin negotiations over a permanent solution to the conflict with Israel. The declaration described the 1947 UN partition resolution "which divided Palestine into an Arab and a Jewish state" as "still providing conditions for international legitimacy including the right of the Palestinian people to sovereignty and national independence."[11] By citing the resolution, mentioning its provision for a Jewish state, and describing the state of Palestine as "peace loving, bound by the principles of peaceful coexistence," and working "with all states and peoples to realize a permanent peace based on justice and respect of rights," the second Palestinian declaration of independence marked a clear step toward a two-state solution.

Much less noticed by external observers was the declaration's description of the political principles that would govern the Palestinian state. The new state belonged to Palestinians throughout the world and would be characterized by a "democratic parliamentary system," freedom of expression, equality, a constitution, the rule of law, and an independent judiciary. Despite the promise of the eventual articulation of constitutional principles, however, the only immediate institutional change was to make Yasir 'Arafat, previously chairman of the PLO, president of the state of Palestine. Since this state controlled neither territory nor population, designing constitutional mechanisms seemed premature. Nevertheless, over 'Arafat's objections, the PNC passed a resolution authorizing its Central Committee to approve a Basic Law. The resolution was ignored in the aftermath of the meeting.[12] The Palestinian leadership satisfied itself with the principles contained in the 1988 declaration for five years.

In September 1993, the situation changed radically with the signing of the Declaration of Principles between the PLO and Israel (the first of the Oslo Agreements). For the first time, the Palestinian leadership anticipated assuming a measure of control over a small (but growing) Palestinian-populated territory. A group from the Legal Committee of the PLO quickly drafted a provisional constitutional document that became public by the end of the year.[13] The beginning of the process was rushed, reflecting the immediate need for a provisional document. But it was never clear how provisional the Basic Law was to be, and many worried that once put in place, the mechanisms it established would be impossible to dislodge.

Further, from the beginning the effort was caught between two very different political foundations. On the one hand, the provisional Basic Law was to be authored and authorized by the state of Palestine (or the PLO), purporting to represent Palestinians everywhere. On the other hand, the purpose was to govern a constrained Palestinian entity (eventually the PNA) emerging from the negotiations with Israel. Viewing the document in this latter context would emphasize its relationship to the Palestinian population of the West Bank and Gaza; it would also reinforce the limitations on Palestinian autonomy in the Oslo Accords. For Anis al-Qasim, the Palestinian jurist who led the initial drafting efforts, this tension could be easily resolved: while the provisional Basic Law was to govern the PNA, it was to be issued by the PLO and draw its legitimacy from the Palestinian people everywhere. The PLO itself was to issue but remain unconstrained by the Basic Law. Thus, it was essential that the Basic Law be issued before the establishment of the PNA.

That condition was not met. The draft issued by the Legal Committee of the PLO contained elements the Israelis found noxious: not only did it adduce the Palestinian people as the source of its authority, but the second draft also proclaimed Jerusalem the Palestinian capital. And while it was designed as a transitional document, it began the move in the direction of a permanent constitution for a sovereign state. Palestinian critics found a different set of flaws, charging that the document was drafted in secrecy, full of loopholes, and unlikely to prevent presidential authoritarianism. The PNA began operation before such constitutional issues were resolved.

Upon assuming leadership of the PNA, Yasir 'Arafat simply issued a declaration affirming laws in force before the Israeli occupation in June 1967 (see Chapter 2). The absence of a Basic Law had real costs for Palestinians by depriving them of one of the accoutrements of statehood, robbing their new institutions of a clear legal foundation, and leaving only the Oslo Accords as a legal basis for authority. But the constitutional vacuum had benefits for the new rulers: it freed them from any institutional constraints as a Palestinian bureaucracy, security apparatus, and legal structure were established. For instance, a restrictive press law was issued in 1995 simply by decree; there was no need to resort to parliament on the issue.[14]

Throughout 1995, the leadership of the PNA ignored the effort to write a Basic Law, instead negotiating issues of constitutional structure with the

Israelis. Anis al-Qasim continued to call for the Central Committee of the PLO to issue the Basic Law, but no action was taken.[15] Instead, the Basic Law was redrafted to reflect the realities of the new round of Israeli-Palestinian agreements. Those agreements proved difficult to negotiate, however. Even though the interim phase was to be limited in time (with final-status talks to be completed by 1999), Israeli and Palestinian negotiators argued over a wide range of matters, extending from postage stamps and passports to border controls and legal structure. The Palestinians were anxious to assert control over as much territory and as many aspects of sovereignty as possible during the transition, and the Israelis resisted them on most points.

In matters of internal governance, the Palestinians attempted to obtain Israeli agreement to symbolic and structural aspects of statehood. An elected Palestinian Council stood as an important marker for both sides of the extent of statehood. For the Palestinian negotiators, the council was to be a parliamentary and legislative body representing the population of Gaza and the West Bank (including East Jerusalem). They pressed for a larger, elected body with full legislative powers. The Israelis resisted, arguing for a body that would act less as a parliament and more as an oversight committee for the Palestinian administration. As with many other aspects of the Oslo Accords, the agreement offered something to both sides but also left a considerable measure of ambiguity, though the final document reflected Palestinian suggestions on most matters not immediately connected with sensitive political issues (such as sovereignty).[16] The September 1995 Interim Agreement on the West Bank and the Gaza Strip established a Palestinian Council that was to "assume all the rights, liabilities and obligations of the Palestinian Authority" (Article 20, paragraph 4). Palestinian residents of Gaza and the West Bank (including Jerusalem) would elect eighty-two council members (later unilaterally amended by 'Arafat to eighty-eight) as well as its president (*ra'ees).* In its structure, therefore, the council seemed to be halfway between a parliament and an oversight committee. On the one hand, the new body was explicitly given both executive and legislative authority (Article 9). On the other hand, the council would have an executive committee, headed by the president (Articles 4 and 5). Perhaps in recognition of these ambiguities, the agreement also called upon the council to write a "Basic Law" to govern its own "organization, structure and functioning" (Article III, Paragraph 7).

In preparations for elections to the Palestinian Council, a Law of Elections was promulgated that gave the liberal principles contained in the declaration of independence a far sounder legal basis.[17] First, the explanatory memorandum attached to the law cited the liberal and democratic promises of the 1988 declaration in justifying its provisions for elections. Second, the law stated in its third article:

> Immediately after its election, the Palestinian Council, as its first task, shall assume responsibility for composing a constitutional order for governance in the transitional period. The constitutional order shall be founded upon the principle of popular sovereignty, democratic principles, separation of powers, independence of the judiciary, equality among citizens, and the guarantee of the basic rights of the citizen.

Thus, in the process of negotiating with the Israelis, the Palestinians seemed to transfer the authority for issuing a constitution from the PLO Executive Committee to the Palestinian Council. Since the council described in the agreement represented a successor to, rather than the legislative element of, the PNA, perhaps Palestinian leaders anticipated that they (as leaders of both the PNA and the PLO) would retain control over the process. Yet the Palestinian Council that emerged was far closer to the original Palestinian conception of a parliament for the West Bank and Gaza than seems to have been provided for in the Israeli-Palestinian agreements. And it took its mission of drafting a constitution quite seriously.

THE THIRD EFFORT: THE BASIC LAW OF THE PALESTINIAN NATIONAL AUTHORITY

Realizing that the constitutional order was about to be taken up by the newly elected PLC, the Palestinian leadership hastened to prepare a draft, referring the latest version to a committee of legal experts formed by the new Ministry of Justice. At this point, however, the leadership lost control of the issue for two reasons. First, because earlier drafts of the Basic Law had been published, constitutional issues were now widely discussed in Palestinian society. Palestinian organizations held conferences, meetings, and workshops to discuss the Basic Law. Constitution writing was turning into a very public process.

Second, measures taken by Israel in response to a series of bombings made the drafting process difficult to coordinate centrally. Israel imposed prolonged closures on the Palestinian-ruled territories during 1996 that made it impossible for the drafting committee to meet. Not only was travel difficult between Gaza and the West Bank, but even travel among West Bank cities was frequently impossible. Individual committee members therefore formed their own local working groups to produce suggested changes and further drafts. In general, most of these suggested changes focused on increasing human rights protections, closing loopholes, and further specifying procedures. Thus, by the time the PLC had convened in the summer of 1996, the Basic Law had attracted a considerable amount of public attention and expert commentary.

In this atmosphere, the PLC felt it could not wait for the cabinet to present a draft formally. Instead, council members enthusiastically took over the drafting process themselves. Many PLC members regarded the matter as critical: up to that point, newly emerging Palestinian institutions based their legal existence only on signed agreements with Israel. Even strong supporters of those agreements wished to root institutions in Palestinian laws rather than agreements with an erstwhile enemy. Many members of the council regularly gave expression to the desire to establish a Palestinian state with a stronger democratic and constitutional basis than prevailed elsewhere in the Arab world. At the beginning of April 1996, the PLC passed a resolution demanding that the cabinet present its final draft of the Basic Law within three weeks.[18] The implicit threat (which was, in fact, carried out) was that the council would begin consideration of the matter on its own if it was not furnished with a cabinet-endorsed draft.

Members of the council found that their efforts drew international interest and support. External aid agencies had focused on the council as an essential instrument for improving Palestinian governance and were willing to bring in foreign expertise. Adrien Wing, a law professor from the University of Iowa with experience in southern Africa, and Muhammad al-Mirghani, an Egyptian law professor, came to advise the council.[19] Palestinian legal experts, such as the law faculty at Bir Zayt University and those associated with think tanks (such as the Center for Palestine Research and Studies) and human rights organizations, also joined in advising the council on its work.

Yet when it began discussion of the Basic Law, members of the council soon found themselves engaged in a very public confrontation with Yasir 'Arafat. 'Arafat claimed that the Basic Law was properly a matter for Palestinians everywhere; thus, the matter should be taken up by bodies representing all Palestinians (such as the PNC, the PLO's Executive Committee, and 'Arafat himself as president of the PLO) before the council (which merely represented residents of the West Bank and Gaza). Members of the council, many from 'Arafat's own Fatah movement, argued that they were simply considering the interim constitution for the PNA, not permanently deciding the political structure to govern all Palestinians. Further, many suspected that 'Arafat's autocratic tendencies motivated his procedural concerns. Council members with a strong interest in human rights and democracy had no wish to have the contents of the law dictated by 'Arafat. And they feared that 'Arafat intended to marginalize the council, still relying on PLO structures that he could dominate more easily. As the conflict heated up in July 1996, council leaders and members of the executive tried to work out a compromise. At the end of the month, 'Arafat made a rare personal appearance in the council and told the members they had no right to be discussing the Basic Law. While addressing the council, 'Arafat and Speaker Abu 'Ala' (Ahmad Quray') exchanged pointed remarks about the rights of the council, and Abu 'Ala' resigned in protest over 'Arafat's behavior.[20] Abu 'Ala' was dissuaded from carrying through on his resignation, and the council resumed its discussion of the Basic Law, but 'Arafat did not retreat from his position that the council was acting prematurely.

The procedural differences between 'Arafat and the council should not be overstated. Both ostensibly agreed on the need for a Basic Law to govern the PNA in the interim phase. Both also agreed that any legitimacy for even an interim Basic Law came from the Palestinian people and that any final determination of matters of governance had to involve structures (such as the PLO and PNC) representing all Palestinians. But this agreement could not obscure the fundamental structural division between 'Arafat and the PLC. Whereas the PLC was strictly a creature of the PNA, 'Arafat remained president of both the PNA and the PLO. He used his dual position to outmaneuver critics: to PLO dissidents he presented himself as president of an embryonic state; to PNA rivals he asserted that his position in the PLO made him a representative of Palestinians everywhere. All orders and decrees from 'Arafat cited both positions, allowing him to slide back and forth between the two roles.

When attention turned from procedural matters to the substance of the draft, the reasons behind the intensity of the debate became even clearer. The draft taken up by the council would have represented one of the most liberal constitutional documents in Arab history. The draft Basic Law allowed for a mixed presidential-parliamentary system not uncommon in Arab republics. More unusual was the strength of its rights provisions as well as the attempt to close loopholes that exist in many other Arab constitutions (involving emergency powers, constitutional interpretation, and the independence of the judiciary). One of the most sensitive issues in Palestinian politics—succession—was addressed explicitly: if the president died or became unwilling or unable to serve, the Speaker of the PLC would succeed him on a temporary basis until a permanent replacement was chosen. This would transfer determination of succession out of 'Arafat's hands.

'Arafat seemed to prefer to keep the matter of succession vague, perhaps as a way of balancing Palestinian factions against each other. (The importance of the succession issue should not be overstated, however, since the provisions in the Basic Law mirrored those 'Arafat had issued by decree in the 1995 Law of Elections. While few Palestinians and even fewer outside observers noticed, there were succession mechanisms already in effect.) And the draft could have led to a diplomatic crisis with Israel by retaining the designation of Jerusalem as the Palestinian capital.

The council debated the Basic Law and approved its first reading on 29 August 1996. The law was then referred to the relevant ministry and president for comment, following Arab parliamentary practice. Rather than comment and refer the draft back to the council, however, 'Arafat failed to act. Relations between 'Arafat and the council became increasingly strained over the matter. In the minds of many council members, the dispute only accentuated the need for immediate passage of a Basic Law: in its absence, the precise delineation of authority between the council and the president remained unclear, leaving the council unsure of whether or how it could pursue the matter further. In 1997, the council finally decided to resume discussion of the Basic Law and passed it on its second and third reading. From the perspective of council members, their work was done. A final draft was approved, requiring only presidential endorsement.

'Arafat simply ignored the Basic Law for five years. Most speculation on 'Arafat's inaction centered less on the process of drafting the Basic Law than on its content. And here the Basic Law contained some surprising (and, from the perspective of a ruler seeking to avoid constraints on actions, problematic) elements. It is true that Arab constitutional models and thought exercised the greatest influence on the first and especially subsequent drafts of the Basic Law. Initially, this augured well for presidential prerogatives. The reliance on Arab models is not surprising: the PNA had set itself the task of establishing a Palestinian political entity that was unmistakably Arab. Most Palestinian legal scholars and political leaders were trained in the Arab world. It should be no surprise, therefore, that the structure, language, and content of the document resemble those of other Arab documents. The Ottoman constitution served as the basis for most Arab constitutional texts of the twentieth century; the Egyptian constitutional tradition has proved particularly influential in addition (particularly because of the number of Egyptian experts consulted in the drafting process in other Arab countries).

The reliance on the Arab constitutional traditions carries strong implications, not all of them desirable from the perspective of Palestinian constitutionalists. The Arab world is rich not only in constitutional texts but also in mechanisms that vitiate their provisions. Arab constitutions generally grant strong executive authority, provide numerous escape hatches (such as emergency rule) and ambiguities, and shy from clear enforcement of basic constitutional principles. For instance, rights provisions are generally vague and without any clear means of enforcement; judicial independence is often mentioned but not given effective institutional expression. Importing Arab constitutional forms and practices seems a poor basis for Palestinian constitutionalism. Indeed, the first draft of the Palestinian Basic Law contained many of the silences and loopholes characteristic of Arab constitutions. Arab rulers are generally authoritarian and effectively unaccountable even while they stay within plausible interpretations of the constitution.[21]

On the other hand, the Arab constitutional tradition provides not only loopholes but also helpful experience. Those who have studied other Arab countries have learned clear lessons on the nature of the gaps and silences that have to be filled for constitutionalist practice to emerge. Palestinian constitutionalists focused intensively on Arab experiences to discover shortcomings of the first draft. In general, the process of drafting and redrafting the Basic Law exposed it to analysis by those sympathetic with constitutionalist ideas, and many of the loopholes and gaps of the first draft were progressively closed. In short, the Palestinian Basic Law not only drew on Arab constitutional models and traditions but (in its final form) turned them sharply in a liberal direction.

With each iteration, the Palestinian Basic Law progressively changed from a skeletal and extremely provisional document into a more extensive and potentially more permanent basis for political life.[22] The relationship between the structures of the PNA and the PLO grew increasingly attenuated, albeit in subtle ways.

Structure

The early drafts of the Basic Law provided for strong concentration of authority in the hands of the president. Subsequent drafts diminished, but did not eliminate, the presidential nature of the document. Initially the president was to serve as prime minister until the first elections; this provision was dropped in intermediate drafts, and the final drafts eliminated the position of prime minister entirely. These changes were partly dictated by the evolving circumstances under which the Basic Law was drafted: initially intended to provide the basis for establishing the structures of the PNA, the early drafts had few details about the council that was to be elected. Thus, in early drafts, officials were held accountable to the PLO Executive Committee rather than the council. Many of the details concerning the council were negotiated with the Israelis; when these were completed, the council was elected and itself took up the draft. It should not be surprising that members of the council insisted on provisions designed to guarantee themselves a strong oversight role. In these drafts, the cabinet receives a vote of confidence from the council, and confidence may be withdrawn from the cabinet or from individual ministers. While this would seem to render the proposed structure closer to a parliamentary than a presidential system, in fact similar provisions exist in most Arab constitutional documents but are rarely exercised. Only a very independent, well-organized, and determined parliamentary body can make use of such provisions to bring down ministers. A provision requiring that most ministers be drawn from the council was inserted in intermediate drafts but dropped from the final document.[23] Financial disclosure requirements, an innovation in Arab governance, were also written into the Basic Law.

While the council was potentially strengthened as drafts progressed, strong authority remained in the hands of the president. Not only was he to be elected directly; he would be difficult for the council to remove. The president was granted an American-style veto authority: a two-thirds majority would be required to pass legislation over his objection. And while serious steps were taken to ensure a strong judiciary, the seeds of presidential domination of the courts were also planted. Elements of a strong judiciary included provisions for a constitutional court and administrative courts.[24] A judicial council was to assume control over judicial affairs; it was even to make a recommendation on the post of attorney general (a quasi-judicial but executive-dominated post in most Arab countries). Earlier drafts had either a stronger presidential role or fewer details on most of these questions.

The various drafts of the Basic Law did take progressively more care to regulate one of the most problematic tools of Arab authoritarianism: emergency rule. Arab governments have used emergency powers to issue harsh or unpopular legislation by decree, to suspend basic rights, or to move heavy-handed and controversial conduct (especially by the security forces) outside the review of normal constitutional institutions. The issue was particularly salient for Palestinians because of their experience in this regard not only with Jordanian and Egyptian practices but more immediately with the Israelis. After assuming control of the West Bank and Gaza in 1967, Israel had taken a series of legal steps that made it virtually impossible for Palestinians to challenge official actions. The authors of the first draft of the Basic Law acknowledged this history only in an oblique way by forbidding suspension of the Basic Law itself or any of the rights it guaranteed. This was unsatisfactory to the more constitutionally minded forces that dominated in subsequent drafts, and more extensive provisions for emergency rule were included. On the one hand, the drafters did not want to hamstring a government likely to be coping with a difficult security situation. On the other hand, the drafters wished to ensure that some constitutional protections and procedures would be immune even during emergency situations and that political accountability would never be lost. Accordingly, the final draft authorized the president to issue decrees during emergencies, but such decrees would lose their legal force if they were not approved by parliament (Article 60).[25] The Basic Law also allowed the president to declare a state of emergency but included some real limitations: the declaration could take effect for only thirty days; further thirty-day renewals required approval of two-thirds of the council; and the council could review actions taken under the emergency authority (Chapter 6). The declaration of the emergency must state the goal, area, and duration. These seemingly unexceptional requirements for a declaration actually represent a bold departure from Arab practice, in which emergencies are often loosely defined and justified in only the vaguest terms. The final draft took one further step toward closing loopholes regarding states of emergency by explicitly repealing all previous states of emergency; Arab and Israeli practice often left such emergency situations lingering indefinitely, allowing future governments to rediscover their extensive powers. In a nod toward political realities, the Basic Law implicitly acknowledged the possibility of suspending constitutional freedoms by barring any restrictions not related to an emergency. The document itself and the council could not be suspended, however.

Rights

The Palestinian Basic Law contained an impressive catalogue of rights, freedoms, and guarantees to a population that had rarely enjoyed them previously (Chapter 2). The list of rights tended to grow modestly with each successive draft, and a requirement that citizens cooperate with the police was finally eliminated. Economic and social rights (including even the right to a clean environment) were included, giving the document a liberal and socialist tinge at the same time. In this regard, however, the Palestinian effort does not stand out from other Arab constitutions. Most Arab documents contain equally lengthy lists of such rights and freedoms. A variety of constitutional and legal shortcomings generally prevent these provisions from serving as the basis for a genuinely constitutionalist order, however. Thus, the real test for the Palestinian Basic Law was not how many freedoms it could name but how it was constructed to defend them. The document was quite mixed in this regard, though it was stronger than almost all of its Arab counterparts.

First, Arab governments often avoid enforcing the constitutionally enumerated rights by allowing them to be defined by ordinary legislation. It is common for constitutions to guarantee a right and then specify that the right will be "defined by law" or even must operate "within the boundaries defined by law." Such language is not an Arab invention but is often included in European constitutions. The effect is to render the constitutional guarantee dependent on ordinary legislation. The Palestinian Basic Law, even in its final form, did employ such formulations for many basic freedoms. Second, Arab governments often rob constitutional guarantees of their meaning by depriving citizens of any means to enforce them. The Palestinian Basic Law contains fairly strong provisions to prevent this tactic from becoming effective. For instance, citizens are guaranteed compensation for any violations of security of the home (through illegal reconnaissance or entry by officials; Article 17). Indeed, one article requires compensation for any violation of basic rights (Article 32). Closing another gap left in some Arab constitutions, the Basic Law barred the exclusion of any administrative act from judicial review (Article 30).

Status of the Basic Law

The original draft of the Basic Law was a far more modest document than the one finally produced by the council. Early drafts made clear that the structures established by the Basic Law (and, implicitly, by the Oslo process) were subservient to the PLO. This was so not only for the structural terms described above but also for provisions that clearly moved the PLO outside the constitutional order being created. An explicit provision in draft after draft stated that the PLO was not subject to the provisions of the Basic Law—even as the structural links between the PLO and the PNA were being dropped. The final draft approved by the council took the bold step of removing this provision completely. The only traces were some references in the preamble to the PLO as the "sole legitimate representative of the Arab Palestinian people," an acknowledgment that the status of the Basic Law and its ratification by the council came from this fact, and a ratification of the flag adopted by the PLO.

Just as the final draft diminished without repudiating the link with the PLO, so it distanced itself from the Oslo process. The preamble briefly mentioned the Oslo Agreement but only to set the historical context in which the document was being written. In a sense, the drafts produced by the council were themselves indirect results of the Oslo process, for they were authored by a council whose existence and structure were negotiated by the PLO and Israel. Yet there was no more than passing acknowledgment of this ancestry in any of the drafts of the Basic Law. Indeed, the final document was bolder than previous drafts in one respect: while Jerusalem was proclaimed the capital, earlier drafts allowed a temporary capital to be established elsewhere during the transitional period. The final draft proclaimed simply, "Jerusalem is the capital of Palestine." The preamble also took care to state that the Basic Law for the transitional period did nothing to diminish the Palestinian right to resume efforts for "return and self determination, including the establishment of the Palestinian state with its capital, Jerusalem." Mindful that many Palestinians regarded the establishment of the PNA with apprehension as a structure representing only those still resident in the West Bank and Gaza, the council also inserted in the preamble an affirmation of the right of "any Palestinian, wherever he exists, to enjoy equal rights along with his citizens on the land of the Homeland."

Those who drafted the Basic Law presented it as a modest document that would govern the PNA only during the transitional period. Yet they clearly hoped to establish a new Palestinian constitutional tradition that would channel permanent arrangements in liberal and democratic directions. They failed in their short-term goal: just as they discovered after they had passed the first reading of the Basic Law, members of the PLC lacked any clear legal mechanism of forcing the president to take action on legislation. Indeed, the drafters declined a suggestion that the document include a clause having it go into effect if the president refused to act within a specified period.[26] 'Arafat's inaction on the Basic Law contributed to deterioration in his relations with the council into a state of near-hostility. In a prolonged confrontation in 1997 and 1998, the council included the Basic Law in a list of grievances and threatened to suspend its own work or remove confidence from the cabinet. Yet the council eventually backed down on most matters (the confrontation is described more fully in Chapter 4). While they still cited the Basic Law on many occasions, PLC members allowed the matter to drop in favor of other work. As one council member said in 2000, "We always cite it; we relate everything to it. . . . But I am not going to waste four years crying over the Basic Law."[27] Having abandoned more confrontational techniques, the members of the council found that the only tools that might otherwise be available to them to force action were contained in the still unenacted Basic Law.[28] Only in May 2002—when the president himself hoisted the banner of reform—did PLC members rediscover their former enthusiasm for the Basic Law. By that time, it had been nearly five years since they had passed it.

Amidst a sudden upsurge of interest in Palestinian reform coming in May and June 2002, 'Arafat suddenly announced that he had signed the Basic Law. By then, many had forgotten the document. And the approval, while significant, was not unproblematic. At first, 'Arafat stopped short of putting it into effect. The Basic Law was not published in the *Official Gazette*, a necessary step for it to become effective, until July 2002. Thus, when 'Arafat appointed a new cabinet in June 2002, his decree did not cite the Basic Law (as would be expected) for its authority. Further, the cabinet contained one more minister than the Basic Law would allow. Widespread speculation that 'Arafat had amended the Basic Law before signing it seemed to explain such odd steps. When the Basic Law was finally published, one significant change was indeed made concerning appointment of the prosecutor general. The Basic Law as passed by the PLC conflicted with a provision of the judicial law (signed by 'Arafat shortly before the Basic Law). The PLC-passed Basic Law provided for a PLC role in the appointment of the attorney general (Article 98), but the judicial law removed a similar provision at 'Arafat's insistence. The version of the Basic Law published in July 2002 dropped the PLC role, apparently because 'Arafat unilaterally removed the provision.

Even given the irregular amendment process, approval of the Basic Law marked a major step for Palestinian constitutionalism. Given the prevailing political crisis within the PNA at the time, however, there was little likelihood of its being easily implemented. Indeed, the drafters and the supporters of the Basic Law may have had more success on their long-term goal of establishing a Palestinian constitutional tradition. As will be seen, the process of drafting a permanent constitution adopted much from their efforts.

But while the Basic Law was being drafted and ignored for so long, an alternative constitutional order was developed for the PNA. While this order was never openly declared as such, it was far more effective in practice than the Basic Law and left a far different legacy for Palestinian constitutional development.

THE UNDECLARED CONSTITUTION OF THE PALESTINIAN NATIONAL AUTHORITY

Although most domestic and international debate on constitutional issues focused on the drafting of the Basic Law, the PNA worked quietly from the beginning to establish a legal framework for governance largely separate from that effort. From the first days of the PNA, the leadership developed a basis for subsequent legislative action. The bulk of the legal order created (and revived) by the PNA is analyzed in Chapter 2; for present purposes it is sufficient to note that the legal order did entail construction of a makeshift but effective constitutional order that enabled the development of a more comprehensive legislative framework.

The Oslo Agreements—with their extensive provisions on matters of Palestinian self-government—provided very little of this constitutional framework. To be sure, the institutions created did not stake out any direct claim to sovereignty, nor did they touch on the matters designated in those agreements to the final status negotiations (refugees, Jerusalem, borders, and settlement). In that way, the Oslo Agreements can be portrayed as forming a part of the Palestinian constitutional order. Aside from the Oslo Agreements, the other elements of the Palestinian constitutional order followed the same path as Palestinian textbooks (see Chapter 6): they sidestepped the sensitive issues of borders and sovereignty wherever possible and treated them extremely obliquely when mention was unavoidable.

The unacknowledged (but very much written) constitutional order of the PNA was created in four steps, all issued directly by Yasir 'Arafat in his dual capacity as president of the PNA and chair of the Executive Committee of the PLO. The first came on 20 May 1994, in Tunis, while the PNA was still being established. In a brief decree, Yasir 'Arafat proclaimed that all laws, regulations, and orders in effect before the 1967 war in the West Bank and Gaza would continue in effect until their unification had been completed.[29] This decree made no immediate change in the legal framework then prevailing in the West Bank and Gaza. But it had an important constitutional component: the source of authority for those laws now derived not from the previous powers that had issued them but from 'Arafat in his dual capacity as PLO and PNA leader. In short, the source of law for the West Bank and Gaza was now the PLO and the body it authorized, the PNA, and 'Arafat had the authority to act in the name of both.

The next two steps in the construction of the constitutional order of the PNA were taken on 17 April 1995. First, in a law issued by decree, President 'Arafat transferred all authorities under all laws, decrees, circulars, and regulations in force to the PNA.[30] This step resembled those taken by previous authorities upon assuming control (the British, Jordanians, Egyptians, and Israelis). The law went beyond merely taking over from previous authorities, however: 'Arafat assigned both legislative and executive authority to himself and the Palestinian Council (which at that point referred to his cabinet). The intent was clearly to move toward establishment of a sovereign entity, but it left internal constitutional questions ambiguous because the relative authority of the president and the council was not explained.

On the same day, therefore, 'Arafat issued a second, far more detailed law establishing the process for making new laws in the PNA.[31] What was notable about the procedure was that the entire process was contained entirely within the executive branch. A ministry or agency was to draw up legislation and refer it to the Diwan al-fatwa wa-l-tashri' (Bureau of Legal Consultation and Legislation), a freestanding body within the Ministry of Justice. The Diwan was then to make necessary changes without affecting the essence or the purpose of the proposal, consulting with concerned ministries, before referring it to the secretary-general of the cabinet. The cabinet was then to refer it to a Ministerial Committee headed by the minister of justice, with the director of the Diwan as a member. The committee was then to study the matter and refer it to the entire cabinet, which could accept, reject, or amend it and then refer it back to the Diwan one more time to put it in proper legal form. The Diwan would bring the final product to the president for promulgation.

These three legal steps formed the basis for most subsequent legal action taken by the PNA. Subsequent laws and decrees routinely cited them as the basis for their authority. Occasionally other sources of authority would be mentioned—the agreement of the PLO Executive Committee, or, on one occasion, unnamed "constitutional and legal principles in operation"—but it was clear from the laws, regulations, and decrees issued that the PNA leadership regarded these laws as providing the basis for governance.[32] And the constitutional order thus created was unmistakably an unbounded and completely circular autocracy. The president assigned all authority to himself, and the critical officials participating in Palestinian governance (the ministers and the director of the Diwan) were presidential appointments. The president even chaired cabinet meetings, meaning that he was responsible for overseeing the body that referred legislation to himself.

The final step in the creation of a Palestinian constitutional order robbed some of the clarity from this system without fundamentally altering it. On 7 December 1995, President 'Arafat promulgated one of the most complex pieces of legislation produced by the PNA, the Law of Elections.[33] Most of the law concerned the process of conducting elections for the presidency and for the PLC, but two unmistakably constitutional elements were introduced. First, the very fact that elections would be held introduced a new source of authority, the Palestinian people living only in the West Bank and Gaza. To be sure, every subsequent legal action taken by 'Arafat continued to cite his dual position as PNA president and PLO leader, meaning that he still maintained a broader source of authority (the Palestinian people throughout the world, as represented by the PLO).

Second, and of far more practical importance, the law assigned some tasks to the PLC: it was to draw up a constitutional order, assume undefined legislative authority, and approve the cabinet. No longer was authority totally circular and contained within the presidency. But the Law of Elections did not offer effective limitations on presidential authority either. First, as described above, the council was free to draft the Basic Law but found it could not impose it on an uninterested president. Second, the law did not supersede the earlier law on the preparation of legislation—a law that made no provision for the PLC. There followed a prolonged wrangle in which the council's authority to initiate legislation stood very much at issue. As described in Chapter 4, the council finally won in the sense that its rights were acknowledged by the executive branch—but very little of its legislation was approved. Finally, the authority of the council to approve (or, by implication, dismiss) the cabinet was firmly grounded in law but extremely difficult to exercise in a way that provided for genuine accountability. It was because of the centrality of the Law of Elections to the Palestinian constitutional order that reformers developed proposals for a revised law in 2002.

Thus the oft-repeated complaint of Palestinians that they remained without any constitutional framework, based as it was on 'Arafat's failure to act on the Basic Law, missed much of the groundwork that had been laid. It was true that some fundamental questions—chiefly relating to relations between the council and the executive branch, but also involving the judiciary as well as fundamental rights—remained unresolved. But the legal and constitutional framework existed for an extreme concentration of authority in the hands of the president.

Even the constitutional ambiguities that remained served presidential autocracy. 'Arafat's dual position as PNA and PLO leader was augmented by his consistent refusal to make clear in which capacity he was acting on a particular measure. And his insistence on convening meetings of the Palestinian "leadership," combining the cabinet with the PLO Executive Committee, blurred distinctions and chains of command still further. It was clear that Yasir 'Arafat stood at the apex of Palestinian governance, but it was not clear how the various structures and institutions below him were to relate to each other. The result could be extremely frustrating for those desiring either clarity or accountability—which was, perhaps, the point of all the deliberately constructed ambiguities.

The outbreak of the second intifada actually obscured matters still further.[34] Members of the security services doubled as members of popular militias, individuals moved among their various PLO, PNA, and party positions, and 'Arafat himself withdrew from a significant public role in decision making. The result was a situation that confused Palestinians and confounded international observers. For all its flaws, however, the constitutional order prevailing fit very well with the leadership's apparent desire to preserve flexibility and avoid limitations on its actions. In this respect, it served as a far more attractive alternative than the Basic Law.

THE FOURTH EFFORT:
CONSTITUTING A PALESTINIAN STATE

The constitutional framework offered by the Basic Law offered clear and largely liberal principles of governance. The alternative constitutional framework offered almost unchecked executive authority within the PNA. Neither offered any symbolic support for Palestinian sovereignty: the Basic Law was explicitly designed for the interim period; the alternative framework was never declared to be the constitutional order at all.

In April 1999, the Central Committee of the PLO quietly moved the focus of Palestinian constitutionalism in a new direction emphasizing internationally recognized sovereignty. Meeting shortly before the target date for a final status agreement, the Central Committee gained international attention by deciding to refrain from an immediate declaration of statehood. Much less noticed by international observers was its decision to move ahead with preparations for statehood. First, the Central Committee authorized a new target date for declaring a state, September 2000. Second, it authorized the necessary preparations. One particular effort was singled out for explicit mention: the committee welcomed the decision of the secretary-general of the Arab League to appoint a committee to assist the Palestinians in drafting a constitution.[35]

The effect of the Central Committee's statement was to transfer constitution writing from the PNA back to the PLO, without even acknowledging the Basic Law. The statement also implied a role for the Arab League and thus the possibility of reintroducing Arab constitutional flaws that had been weeded out over successive drafts of the Basic Law.

Perhaps most frustrating for those who had invested their hopes in the Basic Law, the new effort got off to an extremely slow start. The purpose seemed to be to assure Palestinian and Arab audiences that appropriate preparations were being made without actually making them. An Arab League advisory committee was formed on paper but showed no sign of life and eventually faded. A second Palestinian committee was formed under the leadership of Nabil Sha'th, but even some of its members were initially unaware of what the committee was supposed to do and who was on it.[36] The committee members received little guidance and no budget (financing their limited expenses personally).

Slowly—and largely out of the public eye—the committee formed a clearer sense of mission, generally acting on its own initiative. It began meeting in the fall of 1999. In February 2000, the Central Committee of the PLO met again to hear how the work it had commissioned the previous April was proceeding. Little attention was given to the Constitutional Committee, however, which had at that point engaged only in preliminary debates. In July 2000, the Central Committee met again and affirmed its support for democratic and liberal principles but did not even mention the constitutional effort or the committee.[37] As a result, the committee had to proceed with very little guidance over constitutional issues. Frustrated by the lack of guidance and support from the Palestinian leadership, some members of the committee began drawing up their own drafts. By the summer of 2000, they began to circulate these drafts and hold public workshops to discuss them.[38] Others began to speak of the need for a preliminary constitutional declaration, since there was little chance of finishing work by the expected declaration of statehood in September; they also began to speak of the need to convene a constituent assembly so that the drafting could be truly democratic and participatory.[39]

In September 2000, the PLO's Central Committee met, issuing a statement that criticized the slow pace of preparations for statehood. It demanded completion of a provisional constitutional declaration, a Law of Elections for a Palestinian parliament and the leadership of the state, and a beginning to the process of gaining membership in the United Nations. And it demanded a detailed report by the next Central Committee meeting, scheduled for 15 November 2000, the twelfth anniversary of the 1988 declaration of independence.[40]

The eruption of the second intifada in late September 2000 disrupted and further confused the process of drafting a constitution, but it did not bring it to a halt. The committee drafting a full document managed to continue its work, though its plan for extensive workshops including trips to Palestinian diaspora communities was disrupted. In February 2001, it produced its complete draft.[41] The draft makes clear that it is to be adopted according to a democratic procedure, but no body—from either the PLO or the PNA—drew up plans on how to proceed with the document. Meanwhile, those calling for a provisional and abbreviated constitutional declaration along with preparations for electing a constituent assembly to draft a document reiterated their call but did little in effect to pursue it. Most of this debate remained far out of the public view, obscured by its technical nature, the lack of interest shown by the senior leadership, and the drama of the daily violence of the second intifada.[42] Yet those who had participated in this debate must have been startled when, in May 2002, their efforts received the endorsement of the president of the United States. Palestinian constitutional specialists who had trouble attracting the attention of their own public and leadership heard George W. Bush proclaim, "The Palestinians need to develop a constitution, rule of law, transparency. They've got to have a treasury that is able to battle corruption, so that not only do the Israeli people have confidence in the Authority, but so do the Palestinian people have confidence in the Authority."[43]

The renewed Palestinian and international interest in reform of PNA institutions did lead to an uncoordinated revival of constitution-drafting efforts. A group of Arab-American attorneys, operating with Saudi assistance, worked with an English translation of the February 2001 draft to develop their own proposal (the document was presented to the U.S. government but not the broader Palestinian public and subsequently disappeared from view). The committee that drafted the February 2001 document was called back into existence in the summer of 2002, working individually and by teleconferencing (because of the continued Israeli closure). The Arab League committee, formed on paper in 1999 but never active, was revived in December 2002 to review the work of the Palestinian committee.

Despite such episodic attention, those drafting a constitution encountered a deep skepticism about their work from many Palestinians even when they did manage to attract attention. Such skepticism flowed not only from the experience of the abortive Basic Law but also from a more profound doubt regarding the appropriateness of drafting a constitution before statehood had been clearly achieved. This doubt came in three different forms.

First, some saw the entire process as unrealistic and premature. While the Oslo Accords had allowed the establishment of the PNA, Palestinian autonomy was still severely constrained. Even assuming eventual Palestinian statehood—itself not assured by the accords—critical aspects of the eventual Palestinian state remained unclear (such as borders, security arrangements, capital, and relations with the Palestinian diaspora). To write a constitution for a state in such a context seemed a meaningless gesture to many.[44]

Second, others saw the attempt to design a constitutional order premature in more practical terms. Bringing about a truly liberal and democratic order required time, extended debate, and popular participation. Behind the calls for an elected constituent assembly often stood implicit criticism of the efforts of the small number of academics and officials in the drafting committee: despite their efforts to provoke public interest and debate about their work, such individuals were not true representatives of the people and should not be entrusted with making fundamental choices. Presenting their work to a final plebiscite would allow Palestinians only to accept or reject their work; earlier and more sustained public involvement was necessary. And it would be futile to try to provide for such involvement with the territorial separation, periodic closures, and difficulties of securing the involvement of the Palestinian diaspora (with the PLO outside Palestine largely moribund).

Third, the constitution-drafting effort seems to be regarded by the senior leadership as useful only for its symbolic assertion of sovereignty. No public statements to this effect have been issued, nor are any likely to be. Yet the sustained neglect of any constitutional efforts and the silence of senior leaders—a silence punctuated only by periodic Central Committee statements mentioning constitution drafting as part of the preparation for statehood—give a fairly clear indication of the priorities of the leadership. 'Arafat's inaction on the Basic Law—based partly on the insistence that the PLO must be consulted—combined with his failure to invigorate the Legal Committee of the PLO, which would be responsible for such issues—provides additional confirmation of this attitude. The leadership has relied fairly heavily on the ambiguity of its position to allow it maximum freedom from constitutional fetters. At a climactic moment in the national struggle—a climax initially of negotiation and then of violent confrontation—a constitutional document must seem an unwelcome intrusion indeed.

Yet those pursuing the constitutional path are not persuaded by such views. If the PLO is ever to make the transition from revolutionary organization to statehood—a transition it committed itself to unambiguously in 1988—it must begin the task of structuring its state, making clear the chains of command, organizing relations among public authorities, and defining the relationship between the state and the society. A constitution is a vital contribution to all these tasks. Ignoring constitutional issues would allow the existing constitutional order to continue by default. The effective constitution of the PNA would become the permanent constitutional order, leaving the state of Palestine with a political system less institutionalized and developed even than its authoritarian Arab counterparts. Even a provisional declaration of constitutional principles might—in the eyes of some

Palestinian constitutional activists—become a way of enshrining current authoritarian practices for an indefinite period of time. Constitutional decisions, even those made temporarily, are often difficult to reverse or modify.

The draft document produced by the Constitutional Committee in February 2001 provides—much like the Basic Law—an unrealized but powerful vision of a different kind of Palestine. It is worth examining in some detail as a statement of what a Palestinian constitutional order might look like if it ever comes into being. And indeed, any subsequent drafting efforts will probably have to begin with the draft as a starting point, produced as it was by a committee loosely authorized by the PLO. (In the same way, the committee itself found itself using earlier documents—the 1988 declaration of independence and the PNA's Basic Law—as the starting point for its efforts.)

Structure

The 2001 draft constitution introduced one major structural change in the form of governance operating under the PNA: while the PNA had a strong president with an elected (and self-proclaimed legislative) council, the state of Palestine was to have a prime minister. The decision to separate the head of state from the head of government would bring Palestine into line with prevailing Arab constitutional practice. But its effects might be somewhat different than elsewhere in the Arab world. Throughout the Arab world, the concentration of authority in the head of state is generally only loosely constrained by an elected council. A prime minister effectively answers only to the head of state. (Technically, most, but not all, Arab prime ministers can serve only with the confidence of the parliament. But Arab parliaments do not refuse the head of state's choice, nor do they remove confidence once they have granted it.) Yet the Palestinian parliament might be a more assertive body. Certainly the PLC—which, during its short life succeeded in bringing down a government—proved more active than most Arab parliaments with far longer histories. The full explanation for—and the strong limitations of—the PLC's record are explored in more detail in Chapter 4. For the present it is sufficient to note that the hybrid parliamentary/presidential system constructed by the draft constitution might bring a greater amount of accountability than comparable systems do elsewhere in the Arab world. Such at least was the hope of many reformers as well as some international actors (such as the United States) for whom the chief attraction of constitutional reform was the alternative it might provide to President 'Arafat's leadership.

Beyond moving Palestine toward such a hybrid system, the drafters of the constitution sought to enhance the accountability in several other ways, reacting primarily to the brief experience provided by the PNA. Indeed, the draft constitution contained several provisions with surprisingly detailed and specific requirements on what might seem to be minor matters better left to legislation or evolving practice. Only a seasoned observer of PNA practice would understand the underlying motivation for such clauses. Two examples best illustrate the point.

First, with regard to the promulgation of laws, the draft constitution required that laws passed by the parliament be published in the *Official Gazette* within thirty days (unless returned by the president for reconsideration, in which case the parliament could decide on proposed amendments before resubmitting it to the president). Yet the draft also contained clear provisions in case the president failed to act or the *Official Gazette* failed to publish the law. In both cases the law would go into effect thirty days after passage or after a parliamentary request that the law be published. Constitutional provisions for presidential inaction are not uncommon, but the careful provision that a law could go into effect even if it was not published may be unique. It represents a clear response to the PLC's frustration: not only did the president fail to act on many pieces of legislation passed by the PLC, but the *Official Gazette* would not publish laws that the PLC was convinced should have gone into effect. (This was the case with the Basic Law, which PLC members felt should go into effect after the president failed to reject it, and the Labor Law, which the president signed but failed to have published for a considerable period, rendering its effectiveness in doubt.)

Second, those who drafted the constitution sought to enshrine fiscal accountability of the government to the parliament through correcting practices that had developed under the PNA. The section of the draft constitution covering the fiscal authority of the parliament included ten articles, and there were numerous other references to budgetary and fiscal matters throughout the document. These provisions specified when the budget had to be submitted, what expenditures the government could make if the budget was not approved on time, and when the final accounts would have to be submitted. Most of these detailed provisions were adopted from the budget law for the PNA; many of them had been routinely violated (by submitting the budget late, failing to obtain PLC consent for changes, and neglecting to submit final accounts). The drafters of the constitution offered no remedy for violations, but they evidently hoped that elevating such requirements from statutory law to the constitutional text would help ensure that they were more faithfully observed.

Rights

Like the Basic Law, the 2001 draft constitution provided a catalogue of liberal civil and political rights. It also struck a liberal economic pose in some areas, guaranteeing private property, protecting the right to strike in a very weak way, and proclaiming support for free market principles. Some of the socialist legacy of Arab constitutionalism entered the document as well, with guarantees for free education and social insurance. And the right to a clean environment, introduced in the Basic Law, was retained in the draft constitution. Two controversial issues in the Basic Law—the role of the shari'a and of women's rights—were handled in a similar way: the shari'a was to be a source of legislation, with religious law the basis for personal status legislation. The draft drew back from women's equality, instead declaring women to be "full sisters" of men.

Yet as with the Basic Law, the real test of the meaning of the rights provisions lies in the mechanisms used to defend them. And here the draft constitution's record was mixed, much like the Basic Law (though in some different ways). Many of the basic rights were to be limited or defined by law. International human rights documents received mention, but they would have effect only when ratified by Palestine. At that point they would have the status of regular legislation (which essentially made them self-enforcing but also opened the possibility that later legislation could modify them).

The drafters of the constitution were very much aware of the possible gaps in rights provisions, having learned from the broader Arab as well as the Palestinian experience. They sought to close some of these gaps in three ways. First, the constitution provided for a constitutional court, with its members appointed by the three branches of government (the president, the parliament, and the judiciary) to ensure that it was not dominated by the executive. Second, many of the provisions of the constitution sought to ensure that governance would take place through legal mechanisms, in obvious contrast to the PNA, where large gaps in the legal framework allowed the executive branch to do as it pleased. For instance, monopolies, concessions, and public employment were all to be regulated by law. Searches could be conducted only by court order and during the day. Finally, the constitution was drafted to restrict states of emergency as much as seemed practicable. Previous states of emergency were specifically terminated (as with the Basic Law). Most notably, the provisions for the state of emergency itself were stringent. A state of emergency could be declared only for thirty days, renewable only once with the consent of the PLC. Emergency powers had to be exercised through legal means and could not suspend constitutional provisions. Such limitations, if they actually came into force, would place Palestine in an unusual position in the Arab world, where states of emergency are often the norm and are only loosely constrained by law.

Status of the Palestinian State Relative to Other Palestinian Bodies

Unlike the Basic Law, the 2001 draft constitution was unambiguously a document for a sovereign state. Sovereignty and statehood were declared at the outset and asserted throughout the text. This required that the constitution define the relationship between the state of Palestine and two other entities: the PNA and the PLO. It did so—indirectly in both cases, but also in such a way as to make clear that the state of Palestine was the legal successor to both entities.

First, with regard to the PNA, Article 218 of the draft constitution provided that "the laws, regulations, and decisions currently in force in Palestine shall remain effective until amended or cancelled by corresponding legislation in accordance with the provisions of this constitution." In short, the work of the PNA (including all the laws passed by the PLC) remained in effect until superseded (unless specifically contradicted by the constitutional text). The PLC had been proceeding on the assumption that it was not only legislating for the PNA but also laying the foundation for the Palestinian state.[45] The draft constitution endorsed this view and protected their work.

Second, the draft constitution implied that the state of Palestine incorporated the PLO. The text did not explicitly address the relationship between the two and could thus lead to confusion and controversy later. While the PLO fell into a state of institutional decay after the creation of the PNA, its structures continued to exist and fulfilled some critical functions. The PLO, as the representative of Palestinians everywhere, granted legitimacy to the PNA, which ruled only in the West Bank and Gaza. Under the Oslo Accords, the PNA was not to conduct foreign relations, meaning that the PLO remained the representative of Palestinians internationally. And the bodies associated with the PLO—the PNC, the Central Committee, and the Executive Committee—continued to exist (in varying degrees of viability).

The draft constitution never mentioned the PLO explicitly, but it included two provisions that implied that it was to be superseded. First, the state of Palestine was clearly authorized to conduct foreign affairs, and ambassadors were said to be responsible to the president of the state (not the president of the Executive Committee of the PLO, as under the Oslo

Accords). Second and more importantly, the draft constitution provided for a parliament with two chambers. One was the Legislative Council, elected by those in the state of Palestine. The second was the National Council, representing Palestinian refugees abroad and having a far more restricted legislative role than the Legislative Council. Not only did the National Council share the name of the Palestinian National Council (often referred to as the "Palestinian parliament in exile," it was the body that established the PLO and made pronouncements of basic policy in the name of the Palestinian people). The constitution also provided that the existing electoral system for the PNC would continue until amended by Palestinian law. In short, the state of Palestine would absorb the constituting body of the PLO, transforming it into a chamber of the Palestinian parliament.

Yet as much as the draft constitution posited the state of Palestine as a successor to the PNA and the PLO, in one respect the document asserted a more modest claim. While Palestinian refugees abroad were to be represented in the upper house, this did not imply that the Palestinian state could negotiate their right to return on their behalf. The drafters of the constitution not only asserted a right of refugees to return to their original domicile (and not merely homeland) but also described it as an individual right that could not be delegated. While the state of Palestine was therefore to represent all Palestinians, it would be constitutionally barred from negotiating away the right of each Palestinian to return to the pre-1948 home of his or her ancestors.

CONCLUSION: CONSTITUTING THE RESUMPTION OF ARAB PALESTINE

In May 2002, Palestinian constitutional issues suddenly attracted international attention. President George W. Bush called for a Palestinian constitution, and PLC members renewed long-forgotten calls for approval of the Basic Law (mindful that the draft permanent constitution was probably not yet ready for immediate adoption and might have amounted to a declaration of statehood). The sudden resurrection simply resumed constitutional debates where they had left off when the second intifada had pushed them out of public attention.

These broad debates—concerning the form, content, and timing of the Palestinian constitution—reflect all three senses in which recent years have witnessed the resumption of Arab Palestine. First, the sense in which the PNA—and the state of Palestine when it is declared—represent resumption from past Palestinian history is emphasized by tenuous but carefully preserved legal continuity from the past. The mandate gave way, in this view, to the All Palestine Government. The death of that entity gave birth to the establishment of the PLO, which in turn authorized the establishment of the PNA. Without diminishing its dependence on the PLO, the PNA also drew on the constitutional legacies of Egyptian and Jordanian rule. The state of Palestine—when it is declared—will either succeed to or subsume the PLO and its subsidiary, the PNA. Thus, according to this perspective, Palestine is a continuous entity, fragile and modest as its institutional expression may have been at times. The state of Palestine, when it is declared for the third time, will be not a new creation but a new expression of an older one.

The constitution of Palestine also represents the resumption of full participation in Arab politics and expression of Palestine's Arab nature. The constitutional forms and language proposed—whether in the Basic Law or in the draft constitution—are drawn from the Arab constitutional experience. This is true in the positive sense that the drafters have borrowed clauses, structures, and conceptions from the Arab constitutional tradition and have looked primarily to Arab models in devising Palestinian procedures and institutions. It is also true in the negative sense: the drafters have been attentive above all to the shortcomings in the Arab constitutional tradition and have sought to avoid them. In that way, they have worked not only to draw on the Arab experience but also to contribute to its development.

Finally, those who seek to resume normal political life and end the subordination of all political life to the nationalist struggle have focused much of their energy on constitutional drafting. Behind debates about the content—and even the appropriateness—of a Palestinian constitution lies a more fundamental structure about the nature of Palestinian politics at present. For some—including the senior leadership—constitutional texts offer some attractive rewards (especially those connected with sovereignty) but also entail some costs. They can constrain power and rob the leadership of flexibility. At a time when it must concentrate on an existential struggle, such structures seem at best a luxury and at worst a debilitating impediment to realizing the nationalist cause. For the Palestinian constitutionalists, it is precisely at this formative stage that proper constitutional development must take place. Postponing the matter until the resolution of the nationalist struggle damages not only the Palestinian present but also the Palestinian future: it risks entrenching institutions and practices that will serve future generations poorly. Writing a liberal, democratic constitution furthers rather than undermines the cause of Palestinian statehood; the proponents of this vision of the resumption of Arab Palestine speak of the need to move from *thawra ila dawla,* from revolution to state.

Oddly, the contest between the proponents of constitutionalism and those who view it as premature rarely takes the form of open confrontation. The proponents of constitutionalism have dominated the drafting process for both the Basic Law and the draft constitution for a Palestinian state. The resulting documents are impressive testimony to the ability to provide a framework for a liberal, democratic order out of the Arab constitutional tradition. The opponents—or rather the advocates of delay—have lost much in these documents. Their defeat owes far more to their lack of interest in the text than to any political weakness. The problem for the constitutionalists, then, is often that the more they dominate the drafting process, the more they make adoption of their texts increasingly unlikely. The Basic Law represented an impressive accomplishment in its drafting, but it offered little to a leadership anxious to preserve flexibility. The document was therefore a greater testimony to the constitutionalist ambitions of its authors than to their political realism. And the draft constitution risks a similar fate—ignored by those who commissioned it, not because it was an unsatisfactory effort, but because it was too good.

4 Inventing a Parliament

We are never as steeped in history as when we pretend not to be.
MICHEL-ROLPH TROUILLOT, *Silencing the Past:
Power and the Production of History*

On January 26, 2000, the PLC met in Ramallah for the presentation of the PNA's budget for the year. The budget that the cabinet had forwarded to the PLC marked a departure from past practice in two very significant ways. First, unlike any previous budget, it had been submitted before the beginning of the fiscal year. Second, the budget was balanced for the first time in PNA history. Yet the session seemed likely to be highly charged. No deputy could forget the session held just two months earlier.

In that earlier session, some members of the PLC had attempted to confront the PNA's record over four budget cycles. Year after year, the PLC had criticized the government for failing to deliver the budget until well into the fiscal year, giving skeletal details at best on sensitive areas (such as the security services), failing to respond to requests for additional information, refusing to include a significant portion of PNA revenues, and keeping some of the PNA's activities completely off the official record. The chairman of the Budget Committee in 1999, 'Azmi Shu'aybi, had decided that four years was enough time for the PNA to learn how to submit a budget properly, and he prepared for a public confrontation. While Shu'aybi belonged to a small party (FIDA, or the Palestinian Democratic Union), he was widely respected for his integrity and diligence. Unlike many of the other PNA critics in the assembly, he remained supportive of the leadership's basic approach to negotiations with Israel. And he was tenacious. Thus, his determination to force an open debate on the budget—and even threaten removal of confidence from the minister of finance—was taken quite seriously. Indeed, the 1999 budget had been passed—with the year more than half over—only after Shu'aybi had secured a promise that the PLC would debate the government's failures and broken promises. Members of the Budget Committee had considered submitting their resignations all at once if the debate was

94

suppressed. Yet when members assembled for the debate on the budget on November 24, 1999, Abu 'Ala' (Ahmad Quray'), the PLC Speaker, informed them that only Shu'aybi had resigned from the committee. Abu 'Ala' turned to Shu'aybi, who declined to explain, leading the Speaker to explain that Shu'aybi had resigned "for known reasons." One PLC member leapt up crying, "Point of order! I don't know why he resigned!" The Speaker hissed, "That's not a point of order." When the deputy continued to object, the Speaker shouted, "It's none of your business."

Shu'aybi's resignation did not prevent a noisy debate. The Budget Committee, now chaired by Da'ud al-Zir, informed the council that it had made eighteen requests of the government but that only three had been fully complied with. The matters in dispute were often quite significant—such as the government's inability to give any reliable figures on the extent of the deficit. After the committee presented its report, deputy after deputy condemned the government, sometimes in extremely harsh terms. One deputy thundered that the government's conduct would bring a new intifada and that the PLC should either withdraw confidence from the government or resign. Another claimed he wish to withdraw confidence not simply from the cabinet but from the entire PNA. The Speaker refused to entertain any motion of no confidence, explaining that the PLC had met only to discuss the Budget Committee report. In the end, the PLC decided—by a single-vote margin—to approve a weak motion calling for monitoring the government's compliance closely and working with it on administrative and fiscal reform.

Thus, when the PLC met again in January to discuss the 2000 budget, the angry rhetoric and frustrations of the earlier session could not be forgotten. Al-Zir, the new chair of the Budget Committee, presented a report that began on a conciliatory note, commending the cabinet for submitting a balanced budget for the first time. Yet he then went on to note numerous violations of the law, failure to report information fully and accurately, and continued irregular practices. Symptomatic was correspondence between the committee and the PNA's General Personnel Council (Diwan al-muwazifin), attached to the report. When the committee had asked the council directly why its budget had mushroomed, the council responded in writing that it had been instructed to add a large number of employees to its budget that had nothing to do with its work. The Budget Committee sent a further inquiry, requesting a list of those employees. The council again responded, this time in detail, listing employees assigned to its budget in the president's office, the security services, NGOs, the supposedly private *Al-hayah al-jadida* daily newspaper, and even a children's theater. Most ironically, perhaps, five employees of a committee to oversee reform in the PNA—a committee designed to ferret out and correct such practices—had been tucked away in the Personnel Council's budget.

Once again, deputy after deputy rose to attack the government's behavior. The finance minister appeared almost lost in the details, unable to respond to the committee's criticisms. In the end, however, the PLC voted once again to approve the budget.[1] One PLC deputy explained the combination of confrontational rhetoric and conciliatory action two weeks later: "My role in the Council is so important to me, and I am influenced by the political situation. My main aim is my identity as a Palestinian but we need to insure it on the ground. We need to work for the liberation of the land. I want to empower the negotiators, not undermine them."[2]

Unlike almost any other institution operating under the PNA, the PLC had no clear antecedent on which to base its work. Despite some attempts (such as the 1948 PNC or the Legislative Council operating under Egyptian rule in Gaza), there never was a viable Palestinian parliament prior to the elections of 1996. Nor was there any clear guide on its authorities and functioning. The Oslo Accords did give some indications, but they were quite vague—and deputies were loath to rely on an agreement with Israel rather than the Palestinian people for their authority. The PLC, more than any other PNA institution, had to define itself out of nothing. It chose the role of the legislative branch of the PNA. Yet having made its choice, it faced formidable difficulties in playing that role and convincing other PNA institutions of its authority.[3]

THE BIRTH OF A PALESTINIAN PARLIAMENT

Most institutions of the PNA have antecedents in preexisting political structures. Palestinian courts are lineal descendents of mandatory-era structures. The PNA presidency was based on the PLO presidency, with some legal continuity from the Israeli military governor and the British high commissioner. The various security services are often based on antecedents in the PLO or in Palestinian political movements.

The PLC stands in contrast to these structures because its origins lie in Palestinian-Israeli negotiations. Israel and the PLO began negotiating in the early 1990s—sometimes indirectly and sometimes secretly—on a set of interim arrangements to allow a measure of Palestinian autonomy in the West Bank and Gaza. These interim arrangements were to hold until a final status agreement was reached. While every single aspect of these interim arrangements was hotly contested, one common structural feature prevailed throughout: Palestinian autonomy would be administered through an elected council.

In 1993, Israel and the PLO signed their first, extremely skeletal agreement, the Declaration of Principles. This was followed by more detailed agreements in 1994 that provided for the first stage of the construction of a Palestinian interim authority in Gaza and Jericho. These agreements referred to the construction of a Palestinian Council, but the details were not finalized until the September 1995 Israeli-Palestinian Interim Agreement on the West Bank and the Gaza Strip. That agreement clearly and specifically defined the Palestinian Council and the Interim Self-Government Authority synonymously and provided that Israel would "transfer powers and responsibilities as specified in this Agreement from the Israeli military government and its Civil Administration to the Council in accordance with this Agreement."[4] Those responsibilities not transferred to the council would continue to be held by Israel.

To be sure, the 1995 agreement did not anticipate a council that would directly exercise all these authorities on a daily basis. There was to be a president for the "Executive Authority of the Council."[5] And that "Executive Authority" would consist of ministers (though the term is not used), drawn largely from the council, to exercise "the executive authority . . . on behalf of the Council."[6] The council would have eighty-two members and would be directly elected; the president of the council's Executive Authority would be "directly and simultaneously elected" as well.[7]

Thus, the 1995 agreement contained general language indicating that the council would be the supreme body and most comprehensive expression of Palestinian autonomy. It had "within its authority, legislative, executive and judicial powers and responsibilities" specified in the agreement.[8] All Palestinian bodies mentioned by the agreement—including the presidency and the cabinet—were merely arms of the council. On the other hand, the agreement included provisions for independently electing the president, for the president appointing the cabinet (subject to the approval of the full council), for legislation (which could be proposed by the president but required the approval of the full council), and for independent courts. This seemed to suggest a council that was not coterminous with the autonomous Palestinian Authority after all but was rather a parliament in a mixed presidential-parliamentary system. And even before elections were held, 'Arafat's decrees started to refer to the body as the Palestinian Legislative Council, implying that its role was more limited (though he eventually showed reluctance to consider its actions authoritative even in the legislative arena).

Aggravating the confusion in the 1995 agreement establishing the council was the attitude of many Palestinians, including virtually all members of the council when they were elected: they saw the council not as a product of bilateral negotiations with Israel but as the first and fullest expression of the will of those Palestinians living in the West Bank and Gaza. In short, not only did the council have an ambiguous charter in the agreement, but it also seemed determined to ignore the circumstances of its own birth as fully as possible. Council members were averse to refer to the more ambitious and general elements of the 1995 agreement because doing so would imply that their mandate came only by Israel's agreement and permission. Bereft of any antecedent and unwilling to use the one document specifying its authority, the council, in the words of its Speaker, had to "start its work from nothing."[9] The result was that the council was destined to spend much of its initial efforts simply defining itself, as will be seen.

The signing of the 1995 agreement was quickly followed by a series of decrees from the president (who had ruled by decree since mid-1994) establishing an electoral system. Perhaps because of the importance of the subject and the incongruity of the president issuing by decree the system under which he himself would be elected, Yasir 'Arafat presented the most comprehensive decree, the Law of Elections, to the PLO's Executive Committee and the cabinet for approval.[10] Because of complaints after the system was first introduced, some amendments were immediately decreed. The resulting system provided for eighty-eight members (rather than the eighty-two stipulated in the 1995 agreement) in sixteen multimember districts. The districts were of uneven size but were accorded seats according to their population (so that Ramallah received seven seats but Qalqilya only two). Women were guaranteed five seats, Christians six, and the tiny Samaritan community was to receive a single seat.

The electoral system, with its multimember districts, encouraged a campaign based on personality rather than party organization. The Palestinian political parties virtually guaranteed such a result when they abdicated any effective role in the campaign. Most of the Islamist opposition refused to participate, and most of the leftist opposition, organizationally divided and with a small popular following, stood aloof as well. Fatah had a fully open field, with only a few small parties and a large number of independents running against it, but the party was unable to take advantage of the situation. Many leading Fatah members who were denied the party's nomination (often those with strong local followings were passed over in favor of party loyalists coming in from Tunis) decided to run as independents. The result was a council that initially appeared likely to be fairly tame and dominated by personalities and vague ideological inclinations rather than tight party discipline. The council surprised many observers, however, by displaying a strong independent streak immediately upon its first meeting.

DECLARING INDEPENDENCE BUT LOSING CENTRALITY

When the PLC convened in March 1996, it found itself embroiled immediately in a clash with Yasir 'Arafat. The dispute took place largely on symbolic grounds, but it had long-range implications for the PLC and the way that it operated. 'Arafat, who had served as PNA president and ruled by decree for two years before the PLC convened, seemed to regard the new body not as a replacement for the PNA but as a body explicitly subordinate to the PLO and implicitly subordinate to the executive.

When it first met, PLC members elected Abu 'Ala' (Ahmad Quray') as their Speaker, though he was widely rumored not to be 'Arafat's personal choice for the post. (A negotiator of the Israeli-PLO accords, Abu 'Ala' was not a confrontational choice, however—indeed, PLC members decided not to elect the more respected but far more confrontational Haydar 'Abd al-Shafi.) The PLC then took up the matter of its own internal operations, and a Legal Committee submitted a draft of "Standing Orders" to govern the PLC. The orders made provision not simply for the internal operation of the council but also for its relationship with the president. Most importantly, they gave the council the right to question and remove confidence from ministers, review and approve the budget, and pass legislation. (As eventually adopted, the orders allowed the president the right to withhold approval of a law; if he did so, the council could make the law effective by approving it by a two-thirds majority. In addition, a law would become effective if the president failed to take any action.)

Yet it was not such weighty issues that attracted the initial attention of the council. Instead, the first issue provoking debate was whether members of the PLO Executive Committee had the right to speak in PLC sessions.[11] 'Arafat angrily insisted that PLO Executive Committee members had the right to participate in all PLO bodies and reminded PLC members that only the PLO represented all Palestinians. PLC members did not wish to have their loyalty to the PLO questioned, but some seemed annoyed at according Executive Committee members a status that few parliaments elsewhere would have granted. A more troublesome storm broke out over the oath that PLC members would take. 'Arafat's decree calling the PLC into session had members swearing the oath before the PNA president, but many members of the PLC wished to substitute the president of the High Court or the entire PLC as more appropriate.[12] Since the entire PLC membership had already been sworn in on the basis of 'Arafat's oath, the issue seemed trivial, but debate ensued. 'Arafat stalked out of the chamber at this perceived insult and was absent when the PLC voted in defiance of his wishes. He then invited PLC members to lunch in a conciliatory move. But when the PLC reconvened after lunch, 'Arafat returned to berate the members, accusing them of treating him like "dirt" and slapping him in the face: "The first thing the Council does is break my rules!"[13] His argument was legal as well as personal: his decree had specified an oath that the PLC was now asserting the right to change. Council members deflected the president's anger by referring the matter to committee.

Eventually, 'Arafat lost this symbolic battle, as he lost others: after some hesitation, PLC members successfully insisted that sessions be completely open to the public and that journalists be allowed in, even though 'Arafat seemed to wish to keep some of the discussions more private. Yet the symbolism was significant, and the ramifications for the PLC were far greater than initially appeared: the PLC had demonstrated its independence from the president but had isolated itself from the wielders of political authority in the process. When the PLC approved the Standing Orders, for instance, it transformed the nature of the document. While 'Arafat had initially insisted on a right to approve the orders (and indeed, the council referred them to him for his assent), the council eventually issued them on its own authority. The PLC then turned attention to the Basic Law, which was to govern the PNA and executive-legislative relations more generally. But the Basic Law was not approved until 2002 (see Chapter 3). That left the Standing Orders the only governing document for the PLC, but 'Arafat and the executive regarded them as a matter governing only the council's internal operations. And while 'Arafat's formal position in the Oslo Accords was president of the council, he soon made clear that he regarded himself as completely independent of the PLC—by virtue of his position both as PNA president and as president of the PLO's Executive Committee. In effect, after some histrionic battles, 'Arafat conceded that the council was free to do as it wished in its own affairs but that it could not impose its will on him. Thus, the provisions in the Standing Orders for passing legislation had no binding authority on the executive. 'Arafat would approve no law he did not wish to, and he took as long as he wished to consider any piece of legislation. The council could pass any law as many times and with whatever majority it liked, but only 'Arafat could publish it in the *Official Gazette* to make it effective.

At first, 'Arafat and his cabinet inclined toward the position that the decree law governing legislation (Law 4 of 1995), issued before the PLC's election, still applied and therefore that the council could at most approve legislation rather than initiate it. This position softened over time, but the attitude behind it never disappeared. At the end of the PLC's second year in existence, only one law that it had initiated had received presidential approval.

Council members therefore found that legislate as they might, they could not make their will stick without getting the president's assent. And at the beginning, that was extremely difficult for them to do. Indeed, it seemed impossible for the council members to get the respect or even attention of the executive branch. Requests for information from ministries were often ignored, and ministers—many of whom were council members— would often fail to show for sessions discussing their ministries' affairs. Only in the council's third year did the rate of executive responses to council requests reach 50 percent.[14]

But the council was worried about more than being ignored: sometimes executive contempt could take a more ominous form. Just as the council was forming, some of the members held a press conference in which they denounced the PNA for violating human rights in a crackdown on Islamists. 'Arafat implied that he was lenient in not having the members arrested immediately; instead, he had his attorney general write to the PLC, demanding that it discipline them. PLC members voted simply "to return the letter to the Attorney General."[15] After this clash and some others regarding interference with press coverage, the PLC voted to "approve the formation of a special police squad for the Council," though no such force was ever formed.[16] Intermittent complaints of assaults and restrictions on PLC members continued. In August 1996, the governor of Nablus forbade PLC members from holding a seminar.[17] Members of the security services were accused of attacking deputies on several occasions, sometimes when the deputies were engaged in public protests against detentions. During 1997, PLC members complained of seven assaults, two of them in the PLC building. In December 1999, the most widely publicized attacks took place in the wake of the release of a petition signed by several council members (the *bayan al-'ashrin*, or Statement of Twenty, which sharply criticized PNA corruption as well as the negotiations with Israel, holding 'Arafat partly responsible). One signer, Mu'awiyya al-Masri (perhaps the PLC's most pugnacious member), was shot in the foot during a scuffle with unidentified assailants; another, 'Abd al-Jawwad Salih (a former minister, mayor, and one of the most respected and vocal members of the PLC), was beaten while participating in a demonstration in Jericho. While the assaults may not have been part of a coordinated attempt to intimidate the PLC, deputies charged that the security services generally, and the executive branch more generally, regularly demonstrated their contempt for Palestine's first effective parliament.

Even PLC members most inclined to be deferential to the national leadership admitted that the PNA executive did not take them seriously. Rawhi Fatuh, a Fatah member and secretary-general of the PLC, reflected on the body's first two years in the PLC's own journal:

> The Legislative Council has performed its role well, but there have been obstacles from the Executive Authority. The Legislative Council has an independent will, because its membership believes strongly in the Council's priorities, so we have had no problems with attempts to influence it. But the Executive Authority stalls the implementation of these democratically voted recommendations and resolutions as well as the endorsement of legislation.[18]

Fatuh's description of the attitude of the PLC stands out only for its gentleness. Most PLC members realized from the early days of the council that they could do little to force 'Arafat, the cabinet, and the security services to do what they did not want to do.

MASTER ONLY OF ITS OWN HOUSE: EFFORTS TO BUILD THE CAPACITY OF THE PLC

If the PLC could not enforce its will on others, at least it had achieved a measure of autonomy from the PNA president. It used this autonomy to attempt to build itself into a parliamentary body capable of writing legislation, reviewing the budget, overseeing the executive, and responding to the public. This was an ambitious agenda indeed, and the council's success in achieving some capacity in these areas did not necessarily (or even often) translate into an ability to use the tools effectively.

Starting at the Beginning

Because the PLC began with no institutional predecessor, and because its members and staff almost totally lacked any parliamentary experience, basic features of parliamentary institutions sometimes took years to develop. Early sessions of the council were consumed with prolonged procedural wrangling and arguments, as the Standing Orders gave only general guidance on most issues. While procedures became clearer over time, the chair of the Legal Committee admitted after four years of PLC operations that there was still vagueness over fundamental matters, including how to deal with comments on legislation from the executive branch and the work of PLC committees.[19] It was two years before the council began recording minutes (prior to that time, only official actions such as motions and resolutions were faithfully recorded); those minutes are still not made accessible to the public (nor are they consulted by the members). And while council sessions are public and covered well in the press, basic requests for information are often ignored.[20]

There was much work to do. Committees had to be constructed, staff trained and hired, district offices established, and expertise developed. In general, the PLC modeled many of its procedures and structures on Arab counterparts, but the institution was very willing to reach out more broadly. There was some external support (especially from USAID) for training of staff and even construction of a research arm for the council, the Parliamentary Research Unit. And these efforts began to show some effects: in the realm of the budget, for instance, council members and staff steadily gained experience and boldness in analyzing material submitted by the cabinet, leading to more exacting and demanding reports (though with uneven success, as will be seen below). The PLC steadily gained in the ability to draft its own legislation, consult with key constituencies, and regularize its own operations. The council's procedures were not sufficiently well established to avoid controversies, however. In 2000, members of Fatah joined the Oversight Committee in order to vote out its chair, Hasan Khraysha, a council firebrand and signatory to the *bayan al-'ashrin*. In doing so, the Speaker and council members clearly manipulated (and, according to some, broke) the PLC's internal rules on forming committees. Council members also sometimes complained that the Speaker would drag his heels on holding a session or manipulate the agenda, bending or breaking PLC rules—generally to stave off those seeking to confront or embarrass the president.

Yet the effect of PLC institutional efforts generally made the body more capable of examining issues and making contact with key constituencies. Committee structures are perhaps the best illustration of this. The council's Standing Orders mandated that committee sessions be secret unless the committee decided otherwise. Ministers were also invited to attend meetings of any committee.[21] In short, the PLC seemed to be establishing committees on the Arab parliamentary model, where they are far more effective at coordinating actions with the executive than in taking independent action.[22] Yet with additional training (and some American and non-Arab models to follow), some committees began to experiment with public hearings and consultation with key groups. The NGO Law was virtually redrafted by an external constituency (a coalition of leading NGOs, see Chapter 5). Other organizations, such as the labor confederation and professional associations, began to learn to contact supporters in the PLC.

And the PLC became increasingly ambitious about reaching out to the general public. It voted from the beginning to have its sessions televised (despite some early clashes with 'Arafat and others over press coverage) and encouraged Palestinian newspapers to cover its sessions. Live broadcasts proved too politically sensitive for the executive, which effectively shut them down, but extended excerpts of council sessions were eventually broadcast. The council began its own publication, *Al-majlis al-tashri'i*, to reach the public directly. In all these steps, the PLC was following what other Arab parliaments had often tried (and almost as often failed) to do. And PLC members found themselves—from the moment that they were elected—called upon to perform a more common task for Arab parliamentarians: receiving citizen complaints. The more energetic members of the council handled this task with enthusiasm, contacting Palestinian officials at the behest of constituents to solve bureaucratic wrangles and settle disputes.

Members of the PLC and external observers often found that the body was hampered in its further development by the absence of any firm party structure. The majority of the PLC consisted of Fatah members and sympathizers, yet they rarely met as a caucus (and generally did so only when there was a crisis that caused the leadership to lean on members to toe the line). Even when they did meet—on the irregular occasions that they were called together by party leader Yasir 'Arafat—sessions could be undisciplined and raucous. There were never any sanctions placed on those who broke ranks with the party, even on important votes.[23] With the majority barely able to act as a coherent party body, and the minority consisting of disparate independents and members of small parties, the PLC was marked by a remarkably low degree of partisanship by international standards. Yet while this may have hampered the PLC's ability to organize its affairs, it probably increased the body's independence: firmer party discipline would have likely brought the PLC far more under executive domination (since the president headed the majority party). As it was, the PLC became gradually more reluctant to confront the executive (until 2002, when it rediscovered its youthful enthusiasm). Yet in most matters not involving a sense of crisis and confrontation, the council showed a remarkably independent spirit, and Fatah members often rivaled their nonparty counterparts in willingness to stake out their own positions.

The Second Intifada

When the second intifada broke out in September 2000, the immediate effect on the PLC was to augment its marginalization. Individual PLC members—most particularly Marwan al-Barghuti, the secretary-general of Fatah in the West Bank and a leading PLC maverick—quickly rose to prominence. But the body itself seemed less relevant at a time of armed confrontation. Further, the intifada made explicit challenge of the leadership more daunting to contemplate (as the battle over the budget, examined below, will show). These developments, however, were uncertain and temporary: the nominal leadership of the PNA was itself sometimes sidelined by the actions of various militias and groups, leading many to question the efficacy of the PNA and the PLO. And the failure to resist the Israeli military campaign of April 2002 brought the PNA's institutional failures into even clearer focus. Advocates of institutional reform sometimes turned to the PLC for action, and it was therefore significant that President 'Arafat, on the rare occasions that he adopted the reform banner (in March 2001 and May 2002), did so in the form of a speech to the PLC.

Thus, the second intifada decreased the short-term prominence of the PLC, though it did not necessarily augur ill for the body's future. Most obviously in the short term, the intifada undermined the body's ability to operate. The prolonged closures and restrictions on movement made it difficult for the PLC to hold regular meetings. Some deputies that Israel accused of direct involvement in violence were refused travel permits altogether (and al-Barghuti himself was eventually arrested in the April 2002 military campaign). And for all deputies, travel between Gaza and the West Bank became virtually impossible. In March 2001, Israel allowed travel permits to all but two PLC members so that a session could be held in Gaza. Other meetings were possible with videoconferencing equipment made available by USAID. Yet this method of holding sessions was used surprisingly rarely. Many deputies seemed dispirited, feeling that their work was irrelevant in the face of confrontation. Others viewed the use of technology enabling remote meetings as acquiescence to the Israeli policy of closure. And that closure made it impossible not only for the plenary body to meet but also for committees and their staff to meet, so that the PLC itself could function only very slowly. In March 2002, matters had reached the point that the PLC allowed itself to suffer a procedural indignity. The PLC was scheduled to begin its seventh year of operation, but Israel refused deputies the necessary travel permission to meet in person. With the body unable to convene (and unwilling to use videoconferencing for the symbolically important opening

of a new session), the PLC was forced to accept a presidential decree extending its sixth session for an additional three months.[24] The following month
the PLC fell victim to the conflict with Israel in a far less symbolic way: its
meeting chamber in Ramallah and its nearby administrative headquarters
were ransacked by Israeli forces.[25] Besides damaging some of the premises
and equipment, troops took some computers, records, and videotapes of PLC
sessions. The odd assortment of confiscations was never explained.

It might therefore seem remarkable that the PLC was able to conduct any
business at all. Yet the legislative mechanisms continued to work slowly:
after the outbreak of the intifada the PLC was able to pass and secure presidential approval for some legislation governing court operations and fees;
it was also able to discuss a host of laws related to matters from smoking to
agriculture. Since the pace at which the PLC legislated had never been particularly swift, the slowdown was not all that noticeable.

Even before the outbreak of the intifada, when the council was aug-
menting its capacity and capabilities, the efforts were unable to stem (and
may have aggravated) the PLC's loss of centrality. In all sorts of procedural
and substantive matters, the PLC showed that it would stop only slightly
short of open defiance of the executive. As the executive learned ways to
avoid the council, it increasingly made it possible for PLC members to make
noise without affecting policy. The PLC was neither a model of efficiency
and independence nor completely impotent. But many steps it took toward
efficiency and independence tended to reduce its influence. Despite this
conundrum, Palestinian legislators soldiered on in their twin tasks of oversight of the executive and legislating a new framework for the PNA.

OVERSIGHT OF THE EXECUTIVE

Having defined itself as a parliamentary body and successfully established
a modicum of autonomy from the executive (and the PLO as well), PLC
members saw themselves as charged with overseeing the Executive
Authority. This function had four different aspects: investigations and questioning; formal accountability (through votes of confidence); approval of
the budget; and general expressions of policy and public opinion. In all of
these areas, the PLC flirted with open confrontation with the executive but
ultimately drew back, often under the guise of protecting national unity.

Investigations and Questioning

Almost from the moment they took office, the members of the PLC moved
to use their authority to pose questions of ministers and investigate execu-

tive branch actions in order to realize an effective oversight role. Ministers were peppered with a variety of questions involving local problems, provision of services, and sensitive political matters. As the security services began to take unpopular actions, such as detaining citizens without charges or trying them in state security courts, PLC members attempted to query ministers on the subject.

While the authority to ask questions of ministers was well established in the council's Standing Orders and in Arab (and international) parliamentary practice, PLC members often found the experience frustrating. This was the case even when they trod on less political sensitive turf. After two and one-half years of operation, the PLC had directed at least 136 formal questions in plenary session to ministers. Committees directed approximately another 100 requests for information. Only 69 of these received a response.[26] Members showed some signs of becoming discouraged as their use of parliamentary questions declined. And ministers—even including those drawn from the PLC's membership—showed their own disdain for the body by failing to appear to answer questions. The minister of finance absented himself during some sessions in which the budget was discussed; the minister of justice declined to appear even during special sessions called to discuss legal affairs. Deputies sometimes thundered that they would remove confidence from such ministers, but, as will be seen below, more confrontational PLC members were unable to convince the entire body to go along.

The steady drumbeat of criticism from the PLC did finally lead President 'Arafat to appoint a minister for parliamentary affairs; the role was filled until May 2002 by Nabil 'Amr, who faithfully attended sessions to deliver soothing speeches and promises of greater responsiveness.[27] While 'Amr was able to mediate some crises, the lack of executive responsiveness to PLC questions stemmed from structural and not merely personal causes. This was especially the case on the most sensitive political issue, the detention of individuals without trial or their trial in state security courts. Such individuals generally fell into two categories (and often both): political adversaries of the regime and members of organizations engaged in violent attacks on Israel. Detention or lightning trials stood as an especially noxious reminder to many Palestinians of the days of direct Israeli rule and led to a frequent criticism that the PNA was simply subcontracting for the Israeli government. There was little effective response that senior PNA officials could give that would find any public resonance—so they generally preferred to talk vaguely about threats to national unity or (as time went on) to simply ignore the subject altogether. And many PLC members therefore used parliamentary questions to break the official silence.

They had little success. The PLC constantly sent questions to Farih Abu Mudayn, the minister of justice, about detained Palestinians and often received no response. When he did appear, Abu Mudayn simply explained that he had nothing to do with the subject: he only oversaw the regular courts and civilian prosecutors; the security services, the state security courts, and the Ministry of Interior were outside of his control. At times he would even imply that the council itself was to blame by not passing the necessary legal framework to govern these bodies.[28] Yet the council was powerless to call the security services or State Security Courts to account; they answered directly to the president and not through any ministry. And the entire Ministry of Interior was effectively outside of parliamentary supervision as well. Until June 2002, its minister was none other than the president himself, Yasir 'Arafat. While there was nothing legally preventing the PLC from questioning or even withdrawing confidence from 'Arafat as a minister, the step would have been too confrontational even for some otherwise bold parliamentarians.

Perhaps the most frustrating example of the PLC's inability to use its investigatory authority for oversight purposes involved the report on corruption produced in the council's second year. In 1997, the PLC received a report from the PNA's General Control Institute detailing administrative and accounting irregularities in most ministries and agencies. Council members were sufficiently alarmed by the contents that they established their own committee to investigate and audit official practices. The committee's report, soon dubbed the "Corruption Report," earned international attention and set off a protracted confrontation with much of the PNA's executive branch.[29] A wide range of misdeeds and misconduct were uncovered. Some involved mere inefficiency (such as unclear policies and responsibilities and inadequate monitoring in many government offices); some involved wasteful extravagance (renting of overly lavish offices and furniture). Much of the corruption was personal and small scale (such as overuse of international telephone lines); some was far broader and deeper (such as manipulating border crossings to steer importing business to cronies).

Faced with so many tales of misdeeds, even conciliatory PLC members could not prevent a confrontation. The PLC decided to allow ministers the opportunity to explain their conduct; most responded with defiant denials. Opponents of the PNA overseas quickly turned the report to their advantage. One particularly strident member of the American Congress cited the Corruption Report in his opposition to American aid to Palestinians.[30] For the senior PNA leadership, nothing could prove more effectively that the PLC was damaging the national cause. But PLC members hardly took the refusal of ministers to respond to the report as a nationalist gesture; they demanded (ultimately unsuccessfully) that several be investigated for criminal corruption and that the president form a new cabinet.

Besides the defeat in the cabinet reshuffle, discussed below, the confrontation saw the PLC defeated in other ways. The call for investigation and prosecution was met by a mere promise that the charges would be investigated; in October 1997 President 'Arafat wrote a letter to Speaker Abu 'Ala' promising that the matter would be turned over to the public prosecutor.[31] The PLC did allow those accused in the report an additional opportunity to defend themselves. Nothing was heard on the matter again. And in 1998, members of the PLC discovered that they were not to receive the annual report of the General Control Institute—despite 'Arafat's approval of a law that same year that explicitly required that the PLC receive the report. Indeed, in the aftermath of the Corruption Report, the General Control Institute became the one official Palestinian body that refused to communicate directly with the PLC.[32]

Expressing Public Opinion

The PLC showed great early enthusiasm for a second technique for oversight of the executive: the resolution. From an early date, the PLC began a stream of resolutions expressing the body's position on a host of internal and external issues. For instance, in April and May of 1996, the PLC voted to (among other things) encourage democratic dialogue, speed the release of detainees, educate the security services, condemn a raid on al-Najah University, demand that the cabinet present a draft of the Basic Law, release jailed students, end monopolies, and request the 1996 budget.[33]

The concerns of the PLC tended to focus on specific areas, generally related to PNA actions that members saw as unpopular and illegitimate. On issues connected to negotiations with Israel, the PLC generally backed the line taken by the leadership but provided little basis for supporting compromises; the council had little ability to intervene in the negotiations (even though several of its members, including the Speaker himself, were often closely involved), but many members seemed to wish to strengthen the resolve of the negotiators to resist concessions. Council members represented districts where conflicts with Israeli settlers were frequent, and the PLC regularly issued denunciations of settlement activity. Acutely aware that Israeli negotiators consistently cited domestic public opinion in support of their reluctance to offer compromises, some PLC members sought to have their body play the role of communicating the boundaries that the Palestinian leadership could not cross. In this they were unsuccessful—not only did international audiences (including Israel) take little note of the PLC resolutions, but the council itself lacked tools to enforce its will on such issues. (For instance, the PNA lacked a foreign minister who could be questioned and removed—the Oslo Accords left most foreign relations to the PLO rather than the PNA, and the Ministry of International Cooperation, which operated as something akin to a foreign ministry, was formally responsible for coordinating international assistance rather than negotiations.)

The PLC sought to make its desires felt in other sensitive areas as well, especially detained prisoners. Indeed, no issue caused greater frustration among members than their inability to convince the PNA to follow the law on detentions. When Palestinians were detained without charges (often because they were members of groups involved in violent attacks on Israeli targets), the PLC would call for them to be charged or released. Since, as was made clear above, ministerial responsibility would not function on this matter, the PLC issued resolutions calling for the release of detainees. Such resolutions were routinely ignored. Perhaps more galling, when detainees were able to obtain court orders for their release, security officials would often refuse to obey, insisting that they would only follow a presidential order. PLC members complained loudly and often about the refusal to follow the law and the judgments of the courts, generally to little effect.

The most plaintive PLC resolutions often called simply for laws that the body had passed to be acted upon or laws that the president had approved to be implemented. Some critical pieces of legislation—such as the Civil Service Law—required implementing regulations to become operative; the PLC found that it could do little but periodically remind the cabinet that such regulations needed to be issued. Other crucial PLC functions—such as examination of the budget—required that the executive submit a proposal, but if the official submission was tardy, there was little the PLC could do but pass a resolution asking that the executive fulfill its obligation. On one major matter—the Basic Law—the PLC was so eager to work that it finally decided to take up the matter without an official submission from the cabinet (see Chapter 3). That decision taught many council members the limits of their power—they were able to pass a version of the Basic Law but were absolutely impotent when the president took no action for five years on the draft. Often the PLC simply asked that the Executive Authority respond to its resolutions, but it was generally powerless to do more than appoint a committee to report back on any official actions taken. And on some occasions, the PLC simply passed resolutions reaffirming its past resolutions and asking that they be implemented.

Observers expressed some frustration with the PLC, complaining that its members did not understand that passing a series of resolutions—especially on a matter outside its control—was bound to be ineffective and that the inexperienced deputies did not realize how to implement their will. There was some truth to this observation, though as time went on, the PLC made decreasing use of resolutions and greater use of other mechanisms such as investigations and public debates.[34] Yet in some respects the charge of unsophistication was unjust: PLC members were often aware that their public position would be difficult to implement, and some of the body's resolutions read as if they were attempts to express public opinion (and garner its support) without implementing it. Parliamentary posturing was hardly a Palestinian invention, but PLC members learned how to strike the proper pose. The teachers' strikes of 1996 and 2000 provide the best example of this: on both occasions, the PLC issued vague resolutions indicating sympathy with the teachers' wage demands and calling for release of arrested activists, but the resolutions gave no guidance whatsoever on how to handle the fiscal implications of such a step. In short, striking teachers garnered unenforceable PLC support, but resolutions were so generally worded as to be ineffectual. When matters such as the budget and the Civil Service Law came up, PLC members pressed for greater funds to be made available for education but did not take the necessary measures to implement their will.

Giving Confidence and Threatening to Withdraw It

Stymied in its efforts to oversee the executive through questions, investigations, and resolutions, the PLC was often forced to fall back on threats to use a far blunter instrument: withdrawal of confidence. In most Arab countries, parliaments have never withdrawn confidence from a single minister, much less the entire cabinet; in several countries, mere talk of doing so has led the head of state to close down the parliament.[35] The PLC in that sense struck a blow for Arab parliaments by talking continually about withdrawing confidence without being shut down. It took six years before making good on its threat, however.

Some council members may have been suspicious from an early date that the president did not take sufficiently seriously the need to garner a parliamentary majority for his cabinet. It took two months for the president to present his cabinet to the PLC. The council itself delayed a month before voting confidence in the cabinet and its programmatic statement by a two-to-one margin.

The matter of parliamentary confidence then rested for a year, until the council's committee issued its Corruption Report in the wake of the abuses alleged by the General Control Institute. The Corruption Report set off a yearlong confrontation between the government and the PLC. While the PLC constantly threatened to withdraw confidence and did in fact force a limited cabinet reshuffle (that largely amounted to an addition of new ministers without a dismissal of old ones), it is difficult to understand the affair as anything but a stinging defeat for the council.

The confrontation caused by the Corruption Report came in a context of rising frustrations on the part of council members that the president and the cabinet were ignoring the PLC's oversight roles. Resolutions were ignored; legislation sat on the president's desk with no action taken; the president refused to acknowledge the PLC's efforts to write a Basic Law; and even routine requests for information drew no response. Council members seemed not to know how to enforce their will without taking the drastic action of withdrawing confidence from individuals or the cabinet as a whole. The Corruption Report sufficiently emboldened a majority of the PLC to move toward such a step.

Yet the action the council took in the wake of the Corruption Report was not to withdraw confidence from the cabinet. Such a step would, have in one sense, not gone far enough: some ministers were charged with criminal offenses and deserved, in the PLC's eyes, to be prosecuted rather than merely dismissed. But in other ways a withdrawal of confidence would have gone too far: the Corruption Report was issued at a time of extremely tense relations with Israel, and PLC members were anxious to avoid taking a step that might have been seen as undercutting their president. So instead of withdrawing confidence, the PLC passed a resolution that called for drastic action without forcing it. The PLC resolution demanded that some ministers to be investigated and tried but then went on to cast its demand for a new cabinet in positive terms. Rather than informing the president directly that his cabinet no longer had a supportive majority, the PLC requested at the end of July 1997—with only one dissenting vote—that he form a new cabinet of qualified ministers and technocrats. Most PLC members felt they had passed a functional equivalent of a vote of no-confidence while avoiding a direct insult to the president. And their expectations were initially confirmed when Yasir 'Arafat asked for the resignations of all ministers pending a cabinet reshuffle.

Yet as the months went by, the promised reshuffle did not take place, and all ministers continued to work in their positions. In the autumn of 1997, the PLC again girded itself for confrontation over the reshuffle, the Basic Law, and the failure of the president to act on laws and resolutions passed by the council. New irritants arose: the minister of local government explained that local elections mandated by the council could not be held anywhere because some Palestinian towns and villages remained under Israeli control. (Many saw this as an excuse for indefinitely postponing elections that would be likely to embarrass the leadership.) Members began to raise the possibility of withdrawing confidence once again.

On 8 October 1997, the crisis was sufficiently severe that President 'Arafat made a rare appearance at a closed council session. The leadership struck a conciliatory pose. While 'Arafat himself did not speak about the meeting, PLC Speaker Abu 'Ala' detailed the session in a news conference in which he stressed the need to close ranks at a critical time. According to Abu 'Ala' and satisfied PLC members, 'Arafat promised to sign some legislation passed by the PLC within ten days; submit the already overdue 1998 budget; carry out his commitment to a cabinet reshuffle at an appropriate time; and allow the appointment of a joint committee from the cabinet and the PLC to study implementation of 187 PLC resolutions. He also asked that the PLC grant accused ministers another opportunity to defend themselves.[36]

While many PLC members expressed renewed support for the president and relief at the new cooperative attitude, by the end of the year the atmosphere of crisis returned. By late December virtually none of the October presidential promises has been fulfilled: no legislation had been signed; no budget had been submitted; and no cabinet reshuffle had been submitted. The joint committee had been appointed but had no visible accomplishments to its credit. This time Fatah members took the lead in denouncing presidential inaction and threatening a no-confidence motion. Soothing statements by ministers that the promises would soon be enacted had little effect. Fatah deputies were mollified only when the president met with them and renewed some of his vows.[37]

Even this time, the president's promises were not met. 'Arafat finally approved a few laws passed by the PLC, but most of the prominent pieces of legislation drew no response. The 1998 budget was not submitted until April (see below). Yet the spirit of confrontation seemed to have left most PLC deputies. Some continued to complain about presidential inaction; one group of Fatah members even spoke of setting up an independent Fatah bloc within the PLC, essentially moving them into opposition. Yet no action was taken. The limited steps 'Arafat took were enough to dissuade most PLC members (often quite unhappily) from moving to withdraw confidence from the cabinet. A sense of protracted crisis with Israel made many members unwilling to be seen as adding to the pressures on the president. A noisy minority within the PLC rejected this attitude, claiming that prevailing practices were weakening Palestinian public institutions and undermining public morale. These deputies rejected their colleagues' deference, viewing the council's inaction as either irrelevant or damaging to its position with regard to Israel.

The president's ability to stave off PLC pressure was convincingly demonstrated by the way the confrontation was finally resolved. In August 1998, more than a year after the council had called for the cabinet's dismissal, President 'Arafat finally announced his reshuffle. The only ministers dropped from the previous cabinet were those who had died; all those named in the Corruption Report were returned. New ministers were added, however. Critics in the PLC viewed the new cabinet as a cynical and disrespectful move: the number of ministers in the cabinet would exceed the limit of nineteen in the Basic Law; new ministries were constructed by presidential fiat rather than PLC consent; and several new PLC members were added to cabinet in an effort to silence the parliamentary opposition. Some more independent PLC members (such as 'Abd al-Jawwad Salih and Hanan 'Ashrawi) turned down offers to return to the cabinet (Salih had been minister of agriculture and 'Ashrawi minister of higher education; both were offered different posts). Yet the majority of the PLC chose to regard the new cabinet as a positive step and voted confidence, effectively ending the episode.

Following the grant of confidence in the new cabinet, the PLC took years before confronting the president or the cabinet so directly again. Periodic disputes—over the budget, legislation, PLC resolutions—would recur over the next several years, and individual PLC members (generally independents supported by some more independent members of Fatah) would stand and call for removal of confidence from a minister or the entire cabinet. Yet no motion was ever voted upon, nor did the PLC ever muster a majority for a resolution like that passed in July 1997 calling for a new cabinet. Sometimes these threats would provoke a weak attempt to satisfy PLC demands (especially on the budget; see below). But in 1997 and 1998, the PLC discovered it lacked the will to bring down ministers it had charged with embezzlement. The only sure way to lose a job as Palestinian minister was to die.[38]

The Palestinian September 11

In May 2002, a shorter version of the 1997–98 crisis repeated itself. Amid domestic and international calls for reform, 'Arafat promised a new cabinet. Yet when finally appointed, the new body looked very much like the old. The number of ministers was trimmed to twenty (still one more than the nineteen allowed by the Basic Law), and fifteen of them (including several the PLC had charged with corruption) returned from the previous cabinet. Two of the new ministers (Ibrahim al-Daghma in Justice and Na'im Abu al-Humus in Education) had been accomplished senior civil servants. Two incoming ministers represented the possibility of significant change. 'Abd al-Razzaq al-Yahya, a senior PLO military figure, became minister of interior; for the first time PLC members would have someone in the role they might hold accountable. And Salam Fayad, an economist with experience in international institutions, promised genuine fiscal reform. Yet 'Arafat dallied in presenting the new cabinet to the PLC, showing that his willingness to ignore the body had not changed.

But on 11 September 2002, the PLC accomplished what other parliaments in the Arab world have been shut down for even discussing: it brought down the cabinet and forced a decree for new elections. 'Arafat's call for reform the previous May had been greeted cynically by many in the PLC whose experience with years of unmet or overly vague promises had convinced them that true reform was not likely to be forthcoming from the existing leadership, even as modified. And the decay of Palestinian institutions and lack of clear leadership during the intifada undermined the argument that supporting 'Arafat aided national unity. In the April 2002 Israeli military campaign, the inability of Palestinian institutions to respond made clear to all that reform was needed and that 'Arafat would not be likely to lead such an effort willingly.

In an attempt to respond to these pressures, 'Arafat signed the Basic Law and an important judicial law, promised new elections, reshuffled his cabinet, and had the new body draw up an ambitious reform program. Reformers in the PLC were emboldened rather than placated by these efforts. They drew up their own reform program and began work on amending the electoral law in defiance of the president. In late August 2002, the PLC was finally able to turn its attention to the new cabinet 'Arafat had appointed, with deputies objecting that the body had never been presented to the PLC for approval. After some angry debate, the PLC summoned 'Arafat to present his cabinet and its program.

The session to debate the new cabinet proved difficult to hold. Some Israeli officials viewed the entire matter as a ruse for 'Arafat to obtain approval for his cabinet and were reluctant to allow the PLC members to gather in Ramallah for the session. In the end, the PLC met in both Gaza and Ramallah, connected by American-donated videoconferencing technology. And Israeli suspicions of the meeting allowed 'Arafat to transfer the meeting to his headquarters (arguing that if he left, the Israelis might complete the destruction of the complex), so that instead of an angry PLC summoning the president to explain himself, an embattled president invited the PLC to meet with him.

Yet 'Arafat's symbolic triumph was squandered. On 9 September, he addressed the PLC, attempting to placate deputies with more vague promises of reform and then left to have the cabinet members present themselves and the government program the next day. He met separately with Fatah deputies, urging them to support the cabinet in the name of national unity. On 10 September, the cabinet members faced a rude reception in the chamber, especially when they argued that the PLC should vote only on the new ministers rather than on the cabinet as a whole. This argument stood on shaky legal grounds and also carried little political weight—the most unpopular ministers were the returning ones, not the new ones. The matter was referred to the PLC's Legal Committee.

On 11 September, the PLC session began with two bombshells. First, the Speaker read a presidential decree specifying the date of 20 January for new elections. The step effectively rendered the cabinet an interim body and seemed designed to stave off a vote. But the PLC responded with a counterthrust in the form of the report from the Legal Committee. That report did not simply support the view that the PLC should vote on the entire cabinet. It also observed that the cabinet exceeded its constitutionally mandated size and that all of the ministers were constitutionally barred from exercising responsibility before a vote of confidence. Thus, cabinet and ministerial actions since 9 June 2002 (when the body was appointed) were unconstitutional and void. When the PLC voted to accept the logic of the report, the Speaker called for a brief recess. The break was used to preempt PLC action with a rushed presidential decree accepting the cabinet resignation and ordering ministers to stay in their positions only until a new cabinet was appointed. The Speaker then quickly adjourned the session until the new cabinet could be presented.

The preemptive strike of a cabinet resignation and recess effectively quashed any effort to consider the cabinet retroactively illegal. And it prevented the PLC from meeting to take up other reform efforts. More ambitious deputies blamed not only 'Arafat himself but also the PLC Speaker for blunting their assault on the executive. Still, there was no denying that the PLC had finally refused to back down in a confrontation with the president.

The short-term effects of the PLC action were not impressive. The following month the PLC approved a mildly modified cabinet that was more faithful to the provisions of the Basic Law. And the election decree that the Speaker read at the September session was not published. Indeed,

Palestinian elections were already subject to conflicting international and domestic pressures. The United States and the EU supported democratizing reforms in the PA, but the United States regarded early elections with suspicion because they conflicted with another American goal—the replacement of the current Palestinian leadership. An American-sponsored pre-election assessment supported delay. The EU, by contrast, publicly endorsed elections in early 2003. Israeli officials clearly regarded talk of early elections as a ploy to leverage Israeli withdrawals and perhaps bring about international pressure to allow Palestinian Jerusalemites to participate as they had in 1996. Domestically, PLC reformers were more ambivalent, arguing that elections are overdue but that the Law of Elections law should be revised, a process that the PLC has begun considering but could hardly have hoped to conclude in time for January voting.

Left with a cabinet similar to the one they had rejected and without a clear date for new elections, the PLC attack would seem to have been blunted. But the episode marked the revival of efforts by the PLC to hold the leadership accountable to legal procedures. Having been largely dormant for over a year, PLC committees returned to action, considering matters like budgetary affairs, court structure, and the Law of Elections.

The Battles over the Budget: Winning in Principle but Losing in Practice

If the president and the cabinet could effectively fail to act on resolutions, ignore many questions and requests for information, and parry any effort to withdraw confidence from the cabinet, then most of the normal mechanisms of ensuring executive accountability to the parliament were robbed of effectiveness. The PLC did have one more tool at its disposal, however, and it was potentially comprehensive and powerful: annual review of the budget. According to the council's standing orders the cabinet was to present the budge four months prior to the beginning of the fiscal year. The council was required to act within two months to accept the budget or return it to the cabinet for modification and resubmission.

While neither the president nor the cabinet ever explicitly accepted that they were bound by the council's Standing Orders, they did attempt to comply. And in August 1998, President 'Arafat signed the far more detailed Law of Organizing the Public Budget and Fiscal Affairs for the National Authority, formalizing the cabinet's responsibility to the PLC and making clear that the annual budget itself was to be treated as regular legislation.[39] (The Budget Law attempted to bow to reality and required only that the cabinet submit the budget two months in advance.)

Yet on only two occasions did the cabinet ever submit a budget before the beginning of the fiscal year. Each year, the PLC passed the budget with reservations and demands that mistakes not recur. The following year, the same sorts of problems would arise, leading the PLC only to reiterate its demands. In effect, the PLC successfully established the principle that it had the prerogative to review the budget. And on some occasions, demands for greater information, reformed practices, and more accuracy were met. But after involvement in seven budgets, the PLC cannot be said to have been successful in using the budgetary process to ensure accountability. A review of each year makes it clear how the PLC could claim credit for uneven progress toward its goal while still falling far short of true oversight of the budget.

In 1996, the PLC began to assert its right of budgetary oversight immediately. Although the PLC did not even begin meeting until the third month of the fiscal year, members insisted that they had a right to review the annual budget. In June 1996, the council asked the minister of finance to present the budget.[40] But cooperation was slow in coming. By September the Budget Committee returned to the full PLC to obtain a second resolution requesting that the Ministry of Finance cooperate with them and provide needed information.[41] 'Azmi Shu'aybi, a committee member (and later chair), claims that such pressure became effective only when the PLC made critical concessions and international actors made similar demands on the PNA:

> At the beginning, the Authority was extremely reluctant to publish its budget or even to formalize it. But at the end of 1996, under the combined pressure of the World Bank, the IMF, the donor countries, and the Legislative Council, the PA was obliged to draft a budget and to submit it to the Council. But the PA refused to submit it to the Council until we agreed in advance to approve it without stirring up any trouble. We went along with this because our goal was to pass a law forcing the Authority to submit a budget to the Council as a matter of course. And this is what happened.[42]

In the end, then, the 1996 budget was never approved by the PLC, but members felt that they had received sufficient concessions on matters of future procedure to drop the matter.

In 1997, the PLC began to assert itself more intrusively. It may be, as Shu'aybi claims, that PLC leaders agreed to approve the budget as a condition of its submission, but the PLC Budget Committee—then headed by Sa'di al-Krunz—issued a thorough and often harsh report highlighting many flaws in the budget and the submission process:

- The final accounts for 1996 were not presented.
- The PLC did not receive the budget until March 1997, over two months into the fiscal year.
- The budget included no explanation or justification.
- The revenues of publicly held companies were not included in the budget.
- PNA institutions wasted money on expensive leases when the money would have been better spent on permanent construction.
- Developmental expenditures were not controlled by either the Ministry of Finance or the financial departments of the various ministries. And, the committee noted tersely, there was rampant corruption (though the word was not used): "In most cases, tenders are awarded to companies owned by senior officials in the Ministry of Planning and International Cooperation, or working in the other ministries and public institutions." Some ministry officials received additional salaries from development projects; others collected less than the contract allocated (with the difference presumably siphoned off, though no specific charge was made).[43]

Some of these accusations were taken up by the Corruption Report, but none died with that report: virtually every charge was still being levied five years later.

In 1998, the PLC Budget Committee issued a far less detailed and more restrained report.[44] Some council observers speculated uncharitably that the reason for the report's reticence was connected not with any improvement in the budget but with Sa'di al-Krunz's imminent appointment as a minister. The budget did become tangled with the cabinet reshuffle, stealing the thunder from some threats issued by the PLC for executive noncooperation. The budget was again presented in the third month of the fiscal year; the PLC Budget Committee reported back to the plenary at the end of April requesting some changes. The PLC then requested changes but received no response from the cabinet. The PLC scheduled a session for 15 June to debate withdrawing confidence from the government. Three days before the PLC deadline, President 'Arafat requested a delay to 25 June because of the pending ministerial change. On 24 June, President 'Arafat announced his formal acceptance of the cabinet's resignation and requested another two-week delay from the council. The cabinet finally approved limited measures to answer the Budget Committee's objections, and the committee therefore recommended formal approval of the budget.

The repetition of threats and delays won at best promises of better behavior in the future: the Budget Committee announced that the executive had agreed to submit loans to the PLC, increase funding to universities, give designated funds to local governments, explain the privatization policy, and so on. Yet some of these pledges were forgotten. For instance, the Ministry of Finance explained it could not report on the revenues of publicly held corporations until it received the information and the PLC had developed the necessary legal framework. Yet the less confrontational process seemed to result in some accomplishments. Out of public view, President 'Arafat agreed to shift some funds to the public budget and the Ministry of Finance that he had withheld in previous years.[45] The concessions did little to affect the 1998 budget, however—and the PLC discovered that it had to ask for the same concessions again in the following two years.

The year 1999 saw the most protracted and contentious debate over the budget, lasting throughout most of the year. With al-Krunz having joined the cabinet, the chairmanship of the Budget Committee fell to 'Azmi Shu'aybi. With an eye on the string of broken promises and fiscal irregularities, Shu'aybi eschewed any compromises or private negotiations. The new strategy was based on a feeling that the executive had been given many opportunities to correct its behavior and that the Budget Law and the history of promises gave the PLC a stronger position. Shu'aybi's strategy of confrontation did succeed in moving the controversy very much into public view but in the end wrested only a few more concessions and cost him his chairmanship.

The struggle over the 1999 budget began late, as had earlier budgets: the cabinet did not submit the draft until April, the fourth month of the fiscal year. Shau'aybi did not accept this delay easily: he announced in a PLC session on 5 January that the minister of finance had submitted the draft to the president at the end of November (beyond the deadline for submission to the PLC but at least before the beginning of the fiscal year) and suggested that the cabinet be held responsible. He further requested a special session for interpellating the minister of finance, the step prior to a motion to withdraw confidence. Nabil 'Amr, then minister for parliamentary affairs, attempted to placate the PLC by stating that the cabinet had begun discussion of the budget.[46] On 28 January, the minister of finance appeared in a special session to explain that the Civil Service Law—passed by the PLC but not yet implemented partly because of its fiscal implications—had caused the delay. Shu'aybi was not mollified, levying further charges that loans has been contracted without submission to the PLC and that PNA revenues were still not all passing to the Treasury and thus remained outside of the budget. The PLC reacted to the debate by holding the entire cabinet rather than the minister responsible and threatening withdrawal of confidence if no budget was presented within three weeks.[47] The executive managed to delay further, however, and the budget was not submitted until April.

This time, however, Shu'aybi made clear he would not be satisfied with a reiteration of past promises. He claimed that significant amounts of PNA revenues, development expenditures, and the activity of publicly owned companies were still not included in the budget, and he began to move to investigate these areas more thoroughly. He was sufficiently successful in convincing the executive of his tenaciousness that the government withdrew the budget and resubmitted it in July, claiming that it had now addressed Shu'aybi's concerns. Shu'aybi and his committee pursued their investigative work further, however, and found significant faults even with the revised budget. Most significantly, some of the revenue now being reported (as going to health and education) was not going to the ministries as claimed. Shu'aybi had succeeded in getting resentful ministers to supply his committee with information that allowed him to question the accuracy of the budget as submitted. The result was the most detailed and merciless report on the budget produced by the PLC Budget Committee.[48] The report recounted all the promises and legal provisions (especially from the 1998 Budget Law) that had been ignored and repeatedly broken: the budget was late, it did not include all revenues, all manner of personnel violations occurred (overpayment, underpayment, overhiring, and extralegal hiring), ministries paid high rents rather than undertaking construction, loans were contracted without notifying the PLC and were used for operating rather than capital expenses, revenues promised to local governments were not delivered, there was still no plan for controlling travel expenses, and so on. And the committee dredged up some new issues as well. Most notably, perhaps, the committee complained that it had not received a detailed financial report for 1998. It did receive the final accounts for 1997 and discovered that the ministry had made major changes in the budget without obtaining PLC approval.

The entire PLC struck a more compromising pose than Shu'aybi's Budget Committee. It finally approved the budget on 12 August (seven and one-half months into the fiscal year), but the committee also called for a special session in October to discuss the government's compliance with its past promises. That session was delayed until 24 November and came only after 'Azmi Shu'aybi's resignation (as described in the opening to this chapter). It fell to Da'ud al-Zir, the newly elected chair, to present the committee's report on government noncompliance with the budget and the law. About two weeks before the session, the Ministry of Finance submitted the 2000 budget, the first one presented in PNA history prior to the beginning of the fiscal year. Nabil 'Amr, the minister for parliamentary affairs, pointed out that with the fiscal year virtually over, there was no point in making any amendments in the budget. He spoke of the timely submission of the 2000 budget as a fruit of a new cooperative spirit. And when some deputies tried to force a vote of confidence on the issue, Abu 'Ala' shouted them down, stating that the PLC had assembled only to discuss the Budget Committee's report—a report that came without recommendations and therefore made it difficult to take action of any sort. In the end, the vote was held when the government had a bare majority of deputies, and the resulting resolution (passed 19–18) merely called for continued monitoring of the budget and administrative reform more generally. Once again, the PLC had been dissuaded from a confrontational path by the promise of future changes.

The 2000 budget debate combined the detail and bitterness of the 1999 debate with the acquiescence of the 1998 debate. The budget was submitted before the beginning of the fiscal year and was originally balanced. Corrected figures submitted early in 2000 disturbed this picture slightly (with a deficit of $90 million in a total budget of $1.364 billion). Shortly before the Budget Committee presented its report to the full PLC, the president announced the formation of a new Supreme Development Council to oversee the unified accounts of the PNA; this was coupled with a promise to direct all revenues to the treasury and disclose publicly held holdings. While these reforms came more in response to international pressure than to PLC urgings, they had been long-standing PLC demands that arose in all previous budget debates. In this atmosphere, the PLC was in a more conciliatory mood when it met on 26 January to hear the report of the Budget Committee. The report, described at the beginning of this chapter, was hardly uncritical. The same issues arose that had been raised in previous reports: the lack of detail, failure to comply with the provisions of the Budget Law and other laws, and even the lack of an official travel policy and overreliance on expensive rental properties rather than new construction. On one issue—the PNA's practice of deducting 5 percent from the salaries of employees—the PLC had been objecting since June 1996, only a few months after it began operation. Every budget debate brought new complaints and government promises to begin to diminish the practice—yet the 2000 report found that deductions continued. The debate over the budget was acrimonious, with opponents dominating the discussion. But when it came time to vote, the PLC was sufficiently anxious to protect the gains made that it elected to approve the budget by a 25-to-18 margin.

Those gains were erased by the time of the 2001 budget. With the second intifada erupting in September 2000, accompanied by a closure on travel among Palestinian-ruled areas as well as between them and the rest of the world, and with an Israeli refusal to transfer tax payments to the PNA, the 2001 budget was prepared in an atmosphere of economic and fiscal crisis.[49] Thus, the budget was once again late, submitted only in March 2001. Upon announcing receipt of the budget, the Speaker also told reporters that he expected the Budget Committee to finish its work within one week so that adoption would not be delayed.[50] The PLC was given little choice: continued external funding to compensate for the cancellation of Israeli transfer payments depended on an approved budget; supportive Arab states could not be asked to assist without specifying the state of PNA finances. To prolong the controversy would transform fiscal crisis to total collapse. The PLC had not forgotten past disputes—in March 2001 it had reiterated one more time its demand for a final accounting for previous budget years.[51] But budget chair al-Zir still reported that the Budget Committee recommended approval of the draft:

> We consider this budget as an emergency budget. We took into consideration the blockade and closure imposed on our people and on the National Authority. For that reason, we are recommending approval of the budget so that expenditures will become legal, as long as the Ministry of Finance produces the appendices to the draft in the matters where the committee has requested it.[52]

The PLC complied on 4 April 2001, approving a $1.68 billion budget by a 26-to-8 vote; the total deficit (including some expenditures carried over from the previous year) reached $526 million. Yet it was not the ballooning deficit that gave the PLC pause. The resolution passing the budget restated past demands that the budget be submitted on time, that it include the earnings from publicly owned companies, that employees of such companies not be placed on the state budget, and that the budget follow long-stated but also long-ignored policies on personnel, debt financing, and transfer of revenue to local government. The PLC even found itself forced once again to call for the final accounts for previous budget years. Finally, the resolution approving the budget noted that the document itself should be published once approved.[53]

In 2002, the cabinet once more failed to produce the draft budget before the beginning of the fiscal year. On 14 February, six weeks after the fiscal year had begun, the PLC finally received the draft. Budget chair al-Zir set the end of March as a target for his committee's report; this would have paved the way for an April PLC meeting for final approval. That time line proved impossible in light of the Israeli military campaign; it was not until May that the PLC could resume work, and then broad reform, rather than examination of the budget, filled its agenda. The 2002 budget was eventually simply forgotten.

The 2003 budget began more auspiciously for the PLC. The appointment of a new finance minister and the watchful gaze (and financial contributions) of outside actors coincided with a modest revival in PLC activity. Sa`di al-Krunz returned to head the Budget Committee, where he had operated effectively until enticed into taking a ministerial position from 1998 until 2002. Yet the fiscal crisis that began in 2000 when Israel stopped transferring Palestinian tax revenues to the Palestinian treasury had grown acute, even though the European Union and other donors had filled some of the gap (and Israel had finally agreed to transfer a small portion of the funds). The finance minister cited this situation in explaining his failure to submit the 2003 budget until the last hours of 2002. Despite this delay, he could still claim to be timelier than his predecessor, who had operated in far less difficult fiscal circumstances.

With virtually every budget, then, the PLC girded itself for confrontation but ultimately compromised—sometimes very quickly and sometimes only after protracted conflict—granting its assent to a budget in return for promises about future behavior. What is remarkable is that almost all of this debate took place on procedural grounds. Deputies in the PLC could deliver trenchant criticisms of the budgetary priorities of the PNA: Why was the budget for security greater than that for education and health combined (with police and security receiving 35.1 percent of reported expenditures in 2000, education receiving 18.4 percent, and health receiving 9.8 percent)? Why did the presidency consume such a large share of the budget (in 2000, 6.1 percent)? Why were Palestinian universities, some of them unable to pay their employees or the electrical bills, receiving so little public support? The Budget Committee would raise such uncomfortable questions, sometimes succeeding in eking out modest increases for social services. Yet the PLC never tried to make significant changes in the budget, satisfying itself with insisting (with uncertain effectiveness) that legal procedures be followed. The PLC seemed uncertain of its legal authority to make changes and lacked the political will to test the issue.

Indeed, the ability of the PLC to make changes in the budget was rendered quite ambiguous in the 1998 Budget Law. On the one hand, the law required that the annual budget be passed as a law, implying that the regular legislative process operated for the budget. That process was governed itself by an ambiguous body of law. (See Chapter 3; this included the PLC's standing orders, Law 4 of 1995, the Basic Law, and the Egyptian-era and Jordanian constitutions. The applicability of each of these legal frameworks was often in dispute.) On the other hand, the 1998 Budget Law included its own language that hardly clarified matters:

> The cabinet will submit the draft law of the public budget to the Legis-
> lative Council at least two months prior to the beginning of the fiscal
> year. The Legislative Council will refer the draft to the Committee
> on the Budget and Fiscal Affairs for detailed study and opinion. [The
> Committee] will report its recommendations regarding [the draft] to
> the Council. The Legislative Council will hold a special session to discuss
> the draft law of the public budget in light of the report and recommen-
> dations of the Committee and will approve the budget with the amend-
> ments before the beginning of the fiscal year or return it to the cabinet
> in a period not less than one month from the date of its referral, accom-
> panied by the comments of the Legislative Council so that the required
> changes can be made and [the draft] returned to the Legislative Council
> in a period not less than two weeks from its referral to approve it.[54]

Could the PLC make changes in the budget on its own, or could it only request the cabinet to make them? If the PLC passed the budget "with amendments," were those amendments binding or did they require presi-dential assent, like other legislation? On occasion, the PLC Budget Commit-tee would tinker with the budget, asking the entire body to approve the bud-get with those amendments (as it did in 1999 and 2000). It was never clear whether the cabinet or the Ministry of Finance acknowledged the validity of these changes. And since the Treasury generally failed in its legal obligation to give final accounts for the fiscal year (in 2000 the council found itself reviewing the 1997 accounts), there was little way of discovering whether the PNA had implemented any amendments (or even the budget itself).

AN UNPERCEIVED REVOLUTION IN PALESTINIAN LAW

There was one area in which the PLC found itself in a more powerful posi-tion: legislation. While some members of the executive initially contested the PLC's right to initiate legislation, they reluctantly acquiesced in the PLC's more ambitious view of its own role. And as legislation began to come out of the PLC—slowly at first, but gradually more quickly—it showed a marked difference in both process and content from pre-1996 Palestinian law. Generally, the PLC followed a more open, public, and accessible process in writing law, and the legislation it produced had a far more liberal and less statist flavor than pre-1996 legislation. The openness and liberalism of the PLC can be seen in several areas of legislation, such as the NGO Law (see Chapter 5) and the Law on the Independence of the Judiciary (see Chapter 2). In many ways, then, the PLC was responsible for an unperceived revolution in Palestinian lawmaking. Its effectiveness should not be overestimated: having made law, the PLC was powerless to do anything other than plead with the president to approve it, and, when it did obtain presidential endorsement, the PLC was often frustrated in attempts to get the law enforced.

In procedural terms, the PLC signaled a departure in how it would craft law when it tackled its first major piece of legislation—the Basic Law. By the time the PLC took up the task of drafting the constitutional framework for the PNA, the issue had already moved into public view (see Chapter 3). But the PLC did nothing to turn the debates in a technical direction; instead, it moved to incorporate the public debate into its drafting process. Drafts were publicly circulated, PLC members attended public workshops and town meetings, and the technical help offered by the PLO's Legal Committee and the Ministry of Justice's Diwan al-fatwa wa-l-tashri' gradually faded in importance in the process (though it retained its role in ordinary legislation). Other laws followed a similar path: the NGO Law (see Chapter 5) was drafted initially in Palestinian ministries but then, when taken up by the PLC, came to resemble much more closely drafts produced by NGOs themselves. Professional associations participated in drafting laws that governed their own affairs (see Chapter 5). For the most part, the PLC did not formally institutionalize any public role in the drafting process (though PLC committees did begin to experiment with public hearings). Yet by its very procedures—in which draft laws underwent an initial reading before the entire PLC—it became easy for affected groups to track relevant legislation, and PLC members and committees regularly consulted with affected groups. In most Arab countries, the bulk of legislative drafting work is done in ministries and offices attached to the cabinet; external consultation and lobbying are not unknown, but the task of legislative drafting is seen as a highly technical matter to be left (largely if not entirely) to professional experts. Whatever the source of a law's first draft—the cabinet, an NGO, or a council member or committee—the PLC followed a very different vision of the legislative process: the broader purposes of a law were more likely to be articulated by critical groups and institutions (governmental or otherwise), and the role of technical expertise was simply to articulate those purposes in legal language. To be sure, the PLC could pursue this task fairly easily because it rarely had to deal with competing public constituencies. When it considered professional associations, for instance, there was only one group speaking for the association and no countervailing pressure. (There were some exceptions, such as the Labor Law, in which unions and employers had conflicting visions of its proper content.[55])

The PLC did not only change Palestinian law by opening up the legislative process; it also tended to produce laws with a very different content. In part this was because PLC deputies worked in areas that were not a priority for the executive branch. Such was certainly the case with the Basic Law, which deputies felt was the most fundamental and critical task they faced as an institution, but which the executive in general and the president most specifically were content to live without indefinitely. But there were other areas of law that the PLC took up enthusiastically with little encouragement from the executive. A law on foreigners owning real estate caused the PNA some international embarrassment because it was introduced during a wave of attacks on land dealers. In 2000, the Oversight and Human Rights Committee of the PLC worked with human rights organizations to draft legislation forbidding torture—a measure that would have had a deep resonance among inhabitants of the West Bank and Gaza but would have hamstrung and embarrassed the security services and the president.[56] The plenary managed to bury the draft quietly soon after it was reported out of committee.[57] On other occasions the PLC did not initiate a draft but systematically rewrote one endorsed by the cabinet, generally replacing authoritarian provisions with far more liberal ones. This was the case, for instance, with the Law of Political Parties (which ground to a halt in a PLC committee in 1998 amidst the effort to redraft it) and the NGO Law (passed by the PLC and approved by the president after considerable delay and some procedural wrangling—see Chapter 5). And the Law of Public Meetings, while approved by the president as part of a conciliation with the PLC, gave PNA officials far fewer legal tools than they would have liked to control politically troublesome gatherings.

The problem with initiating such liberal laws, or redrafting statist and authoritarian provisions in a more liberal fashion, was that the PLC was powerless to ensure that a law it passed was actually implemented. On occasion, forces within the PLC more conciliatory toward the executive (including the Speaker and other leaders as well as some, but not all, Fatah deputies) shied away from pursuing a matter or shelved a controversial issue. Such an attitude may explain the indefinite postponement of the Law on Political Parties or the decision to accept a presidential amendment to the NGO Law despite the weak legal basis for doing so (see Chapter 5). Far more often, the PLC deputies received no presidential discouragement or ignored the signals they did receive (as with the Basic Law). Yet passing a law was hardly the end of the legislative process for the PLC. On most occasions, intensive lobbying with the president was necessary before his assent was given. The most striking example is the Law on the Independence of the Judiciary. After a prolonged legislative process, including particularly wide-spread consultation with international experts and Palestinian officials (lasting through much of 1997 and 1998), the PLC approved a law on 25 November 1998. Far from being finished with the matter, however, PLC members found that their work had just begun. They obtained the support of leading legal officials for the law and repeated assurances that the law would soon be approved.[58] And the PLC began work on supplementary legislation, governing the formation and administration of the courts. Yet the Law on the Independence of the Judiciary still sat unsigned. PLC members continued to lobby for approval.[59] In February 2000, the PLC made a concession as part of the effort to obtain presidential approval: the cabinet had requested that the PLC take itself out of the approval process for the Al-na'ib al-'amm, the attorney general.[60] Since this change came after the third reading of the bill (before which cabinet comments had been received), this was a procedural as well as substantive concession. Still no approval came. In March 2000 the minister of justice arrived late to a session discussion judicial legislation and described the judges themselves as the obstacle to approval of the law.[61] Yet even the appointment of senior judicial personnel and the formation of the Supreme Judicial Council (mandated by the law but appointed by presidential decree in lieu of approval of the law) did not seem to resolve the matter. In March 2001, with the opening of the sixth year of the PLC, President 'Arafat dramatically called up the chief justice to sit on the podium with him as he opened the PLC session. He promised that the law would be approved within hours, but he still did not take action until May 2002 (see Chapter 2).

The saga of the Labor Law displayed even more irregularities. After considerable controversy (including some opposition from labor union officials), the Labor Law was passed in March 2000. Two months later, the minister of labor announced that the president had signed the law. Yet it was not published in the *Official Gazette*, rendering it inoperative. Over a year later, Yasir 'Arafat announced in a May Day message to workers that the law would be published and had gone into effect.[62] After three months, however, the law's supporters saw no sign of this and spoke of going to court to have the law published and implemented. Not until November 2001 was the law finally published in the *Official Gazette*—and without a trace of embarrassment or explanation, the effective date of the legislation was listed as April

2000. This was hardly the end of the story, however. In February 2002, in a meeting with labor leaders, the minister of labor admitted that the law required additional efforts (such as the construction of labor courts) before it could be applied.[63] And the following month, the Diwan al-fatwa wa-l-tashri' forwarded an amended Labor Law to the cabinet, designed to clarify matters left vague in the recently published law.[64] That law was still not fully in effect, however, because implementing regulations had not yet been written.

Indeed, for many laws, even after presidential approval was secured, enforcement required further lobbying and effort. The Budget Law, for instance, was passed by the PLC in April 1998 and approved by the president four months later. Yet as the discussion above shows, the PLC had to launch a yearly battle to ensure that the Ministry of Finance and the cabinet would meet the provisions of the law—and with a very uneven record of success. The Law of Public Meetings was passed in 1998, yet in 2000 governors felt comfortable clearly violating its provisions, as will be seen below.

The arduous road that the PLC was forced to follow in legislating for the PNA in all steps (from drafting to implementation) can be seen in three areas of its earliest activity: local government, civil service, and public meetings. Local government seemed to be an area of early success for the PLC; indeed, the first two pieces of PLC legislation approved by the president involved local government.

In December 1996, the PLC passed its first law, governing elections for local government. (The PLC had taken up the Basic Law earlier but not yet passed it in final form.) The experience was deceptively easy: the matter provoked little controversy, and the president approved the law within weeks. Law 5 of 1996—the first legislated by Palestine's new parliament—was published and (theoretically) went into effect before the end of the year. The following month, President 'Arafat issued a decree establishing a body to oversee local elections. (Oddly, it took one year for the order to be published in the *Official Gazette*—or perhaps not so oddly, because the body never met.).[65] The law governed the electoral process, but it covered little else relevant to local government.[66] Accordingly, the PLC took up another major piece of legislation, the Law of Local Palestinian Government. This work proceeded only slightly more slowly, with the PLC passing the law in July 1997 and obtaining presidential approval on 12 October 1997.[67] The law was very detailed in some aspects, assigning considerable jurisdiction to local governments, including planning, zoning, provision of services (such as water and electricity), control over public buildings and markets, and monitoring of weights and measures. Half of all traffic fines were designated for local governments, and provisions for other sources of revenue were also made. Yet the law also provided for a strong measure of oversight by the cabinet and the Ministry of Local Government. It was unclear how autonomous local governments would be in practice; this would necessarily be determined less by the provisions of the law and more by the extent of fiscal and electoral independence local governments would be able to achieve. In short, the legislation passed by the PLC would have allowed for strong, democratic, and autonomous local government but would not necessarily have required it.

Indeed, it was precisely in enforcing these provisions that the PLC's two laws began to break down. While the first law provided for democratic elections for local government, those elections were never held. Given the speed with which the cabinet submitted a draft law to the PLC and the immediate presidential assent, there is no reason to doubt that the PNA leadership initially inclined toward holding elections, to the extent that the matter was given much thought. Yet promises of implementation became progressively vaguer. Two reasons were generally given for the delay. In public, PNA officials (especially the minister of local government, Sa'ib 'Erakat) explained that large areas of the West Bank and Gaza remained under Israeli rule and that the PNA did not wish to administer elections under occupation (though it had done so for the PNA president and the PLC); neither did it wish to hold elections in some areas only, afraid that this would signal acceptance of limited Israeli withdrawals.[68] A second reason was spoken in private by PNA critics: local elections might result in opposition-dominated bodies that would make life difficult for the leadership and even embarrass it internationally. The PLC regularly expressed frustration on the issue, periodically questioning 'Erakat or passing resolutions calling for elections. In December 1998, the PLC called for local elections to be held before 4 May 1999 (the presumed date at the time for the declaration of Palestinian statehood).[69] One year later, the PLC was still asking why elections had not been held.[70] Yet a truly determined parliament might have pursued the matter further by withdrawing confidence from the minister or taking other steps to signal rejection of executive branch justifications. Instead, the PLC simply periodically nagged the executive, ultimately accepting that on matters of national importance the PNA leadership might be gently criticized but should not be undermined. Not until May 2002, when the leadership was desperate to show its commitment to reform, were local elections placed back on the agenda. Since the amount of Palestinian territory under Israeli control had actually increased, previous justifications for delay were revealed to be excuses. The elections were tentatively scheduled for early 2003.

The PLC was no more successful in pressing for fiscal autonomy for local government. Budget Committee reports regularly noted that the designated portion of traffic fines was not delivered to local governments as required by law. At times the Ministry of Finance would complain that local governments tended not to pay their electricity and other bills, meaning that the ministry had to retain the funds to cover the obligations that local governments had incurred, but no total accounting was given. Neither did the Ministry of Finance explain why all local governments were deprived of an instrument of fiscal autonomy because of the sins of a few.

The Civil Service Law stands as one of the most complex pieces of legislation the PLC every produced. In May 1996, shortly after the PLC began operating, the cabinet approved a draft to submit to the new parliament for consideration. The PLC worked on the legislation for a year, passing the final version in June 1997. Covering all sorts of areas—vacations, ranks, employee rights, hiring procedures, and so on—the Civil Service Law looked to become a fundamental building block of the construction of a new Palestinian bureaucracy and thus of the emerging Palestinian state. Despite the breadth and complexity of areas covered, the law occasioned little controversy. In one respect, however, the PLC introduced changes that proved problematic: it granted a generous pay schedule. Consideration of the Civil Service Law came in the midst of a bitter strike by teachers; PLC members viewed public sector wage demands fairly sympathetically. The law allowed the cabinet a year to issue implementing regulations; it also allowed government agencies to move employees to the new salary schedules gradually. Still, the president was still reluctant to sign a law that his Ministry of Finance—and international donors—worried would be fiscally irresponsible. Those claiming to speak for the president issued periodic promises that the Civil Service Law—among other laws passed by the PLC but not receiving presidential endorsement—would soon be approved.[71]

Members of the PLC continued to lobby for adoption of their law, arguing that the pay schedule could be implemented gradually.[72] The president finally succumbed to this argument and signed the law in May 1998. With public employment mushrooming, the PNA moved to implement the law gradually. Yet this strategy soon sparked resentments among those not targeted for initial raises (and in a few cases officials complained that the new salary schedule would actually result in a decrease). In February 1999 public sector health workers in the West Bank went on strike and demonstrated at the PLC over the delayed implementation of the law.[73] The strike backfired—the result was that the PNA retreated from its promise to implement the law gradually and the operation of the law was suspended in its entirety.

And the leadership seemed immune to pressure on the issue. Periodic public sector strikes (especially a second strike by teachers in 2000, occasioned by a decision to introduce higher deductions for pension funds for the West Bank while still delaying the salary raises occasioned by the Civil Service Law), pressure from the PLC during the budget process (including demands that funds be designated for gradual implementation of the law), and even World Bank endorsement of the nonsalary provisions of the law provoked only vague promises.[74] Four years after passing the law and three years after receiving presidential approval, the PLC still found itself passing resolutions demanding that the law be applied.[75]

A third, and far less noticed, example of the difficulties faced by the PLC in having its laws effectively adopted and enforced was Law 12 of 1998, related to public meetings. The legislative process was more extended for this law, beginning in March 1997 and ending with passage on the third reading in December 1998. Despite the protracted legislative process, the law did not provoke an enormous amount of public debate, and the president approved it shortly after it passed. The law itself was brief (with nine short articles) but very liberal: essentially it allowed citizens the right "to hold public gatherings, meetings, and marches in freedom," subject only to the limitations contained in the law. Those limitations required only that that the governor or police commander be given written and signed notification at least forty-eight hours in advance. The official could, within twenty-four hours of receiving the notice, give a written order regarding the time period or the course of a meeting or march, but only in order to organize traffic and not in such a way as to infringe the freedom to hold the meeting. Other protective measures could be taken as long as they did not harm the freedom of those meeting or the meeting itself. As was generally the case with Palestinian legislation, all older legislation (Ottoman and Jordanian) or unspecified contradictory laws were canceled.

It would have been difficult to write a more permissive or liberal law. In February 2000, however, a far more restrictive interpretation of the law was put forward by PNA security officials. A demonstration at Bir Zayt University on the occasion of a visit of the prime minister of France had led to a clash between students and security forces. The prime minister himself was jostled, and the PNA felt publicly embarrassed. A group of students was arrested and the university was briefly closed. A few days later, the Palestinian Police commander, Ghazi Jabali, published an announcement in Palestinian newspapers forbidding any demonstrations, meetings, or marches that did not have prior police authorization.[76] Not only did the requirement that organizers obtain permission directly contradict Law 12 of

1998 (which required only notification, not permission), but the order brazenly cited Law 12 as the basis for its authority. Human rights organizations and some opposition political parties immediately filed suit against the order in the Palestinian High Court. Acting with uncharacteristic alacrity, the court canceled the order on 30 April 2000.[77] The victory for liberal freedom lasted mere hours. On the same day, the minister of interior (Yasir 'Arafat) issued an administrative decision regarding implementation of Law 12.[78] This decision did not so obviously contradict Law 12, but it did implement it in the strictest way possible, violating the spirit (and probably the letter, though it has not been tested in court) of Law 12. The written notification of the meeting had to be delivered by hand and had to describe the purpose of the meeting. If the governor rather than the police commander received the notice (as the law allowed), he was to turn it over to the police commander. The police commander could demand a meeting with the organizers to find out additional information about the meeting and its purpose. He was then to respond with written permission, mentioning the time, place, duration, and purpose, and "any other conditions." A meeting could not be held in a tense place, nor could the meeting's purpose (and not merely the meeting itself) be in conflict with the law or public order. The police commander could end the meeting if it exceeded its stated purpose, and the organizers of the meeting were to be held to Presidential Decree 3 of 1998, concerning national unity and forbidding incitement. Organizers were to be held personally and criminally liable for violations. In short, the PLC had legislated as liberal a law as possible, and the security authorities, including the police and Ministry of Interior, made clear that the law would be interpreted (or misinterpreted) as restrictively as they wished. The interior minister's Order 1 of 2000 occasioned little debate from the PLC. The most obvious countermeasure the council could take in response—questioning the minister himself—was unthinkable. As Order 1 made clear in the text, it came not simply from the minister but from the president of the PNA and the president of the Executive Committee of the PLO, all the same person.

The PLC was therefore successful in changing Palestinian law dramatically in two ways: the legislative process became far more open to various societal groups, and the content of the law became far more liberal. Yet it failed in having many of its laws approved. Those that were approved were often ignored: implementing regulations were not issued; prescribed procedures were not followed; and new bodies were to be formed but never convened. The revolution in Palestinian legislation was real, and many of its accomplishments are actually on the books. But its subjects have never felt the effects.

CONCLUSION

While the PLC seemed at its founding to mark a sharp break in Palestinian history, it soon found itself a victim of that history. It is true that the PLC was an institution without antecedents: no Palestinian parliament had ever been effectively convened. What antecedents might be cited provided little guidance. A body called the Palestinian National Council had convened in Gaza in 1948, but it was able to accomplish little and was soon forgotten. Palestinians in the West Bank had participated in the Jordanian parliament (and helped transform and embolden that body in the 1950s until King Husayn brought it under firmer control in 1957); those in Gaza had participated in a largely consultative chamber formed under Egyptian rule. The PLC stood as an institutional successor for neither of these, and in both these cases, the individuals participating had largely passed from the scene (the most significant exception was Haydar 'Abd al-Shafi, who chaired the Gazan body and briefly held a seat in the PLC before resigning in protest at the body's powerlessness[79]). In 1964, a new PNC was convened in Jerusalem, meeting periodically and forming the source for the PLO's authority. Yet that body was composed haphazardly, generally by appointment, and developed no structures that allowed it to do anything other than ratify decisions hammered out by senior leaders.

The deputies of the PLC therefore seemed to be starting from scratch, armed with an agreement that constituted the PLC itself as the governing body for Palestinians in the West Bank and Gaza. Yet the deputies found very soon that they did not fall outside history after all. First, it was clear that some of the senior leadership—including Yasir 'Arafat himself—regarded the PLC's role the way they had viewed the PNC. They argued that the PLC could discuss legislation but not initiate it and that the PLC should support rather than undermine the leadership at a time of the culmination of the nationalist struggle. Second, the PLC fell victim to the short but decisive history of the PNA. On paper, it was the Palestinian Council that constituted the Palestinian Authority, and the president simply headed the executive branch of the Palestinian Council. In reality, however, the president preceded the council: Yasir 'Arafat had returned in 1994 and operated as PNA president for two years before the council even met. It was his signature as PLO leader that had resulted in the agreement that formed the council. And it was politically impossible for the PLC deputies to use the Oslo Accords—with their sharp restrictions on Palestinian freedom of action—as a tool against their president. Third, the broader Arab historical experience with parliaments soon proved to govern the Palestinian case. To

be sure, Arab parliaments have, on occasion, proved to be important political arenas.[80] Yet the most successful of them go no further than what the
Palestinian parliament has accomplished: moving issues into the public
view, affecting the legislative process, and bringing government and opposition into dialogue. PLC deputies share many frustrations with their counterparts in some of the more active Arab parliaments, such as those in
Jordan, Kuwait, and Lebanon, in their inability to gain more control over
legislation or institute real accountability.[81]

The PLC therefore resumed Palestine's participation in Arab history
more than its deputies would have liked. But the real struggle in the PLC
came between the two other senses in which the PNA marks the resumption
of Arab Palestine. On the one hand, the PLC was a body that strove, especially at the beginning, to resume normal politics, divorced as much as possible from the negotiations with Israel. To be sure, the deputies staked out
positions on nationalist issues and seemed anxious to play the role of speaking for Palestinian public opinion and shoring up the resolve of the negotiators on critical issues, such as Jerusalem and settlements. In the debate
over the 2000 budget, for instance, deputies criticized the scant funds
devoted to Palestinian institutions in Jerusalem. (PNA leaders probably
cringed at this debate, aware that any PNA activity in Jerusalem succeeded
often when Israel chose to ignore it, something that a noisy PLC discussion
or a series of line items in the budget would make difficult.) But PLC
deputies were happiest when ignoring the Oslo Accords altogether. They did
so when they drafted laws on firearms and property ownership that Israeli
officials claimed violated signed agreements. But more significantly, they
did so when drafting fundamental pieces of legislation—the Basic Law, the
Budget Law, the NGO Law, or the Law on the Independence of the
Judiciary—that formed the basis for politics in a normal (and largely liberal) state. In drafting legislation, the PLC pursued a vision of Palestine as a
political entity that differed little from existing democratic states.

Yet this vision was either defeated or deferred by another vision of the
PLC's role: one that did not assume that the body could operate independently of the nationalist struggle. For the senior PNA leadership, the PLC
was an important marker of the resumption of Palestinian history, but the
parliament's youthful enthusiasm should properly be tempered by a realization that the nationalist issue must take priority over all other concerns.
The PLO (and the chair of its Executive Committee, Yasir 'Arafat), not the
PLC, was to negotiate and lead on such issues, and only the PLO could represent Palestinians throughout the world. PLC overzealousness in some of
the causes it pursued would only embarrass, weaken, or undercut the lead-

ers at a time when their strength lay only in their claim to represent Palestinians.

A few PLC members (such as those who signed the *bayan al-'ashrin*) angrily rejected this argument. A few others were highly skeptical, arguing that strengthening Palestinian political institutions would only make Palestinian negotiators stronger (and might even allow them to cite their own public opinion when refusing to make concessions). But the dominance of Fatah deputies, the position of 'Arafat as the symbol of Palestinian nationalism, and the large number of ministers in the PLC all combined to make most deputies accept the leadership's argument. Some seemed to do so reluctantly. The Speaker himself, while a member of the senior leadership, initially took a more confrontational tone in insisting on the council's prerogatives. But as time wore on, he worked increasingly to settle disputes before they broke out in public, delay consideration of controversial issues, and broker settlements with the vague promises that so frustrated council members.

The result was that nearly every time the PLC found itself in a contest with the executive it has lost. Even more striking, it grew more gracious in accepting defeat. And with the eruption of the second intifada in September 2000, the PLC found it increasingly difficult to operate. For the first year and a half of the intifada, the initiative passed from official bodies (including the PLC) to more shadowy militias and security services. In such an atmosphere, the PLC had far less to contribute.

It may be that the PLC's record did its cause more harm than good, at least in the short term. By insisting that any law passed be liberal in content, the PLC unwittingly encouraged the Palestinian leadership to give little respect to the legal framework more generally. Knowing that the PLC would not enact a more statist (and authoritarian vision) of the proper legal order, the leadership developed a series of extralegal tools that avoided even much of the pretence of the rule of law (see Chapter 2).

It must be noted that it is entirely possible that the PLC accomplished much more than a short-term focus can reveal. On a series of issues, the PLC legislated a far more liberal framework than has ever governed Palestinians. That framework has not yet made itself felt in Palestinian public life, but it may have laid the basis for a new legal order. The current Palestinian leadership has obstructed the effectiveness of new laws, but it has placed many of them on the books. At present, the Palestinian judiciary and the legal system are tremendously weak, not simply by the standards set by liberal states but even in comparison to Palestine's Arab neighbors.

More effective legal and judicial institutions may, at some later date, bring Palestine's legal legacy to more effective life. And if that happens, Palestinian legislators, judges, and lawyers will discover the work of the PLC. The battles that Palestinian parliamentarians fought and lost over the past few years may not have been definitively resolved.

5 Civil Society in Theory and Practice

> Put bluntly, the new "regime" did not trust its own society because it had so few connections with it.
>
> GLENN E. ROBINSON

For many Palestinians and non-Palestinians, associational life offered the greatest possibilities for a new kind of politics in the Arab world. The PNA, while striving to create a state, was not operating in a vacuum; it was imposing itself on a society that had learned to organize many of its own affairs under occupation. According to more optimistic views, the prior existence of a vital and energetic civil society would constrain the development of state institutions, leading to a far more liberal and democratic political order than was the norm for Arab countries. More pessimistic observers focused instead on the conflict between the state in the making (based on authoritarian external structures and individuals, imported from PLO headquarters in Tunis) and local society in the West Bank and Gaza.

Remarkably, both optimists and pessimists have been proven right. As optimists hoped, strong associational life did limit the authority and the actions of the PNA in important ways. And, as pessimists feared, the external PLO leadership had difficulty accepting the autonomy of Palestinian social and political organizations in the West Bank and Gaza. Neither side was able to impose its vision of appropriate state-society relations on the other. As the PNA struck deeper institutional roots, the relationship between associations and the state remained unsettled. A law governing NGOs, for instance, took nearly six years and numerous iterations before it was promulgated and then was forced through by a dubious parliamentary maneuver. Nine years after the signing of the Oslo Accords, most professional associations had yet to consolidate into single bodies (in most cases, consolidation involved unification among separate organizations based in Jordan, the West Bank, Gaza, and the external PLO). Labor conflict was rife in the PNA, but it was often those sectors where unions were weakest that were most able to organize strikes. Efforts among various NGOs to coordinate positions often provoked rival efforts among other NGOs. The confusing welter of Palestinian associations became even more pronounced after the creation of the PNA.

What is truly striking about the relationship between the PNA and Palestinian associations, however, is something that neither the optimists nor the pessimists fully expected: the continued interdependence of the two, an interdependence that was far greater than either side anticipated, wanted, or ever fully acknowledged.[1] The PNA relied on various kinds of associations, NGOs, and other bodies to provide services, links to the key constituencies, and external credibility. Official heavy-handedness often obscured the degree of this reliance.

Even less expected was the way that Palestinian associations turned to the PNA for support, licensing, recognition, and legal protection. (Most associations learned fairly quickly that it was futile to turn to the PNA for funding, however.) The interdependence was not unlimited: while each side needed the other, both also had strong sources of independent support (especially financial) that prevented one side from being captured by the other.

It is this interdependence (and its limits) that draws our attention in this chapter. Associational life, NGOs, and civil society have received a large amount of attention from scholars in recent years. Yet this substantial body of scholarly writing equips us far less well to examine associational life—at least in the Palestinian setting, though perhaps elsewhere—than should be expected. We are forced to draw on a variety of concepts and approaches, some of which have faded from writings on state-society relations.

This chapter will thus open with an exploration of those approaches that will guide our understanding of Palestinian civil society more broadly. Following that discussion, four sorts of organizations will be analyzed: political parties, NGOs, grassroots organizations, and professional associations.

CIVIL SOCIETY: ITS ADVOCATES AND ACTIVISTS

Scholars writing from a variety of perspectives have converged on civil society in the past decade. This renewed interest is especially powerful because of a simultaneous (and not entirely coincidental) surge of interest on the part of policy makers and political activists. The enthusiasm for civil society has spread to the Arab world, where intellectuals and activists have latched on to its implicit challenge to unlimited state authority.

Are the now voluminous writings on civil society helpful to us in our attempt to understand the relationship between associations and the PNA as well as the way that relationship has changed? Two dominant strains in these writings have recently emerged—one emphasizing the constraints posed by a strong civil society, the other focusing on the behaviors it fosters. Both approaches betray a blind spot to the reciprocal nature of the influence between various organizations and the state. After reviewing the newer approaches, we will therefore turn to an older approach: corporatism. Even the resurrection of corporatism will not help us understand how state-society relations change, however. That task will lead us to consider the insights provided by civil society activists who see the relationship between state and society as far more malleable than theorists expect.

Civil Society as a Bulwark against the State

The approach that initially dominated scholarly writings on civil society stemmed from the enthusiasm connected with the collapse of authoritarian and communist regimes. It emphasized the impact that vibrant social institutions could have in providing a counterweight to state authority. Given the nature of Palestinian NGOs and professional associations during the Israeli occupation—when they formed an important locus of nationalist identity, mobilization, and political action—this image of civil society grew especially influential among Palestinian intellectuals and activists. References to "civil society" *(al-mujtama' al-madani)* and NGOs *(munazzamat ahliyya* or *munazzamat ghayr hukumiyya)* have become ubiquitous in both academic and journalistic Palestinian political writings.[2] Such an image led to an implicit contrast between the external PLO and internal Palestinian activists even before the creation of the PNA. Writing on the period of the Israeli occupation (from the perspective of the early 1990s), Baruch Kimmerling and Joel Migdal observed: "PLO leaders saw themselves as building the foundations for a Palestinian state. Local organizers, although talking of their role in this state, were in fact engaged in a very different project—erecting a civil society out of the diverse Palestinian population."[3]

This perspective equips us to understand something about the conscious mission of many involved in Palestinian associational life and the resulting clash between many NGO leaders and the newly created PNA. But the approach is less helpful in the specific issues that concern us now. First, if we wish to understand how associational life not only opposes but also interacts with the state, we are given less guidance. Second, the perspective gives us little help in understanding the tremendous changes in the relationship between political authority and the organizations of civil society, especially those that occurred with the creation of the PNA.

Social Capital

A second, increasingly influential perspective of associational life focuses on the effect that participating in social organizations has on social behavior. Rich associational life is taken sometimes as an indicator of "social capital." Indeed, sometimes associational life is seen not merely as an indicator of social capital but as virtually synonymous with it. The precise meaning of *social capital* has shifted over time, but in its current incarnation it involves the level of trust in a society that underlies the ability to organize collectively. Robert Putnam defines it as "features of social organization such as networks, norms, and social trust that facilitate coordination and cooperation for mutual benefit."[4]

For Putnam and its most enthusiastic proponents, social capital is all but a panacea for a host of social ills (and with proclaimed health benefits, social capital may indeed be a cure-all): "Researchers in such fields as education, urban poverty, unemployment, the control of crime and drug abuse, and even health have discovered that successful outcomes are more likely in civically engaged communities."[5] While systematic research is only beginning, impressionistic evidence suggests that Palestinians may be fairly fortunate if social capital has so many benefits. Membership in NGOs is fairly high, and extended families remain fairly strong.[6] Certainly there is a strong mythical basis for social capital in Palestinian society, with an idealization of village life analogous perhaps to American pride in a town meeting.[7] In the recent past, Palestinians often speak of the intifada as a period in which individuals cooperated spontaneously and altruistically.

To be sure, many scholars are uneasy with the current fascination with social capital and the uncritical celebration of all forms of voluntary association.[8] It is not simply the ambitious claims of its advocates that lead to suspicion. It is also the way the concept leads attention away from differences among various organizations: it is based on the view that the fact of participation matters far more than the organization itself.[9] Most important for present purposes, social capital is understood as the product of deeply rooted and long-term historical or cultural trends. Social capital is cast as cause and rarely as effect of politics.[10] Our interest in the relationship between governance and associational life and in understanding change in that relationship is unlikely to be met fully by concentrating solely on the levels of social capital in Palestinian society.

Corporatism

Thus, those who see civil society as hemming in the state and those who see the experience of participation in associations as bringing numerous social

benefits do not provide all the tools we need to understand Palestinian associational life. They will be helpful to be sure, but we must turn even more
to an earlier rediscovery. In the 1970s and 1980s, political scientists made
great use of corporatism, a mode of interest group representation. Definitions remained fairly cumbersome but centered on state creation or licensing of organizations within the society and granting them exclusive rights
to represent their sector. The most widely used definition, introduced by
Philippe Schmitter, cast corporatism as

> a system of interest representation in which the constituent units
> are organized into a limited number of singular, compulsory, non-
> competitive, hierarchically ordered and functionally differentiated
> categories, recognized or licensed (if not created) by the state and
> granted a deliberate representational monopoly within their respective
> categories in exchange for observing certain controls on their selection
> of leaders and articulation of demands and supports.[11]

From the beginning of the renewed interest in corporatism, scholars noted
the existence of different varieties. For Schmitter, for instance, state corporatism involved systems in which interest groups and associations were created and dominated by the state. Such corporatist arrangements worked to
help minimize class and other political conflict as the senior political leadership pursued its goals. Societal corporatism, by contrast, referred to those
political systems in which the organizations originated in society and
retained more autonomy. Corporatist arrangements in such a setting still
helped to minimize political conflict, but more through bargaining among
societal leaders than through command by high officials.

Interest in corporatism receded for many reasons. First, political scientists
began to feel that the idea was being overused, with corporatism being spot-
ted so frequently that it lost its analytic utility. Second, models of corporatism were remarkably static: once the existence of corporatist arrangements was detected, it was not clear what might induce change or lead to
breakdown in corporatist arrangements.[12] Those who discovered corporatist
arrangements generally linked them to either underlying historical and cultural patterns or the stage and nature of economic development. This suggested that they would change slowly if at all. Studies of corporatism could
slide into a functionalism that assumed that it was required by the nature of
economic development. In the Arab world, corporatist arrangements were
commonly devised but worked far less well than the enthusiastic proponents of the concept expected.[13]

In the Palestinian case, introduction of the concept of corporatism is help-ful, though it is hardly sufficient for understanding the politics of associa-tional life. Since the creation of the PNA (and, in different ways, often before), most Palestinian political parties, NGOs, grassroots organizations, and professional associations have striven far harder to negotiate favorable relationships with the emerging state than to insulate themselves from it. Most Palestinian organizations have sought state licensing, recognition, support, and a degree of coordination. The PNA has eagerly asserted its role in recognizing and coordinating the work of such organizations, though its conception of its role gives it far more dominance than most organizations desire. In short, the struggle over associational life can be cast largely as one between advocates of societal and state corporatism. In a few but highly notable cases, societal leaders have eschewed such arrangements and pur-sued an explicitly oppositional mission, though such attitudes have mel-lowed over time (and they have largely disappeared at moments of nation-alist crisis).

Molding and Bending State-Society Relations

Yet while corporatism and its variants help us describe the contest over Palestinian associational life, we must avoid the static nature of corporatist models of politics. Palestinian associational life has undergone dramatic changes; even after the creation of the PNA, few firm or systematic arrangements have emerged. Remarkably, the least reflective writers on the topic may help us the most to understand such fluidity here because they ignore the near-fatalism of the academic models. Unlike scholars, activists and policy makers have little time to delve into history and deeper eco-nomic structures (though they often make assumptions about both). Yet they have leapt into the effort to create new patterns of associational life with enthusiasm. Even as many take up themes from the scholarly litera-ture (on "social capital," for instance), they implicitly (and generally uncon-sciously) reject its determinism: they insist that current patterns can be changed quickly and work hard to change them. External donors hardly take existing arrangements as given but seek to build a rich associational life (with significant effects, as will be seen). And activists aim not to remake all of society but to better their communities. They seek to maneuver into a relationship with political authority that will allow them to do that.

The remainder of this chapter will focus on the relationship between the PNA and various forms of associations. In particular, political parties, large NGOs, smaller grassroots organizations, and professional associations and syndicates will receive attention. Because of the unsettled nature of Palestinian political life and the large variety of perspectives analyzing associational life, a few prefatory definitional remarks are necessary.

First, although the PNA is not a state, it will be treated as one for most purposes in the analysis that follows. There is no doubt that the PNA has exercised most state functions from the perspective of most organizations, providing the legal framework and undertaking policing and licensing functions. It should be noted, however, that the PNA's lack of internationally recognized status as a state has had at least one important effect: it has given external donors far more freedom (in ways that have affected the operation of many of the NGOs). In addition, the decay of some (but not all) PNA institutions following the eruption of the second intifada changed the environments in which parties, NGOs, and grassroots organizations operated.

Second, political parties are included in this chapter, even though they are typically excluded from most definitions of civil society, largely because of their close links to many leading Palestinian NGOs. Palestinian politics stands starkly anomalous in that political parties seem most significant when electoral politics is least important and fade when elections loom more significant. Indeed, some leading NGOs noted the declining role of political parties in Palestinian politics during the 1993–2000 period and deliberately crafted their activities to serve as surrogates. Perhaps the peak of this effort came in September 2000, when, on the brink of the second intifada, a number of NGOs responded to rumors of impending local elections by quickly forming an election monitoring committee.[14] Besides this odd phenomenon—explored in more detail below—NGOs and political parties have often been closely connected. Leading NGO figures have linked political parties to civil society.[15] NGO activists often repeat the phrase "Civil society is the opposition." In short, the distinction between NGOs and political parties exists in theory but often becomes blurred in Palestinian practice. Accordingly, some coverage of the role of political parties seems appropriate, though that coverage will not be comprehensive.

Finally, a distinction is drawn here between NGOs and grassroots organizations. Such a distinction is common in writings on other regions (such as Latin America) but uncommon in the Arab world, even in writings by participants. It is employed here because NGOs and grassroots organizations have very different sets of relationships with the state. Organizations that have a national focus or a large professional staff will be considered NGOs; local organizations that have no (or, at most, a few) paid staff members will be considered grassroots organizations.

POLITICAL PARTIES AND THE FAILED TRANSITION TO ELECTORAL POLITICS

Perhaps the most ironic feature of political life under the PNA is that political parties have declined precipitously in importance just as electoral politics has been introduced. Most have even declined the "party" label, preferring to be called "movements" or "fronts." During the 1960s and 1970s, Palestinian political parties rose to prominence, though the leadership of most parties remained outside the West Bank and Gaza and though parties disdained elections held under occupation.[16] In the 1980s, the presence of parties in political life grew still further as many launched efforts to mobilize the West Bank and Gaza population through trade unions and other organizations. These efforts paid off during the intifada by laying the groundwork for organizing protest activities.[17]

Palestinian political parties therefore devoted their energies toward organization and direct action rather than elections. The few opportunities for electoral competition during the period of Israeli occupation were generally avoided. Even representation in the PLO and other bodies was generally negotiated rather than subject to a popular vote. Rare municipal elections held under the Israeli occupation were generally dominated by personalities rather than parties. Professional associations and other bodies often suspended elections during the occupation; only the student councils saw true party competition.

When the PNA held its elections in 1996, most political parties continued in their refusal to participate before the termination of the Israeli occupation. Moreover, the electoral law was structured to discourage party competition. In some cases, parties split into factions willing to participate and those opposed. Often those in favor of participating came from inside the West Bank and Gaza; they lost in the struggle (though a few party members ran as independents).[18] The exception to the party boycott was Fatah, the largest by far; several very small parties ran candidates as well. Yet while most victorious candidates were unsurprisingly affiliated with Fatah, the party itself hardly proved itself a powerful electoral machine: many of the victorious candidates were members who had failed to win party endorsement. (See Chapter 4 for more detail on the elections.) After the elections, the role of parties in the electoral sphere declined even further. Fatah leaders proved both unwilling and unable to form a cohesive bloc in the PLC, and public opinion polls showed generally declining levels of popular support for opposition political parties.

Yet political parties continued to play a prominent role in Palestinian politics in two ways. First, the parties remained the most prominent and credible political organizations able to articulate a political vision distinct from that of the leadership. With the exception of Hamas, their underlying ideologies no longer informed their positions (especially for the leftist parties after the collapse of communism), and even their stance on Arab-Israeli negotiations often softened in the 1993–2000 period. Yet at times they could pose as the strongest independent political voices in Palestinian society. This was especially the case when they worked to coordinate their positions. Dialogue among the "factions" became a feature of Palestinian political life. At times Fatah itself would participate in issuing statements that sought to pressure the PNA leadership or oppose its actions.[19] The forum for most of these efforts—the National and Islamic Forces—often took a position at odds with that of the senior leadership.

Thus, rather than switching to electoral politics, most parties continued the sort of politics that had characterized PLO life: parties would not compete against each other for votes. They would negotiate with each other rather than resort to the voters to determine the content of the national program. And in times of national crisis, when the operation of nascent state institutions was heavily impaired, party organizations re-emerged as leading political actors. In the fall of 2000, Fatah party instruments and leaders that had played secondary roles in PNA politics became leaders of the second intifada.

Indeed, the second intifada witnessed a return to prominence for several political parties. Fatah party leaders (most famously Marwan al-Barghuti, the party's secretary-general in the West Bank[20]) took some of the lead in pursuing confrontation with Israel in the early months of the second intifada. As the violence wore on, political parties formed units and cells that undertook direct attacks on Israeli targets, including civilians and those living within the 1967 lines. Harsh Israeli responses (and anticipatory attacks) took a toll on the violent activists but hardly stemmed the tide. Indeed, parties competed against each other in launching attacks more effectively than they had ever competed in elections. Hamas and Fatah were most notable in this regard, but they were soon joined by factions that had earlier seemed in decline (and in confusion over how to respond to the Oslo Agreements), most prominently the Popular Front for the Liberation of Palestine.

But the second intifada witnessed not only party competition but also a revival of attempts among party leaders to coordinate positions. The preexisting forum of National and Islamic Forces stepped to the fore in articulating the Palestinian position on various matters, such as negotiating terms, goals, and diplomatic positions. In some areas it posed as the "field leadership" of the second intifada. In March 2001, the coalition even launched a brief attempt to transform itself into a more popular body, enlisting the support of unions and professional associations as well as political parties.[21] By 2002, the forum's independent streak led one ranking PLO official to attempt to draw it into the PLO. The attempt was unsuccessful; the coalition continued to stop just short of openly challenging 'Arafat.[22]

The second significant role played by Palestinian political parties involves NGOs. Especially in the 1980s, leftist parties (later joined by Fatah and then by Hamas) organized a host of unions, women's associations, relief committees, and grassroots organizations. Some of these organizations formed the backbone of the first intifada. With the formation of the PNA, these organizations developed in three different directions. First, a small number were absorbed into ministries. Second, many became far more independent of the party (a trend actually in evidence even before the PNA was created). As international, non-Arab funding became more available, many NGOs increasingly professionalized (a development discussed more in the following section) and loosened ties to the mother party. Yet even in such cases, the NGOs often retained a strong oppositional character (especially but not exclusively in their reputations). The most prominent example was the Union of Palestinian Medical Relief Committee, whose leader became a leading critic of the PNA both domestically and internationally.[23] Third, some NGOs (especially those less likely to draw non-Arab funding) retained their direct partisan character. Hamas in particular increased its emphasis on social service activities.[24]

Palestinian political parties thus have never been primarily organizations engaged in democratic politics. They have shown a lack of interest in electoral politics, and their internal operations have always been undemocratic.[25] Despite this, they have generally sought varieties of liberal arrangements under the PNA (while the Islamist parties have often eschewed liberal ideologies, they have worked in practical terms to build areas of autonomy that draw on such liberal arrangements). On the one hand, all except for Fatah have tried to carve out a significant area of autonomy from the state for their own activities; those activities are often broadly social rather than strictly political. (For this reason, the distinction between civil society and the arena for political party life becomes particularly hard to draw in the Palestinian case.) On the other hand, all (including at times the Islamist parties) seek arrangements within the PNA that can best be described as consociational, in which leaders bargain among themselves to determine the direction of policy (and in the extreme, especially in PLO institutions, the share of representation for each group).[26] Consociationalism did not work smoothly in the PLO before the establishment of the PNA, and attempts to make it work in the PNA have hardly been more than episodic. But the parties themselves continued to focus their efforts in that direction. And they bequeathed a similar set of goals and strategies for relations with the state to the NGOs that many of them founded.

NONGOVERNMENTAL ORGANIZATIONS: FENDING OFF THE STATE WHILE USING IT

Palestinian NGOs are remarkably strong and autonomous by the standards set by the Arab world.[27] Often emerging out of conflict with the Zionist movement and Israel, NGOs played an increasingly important role under the Israeli occupation. Their importance stood as testimony not simply to the energies of NGO activists, however, but also to deliberate decisions made by nationalist leaders and external funders.

The creation of the PNA caused confusion and conflict over the roles of NGOs. High PNA officials regarded the steps toward statehood as the occasion to resume broader Arab patterns of state-NGO relations, in which NGO officials operate within a framework established by national authorities. Leading NGO figures saw the creation of the PNA as the occasion instead to resume normal social and political life, with NGOs no longer beholden in all their actions to a nationalist agenda established by political leaders. The early acrimony between the PNA and leading NGOs (which re-erupted—and will likely continue to re-erupt—on occasion) should not obscure the widespread recognition that some coordination was necessary. The PNA sought not to destroy NGOs but to bring them into line; the NGOs sought not total independence from the PNA but merely autonomy and a willingness to use state authority to support their work without dictating it.

The Historical Development of Palestinian NGOs

It is sometimes observed that Palestinian NGOs are so significant because they emerged in the absence of a state. Elsewhere in the Arab world, it is often held, strong states emerged first, greatly limiting their political and social space and autonomy for NGOs.

It is true that Palestinian NGOs display greater autonomy than their counterparts in the region largely because of the prevailing political situation, but it is not true that they have been organized in the absence of a state. A variety of states (Jordan, Egypt, and Israel) have governed them, each one imposing its legal framework and regulatory and policing powers in significant ways. And the PLO (as well as Palestinian political movements) acted for a long time as a state surrogate, providing a nationalist framework as well as material and organizational support.[28]

The earliest Palestinian NGOs were formed in the period of the mandate, generally focusing on nationalist work or support for those affected by the nationalist struggle. Most of these were local voluntary organizations, more akin to the grassroots organizations discussed in the following section. Some showed remarkable staying power, however.[29] After 1948, Palestinian organization proved stronger in the area outside mandatory Palestine, as bodies for women, students, teachers, and others were formed.[30] These organizations tended to have a symbiotic relationship with the PLO. Some antedated the formation of the PLO in 1964 and assisted in its founding; others were founded partly on PLO initiative. Most attempted to work closely with the PLO and focused their energies on the nationalist struggle. The result was that building civil society and building a state were not distinguished.[31]

In the late 1970s and early 1980s, a combination of international events turned the focus of efforts to the West Bank and Gaza. First, in 1978, Egypt and Israel signed the Camp David accords, which included a framework for Palestinian autonomy. The PLO and the broader Arab world rejected the framework as insufficient, leading to a struggle over influence in the West Bank and Gaza. Israel's Likud party, then in power, moved to create a "civil administration" attempting unilaterally to normalize the Israeli occupation while allowing some appearances of autonomy. Israel's Labor party, then in opposition, hinted at a "Jordanian option" for resolving the dispute over the West Bank. The PLO and the Arab League moved to counter these efforts. The Arab League agreed to contribute hundreds of millions of dollars to support Palestinian society in the West Bank and Gaza; these funds were given to a joint PLO-Jordanian committee to distribute on the ground. The inclusion of Jordan had the effect of rewarding the Jordanian rejection of participation in Camp David; it also made the funding more feasible because Israel generally allowed Jordanian institutions and official ties to the West Bank to continue. There was another effect as well: the funding supported a tense alliance between Jordan and Fatah (which dominated the PLO) and resulted in support going to conservative and centrist Palestinian organizations with a strictly nationalist agenda (and not to the more revolutionary leftist organizations). In 1982, the Israeli eviction of the PLO from Lebanon intensified the Palestinian determination to develop institutions in the West Bank and Gaza. All throughout this period, therefore, Palestinian social organizations were closely linked to the PLO and were deeply affected by the actions and policies of other states (Israel and Jordan).[32]

The first intifada was partly built on the organizational efforts that preceded it; it also provided an atmosphere in which further organizational efforts (by Fatah, the Islamist groups, and leftist parties) flourished. A series of new organizations arose, dedicated to providing a host of services (such as health and agricultural assistance) to a population suffering deprivation during the intifada. Some were able to attract funding from European sources and moved to professionalize their operations. NGOs showed growing autonomy during the period, but most proclaimed fealty to the PLO (or to a leftist or Islamic party). In this sense, the close association between NGOs and the state surrogate continued. And relations with the Israeli state worsened, with Israel shutting down or obstructing organizations deemed supportive of the intifada. New Palestinian human rights organizations arose (and older ones gained prominence), developing skills in documenting and publicizing abuses by state authorities.

Yet as the intifada wore on, the environment became less favorable for those NGOs reliant on external support. In 1988, Jordan announced its disengagement from the West Bank, ending the effectiveness of the joint committee distributing funds. A prolonged decline in oil prices undermined the ability of the wealthier Arab states to make contributions. And the Iraqi invasion of Kuwait in 1990 destroyed the willingness of the same states to assist: the states of the Arabian peninsula viewed the conduct of the PLO in the aftermath of the invasion as treacherous. Many Palestinians in the peninsula who had supported Palestinian institutions in the West Bank and Gaza themselves came to need assistance in the tremendous dislocation following the second Gulf War. This crisis affected the PLO and Palestinian NGOs equally: both lost important sources of funding.

In 1994, when the PNA began operation, its leaders had long experience working with some Palestinian NGOs. They had operated largely on what might be viewed as state corporatist lines, attempting to create or license organizations and having them hew to the nationalist line as sketched by the PLO. Palestinian NGOs had shown increasing vitality and autonomy in the 1980s, however. They had become vital providers of social services. Some had realized success in building professional staffs, external sources of funding independent of the PLO or existing parties. Others had weathered and even flourished under harsh political conditions, learning how to document government abuses. The PNA began operation expecting to continue arrangements built by the PLO, while NGO leaders felt that they had new opportunities to define their own agenda.

Negotiating a Relationship with the State

Relations between the PNA and leading NGOs began very inauspiciously. Soon after the PNA began operation, its officials moved to assert their control by claiming that public meetings needed prior permission; they even insisted that they must grant permission before political groups contracted for transportation.[33] NGOs were specifically targeted for monitoring the following year when Palestinian General Intelligence distributed two questionnaires that seemed excessively intrusive to activists. Selective audits followed.[34] The PNA produced a draft NGO Law that many NGO leaders found excessively restrictive. NGO leaders pressed their complaints not only domestically but also internationally among donor states, aggravating the PNA's already developing reputation for authoritarian tendencies. A network of leading NGOs admitted in 1998 that after the return of the "national leadership" from the outside, "an unhealthy environment between the NGO community and the PNA emerged. Without delving into the causes of this estrangement, the result was that each side felt an encroachment by the other on its domain of activities."[35] In essence, the PNA regarded NGOs as recalcitrant and unwilling to accept leadership; NGOs regarded the PNA as overly quick to impose state dominance in a manner all too familiar in neighboring Arab states.

Beyond the general struggle over the proper pattern of state-NGO relations, two specific irritants greatly heightened tensions. First, the PNA and NGO leadership each viewed the other as siphoning off control of international funds. Second, the PNA regarded NGOs as allowing its political opposition to don an altruistic disguise—and many NGO leaders made no secret of their displeasure with PNA policies and the Oslo Accords.

The first area of contention—funding—arose immediately after the Oslo Accords. The creation of the PNA came as the crisis of international funding for Palestinian NGOs had reached its peak, and the PNA threatened at first to aggravate matters. In 1994, when the PNA was created, Palestinian NGOs had weathered the practical disappearance of the joint Jordanian-PLO committee and the downturn and then collapse of Gulf funding. The most successful NGOs reacted swiftly by reorienting themselves toward Western donor states and international NGOs (generally headquartered in the West). The requirements of such Western funders differed from those in the Arab world. Aid was more likely to be tied to specific projects, accounting and reporting expectations were more stringent, application procedures were more complex, and political considerations shifted. Arab funds, often channeled through the PLO and Jordan, had been based on general nationalist loyalties; leftist agendas were often viewed with disfavor. Western funds often demanded by contrast that beneficiary NGOS be formally non-partisan, whatever the ideological inclinations of their leaders. Many leading Palestinian NGOs learned to present and organize themselves in new ways. Yet just as many had learned this new set of skills, the PNA emerged and attracted significant international pledges of aid. Many donor states reasoned that the Ministries of Health, Education, Social Affairs, and Agriculture would now assume the services provided by NGOs. International funds for Palestinian NGOs dropped precipitously.[36]

Yet while initial funding patters led some NGOs to feel that the PNA was edging them out, ongoing funding patterns fueled PNA suspicions of NGOs. Some international donors preferred to work directly with NGOs, marginalizing the role of the PNA. For instance, the World Bank, reacting to complaints that NGOs were passed over, agreed to strengthen the NGO sector with a three-year $15 million initiative labeled the NGO Project. While the PNA consented to the initiative, its design was necessarily based on an irksome fact: the World Bank was able to make grants directly to NGOs only because the PNA did not enjoy recognition as a state (normally the World Bank makes loans rather than grants, and it does so to—or through—member states).

The flow of aid funds going directly to Palestinian NGOs was not large, but it often fell outside PNA oversight. The precise amount is difficult to calculate because of the diversity of funding sources and NGOs. Funds came not only from donor states but also from international NGOs; even funds from donor states sometimes came not from funds pledged directly to the West Bank and Gaza but from regional or thematic initiatives. NGO advocates cited these facts to fend off PNA critics who claimed that NGOs were siphoning off funds designated for the PNA. Yet Palestinian NGOs were never able to mollify all PNA leaders. In 1999, several leading PNA figures launched a brief but bitter wave of public criticisms against Palestinian NGOs in the wake of a UN report on international legal and judicial assistance.[37] The minister of justice led the assault, claiming (inaccurately) that the report indicated that human rights and other NGOs had received $100 million of funds designated for the PNA while the ministry itself received a small fraction of that amount. When NGO leaders pointed out errors in official interpretations of the report, critics at first responded by leveling further charges of corruption and excessive salaries, painting NGOs as "fat cats" living off funds dedicated to helping the Palestinian people. And because some funding went to Israeli human rights NGOs, Palestinian NGOs were tainted by association on nationalist grounds.[38] In a sense, the amount of funding was not even the central issue for the PNA: instead, officials found noxious direct grants from donors to Palestinian NGOs that completely bypassed the PNA. Because the PNA was not a state, it lacked some of the legal tools and international standing to demand that all international assistance go through its agencies. Neither were PNA leaders willing to risk the domestic and international repercussions of pressing a demand that Palestinian NGOs follow an agenda laid out by the PNA. Accordingly, even as the crisis of June 1999 receded, the same issues periodically re-emerged in less virulent form. In June 2001, a Palestinian cabinet minister abruptly announced that USAID had failed to coordinate a new NGO program with the relevant PNA structures and distributed an open letter laying down a deadline of forty-eight hours for the problems to be corrected.[39]

Underlying the ongoing feud over funding was the second irritant in PNA-NGO relations: the perception that NGOs were closely tied to the opposition. Indeed, many of the most successful NGOs were founded by political parties, as discussed above. The Union of Medical Relief Committees was perhaps the most prominent Palestinian NGO internationally; its head, Dr. Mustafa al-Barghuti, often spoke out in opposition to PNA policies. The president of one of the largest Palestinian NGOs, In'ash al-usra (Reviving the Family), was Yasir 'Arafat's only opponent in the race for PNA president. NGO leaders would often pose as the only effective domestic monitor holding the PNA accountable. (It is worth noting that Palestinian intellectuals attracted to the concept of civil society often focused more on Gramsci—with his interest in civil society as a potential ground for opposition—than Tocqueville, with his less confrontational understanding.) The rapid rise of human rights groups fueled this association between NGO activity and political opposition. Human rights NGOs were hardly new, but they flourished in the aftermath of the Oslo Agreements. They quickly received great external attention and some external funding as well, leading many PNA leaders to view them as an unwelcome presence working for foreign powers. One of the leading and most thorough human rights organizations, the Palestinian Society for Protection of Human Rights and the Environment (LAW), was headquartered in Jerusalem, where it lay largely outside of PNA control. The PNA did attempt to charter its own human rights organization, headed at first by an internationally prominent Palestinian political leader, Hanan 'Ashrawi. When she accepted a ministerial position, however, the organization was taken over by Eyad Sarraj, whose activities were sufficiently annoying that the Palestinian attorney general announced the bizarre and shocking (though highly dubious) discovery that

Sarraj was dealing drugs. No charges ever stuck to Sarraj, and the affair only blackened the PNA's reputation internationally. Human rights NGOs competed against each other in pointing out human rights abuses in the PNA, and PNA officials responded very unfavorably to what they felt was a drumbeat of hostile criticism. When PNA leaders were at their most polite, they emphasized the importance of human rights work but complained that the NGOs were circumventing PNA structures.[40] But at their most ill-tempered, the same leaders would dismiss human rights organizations as corrupt fronts for political opposition; they would also call their nationalist credentials into question.[41]

In preparation for the ongoing conflict with the PNA, approximately seventy leading NGOs banded together to form the Palestinian NGO Network (PNGO). PNGO quickly emerged as an effective lobbying organization for NGOs, successfully blocking an early PNA draft of a new NGO law and pressuring the PLC for a friendlier version (the controversy is discussed more fully below). PNGO purposely restricted its membership from the beginning: it included larger, more internationally oriented, secular NGOs. It therefore took on a leftist and oppositional coloration. Smaller NGOs, grassroots organizations, Islamic NGOs, and those founded with the encouragement of the PNA were excluded, enhancing the organization's coherence and effectiveness but also giving it a somewhat elitist character. Charitable societies, older and more locally based, formed their own network, the General Union of Palestinian Charitable Societies.[42] PNGO and the union kept their distinct identities but cooperated (especially on lobbying over the NGO law). PNGO brought visibility and professionalism to the alliance, and the union brought broader nationalist credibility and respectability. The PNA reacted by attempting to set up its own networks of NGOs in the West Bank and Gaza. These networks were organized under the aegis of the Office of National Organizations in the PNA presidency; they attracted many (over one thousand) grassroots organizations, generally associated with Fatah or the PNA.[43]

Having girded themselves for battle, PNGO and the PNA clashed first on the legal framework to govern NGO activity. A protracted battle finally resulted in a compromise, after which the relationship between leading NGOs and the PNA became less consistently confrontational, though it remained guarded. Leading NGOs continued to reject a tutelary relationship that the PNA seemed to wish to impose, but over time the two sides realized that international and domestic circumstances forced them into a reluctant and uneasy partnership. NGOs required a supportive legal framework and realized that Palestinian statehood would leave them in an even more exposed position. Thus, NGOs never attempted to ignore or bypass the PNA; instead, they attempted to secure a set of legal and institutional arrangements that would support their work without encroaching too much on their autonomy. For its part, the PNA realized that NGOs were often well connected internationally; more important, they were critical in providing basic services that the fiscally strapped PNA could not. For example, the bulk of the health care system and almost all of the preschool day care services were provided by the not-for-profit sector.[44] Accordingly, the conflict between the PNA and NGOs concerned survival and separation far less than it involved the negotiation of the proper relationship and zones of autonomy and authority.

The protracted battle over the NGO law fully illustrates the evolution of this guarded and reluctant partnership.[45] Shortly after it began operation, the PNA demanded that all existing NGOs—many of which had registered with Israel, Egypt, and Jordan—renew their registration with the PNA. Failure to comply would result in cancellation of the registration. The legal framework for NGOs presumably remained a combination of Ottoman, mandatory, Jordanian, Gazan, and Israeli law. Some leading NGOs on the West Bank refused to register, regarding the PNA's demand as heavy-handed and a possible first step toward asserting more direct control over their operations. The PNA reacted by trying to develop a new legal framework for NGOs. The Ministry of Social Affairs took the lead, working with the Diwan al-fatwa wa-l-tashri' in the Ministry of Justice (see Chapter 2 on the legal drafting process). The draft NGO Law produced most closely resembled the Egyptian law, which NGO activists regarded as heavily authoritarian. NGOs would have to receive permission to operate rather than merely register, licensing was the authority of the Ministry of Interior (a bastion of authoritarianism and often even paramilitary in style in much of the Arab world), and NGOs would need to receive official permission before receiving foreign funds. The newly formed PNGO lobbied heavily against the law, not only domestically but also among donor states. The Palestinian Economic Council for Development and Reconstruction (PEC-DAR), the newly formed agency for coordinating development efforts, feared the law would alienate donors and inhibit badly needed NGOs. Under heavy domestic and international pressure, the PNA promised a new draft. PNGO decided to begin work on its own draft, which retained the basic outline of the PNA version but changed its most noxious provisions: NGOs would merely register rather than apply for a license; they would do so with the Ministry of Justice; they would merely be required to report their funding; and ministerial decisions could be appealed to a Palestinian court.

When the PLC was elected in 1996, it immediately asserted its central role in the legislative process (see Chapter 4). It had before it two draft NGO Laws—one a slightly revised draft from the PNA, the other a far more liberal version issued by PNGO. PNGO began to lobby deputies both heavily and successfully. When the matter was referred out of committee to the full PLC in 1998, the body adopted most of PNGO's recommended text. The law was referred to the PNA executive (the cabinet and the president), which returned it, asking for some changes to bring it closer to original PNA draft. The most contentious issue involved registration. The PNA executive insisted that the Ministry of Interior was the proper agency; PNGO greatly preferred the Ministry of Justice. The insistence seemed odd in light of the minister of justice's leading role in criticizing NGO practices, but PNGO continued to lobby PLC members on the issue. The PLC was sympathetic, perhaps partly because the minister of interior was Yasir 'Arafat himself and thus stood effectively outside any parliamentary oversight. In December 1998, the PLC passed the law on its third reading, rejecting most of the cabinet recommendations.

The PNA executive refused to drop the matter, however. Leading ministers explained that they were reviewing the draft to suggest amendments, an odd position because cabinet-suggested amendments had already been submitted and rejected on the bill's final reading.[46] It was presumably up to the president to accept or veto the law, not to change it. Yet by June 1999, in the midst of the flurry of charges and countercharges between the PNA and NGOs over foreign funding, a ministerial committee was appointed to review NGO activity and recommend changes in the law. The effect was to convey to both the PLC and PNGO that no law would be approved without some modifications. Mediating figures—including, most notably, Abu 'Ala', the Speaker of the PLC, worked to find a solution. In August 1999, a very dubious one was found. At the end of the last meeting in the PLC's summer session, the speaker read out a report from the legal committee explaining that the PLC's actions in December that rejected the cabinet changes had not passed by the necessary majority. Before deputies could query this curious ruling, the session was declared over. For PNGO and its allies—as well as more punctilious members of the PLC—the ruling made no sense. It reversed the relationship between the PLC and the executive on draft legislation, essentially allowing the executive to make changes at will in a text subject only to a veto by an absolute majority of PLC members. It required a remarkably creative reading of the council's Standing Orders to support such a procedure. Yet the advocates of the law had to consider their position carefully: fighting the issue might result in the president's refusing to sign the law, leaving NGOs only with the collection of preexisting laws that gave them fewer protections. PLC members worried about the precedent were reassured that the questionable ruling would not set a precedent. PNGO and its PLC allies decided to accept the maneuver, and in January 2000, President 'Arafat signed the oddly amended draft.

When NGO activists looked back on the outcome, they were convinced they had won a near-total victory. Their draft had essentially prevailed, with the significant but largely symbolic exception of the ministry where they would register. Shortly after the law was signed by the president, Mustafa al-Barghuti proudly endorsed it and proclaimed it as "the most progressive in comparison with the rest of the Arab world."[47] The PNA could also claim victory—not only over the designated ministry but also over the fact that the NGO activities were now to be governed wholly by PNA law.

Indeed, when the final law is examined in detail, it becomes apparent that the acrimony surrounding the adoption of the law obscures a fundamental acceptance on the part of the NGO community that the state has a significant role to play in monitoring NGO activity. It is true that NGOs need merely register (though even this achievement may be less than it seems—while the minister may refuse registration only for cause, no explanation of acceptable causes is given; the decision of the minister may be appealed to a court, but no grounds are given for reversal of a decision). While PNGO received most of what it wished, the tools it had invented still left the state some room for intervention. Indeed, in May 2001, the Ministry of Interior used the law to shut down two organizations for failing to comply with reporting requirements. Both had been involved in joint projects with Israeli organizations, leaving PNGO—which had disavowed such projects at the beginning of the second intifada—unwilling to take up their cause.[48]

More generally, the reporting requirements for NGOs are significant and the governance requirements fairly intrusive. NGOs are told the acceptable size of their boards of directors (between seven and thirteen), the quorum (two-thirds), and the frequency of meetings of the general assembly (once a year, with the meeting consisting of all members of the organization). Preexisting organizations were allowed to maintain their registration but had only nine months to bring their operations into compliance with the law. The specificity of these requirements and their possible unsuitability for certain kinds of organizations (for instance, those without a definable general membership or those with boards that are more supervisory and less managerial) drew little attention. The battle between PNA and NGO leaders was carried out in the field of law, and the PNA therefore successfully established the principle that it was to govern the operation of NGOs.

The nature and extent of that governing authority were debated, and NGOs were successful in obtaining a law that allowed them significant autonomy. NGOs neither sought nor obtained independence from the PNA; they only sought some freedom in setting their own agendas and some autonomy in daily practice.

The later stages of drafting the NGO law were accompanied by a shift in the tone of NGO-PNA relations. The confrontational views arising earlier were more rarely expressed (though the June 1999 controversy showed that vitriolic exchanges could recur). Several initiatives were launched to bring NGOs and the PNA together to coordinate development efforts, discuss the division of labor between them, and cooperate over a common set of goals. Sometimes these initiatives came from individuals or institutions within the PNA, but most came from leading NGOs or academia.[49] On one occasion, a minister successfully scheduled a conciliation meeting between intelligence officers and a leading human rights group.[50] Such efforts at coordination and dialogue varied in effectiveness by field: in health and agriculture, cooperation was sometimes high. In other areas, such as education and poverty relief, cooperation was less institutionalized, and meetings aimed at cooperation were rarely followed up effectively.

Despite the uneven success of such efforts, the PNA showed a gradually increased willingness to contract services out to NGOs in specific fields. When the PNA began operation, it absorbed a number of NGOs but to a lesser extent than either side had anticipated. Most PNA ministries spoke of desires to coordinate provision of services, but actual policy varied considerably by field. Health was probably the leading sector in this regard, with the Ministry of Health recognizing the leading role of NGOs in provision of health services.[51] But cooperation could occur even in unexpected places. The Ministry of Education's Curriculum Development Center turned to an educational NGO to review parts of its draft textbooks (otherwise kept tightly under wraps—see Chapter 6) and train teachers in civic education. Perhaps more remarkable, the Ministry of Justice's Diwan al-fatwa wa-l-tashri', responsible for legal drafting (see Chapter 2), sent its employees to an extended human rights training workshop run by the Palestinian Independent Commission for Citizens' Rights.[52]

A major step toward building an institutional framework for cooperation came in June 1999, when President 'Arafat created a new ministry for NGO affairs, headed by Hasan 'Asfur, a leading negotiator with Israel. The ministry was greeted reluctantly by NGO leaders, however, who regarded it as far less than it purported to be.

To begin with, there were some problems with the legal status of the ministry itself. The matter was not presented to the NGO-friendly PLC, meaning that 'Asfur could only serve as minister of state. (A minister of state has charge of no ministry but is often designated in Arab political practice to deal with a specific issue area. Actually, 'Asfur already served as minister of state, meaning that the legal effect of the appointment was only to give him a specific area to work on as well as a skeletal support staff.) 'Asfur nevertheless attempted to ignore the distinction, referring to his staff as a ministry.[53] Many NGO leaders viewed 'Asfur with suspicion, claiming that he had worked to show a friendly attitude toward NGOs in the past only to be able to report on their activities to the president.[54] 'Asfur reacted to the skepticism by working to soothe the crisis that had recently erupted over funding and to mediate the dispute over the NGO Law.[55] He also distanced himself from the office attached to the presidency for government-sponsored NGOs, signaling that he recognized the legitimacy of NGO desires for autonomy.[56] With no legal mandate, a small staff, an ambiguous status, and a sometimes distracted minister ('Asfur eventually returned to negotiations with Israel), the Ministry of NGO Affairs had little left to do but hold meetings among NGOs seeking to coordinate their work with the government.[57] NGOs had little to object to in this activity, but the new ministry hardly forged an effective partnership. After six years of operation, the PNA and leading NGOs still regarded each other with suspicion tempered by uneven efforts at coordination and cooperation. When 'Asfur lost his position as minister in the 2002 reshuffle (and had his office shifted outside the cabinet), few in the NGO community remarked on the change.

Three Models of Working with the State

NGOs could not ignore the PNA, but they devised different strategies on how to deal with it. The resulting variety can be seen in three different models developed by *zakat* (alms) committees, the Welfare Association, and In'ash al-usra. West Bank zakat committees formally affiliated themselves with the PNA, becoming quasi-governmental while retaining some autonomy. The Welfare Association worked to build a partnership with international funders and the PNA while maintaining its independence. And In'ash al-usra maintained its distance from the PNA and even dabbled in opposition politics.

Zakat committees exist in all Palestinian areas to distribute charitable funds and provide other services to the poor and needy.[58] Payment of the zakat is obligatory from a religious perspective but voluntary from the perspective of the state (in that the state has never enforced payment). Thus, funds come primarily from pious individuals, though businesses also make

contributions in cash or in kind. Zakat committees have also worked to collect funds from Israeli citizens (the "Palestinians of the inside") as well as
diaspora Palestinians and Muslims in other countries. Zakat committees
enjoy a tremendous amount of legitimacy. Even secular leftists admire their
authenticity and ability to operate without reliance on Western funding.[59]
They remain one of the most trusted institutions in Palestinian society.[60]

Zakat committees focus most of their energies on receiving funds, assessing the needs of the poor, and distributing funds directly to beneficiaries.[61]
Some committees undertake other activities (such as providing low-cost
medical services or engaging in other fund-raising activities), but these tend
to be fairly modest. For the most part, zakat committees operate as conduits
of funds between more fortunate patrons and needy beneficiaries. Their
staffs are small, as are their administrative expenses.[62] Despite their reputation as independent organizations, zakat committees in the West Bank are
very much creatures of the state. The Jordanian government worked to create zakat committees in the West Bank during the Israeli occupation on a
regional basis. The Ramallah Committee, for example, was formed by a decision by the Jordanian minister of awqaf in 1978; the Central Zakat Committee for Jerusalem was formed in 1990 (neighborhood committees in Jerusalem antedated the Central Committee by several years). West Bank zakat
committees were transferred to the PNA when it was formed. (The Jerusalem committee has a more ambiguous status. Some of the neighborhood
committees fall under PNA control, and the Ministry of Awqaf—which
oversees the committees—has its West Bank headquarters in 'Izariyya, as
close to Jerusalem as the PNA can openly operate. Yet other neighborhood
committees fall under Israeli control and maintain registration with both
Israel and Jordan.) Zakat committees remain under governmental oversight:
their directors are appointed by the minister of *awqaf;* they are chartered by
the ministry; and they operate under a distinct law (a Jordanian law promulgated in 1990) rather than the NGO Law. Yet in other ways they remain
independent: their employees are not regarded as governmental, and they
receive no regular financial assistance from the PNA. (Indeed, under
Jordanian administration, zakat committees were expected to turn over 10
percent of their collections to the Ministry of Awqaf; the PNA has not yet
adopted this practice). And the legal status of zakat committees remains
ambiguous: the 1990 law under which they operate has never been formally confirmed by the PNA, which generally recognizes only pre-1967
Jordanian legislation. In sum, West Bank zakat committees have conformed
to the PNA's preferred model of NGO activities: they accept PNA oversight
and leadership but expect no financial support. The PNA does provide a reg-

ulatory framework and an official charter that helps regularize and legitimate their work.

The Welfare Association, the largest Palestinian NGO by far (in terms of budget), has chosen a different strategy toward the PNA. It has maintained its independence and positioned itself as a critical link between international donors and Palestinian NGOs. On the other hand, it has worked to build a constructive relationship with the PNA and even sought to lead other NGOs in the same direction.

The Welfare Association was founded in Geneva in 1983 by a group of diaspora leaders and intellectuals (including Hisham Sharabi, Edward Said, and Ibrahim Abu Lughod).[63] They were joined by some leading Palestinian and Arab philanthropists in an effort to build a $100 million endowment to support Palestinian development in the West Bank and Gaza (and to give humanitarian assistance to Palestinians in those areas as well as in other Arab countries on an emergency basis). The endowment has grown more slowly than the founders had hoped; by 2000, it had only passed one-third of the way to the final goal. In the mean time, however, the Welfare Association engaged in direct fund-raising and emerged as one of the leading Palestinian development organizations (by 2000, it had disbursed approximately $100 million). The organization worked from the beginning to support smaller grassroots groups and NGOs working among Palestinians. While it concentrated its efforts on the West Bank and Gaza, it retained its headquarters in Geneva, maintaining its independence not only from Israel but also from the PLO and other Arab governments.

The founding of the PNA in 1994 led the Welfare Association to shift its efforts without redefining its central mission. It moved most of its operations to a location overlooking the northern entrance of Jerusalem.[64] In the mid-1990s, international donors came under criticism for abandoning Palestinian NGOs and redirecting funding toward the PNA; the World Bank reacted by establishing its own NGO Project. Despite PNA suspicions (and Israeli objections to the inclusion of Jerusalem NGOs in the mandate of the project), the World Bank pressed ahead and sought an organization to administer the project locally. Some internationally prominent NGOs entered the bidding, but the Welfare Association offered local experience as well as political independence. A British organization (the Charities Aid Foundation) was to assist the Welfare Association in forming a new consortium to manage the project. While funds came from the World Bank and other international donors (Italy and Saudi Arabia), the local administration has been dominated by the Welfare Association, whose director, Muhammad Shadid, doubles as the managing director of the NGO Project.

The decision to bid for management of the project might have been seen, not simply as a departure for the organization (founded by those who tilted toward the secular left and might have been suspicious of the World Bank), but even more as a challenge to the PNA. A leading observer of Palestinian NGOs wrote, "The control of the $15 million World Bank fund by a vocal and oppositional group of NGOs was clearly seen as an incipient threat to the PA's financial hegemony."[65] Yet the newly created Welfare Consortium worked hard both to maintain its political independence and to simultaneously foster good relations with the PNA. The director had solid nationalist credentials (he had helped found the political science department at al-Najah University and been dismissed after angering both the Israelis and Jordanians) but also a conciliatory approach (in contrast to the confrontational style favored by some leading NGO figures). The Welfare Consortium satisfied its World Bank patrons that its choices were made in a professional and apolitical manner, and PNA suspicions diminished. By February 2000, the Welfare Consortium was sufficiently well positioned as a mediator among the PNA, international donors, and the NGO community that it was able to host a major conference bringing leaders from the three fields together.[66] The World Bank agreed to renew funding in 2000, though the prospect of Palestinian statehood rendered the long-term viability of the NGO Project questionable: if Palestine were to be recognized as a state by the international community, World Bank funding would have to end or be radically reconfigured in accordance with patterns prevailing for other states.

In'ash al-usra is one of the most prominent wholly Palestinian NGOs; it has twice faced radical transformations in its political environment and has kept at best an arm's-length relationship with political authorities.[67] It was founded under Jordanian rule in 1966 as a philanthropic effort to promote training and self-sufficiency. Shortly after it began operation, the organization found itself under Israeli rule and gradually transformed itself into a participant in the Palestinian national movement. It founded a center for Palestinian folklore in an effort to support Palestinian culture alive under occupation; it also began to work to support the families of those killed or imprisoned in the nationalist cause. Its founder and president, Samiha Khalil, became a leading nationalist figure and was arrested six times by Israel. With an exclusively female membership, In'ash al-usra became a leading symbol of women's participation in the nationalist movement. Its nationalist reputation exposed it to risk (it was closed by Israel for two years during the first intifada) but also afforded opportunities—it was able to use its credentials to support its fund-raising activities externally. In'ash al-usra was more successful than many similar organizations in training women in traditional handicrafts and selling their products to Palestinians outside. The founding of the PNA radically changed the situation for the organization, however. No longer could it rely on nationalist sentiments to create a market for traditional embroidery; the major customers for such work (such as the PLO itself) were hardly able to sustain past demand. Other donors were facing financial hardship. The organization continued to guard its independence fiercely, however, and its leader decided to enter the 1996 Palestinian elections as Yasir 'Arafat's only opponent for the presidency. In'ash al-usra attempted to raise more funds through profitable projects; it turned its attention from traditional embroidery to meeting local demand for baked goods, food processing, and clothing. Unlike the zakat committees (which are quasi-governmental) and the Welfare Association (which has worked out a tenuous partnership with international donors and the PNA), In'ash al-usra maintains the same independence that it did during the Israeli occupation, insistent that NGOs must maintain their distance even when a nationalist state is being built.

GRASSROOTS ORGANIZATIONS: VOLUNTEERS STRUGGLING IN A PROFESSIONALIZING ENVIRONMENT

While larger NGOs spent much of the period after 1994 negotiating a suitable relationship with the PNA, smaller grassroots organizations have instead longed for any kind of assistance from the proto-state. For such organizations, the PNA has hardly been a source of unwanted attention; the problem is that the PNA has not paid them much attention at all. The resulting crisis has forced some into undesired retrenchment and financial crisis; others have weathered the transition far more successfully by professionalizing their operations to a degree unnecessary in earlier years.

Grassroots organizations developed in a pattern similar to their larger counterparts, the NGOs. Indeed, many leading NGOs, such as the Union of Medical Relief Committees and In'ash al-usra, began as local, largely volunteer grassroots organizations. Most grassroots organizations have chosen a few local activities, such as a school, day care center, or vocational training center, to administer. Until the 1970s, most were founded and administered by socially prominent and prosperous individuals. They operated on a largely volunteer basis; they received their funds from their own activities, modest local donations, and small-scale fund-raising activities. Some were able to solicit contributions internationally on an episodic basis (such as through a fund-raising appeal to Palestinians overseas), but few had administrative support and necessary funds to be able to turn such donations into a regular source of income (and those that did manage some success often transformed themselves into broader and more professionalized NGOs).

In the 1970s and especially the 1980s, grassroots organizations expanded because of several broader political changes. First, the Israeli occupation led (indeed, forced) Palestinians to rely less on the state for the provision of social services and thus created a far greater demand. Second, the rise of nationalist sentiments helped create the atmosphere in which charitable and voluntary work was more highly valued. Indeed, the 1970s and 1980s saw the emergence of a new form of grassroots organization: local work committees of students or professionals sometimes formed to support agriculture or provide basic health care.[68] Sustained by youthful or nationalist enthusiasm, and sometimes backed by political parties, the new organizations marked a sharp contrast to the patrician and philanthropic charitable societies. Third, fund-raising actually became easier during the period. The PLO and Jordan both sought to support organizations in the West Bank, and the joint Jordanian-PLO committee channeled much of its funding to grassroots organizations. Some of these funds went to grassroots organizations through the General Union of Charitable Associations, a Jordanian-based organization that enrolled many Palestinian organizations.[69]

The same period saw the emergence of a new kind of grassroots organization, the cooperative. Some cooperatives had been formed during the mandate and under Jordanian rule, but not until the 1970s and 1980s was there a sustained effort to expand them.[70] Palestinian cooperatives were remarkably diverse: some centered on marketing, others on olive oil production; and still others operated in poorer areas and refugee camps. Cooperatives emerged among farmers and handicraft manufacturers. Gaza saw fewer cooperatives emerge, partly because the Jordanian government restricted its work encouraging their formation to the West Bank.

The resurgence of these organizations became especially marked during the intifada. With an increased nationalist ethos of self-reliance, cooperatives and neighborhood associations sprang up in all Palestinian areas. The desire to build alternatives to the Israeli occupation led grassroots organizations to widen their focus, often attempting to provide a far wider range of services to residents of an area than the formerly restricted charitable societies and work committees.

When the PNA was founded, there were close to four hundred registered charitable societies and seven hundred cooperatives.[71] They immediately found themselves confronted with a radically changed political environment that endangered many of them even as it offered a few enormous new opportunities. First, the sources of funding that had been so helpful in the 1980s dried up. The demise of the joint Jordanian-PLO committee and the decimation of the comparatively wealthy Palestinian community in Kuwait hit the charitable societies very hard. Cooperatives faced a slightly different set of challenges: less dependent on donations, they still relied on access to external markets for inputs and marketing. Those that relied on traditional handicrafts found diminished international demand; tourism proved itself an unreliable alternative. Those seeking to shift to newer products (in areas such as clothing) found stiff international competition. And the changed political situation made access to international markets difficult: Jordan was no longer willing to treat Palestinian producers as its own, and physical access to external markets was often hostage to broader political relations with Israel.[72]

More subtly, the changed political situation created an entire new set of rewards and incentives for grassroots organizations. The intifada's nationalist enthusiasm and emphasis on self-reliance waned, and vaguely focused community organizations found themselves stretched too thin, drawing far fewer volunteers and wealthy admirers. At the same time, grassroots organizations faced an entirely new set of opportunities: international donors, flush with enthusiasm for all sorts of NGOs, suddenly discovered that Palestinian society was rich with organizations speaking in the prose of civil society. A few international NGOs (such as American Near East Refugee Aid [ANERA] and several religious organizations) had worked supporting Palestinian grassroots organizations for some time; major international funders, such as USAID and the World Bank now joined them. Such donors often preferred not to work directly with grassroots organizations, instead channeling their funds through umbrella groups, consortia, or larger NGOs (such as the Welfare Association, as discussed above, or international NGOs, such as ANERA). Yet to take advantage of the new opportunities, many grassroots organizations had to learn to present themselves in new ways. Donors were not interested in providing general ongoing support for such organizations; they generally concentrated on funding specific projects or building institutional capacity. An organization wishing support for its vocational training might be asked to demonstrate that there were adequate opportunities for those completing the training; a cooperative wishing to buy a piece of equipment might be asked to demonstrate that it would bring the benefits promised. Applicants for World Bank NGO Project funds had to fill out an application that many found daunting. Nationalist enthusiasm and social consciousness mattered far less in this newer world than administrative capacity and professionalism. Yet grassroots organizations, by their very nature, were often sorely lacking in precisely these features. Some organizations did make the transition, a few so successfully that they built up professional staffs and often took on a national rather than local focus; in a sense, they became NGOs rather than grassroots organizations (In'ash al-usra underwent this kind of transition, beginning even before the establishment of the PNA).

Grassroots organizations adopted some of the same strategies followed by their larger NGO brethren to confront this new situation. They banded together (the General Union of Palestinian Charitable Societies, for instance, broke off from the Jordanian organization in order to focus exclusively on the Palestinian environment). And they worked as well on creating a supportive legal environment. The General Union of Palestinian Charitable Societies joined PNGO to lobby on the NGO Law. Cooperatives joined in working on a draft law; they finished their work in 1998 and forwarded it to the Palestinian Ministry of Labor.[73] Yet they lacked the political muscle and sophistication of PNGO, and the law languished in the relevant ministries.[74] In making such efforts, grassroots organizations discovered collectively that the PNA had little to offer beyond general encouragement. Most individual organizations that turned to the PNA for assistance made the same discovery: the relevant ministries had no funds to offer and precious little expertise. (In a series of visits I made to grassroots organizations in 1999 and 2000, I heard the same joke every time I asked whether the PNA had provided assistance: I was told, "They do not help us; they need our help.") Palestinian grassroots organizations were left to their own devices to decay, survive, or flourish under the new circumstances.[75] PNA ministries offered sympathy but felt powerless to lend support. The following cases illustrate the nature of the new environment.

Charitable Societies

The Women and Childcare Society in Bayt Jalla (adjacent to Bethlehem) was founded by a group of leading local women in 1944.[76] The society worked first to establish a clinic; it later expanded to include child care and vocational training. The 1948 war greatly changed the nature of the area: while the population in the center of Bayt Jalla itself remained largely Christian and fairly prosperous, large refugee populations moved nearby, and the society felt an increased demand for its services. The clinic became too expensive to operate, and in 1958 a local member of the Jordanian Senate (the father of an activist in the society) arranged to have it transferred to the Ministry of Health (though the clinic continued to operate on the society's premises). The society began training programs in local refugee camps, concentrating on handicrafts (such as appliqué work) that could be carried out in the home. The large number of Bayt Jallans overseas helped the society's fund-raising: in 1964 a delegation traveled to South America to raise funds among Bayt Jallan diaspora communities for a building; funds from diaspora communities in South America and the Gulf also helped fund a housing project and a loan project. These projects were designed to be self-sustaining, but the loan fund was depleted by defaults, and the housing project (designed for new couples of modest means) was undermined by the housing law, which fixed rents and made it nearly impossible to terminate the leases of those no longer needing assistance. The 1970s and 1980s improved the fund-raising position of the society, with assistance coming from the General Union of Palestinian Charitable Societies; USAID gave some modest funds for vocational training; and ARAMCO (the Saudi oil company) donated funds as well. The society was less well connected with the PLO, however, which made it more difficult to find an external market for its handicrafts (the PLO was a major customer for other similar organizations). The dislocation following the Iraqi invasion of Kuwait motivated diaspora Bayt Jallans to contribute $60,000 but only for distribution to local families. The 1990s brought harder times for the society, which was unable to maintain its building and finally had to close its school in 1999. Yet the society also attempted to take advantage of new opportunities. It shifted its emphasis on vocational training from traditional handicrafts to production of underwear; when this proved difficult to market, the society turned toward stitching together garments (with the pieces cut elsewhere). The society attempted to interest international donors but could not convince them that proposed projects would be self-sustaining (marketing of products was the primary concern). Located on a scenic hill near the main road to Bethlehem, the society worked to contract with local tour operators to bring tourists to visit its handicraft shop but realized no success even before the second intifada eliminated tourism. In all these efforts, the society hoped for some help from the relevant PNA ministries (such as Social Affairs and Tourism), but its leaders complained that no PNA official had exhibited any interest in the society's work.

Cooperatives

Cooperatives have faced a similar set of constraints and opportunities since the founding of the PNA. Perhaps because they are motivated by the self-interest as well as the altruism of their members, some have been more successful in professionalizing their operations sufficiently to take advantage of the new opportunities. In the process, they have exposed themselves to greater risk. While they have sometimes hoped for help from PNA officials, they have received no more than the charitable societies.

The Qalandiya Camp Handicraft Cooperative Society was formed in a refugee camp midway between Jerusalem and Ramallah in 1958.[77] The society has always straddled the distinction between charitable organization and cooperative: it exists for the benefits of its 185 members but also works to benefit the broader population (Qalandiya camp has close to eight thousand residents; women in surrounding neighborhoods and villages also participate in programs). The Qalandiya Cooperative pursues three major activities: vocational training, services (concentrating on a kindergarten and nursery), and production (food processing, traditional embroidery, and modern quilting). Before the establishment of the PNA, the society was able to support its activities by selling its products (chiefly traditional embroidery) directly to the PLO; it had a close personal connection with Abu Jihad. When Abu Jihad was assassinated, the society lost its major patron (and even had trouble collecting for some products the PLO had ordered). The society did receive some support from the joint Jordanian-PLO committee in the form of a loan to add to their building; because of the demise of the joint committee, the Qalandiya Cooperative has yet to repay the loan (in this and other cases, the PNA has unsuccessfully asserted that it succeeded the joint committee as the creditor).

Unlike many other grassroots organizations, Qalandiya was well positioned to take advantage of the new opportunities opening up in the 1990s: with a professional general manager and a paid staff of twenty-five (mostly teachers), the society could cooperate with international donors and develop attractive proposals. Beginning as early as 1989, society leaders developed a proposal for the European Union to buy a quilting machine; the proposal was accepted in 1992 and the machine purchased in 1996. The machine makes it possible for the society to produce quilts and pillows at competitive prices (mainly for the local market). The cooperative expanded its grantsmanship with a successful $50,000 application to the World Bank NGO project. Continued interest of international donors led the society to take some bolder steps. A Swedish organization of cooperatives sought promising Palestinian cooperatives to work with; Qalandiya appeared a likely candidate. The donors insisted that a marketing study be carried out, which the society agreed to; this deepened the organization's professionalizing turn. In 1998, the society submitted three grant proposals to support the opening of a nursery; all three proposals were successful, allowing the society to cover $31,000 of its start-up costs. Society leaders remained ambivalent about the move because they were not certain they could cover the operating costs of the nursery. Despite taking greater risks, the Qalandiya Cooperative was on a fairly sound footing. Most of its operations were self-supporting, and a steady stream of donors offered to fund new initiatives.

In all this ambitious expansion, the PNA played very little role. The international donors largely bypassed the PNA, and some of the key contacts were even forged before the PNA was created. The society did approach the PNA to ask it to pay the PLO's debt and to supply a separate amount to support a trip to Dubai to explore marketing possibilities. On both occasions, the society was successful, but both times because of political connections. Society leaders wish for more help soliciting international donors (especially in the proposal-writing phase), but they have discovered that they possess greater sophistication and experience in this regard than PNA officials in the Ministry of Labor (which oversees cooperatives). The Qalandiya Cooperative appears a success story, but the PNA can claim little of the credit.

PROFESSIONAL ASSOCIATIONS AND SYNDICATES: SEEKING A STATE CHARTER AND A PROFESSIONAL MISSION

Professional associations and syndicates have begun to undergo a fundamental change since the formation of the Palestinian Authority. Most were founded (or operated since 1967) to meet nationalist rather than professional goals. Between 1994 and 2000, most professional associations were divided by struggles to free the organization from domination by the nationalist agenda and leadership and to reorient it toward meeting the professional needs of the membership. No organization completed this transition, and a few came close to collapsing in the attempt. The older generation of leaders of these organizations, sometimes ensconced in new positions in the PNA, yielded reluctantly to the changes if at all. In essence, they opted for state corporatist arrangements in which the PNA dominated and shaped the agenda of professional associations and syndicates. But reformers sought not to disengage their associations from the state but only to negotiate more autonomous arrangements (that still gave them legal protection and often exclusive rights to represent their sector of society). In short, the newer generation often strove to create societal corporatist arrangements. The second intifada froze most of these efforts but reversed very few of them: most professional associations had not yet resolved the generational struggle, but with nationalist issues reasserting themselves so forcefully, efforts to reform the bodies were generally suspended but not forgotten.

Palestinian professional associations and unions occasionally date back to the mandate period but more frequently began effective operation after 1948. Those that began on the West Bank between 1948 and 1967 were formed not as Palestinian organizations but as Jordanian ones. Gaza saw more limited development of professional organizations under Egyptian rule. Some associations began after 1967, and in the 1980s the PLO began to encourage new organizations and strengthen existing ones. It did so as part of a larger effort to mobilize the population of the West Bank and Gaza; the organizations were thus to serve nationalist goals and accept general PLO guidance (and sometimes specific directives). In an era in which PLO leadership was hardly contested and in which nationalist issues predominated, most professional groups loyally accepted PLO leadership and specific directives.

Alongside the unions and professional associations operating in the West Bank and Gaza, numerous organizations sought to represent Palestinians in the diaspora. Some of these organizations were established by the PLO, others actually predated the PLO and assisted in its founding.[78] Writers, teachers, students, and women, for instance, all had unions or associations that were closely affiliated with the PLO; even when they retained limited autonomy, they operated under PLO leadership.

In 1994, the relationships among these various structures were thrown into confusion with the creation of the PNA. Often three different associations existed in the same field: one based in Gaza, one based in the West Bank (often still formally linked to Jordan), and one associated with the external leadership of the PLO. The idea that such diversity and overlap might be healthy—based perhaps on a pluralist vision of society and politics—was rejected by all involved. This was particularly the case for leaders of professional associations, who saw their potential membership disorganized and divided among many organizations. Accordingly, efforts toward unifying the various associations and unions began. Yet in almost all fields, such efforts immediately set off deep conflicts over the leadership and very purpose of the organizations.

In essence, these divisions all related to the degree to which professional concerns could rise to dominate the agenda of professional associations. First, some of the leadership of these organizations regarded their nationalist mission as unfulfilled—and that meant that it was still appropriate to view themselves as part of the national leadership. For others, the creation of the PNA and the opportunity to create unified organizations finally freed up professional associations to pursue their natural mission—meeting the professional needs of members. Those who advocated such a path did not dismiss nationalist politics (in many cases, they were less inclined to support compromises with Israel than their counterparts), but they favored other themes, such as health benefits, continuing education, pay, and working conditions. Second, a generational struggle often accentuated this first split: older activists who rose to prominence under PLO leadership saw younger colleagues as pursuing a self-interested and short-sighted agenda; younger, more professionally oriented leaders saw the older generation as dated PLO apparatchiks. A third set of divisions related to the origin of the activists. The oft-cited split between "insiders" from the West Bank and Gaza and "outsiders," often from PLO headquarters in Tunis, certainly operated. Yet the divisions were often more complex than this implied. Some of the older inside leaders were as closely tied to the PLO leadership as the outsiders. Often West Bank associations—which had operated under more liberal Jordanian law and with assistance from their Jordanian parent organization—regarded their Gazan counterparts as less developed and independent. (Indeed, Gazan organizations were more likely to be called "associations" [jama'iyyat], whereas West Bank organizations were usually "syndicates" [niqabat], implying a greater level of official recognition and formalization, even including exclusive right to represent the sector.) A strong ethos of national unity prevented such divisions over origins from being publicly articulated on most occasions, but younger, West Bank, professionally oriented activists were often barely able to conceal their frustration with older, "outsider" or Gazan, PLO-affiliated leaders.

The struggle over unification and professionalization of these organizations generally focused on three sets of issues. First, many leaders held dual positions as members of their professional associations and as PNA or PLO officials. This was especially the case with the heads of organizations that had been founded in exile, as their leaders were rewarded for their work with PNA positions upon their return. Others who had served long and loyally in West Bank (and especially Gazan) organizations were rewarded with official posts as well. For the professionally oriented, this left professional associations in the hands of government employees, a condition guaranteed to maintain their subordination and dependence. In 2000, an opposition periodical noted that the head of the Engineers Association in Gaza, the president of the Accountants Society in Gaza, the president of the Auditors Society in Gaza, and the secretary-general of the Teachers Union in the West Bank and Gaza were all officials of various PNA ministries; this list was hardly exhaustive.[79]

A second area of contention focused on the law governing associations. Virtually all existing associations and syndicates, as well as those seeking to unify, sought to have a special law written to govern the affairs of their sector. Especially for those wishing to professionalize their organizations, such a law would offer several benefits. First, it would confer official recognition on their organization; indeed, the law would constitute a virtual charter. Second, questions of governance would be resolved in the text of the law (including, for instance, the requirement that officers not be employed by the government). Third, the law would give the syndicate a monopoly over representation of that sector. Finally, questions of how to unify disparate organizations into a single Palestinian syndicate could best be resolved in the text of the law. Association leaders, whatever their orientation, guarded the drafting process quite jealously. Most associations insisted that they should draft the initial law themselves and then work with the relevant legislative organs of the PNA (such as the Diwan al-fatwa wa-l-tashri‘ and the PLC) to ensure that any changes would be approved by the association's leaders. The process of drafting the law sometimes proved quite difficult. The desire to maintain close control over the legislative process combined with the slow pace of Palestinian legislation more generally to delay the process for most associations; the PNA closed its eighth year of operation with virtually all professional associations still working on securing desired legislation.

A final area of contention has concerned elections for the leadership. Most organizations attempting to unify have been held up by the perceived need for a law; in the meantime, existing leaders have served extended terms. In at least two cases (the teachers and the journalists), this has frustrated some activists so deeply that they have moved to form their own separate organizations. The three lawyers' associations were so badly divided about the proper way to hold elections that they needed a series of presidential decrees as well as a law organizing their profession before they could begin the process of scheduling elections; even then the disputes were sufficiently disruptive to postpone the elections indefinitely and lead to a series of lawsuits, as will be seen below.

Journalists

The struggle occasioned by the attempts of younger activists to form more professionally oriented and autonomous syndicates is probably best illustrated in the field of journalism. No formal organization existed for Palestinian journalists prior to the 1990s, though there was a broader Palestinian Writers Union affiliated with the PLO. A more specialized association for journalists, the Journalists' League (rabitat al-sahafiyin), formed toward the end of the Israeli occupation. When the PNA was established, the league began at times to call itself a syndicate *(niqaba)*, though little changed in its structure or legal status.

The profession of journalism was shifting in this period, however. Under the Israeli occupation, Palestinian newspapers operated under heavy censorship and in precarious financial positions (generally propped up by subsidies, the source of which varied according to the political stance of the newspaper). Most newspapers relied heavily on wire services for content; journalists on staff were few in number and poorly paid. In the West Bank and Gaza, broadcast journalism—like broadcasting more broadly—did not exist. The first intifada began to change the face of Palestinian journalism because of the sustained international interest in news from the West Bank and Gaza. Many external news organizations hired some local Palestinian staff, effectively giving a new generation of Palestinian journalists the opportunity to serve apprentice roles. The establishment of the PNA brought further changes in the structure of journalism. Israeli censorship came to an end.[80] Some external subsidies were removed, and one established newspaper, *Al-fajr*, closed, but the PNA began direct subsidies to a new daily, *Al-hayah al-jadida*. A second new daily was founded, *Al-ayyam*, by a senior PLO negotiator whom the Israelis had once deported from the West Bank. The two new dailies hired larger staffs and prided themselves on offering a higher and more professional level of journalism.[81] New broadcast outlets emerged, some operated by the PNA and others privately owned.

The effect of these changes for the journalism profession was to offer many more opportunities and virtually guarantee a generational battle: older journalists had seen their role as supporting the Palestinian national movement and the PLO; younger journalists saw themselves as practicing a profession more than engaging in a national struggle. One of the leading figures of the newer generation explained: "The old syndicate is concerned only with the occupation and the battle of liberation. [Its leaders] are not concerned with training for journalists or for their families"—that is, working conditions and benefits.[82] The task of NGOs and professional associations before the PNA, in the eyes of the dissidents, was to lead nationalist action and channel PLO funds to the West Bank and Gaza. Now a more independent body was needed. In 1999, the dispute finally broke into the open over elections for the existing syndicate. Na'im al-Tubasi, the head of the syndicate and a Fatah loyalist, came under fire for postponing elections for the leadership.[83] Finally agreeing to hold elections in December 1999, al-Tubasi hardly satisfied his critics: according to dissidents in the organization, the elections were riddled with irregularities.[84] Foremost among the complaints were the membership rolls themselves: dissidents claimed that they were dated, including many non- or former journalists who currently worked in PNA positions and loyally supported the leadership. The dissidents formed a "preparatory committee" to explore a new union. Given their strategic location in leading newspapers (especially *Al-ayyam* but also *Al-hayah al-jadida*, where they enjoyed the protection and tacit support of powerful editors), the dissidents were able to have their activities covered regularly in the press and even have their announcements printed without charge. Preparations for a general assembly to create the new union continued throughout 2000.[85] The meeting was finally scheduled for the end of September, only to be disrupted (quite ironically, given its proclaimed interest in avoiding domination of nationalist issues) by the outbreak of the second intifada.[86]

For the dissidents, the issues motivating their attempt to form a new syndicate were fairly clear: the older body was politically dependent on the PNA; lacking any independence, it could hardly advocate on behalf of journalists. When journalists were arrested, Na'im al-Tubasi often attempted to arrange for the release quietly, but he was not an independent figure willing to confront the PNA on general treatment of journalists.[87] Working conditions for journalists (pay, benefits, and often the lack of any written contracts) were a major concern as well; the dissidents did not view the older syndicate as sensitive to such concerns. One leader of the new group described its aims:

> After we arrived at the conclusion that our attempt to change from within was useless, we decided that the situation required work on forming a new syndicate, built on a professional basis, focusing on promoting journalist work and defending the rights of journalists.
>
> And it is clear that the current body—known as the Journalists League, though it sometimes calls itself the Journalists Syndicate— is an ineffective body disconnected from the journalists, distancing itself from their professional problems, and concerned only with working for personal interests.[88]

Yet for the older syndicate the nature of the dispute was different: the dissidents were guilty of high treason.[89] Al-Tubasi blasted the attempt to start a new syndicate as the work of upstarts with no history of contributing to the nationalist cause or standing up to the Israeli occupation: "Where were these people ten years ago, or even two years ago? . . . Where were they when we demanded our rights and were punished?"[90] He accused the dissidents not only of refusing to accept a democratic election but also of working to normalize relations with Israel. The dissidents—some of whom had been imprisoned by Israel during the intifada—scoffed at these charges, which they regarded as a diversionary tactic. They also pursued their own complaints against Israel, focusing on its refusal to allow many Palestinian journalists to work in Israel on security grounds. Thus, the gap between al-Tubasi's syndicate and the new organization was less severe than the older body claimed. Yet beyond his inflammatory rhetoric, al-Tubasi was expressing an authentic difference between his position and that of the dissident organization: for al-Tubasi (and many of his generation) the task of the syndicate was to defend Palestinian national rights. Journalists were very much part of the national struggle, so there was no tension between working on behalf of Palestine and representing its journalists. Opting out of this structure therefore needlessly split the Palestinian nation and pretended that the central conflict, over establishing the state, was over. Al-Tubasi and the rebels agreed on one point: the battle among the journalists was similar to that taking place in other professions.

The Bar Association

Bar associations in the Arab world, like their counterparts elsewhere, generally are accorded a central role in actively governing the legal profession. The law generally grants the bar association such a status, allowing it oversight of licensing, training, and discipline of lawyers. By granting the bar association exclusive right to represent and govern the legal association, Arab governments turn it into a semiofficial organization. Palestinian lawyers have sought such an arrangement since the days of the British mandate, but even the creation of the PNA in 1994 did not allow such a body to emerge immediately. As with other professions, the problem was not too little organization but too much: Palestinian lawyers were divided among several different bodies that accepted the idea of unification but could not agree on how to implement it.

Under the British mandate, the legal profession was governed by the Law Council, a wholly governmental body.[91] There were efforts to construct a full Palestinian bar association (or *niqaba*), but they foundered on broader political considerations. Jewish lawyers organized their own association, and the Palestinian lawyers followed. Both pressed for official recognition, but the mandatory government wished to have a single, unified body. After the 1948 war, Palestinian lawyers in the West Bank finally were able to form a bar association, but they did so as Jordanians. The Jordanian Bar Association was generally dominated by West Bank lawyers and took on an Arab nationalist, often oppositional character. Gaza lawyers saw no change, however, except that oversight of the Law Council was transferred from the British high commissioner to the Egyptian military governor.[92]

When Israel occupied the West Bank in 1967, the Palestinian members of the Jordanian Bar Association announced a strike in protest over Israeli annexation of Jerusalem and control over Palestinian courts. It took nearly three decades for the strike to end. Israel reacted by allowing its lawyers to practice in Palestinian courts and assigning oversight of the legal profession to an Israeli official. In the 1970s, a few Palestinian lawyers broke the strike, and by 1980 there were sufficient practicing attorneys to form an alternative to the Jordanian Bar Association, the Arab Lawyers Committee. The Jordanian Bar Association expelled the members who practiced, and the dispute between the striking and working lawyers turned bitter.[93] Meanwhile, in Gaza, practicing attorneys formed an association in 1977 without offending nationalist sensibilities but lacking the full status of a bar association or syndicate.[94]

The PNA therefore inherited a legal profession divided along geographical and political lines.[95] It took three years for the three bodies to agree on some principles of unification, following which President Yasir 'Arafat issued a decree appointing three members from each body (the Jordanian Bar Association, the Arab Lawyers Committee, and the Gaza Lawyers Association) to an interim board. Yet the step toward unity provoked as much controversy as it settled: the decree had at best an ambiguous legal basis, and no lawyers associated with any opposition party gained appointment. The newly unified bar leadership was authorized for one year to assume all the authority of the previous bodies for lawyers and to draft a law organizing the legal profession.[96] After one and a half years, however, the interim board had not completed its task, leading 'Arafat to issue a second decree extending the board's life until a law was passed and elections for the bar association were completed.[97]

In June 1999, President 'Arafat signed the law organizing the legal profession; the law went into effect in November.[98] The legislation established a framework for an autonomous body, granted exclusive right by the government to represent and govern the legal profession. Mindful of the experience of other Arab countries, where bar associations have been subjugated by admitting government employees with law degrees, the drafters stipulated that membership in the Palestinian Bar Association exclude those employed by the government or the private sector. Elections for a new board were to be held within six months. And the existing bar association began to work to show itself to be a voice for the rule of law, demanding an end to security courts, promulgation of the Law on the Independence of the Judiciary, and proper administrative and budgetary supports for the courts.

Thus, the law represented a tremendous step forward for the formation of a unified and independent Palestinian Bar Association, which seemed poised to become the first professional association to reorganize successfully. Instead, the law raised new problems. Some of these resulted from sloppiness in the drafting process—the version that was finally passed neglected to allow clients to assign their lawyers power of attorney in their offices, resulting in long lines at courts for anyone wishing to deputize an attorney in any kind of legal matter. The bar association sprang into motion, calling for a strike protesting the provision they themselves had drafted. The lawyers demonstrated at the PLC, which dutifully amended the law.[99] But then a second, less tractable problem developed. The law required that elections be completed during or before May 2000 but left it to the bar association to develop detailed procedures. Those proved slow in coming. Meanwhile, slates formed for the anticipated elections. A group of lawyers styling themselves "Lawyers for Change," many active in human rights organizations, began to assemble a slate to run against the existing leadership (whom some regarded as inefficient and too close to the Palestinian leadership). On 6 May 2000, the general assembly of the bar association (which all registered members were eligible to attend) broke up in a noisy dispute when members of Lawyers for Change charged the interim bar president with forcing an electoral procedure against the wishes of the membership. In apparent retaliation for such troublesome charges, the interim board decided that employment by an NGO was incompatible with full bar association membership. Unsurprisingly for professional litigators, the squabbling attorneys took the issues to court.

By May 2000, therefore, instead of holding new elections, the bar association found itself embroiled in a series of lawsuits. Those dropped from full bar association membership resorted to the High Court, which ordered their reinstatement. Some dissident lawyers claimed that the interim board's term had expired and therefore was no longer a legally valid body; that issue also went to the High Court, which this time supported the interim board. In September 2000, the bar association was finally able to issue the rules that would govern its elections. As befitting the bar's status as a semi-official body, its bylaws were published in the *Official Gazette*.[100] Elections were scheduled for March 2001. Yet the bar still was unable to escape litigation. The new elections were scheduled after the outbreak of the second intifada, and some lawyers who would have been unable to get to polling stations because of the Israeli closure successfully convinced the High Court to delay the elections once again until more inclusive procedures could be designed. Nine years after the creation of the PNA, the bar was a success story compared to its counterpart professional associations: it had obtained legal recognition, moved toward unification, demonstrated some independence, written bylaws, and succeeded in having a law organizing its affairs promulgated. Yet despite all these successes, Palestinian lawyers had not yet succeeded in electing their leadership and moving their affairs out of the courts.

The Medical Syndicates

For the medical professions, the problems of unification were less contentious but in many ways just as complicated.[101] In all three professions—doctors, dentists, and pharmacists—branches of Jordanian syndicates operated in the West Bank and Jerusalem dating back to the period of Jordanian administration. That gave these associations a firm basis: they generally had legal recognition (by virtue of Jordanian law), official standing (even an official charter, in the sense that all who practiced the profession had to be syndicate members and that the syndicate was allowed to play some role in determining entry into the professions), and sounder financial status (with established dues and pension funds).

Yet the medical syndicates faced a series of complicated problems in the transition to Palestinian professional associations. First, the unification of the profession into a single syndicate faced hurdles both in the West Bank and Gaza. In the West Bank, the syndicates had to disengage from the Jordanian parent organizations, a complex task because their stronger legal status was based on Jordanian law and their pension funds continued to be held by the Jordanian syndicate. The Palestinian branches worked to resolve this separation by allowing their members to continue affiliation with both the Jordanian syndicate and the soon-to-be independent Palestinian syndicate (rather than attempting to disentangle the organizations and pension funds). In Gaza, on the other hand, a very different problem existed: the Gazan organizations were far weaker (generally "associations" rather than "syndicates") and were often dominated by government employees. West Bank syndicate leaders insisted that their new, unified body be autonomous and thus opposed allowing government employees to serve as leaders—effectively forcing Gazan leaders to find new employment or leave syndicate work. Unifying a syndicate thus involved not only a complex divorce from Jordan for the West Bank but also a politically sensitive divorce from the PNA for Gaza.

A second problem—connected with unification—was the need for a Palestinian law to establish the syndicate more firmly and give it control over its members. The existing Jordanian laws were fairly favorable to association autonomy, but they had no authority in Gaza and provided no basis for a unified syndicate. In drafting legislation, the syndicates generally turned to existing Arab models (especially Jordanian and Egyptian) but were careful to avoid any provisions that would lessen their autonomy. (Provisions in Jordanian laws generally barring government officials from high syndicate offices were therefore adopted; provisions that allowed ministries to supervise the elections within the syndicates were avoided.) Just as important as fending off state intervention was invoking its authority, however: syndicates were to have authority to examine new members, set qualifications and entrance requirements, and prevent nonmembers from practicing the profession. Leaders felt a particular need to develop uniform examinations and standards because of the diversity in training of members of the profession (many having gone to various Arab countries, Europe, or the Soviet bloc for education). The syndicates reacted harshly when they discovered legislation being drafted without their participation.[102]

While the divisions in the medical syndicates were thus less politicized than those among the journalists, the underlying dynamic remained remarkably similar: a group of leaders wished to restructure the existing organizations to allow far more effective concentration on professional concerns. Those pursuing such a path did not stand opposed to any nationalist agenda but saw their role as primarily professional. Years of occupation, legal ambiguity, and division had robbed the profession of some ability to organize its own affairs; in addition, the interests of members of the profession were not adequately defended. The situation varied according to the syndicate, but all worried that their profession was in danger of being flooded by too many practitioners and that the syndicate had not been able to police its members effectively. The pharmacists had the greatest reason for complaint: they claimed that there were approximately two times as many pharmacists as the society needed.[103] The leader of the Dentists Syndicate denied any current oversupply but also expressed the fear that their situation could resemble that of the pharmacists by the middle of the decade.[104] Medical professionals also worried about competition from government and NGO health services, though these concerns were often expressed more gingerly.[105] Syndicate leaders feared that the pressure of competition was leading some members to extend their practices in specialized areas where they were not qualified; they insisted that the syndicate alone could license specialists.[106]

The Engineers Syndicate

The Engineers Syndicate followed a pattern very similar to that of the medical syndicates, though it made slightly swifter progress toward the goal of unification.[107] Engineers on the West Bank began the effort to form a syndicate in 1958; they succeeded in 1959 after traveling to the East Bank and forming under the new Jordanian law for professional associations. The Jordanian syndicate formed a Jerusalem branch in 1963, renamed the Jerusalem Center in 1976 to make it coequal with the 'Amman headquarters. In Gaza, attempts to form a body began in the 1960s, and the association renamed itself as a syndicate in 1995. A third organization, the General Union of Palestinian Engineers, was formed by the PLO in Baghdad in 1973. Before the signing of the Oslo Accords, all three organizations took pride in their role in the nationalist struggle.

Immediately after the PNA was founded, the organizations began to work toward unification. The obstacles were the same as those that confronted the medical syndicates: not only were there multiple organizations, but one was tied to Jordan, while the other two lacked much independence from the PLO and PNA. Perhaps because of its longer history and larger membership, as well as the greater independence of the Jerusalem Center, the Engineers Syndicate was able to proceed more quickly with its draft law for unification and presented it to the Diwan al-fatwa wa-l-tashri' in February 2000. The draft barred government employees and officials from heading the association; it drew most of its clauses from the corresponding Jordanian law. The Diwan referred the draft to the cabinet, which passed it on to the PLC to discuss. The PLC took up the draft in March 2001, but given the torpid pace of the legislative process after the eruption of the second intifada, the matter proceeded slowly. Still, this placed the engineers far ahead of the other professional associations, most of which had not yet finished drafting their laws.

Chambers of Commerce

The same transition from nationalist to professional work has taken place in the thirteen Palestinian chambers of commerce, though it has taken a different form because of the different structures of the chambers.[108] While there is an umbrella organization for Palestinian chambers of commerce (headquartered in Jerusalem until shut down by Israel in 2002), the issue of unification has been far less prominent—the various chambers aspire to coordinate their operations but do not seek to form a single, unified organization. Instead, the chambers have attempted to shift from a broadly political role to a narrowly commercial one. Many look to the legislative process and the PNA to assist them in this task, but their success has been uneven.

The first Palestinian chamber of commerce was formed in Jerusalem in 1936. The existing chamber in Jerusalem at that time had British and Jewish members, and in the atmosphere of the 1936 general strike, Palestinian Jerusalemites decided to establish their own organization. Its first leader, Ahmad Hilmi, later became the leader of the All Palestine Government, the abortive attempt to establish a Palestinian state in 1948 and 1949. Established for nationalist reasons, the chamber became far less political under Jordanian rule (when it was joined by chambers for other Palestinian cities). Yet with the Israeli occupation in 1967, the chambers found themselves among the few functioning autonomous Palestinian organizations and quickly took on some political functions. They took the lead in protesting the imposition of Israeli taxes (though they were completely unsuccessful in that regard). They also took on some quasi-governmental functions, issuing Jordanian passports and other documents to be used in various Arab states unwilling to recognize Israeli documents (the chamber in Jerusalem, for instance, provided documentation and notary services that Palestinians could use in the Arab world). Yet despite this expansion in focus, most chambers declined under Israeli rule: most refused to hold elections under occupation, and their leadership grew older and less energetic.[109] As a result, when the PNA was established, the various Palestinian chambers of commerce drafted a law as the first step to rejuvenating themselves, but that draft has languished for several years without approval. Some chambers wished to hold elections as well, but the PNA leadership viewed this as premature (perhaps reluctant to face the possibility of opposition-dominated chambers). Stymied at the legislative and electoral level, some chambers have still attempted to use the existing law as a basis for renewed vitality. The possibility of attracting foreign investment and of working with a government more sympathetic than the Israeli occupation authorities led many chambers to attempt to resume full-scale operations, focusing on educating business leaders and lobbying for their interests. In short, the same desire to concentrate on narrower professional concerns seen in the syndicates has arisen in the chambers. Yet the chambers complain that they have not received the necessary governmental support. Not only has their draft law been ignored, but they also find that government officials deal directly with business leaders rather than with the chamber as a corporate group. The provision in Jordanian law that requires licensed businesses to join the chamber has not been enforced, robbing the chambers of the counterpart to an official charter held by some of the professional associations.

Labor Unions

Palestinian unions grew quickly in the difficult conditions of the 1980s but had enormous difficulty when the time came to adjust to representing workers under the PNA in the 1990s. Leftist political parties scored some early successes organizing workers in the West Bank and Gaza in the 1980s, leading Fatah to launch its own separate effort.[110] One student of Palestinian unions observes that during this period "trade unions were overtly political organizations more concerned with national liberation than class struggle."[111] The common nationalist struggle did not overcome partisan affiliation, however: Palestinian trade unions maintained close relations with their patron political party but could not coordinate with each other. A Palestinian General Federation of Trade Unions (PGFTU) was formed but split into two rivals claiming the title. In the early 1990s the political parties finally brought the PGFTU back together, but the founding of the PNA brought new problems. First, representatives of external unions returned, taking up senior positions. The secretary-general of the PGFTU, Haydar Ibrahim, was a returnee appointed by Yasir 'Arafat. A rivalry quickly developed between the returnees and the West Bank and Gaza leadership. Second, the PNA rewarded activists (especially those in Fatah) with government jobs; the result was that some trade union leaders found themselves working for the government. As with the professional associations, this led to complaints from the membership that their leaders had been coopted and that the organizations had lost their independence. Ibrahim, for instance, remained a senior official in the Ministry of Labor until March 2000.[112] And at least thirty-eight officials of the PGFTU were sneaked onto the government payroll.[113] The resulting cooptation and divisions left the union movement fairly ineffectual. A new Labor Law was drafted; the PLC introduced changes in the draft that were sharply opposed by the union leadership. But while the PLC was generally fairly responsive to lobbying from outside organizations and deferential to other sectors in writing legislation governing them, the PGFTU found a much less sympathetic ear. Unlike the professional organizations discussed above, Palestinian labor unions have been completely unable to free themselves of structures and practices that grew up when the labor movement was part of a broader national struggle.

This does not mean that there has been labor harmony under PNA rule. Indeed, in the 1994–2000 period, Palestinian newspapers regularly carried news of strikes and demonstrations. Yet the unions representing these striking workers generally stood in the background. The most prominent strikes in the short history of the PNA—the teachers' strikes of 1997 and 2000—were carried out by "coordinating committees" and not by the unions (see below). Union leaders felt caught in a very awkward position, unwilling to confront their patrons in Fatah and the PNA but also embarrassed in front of their membership for their meekness. By contrast, those in fields where there were strong but informal bonds—such as taxi drivers or merchants—were able to organize effective strikes. Those who worked through the PNA- or Fatah-dominated unions posed as supplicants occasionally able to win at best limited concessions. Under the PNA, labor militancy and trade union activity seem at times to be almost inversely related.

Teachers

Palestinian teachers engaged in two bitter confrontations with the PNA, both times setting their sights not only on official policies but also on the union that claimed to represent them. On both occasions, the confrontational poses of strike leaders provoked a harsh response and resulted in a tactical retreat. Despite their failure to win either battle, teachers presented the PNA with one of its most significant challenges in its effort to assert its primacy in Palestinian society.

As in other sectors, a confusing array of organizations represented teachers when the PNA began operation in 1994. Palestinian teachers had lived without a general union under Egyptian and Jordanian rule. Jordanian law specifically forbade unionization of public sector workers, and Israel enforced this ban after 1967. However, teachers in the UN Relief and Works Agency (UNRWA) schools in several Arab countries moved to form committees to press political and professional issues immediately after 1967. The PLO worked to consolidate the work of these committees, forming them into a General Union of Palestinian Teachers (GUPT), led by Jamil Shihada.[114] Yet GUPT faced formidable problems representing its constituency: it could not operate in the West Bank and Gaza; it was regarded warily by the governments of Arab countries where it could operate; and even UNRWA often preferred to avoid it.

Teachers in the West Bank (and, to a much lesser extent, in Gaza) moved to organize their own affairs. Teacher unions for UNRWA schools and private schools could form, but this left the vast majority of teachers in government schools with no effective union representation. Israel successfully suppressed sporadic teachers' strikes (perhaps the most significant coming in 1980). In the mid- and late 1980s, efforts to construct Palestinian organizations and unions under Israeli occupation became more sustained. Local groups of teachers—often associated with specific political parties—formed "coordinating committees." These committees were then gathered under the general umbrella of a Higher Coordinating Committee. In 1990 a group of teachers launched an effort to start a union. To distinguish itself from GUPT—then in exile—the new group called itself the General Union for Palestinian Teachers in the Occupied Territories (GUPTOT). Led by Muhammad Suwan, a Jerusalem teacher twice held under administrative detention by Israel, GUPTOT was successful in attracting PLO financial support.[115]

Thus, when the PNA assumed control over education in 1994, four different sorts of structures existed, none with an easily defined role. First, the formerly Tunis-based GUPT worked to establish itself as a union in the West Bank and Gaza. Its leader, Jamil Shihada, returned from exile. But the organization had little constituency inside the West Bank and Gaza, and when Shihada accepted a position in the PNA's Ministry of Interior, his claim to independence was seriously undermined. Second, the Suwan-led GUPTOT had a stronger basis among West Bank and Gaza teachers but faced different problems. Its leader and headquarters were based in Jerusalem, where the PNA and Israel both exercised control over schools in an uneasy, undeclared arrangement. The body attempted to convert its focus from nationalist politics to labor issues, but this raised new difficulties. Suwan himself was a PLO loyalist and thus was caught between the teachers and their major employer, the PNA. In 2000, he explained (in a mixed metaphor accurately expressing the dilemma faced by many other syndicate and union leaders): "I have to keep on glasses with two lenses. One is on the whole homeland, and one is on the interests of the teachers. How do I balance these? It is not easy."[116] Third, UNRWA and private school teachers retained their unions, but these bodies were unable to represent the vast majority of Palestinian teachers. Fourth, the activists who established coordinating committees during the intifada were unsure of their new role. As opposed to the Fatah-dominated GUPT and GUPTOT, the coordinating committee leaders were often associated with political movements harshly critical of the Oslo Accords and unwilling to abandon a stress on the nationalist struggle. At the same time, their constituency now was employed by the PNA, separating nationalist and union issues. Demands for an end to occupation and demands for higher wages now were directed to different addresses.

In 1997, teacher demands burst to the forefront.[117] In the spring, the coordinating committees went back into action, claiming that steady inflation had reduced teachers' wages. When the Ministry of Education offered only a modest raise (pleading fiscal exigencies), strikes broke out in several West Bank locations. The PNA—which preferred to work with the more pliable leadership of GUPT/GUPTOT (which had moved uneasily to consolidate operations)—managed to obtain a call for the strike to end, but the Higher Coordinating Committee insisted that nothing had been resolved. Teachers resorted to the PLC, where some deputies indicated that they were sympathetic with their plight. The PLC, however, directed its efforts toward writing a generous law governing the entire civil service (see Chapter 4) and thus offered little to the teachers in the short term. In late April 1997, the PNA increased the pressure on teachers to end the strike by bringing the security services into the matter. When the PNA announced that Higher Coordinating Committee members had called for an end to the strike, local committees charged that the statement had been issued under duress and that some leaders had been arrested and others dismissed, transferred to rural schools, or threatened. Ultimately, the coercive tactics worked, though they left a very bitter residue: the strike ended with only modest concessions to teacher demands. And when the Civil Service Law finally passed the PLC and obtained presidential endorsement, its salary provisions were not implemented, leaving the teachers with no substantial victory to claim.

In 2000, however, the PNA provoked a new and more protracted confrontation with teachers when it moved to implement a different provision of the Civil Service Law.[118] In January, West Bank teachers became subject to a new pension system under the law that involved a deduction of 10 percent from their pay. (Gazan teachers had already been subject to a similar withholding system dating back to the 1970s.) GUPT attempted to use its political connections to pressure the PNA to grant a compensating salary raise but dissociated itself from strike calls. Its efforts were unsuccessful, however: the PNA claimed to have brought its budget in balance for the first time and assured international donors that it would keep its burgeoning salaries in check. Beginning in Bethlehem and Hebron and spreading to northern parts of the West Bank, the local coordinating committees bucked the GUPT leadership and launched a strike. They demanded that the PNA apply the generous salary scale of the Civil Service Law if it was also to apply the increased withholding. They also demanded a "democratic" union, attacking GUPT as unrepresentative of teachers. Some opposition parties and PLC deputies backed the teachers, and Na'im Abu al-Humus, then deputy minister of education, took a conciliatory line. (Since Yasir 'Arafat held the education portfolio at the time, Abu al-Humus effectively headed the ministry.) The PNA leadership reacted to the pressure by appointing a committee of ministers and parliamentarians to study the matter and called on the teachers to return to work and allow the committee to do its work. Senior PNA leaders refused to meet with the Higher Coordinating Committee. Some strike leaders were summoned for questioning while others were transferred. More gently, the Ministry of Education threatened that continuation of the strike might lead to cancellation of some of the summer vacation.

In early April, two months into the strike, the Higher Coordinating Committee decided to accept promises from the joint ministerial/parliamentary committee that it would find a solution. Some support for the teachers had begun to waver, with sympathetic PLC deputies and the Nationalist and Islamic Forces (the multiparty forum) calling on the teachers to give the committee a chance to do its work. PNA officials talked about a significant raise for teachers. Yet just as the confrontation seemed to ebb it reemerged with new bitterness. On 1 May, the committee forwarded its recommendations to the cabinet without publicly declaring them. The leaders of the Higher Coordinating Committee began to suspect that the cabinet would fail to endorse a significant salary increase and called for the strike to resume. The security services began again to summon strike leaders for questioning. And when a leader of the Higher Coordinating Committee, 'Umar 'Assaf, harshly criticized the PNA in a radio interview, the security services arrested him without charges and closed the radio station. Since 'Assaf was a member of the political bureau of the opposition Democratic Front for the Liberation of Palestine, those opposition forces that had called for the teachers to suspend the strike resumed a harder line. Abu al-Humus, the highest official of the Ministry of Education, was powerless to prevent the confrontation and resigned (his resignation was eventually rejected, and indeed he was later appointed minister).

The confrontation ended only when nationalist violence broke out throughout the West Bank and Gaza on 15 May 2000. That violence—a foreshadowing of the second intifada—led the Higher Coordinating Committee to decide that nationalist issues were more important than union demands. The decision to end the strike was greeted by renewed promises to raise teacher salaries. But no decision was taken, and the director of the General Personnel Council (which oversaw salaries and benefits for public employees) cast doubt on how much political conditions would permit a raise and full implementation of the Civil Service Law.[119] 'Assaf was not released until late June, after the Nationalist and Islamic Forces called publicly for his detention to end.

Not until the next school year had begun did the issue arise again. The Higher Coordinating Committee held a partial strike on 21 September 2000 to protest the government's failure to provide the expected raise. At the same time, the various teacher organizations finally moved to consolidate their operations. GUPT convened a general meeting of the various bodies representing Palestinian teachers, managing to convince them to form a joint committee to coordinate their actions. All member organizations retained their autonomous existence, but the committee seemed to pave the way for a unified and responsive teachers' union. Elections were scheduled for the end of the year. All political parties endorsed the move, and a PLC member introduced legislation to support the formation of a unified teachers' union.[120] Perhaps to indicate its seriousness to skeptics, the new committee called for a strike throughout the educational sector on 1 October 2000. By that time, however, the second intifada had already begun, and union demands were suspended.

The dilemma facing Palestinian teachers in the 2000 strike—choosing between nationalist loyalties and unionist demands—was sharper and more public than it was for other unions and professional associations, but the underlying logic was no different. Bodies that had operated for at least a generation in the context of occupation and nationalist resistance were forced to convert to serving the professional needs of their membership. That task was difficult enough because it often meant revamping organizations, battling among generations, and forcing out leaders with nationalist credentials. But it was made still more difficult by the unresolved nature of the nationalist issue at the core of Palestinian politics. Twice in 2000 (May and October), teachers felt forced to shelve demands for better pay in the face of Arab-Israeli violence. Yet despite the perceived necessity of temporarily suspending normal union activities, teachers had established a record of labor militancy unequaled in the PNA. Like other unions and professional organizations, the efforts of teachers to pursue professional demands were punctuated with other concerns but probably only temporarily deflected.

CONCLUSION

The Oslo Accords did not create a Palestinian state, but they did create a Palestinian "Authority" that acted like a state for the purposes of most associations in Palestinian society. The relationship of the proto-state to Palestinian associations was different from what other regions or previous Arab experience indicated was likely.

Those who see the institutions of civil society as a bulwark against state authority could find much to support their perspective, especially in the conduct of the largest and most successful NGOs. Some of these organizations posed as the true opposition to the PNA, and many worked to support the principle of accountability in political (and especially human rights) practices. The information gathered and provided by the most sophisticated NGOs often could be more current and reliable than officially provided data, so international and domestic activists, researchers, and organizations relied on them. Much of what was known about the PNA both internally and externally came from the reports of some of the largest NGOs. Governance in the PNA was different and more transparent because of the work of these organizations—far less than they would have liked, of course, but enough so that it cannot be denied that NGOs made a difference in Palestinian politics.

Yet the activity of a small number of organizations should not obscure the degree to which Palestinian associations of all varieties sought PNA assistance and recognition. Grassroots organizations were starved for attention from the PNA, and many foundered in its absence. Professional associations sought a clear legal charter from the PNA in order to professionalize their operations. Ironically, most felt that they could not be truly autonomous actors without full legal and institutional recognition by the PNA. Thus, those who look to civil society as a guarantor of democratic politics would not be wrong, but they risk missing important aspects of state-society relations.

Those who speak of the "social capital" provided by rich associational life also have much to point to in the Palestinian experience. The period of the intifada does seem to have forged some bonds that the PNA could bend but not break. Yet associational life in general does not seem to follow the pattern expected by social capital enthusiasts—that of cultivating trust, expectations of cooperation, and capacity for collective action. Indeed, such aspects of Palestinian society seem to have been stronger in the intifada years when associational life was less structured and formal. With the founding of the PNA, associational life became more formal and professionalized in all sectors—but not in a way that augured well for cultivating democratic and activist practices. If anything, many organizations lost their voluntarist and participatory spirit, operating internally in an undemocratic manner (most organizations remain dominated by a leading personality).[121] The most successful organizations were often those that could court international rather than domestic constituencies. Many of these developments had very positive effects in helping organizations meet their missions—but perhaps at the expense of inculcating the sorts of practices that "social capital" enthusiasts expect to develop out of rich associational life.

Those searching for corporatism will find many telltale traces in the patterns developing in the PNA. Professional organizations provide the strongest example, as they strove to create bodies that would have the exclusive right to represent their sector and a privileged relationship with the state. Even NGOs sought a similar relationship that involved licensing and recognition without any loss of autonomy. If there was any surprise in the nature of the corporatism developing, it was the strength of societal over state corporatism—that is, the various associations displayed far more autonomy and engaged the state on a more equal basis than is the norm in Arab politics.

These various approaches, however, do not lead us to expect the extent to which the structure of Palestinian civil society was malleable: deep historical or cultural forces may have been at work, but the chief forces for change arose out of the immediate political context. The shift from Jordanian and Egyptian rule to Israeli occupation, the attempt to build strong organizations to aid the nationalist struggle, the shift in finances and legal framework, and the demands of state building all left their strong mark on the development of Palestinian associations of all kinds.

The same senses of resumption evident elsewhere in Palestinian politics certainly operated in associational life. Those who saw the Palestine emerging as simply a resumption of past forms of Palestinian politics could point to the strong continuity in Palestinian NGOs, grassroots organizations, and professional associations. The creation of the PNA affected the development of these organizations, but it did not create them; almost all associations could trace their existence back, sometimes for decades.

Those who saw Palestinian politics under the PNA as the resumption of Arab forms of politics could adduce much in the emerging pattern of relationships between various associations and the proto-state.[122] The NGO Law began on an Egyptian model; professional associations were clearly based (and sometimes rooted in) their Jordanian and Egyptian counterparts, and the attitude of the Palestinian leadership toward associations—and their appropriate national role—seemed familiar to students of Arab politics (though, despite the PNA's reputation, it was probably slightly more liberal).

And those who saw the PNA as the occasion to resume normal political life could point to associational life as the linchpin of their efforts. By and large, the major shift in associational life between 1994 and 2000 was the decline of the domination of the nationalist issue. As NGOs turned their attention from supporting the intifada and nationalist struggle to providing services in more peaceful conditions, as grassroots organizations struggled to define their role in a society no longer characterized by revolutionary mobilization, and as professional associations turned much of their attention away from denouncing Israeli settlements and more toward providing retirement benefits and professional education, the shape of a normal Palestinian polity became evident.

To be sure, the eruption of the second intifada in September 2000 set that effort back. And unlike the earlier stages of the first intifada, the emphasis on armed confrontation pushed many NGOs, grassroots organizations, and professional associations to the side. Some began to demand "democratization of the intifada," by which they meant conversion to an uprising based less on ad hoc militias and more on the participation of unions, syndicates, and other popular organizations. While these calls seemed to have some resonance even among some in the Palestinian leadership, the second intifada forced many associations into hibernation. The attempt to form a new journalists syndicate was suspended (and an organizational meeting planned for Jerusalem had to be canceled). The bar association tried to hold elections, but some lawyers in outlying areas claimed that the Israeli closure would make it impossible to vote and obtained a court order postponing the elections. When the Engineers Syndicate held its annual meeting in 2001, its attention focused largely on nationalist rather than professional issues.[123] Two of the grassroots organizations mentioned above—the Women and Childcare Society in Bayt Jalla and the Qalandiya Camp Handicraft Cooperative Society—found themselves quite literally in the line of fire.[124] In such an environment it might be more remarkable how many associations and organizations continued operation. Despite the widespread violence and the complications it posed for those seeking to build a normal political entity, the patterns established under PNA rule from 1994 to 2000 seemed likely to re-emerge whenever the shooting finally stopped.

6 Democracy, Nationalism, and Contesting the Palestinian Curriculum

> One of the signs of the time that frightens me is the insistence, in the name of democracy, freedom, and efficacy, on asphyxiating freedom itself and, by extension, creativity and a taste for the adventure of the spirit. The freedom that moves us, that makes us take risks, is being subjugated to a process of standardization of formulas, models against which we are evaluated.
>
> Paulo Freire, *Pedagogy of Freedom*

Modern Arab states are widely known—both inside and outside their boundaries—for their highly developed (and overlapping) security services, extensive bureaucracies, and closed decision-making structures. The Palestinian Authority quickly obtained a reputation for following this pattern in most respects.

One feature of Arab states has generally received far less attention: their concentration on education. In the twentieth century, all Arab states have built extensive networks of schools at all levels, required education for both boys and girls, and supervised the content of classroom instruction extremely closely. As will be seen, Arab educational systems have unsparing critics, but none question the centrality of education to the mission of the state. In many ways, Arab states present themselves to their citizens as educators of their populations more effectively than they present themselves as defenders of national territory or guarantors of internal security. The PNA has devoted just under one-fifth of its budget to education and employs approximately thirty thousand teachers.

This chapter will focus on the Palestinian educational system and the political contests concerning it. Some of the conflict over Palestinian education has been international (especially because of the charge that Palestinian textbooks incite violence against Israel and Jews). That issue must be confronted (see the appendix to this chapter) because of both the attention it has attracted and the number of people it has misled on the content of Palestinian education. But the fundamental purpose of this chapter is to understand the efforts of Palestinians themselves to define the purpose of the educational system and the content and methods of the curriculum. Not only is this chapter designed to turn attention from incitement to domestic political contests; it also marks a departure in writings on Palestinian education in two other ways.

First, writings on curricula—especially those motivated by an interest in broader political concerns—often take a surprisingly unsophisticated view of causality. The content of a curriculum is assumed to translate easily into childhood (and later adult) political attitudes and actions.[1] Such a view of curricular effectiveness is rarely taken by those who recall their own experience in school; it is still rarer among those who have ever taught (or graded a final examination). It is a mistake to assume efficient transmission: teachers working with official texts can lend them surprising inflections; students are molded less automatically and even predictably than textbook critics often assume.

Second, writings on education—especially as it relates to political concerns—are often surprisingly univocal. Educational systems would seem to be designed to meet a unified vision and to realize that vision. Such a view erases the controversies and struggles involved in creating or remolding a system; in many cases (and certainly the Palestinian), the system is constructed through struggle among contending parties. Academic writings, especially in the discipline of anthropology, have begun to approach these questions with far greater sophistication.[2] The aims here are far more modest: the purpose is not to recast our understanding of how education works but only to understand the political forces at play and the battles that have taken place in the Palestinian educational arena.

While a recent innovation, universal state education has already attracted considerable symbolic and ideological force throughout the world. In Arab countries, education often became a battleground during the colonial period: local elites saw education as a critical tool for promoting national consciousness and economic progress. Colonial powers often saw education as a drain on the budget and schools as loci of nationalist agitation. Thus, the colonial state often restricted its support for education geographically (concentrating on the capital city) and qualitatively (focusing on training for a few professions and government service). Postsecondary education was generally extremely restricted; with only a few exceptions, Arab universities date to the postcolonial period. Freed of colonial fetters after independence, states rapidly expanded educational systems into the countryside and expanded quickly into postsecondary education, all the while maintaining a tight grip over content and structure.

Arab educational systems have been built on the principle that schools are a critical locus for the establishment of political authority and the transmission of political loyalties. Such an approach is neither unique nor surprising: most residents of the Arab world make their first sustained direct contact with political authority in the classroom. Teachers, employed by the state and operating under the watchful eye of the Ministries of Education, are expected to hew closely to textbooks authored within those ministries. Such books represent authoritative truth; the task of the teacher is to assist students in assimilating the information. Both students and teachers are evaluated solely on the success of this process of transmission and assimilation. In this respect, Arab educational systems resemble their counterparts throughout much of the world. However, Arab educational critics in some countries have begun to stigmatize the resulting system as reproducing authoritarianism within the classroom. Such criticism sometimes receives a sympathetic hearing from official educators. Nevertheless, the charge that education supports authoritarianism is hardly likely to horrify most Arab governments.

Arab countries are hardly unique in placing education at the core of state functions. Indeed, it might be that the ubiquity of large official educational establishments has led scholars to pass over their significance: they constitute an obvious and thus overlooked part of the institutional landscape of a modern state. Yet even if the Arab world is participating in a global trend, Arab educational establishments show some strong common features that lead them to resemble each other to a surprising degree.

None of these features alone—or even in combination—is unique to the Arab world, but their repetition in each Arab state is striking. In some ways, the initial efforts of the PNA was to further the replication of these features, many of which were already well ensconced in the educational structures of the West Bank and Gaza.

First, educational establishments are highly centralized in Arab countries. Generally there is a single set of authoritative textbooks for each subject at all primary and secondary levels. Little or no room exists for elective subjects. Curricula and hours of instruction are similarly set nationally by the Ministry of Education. Ministries might consult outside experts, but they generally author and even print texts internally. Teachers may not be formally barred from introducing supplementary material, but they are effectively discouraged from doing so. Education ministries evaluate teachers on how well their students have mastered authoritative texts; since teachers often complain that the texts contain more information than they can teach in the allotted time, they feel little latitude for individual experimentation. Formal education culminates in a single examination at the end of secondary school (the *tawjihi* or *thanawiyya 'amma*); the results of the examination determine entrance into university (and specialization as well), leading to enormous pressures on both students and teachers to hew closely to officially sanctioned forms of knowledge.

Second, Arab educational establishments have stressed quantity over quality: the stress on universal literacy and attendance leads most to expand throughout the country (elite education is available but often private rather than public). They have striven to expand educational establishments even when this has led to poorly equipped, overcrowded classrooms staffed by underpaid teachers. This emphasis is not surprising for strapped governments fending off multiple claims for scarce state resources. Yet it is not simply fiscal exigencies that have encouraged this result. The sort of egalitarian nationalism that dominated the Arab world shortly after independence in many countries (often but not always portrayed as socialism) and the ambitions of newly dominant elites encouraged an expansive educational vision. Many Arab states turned to Egypt for educational guidance (and teachers), meaning that policy choices made by a poor country were adopted by those (especially in the Gulf) who may have been able to afford different options. One by-product of this emphasis has led to large classes, increasing the already strong tendency of teachers to devote their energies to discipline and order.

Third, officially sanctioned educational techniques have stressed mastery of approved material over originality and individuality. One Palestinian educator claims that "the purpose of education in the Arab world has been to transmit information from one generation to the next."[3] Modes of instruction and examination, systems of school inspection, and perhaps class size all support this emphasis. Similarly, Arab educational systems are designed to classify students as well as educate them. Tracking begins generally at the secondary level, in which numerous countries divide students into "literary" and "scientific" streams based on past performance and examinations. The general secondary examination does not simply classify students as qualified for university education or not; it also determines what subjects they may study. At all levels, decisions are made on the basis of examination results far more than individual interest.

Finally, state-sponsored education in the Arab world incorporates instruction in the Islamic religion. Non-Muslims are generally excused (or have their own schools); all other pupils are taught a state-sanctioned form of the religion.[4] Occasionally, officially authored texts will spark national debate (for instance, the Egyptian Ministry of Education came under severe criticism in 1999 for a set of religious textbooks), but the inclusion of Islam as a discrete subject into the curriculum provokes virtually no opposition.

In the eyes of its critics, Arab education is designed to build subjects more than citizens. Yet these common features can be portrayed in some cases (especially the Palestinian) as an outcome of democratic politics: the current Palestinian educational system operates under the auspices of a democratically elected leadership and works to hew closely to the national consensus. For the critics, this brand of democracy misses the point: education should cultivate democratic practices rather than inculcate the beliefs of the majority. As will be seen later in this chapter, contesting visions of democratic education lie at the heart of the current domestic contest over the Palestinian curriculum.

While education might be central to the state mission under most Arab governments, Arab educational systems generally draw little attention from outside observers. Palestinian education is a stark exception to this, however: the president of the United States raised the issue with Yasir 'Arafat; many members of the U.S. Congress have expressed opinions on the topic; and activist groups and external donors have expressed an interest in remolding the Palestinian educational system to promote peaceful relations among Palestinians and Israelis.[5] Much of the public debate on Palestinian education has generated more heat than light. More to the point for present purposes, however, the current Palestinian curriculum has few defenders. The Israeli government denounces it as hostile to peace, the Palestinian leadership regards it as undermining any sense of a Palestinian national identity, and many Palestinian educators regard it as outmoded and exhibiting the worst features of Arab educational systems.

In short, the Palestinian educational system is much-contested terrain. The PNA assumed control over education throughout the West Bank and Gaza (and to a significant extent even East Jerusalem) immediately after it was established in 1994. The system that it found itself administering bore all the hallmark traits of other Arab educational systems. The centrality of education to the Palestinian nationalist vision resembled the situation in other Arab countries that had wrested their independence in protracted struggles. Nationalist leaders throughout the Arab world have claimed that their uninvited rulers starved the educational system of the resources they needed. Schools were not simply seen as possible sites of cultivating national identity; they had also served in the intifada (as they had to a lesser extent under the mandate) as loci of nationalist resistance. And Palestinian education resembled neighboring Arab systems in method and substance; indeed, the curriculum was a direct copy of the Jordanian (for the West

Bank) and the Egyptian (for Gaza). The PNA immediately affirmed the continuity between the educational system and that which existed on the eve of the occupation by restoring subjects and textbooks that the Israeli civil administration had not allowed. However, the pre-1967 system in education in some ways denied a Palestinian national identity (unlike the legal system, which simply ignored it) by subjecting Palestinians to Egyptian and Jordanian national curricula. Thus, the question for Palestinians was not whether to reform the system but how.

RESUMING PALESTINIAN EDUCATION

The current system of Palestinian public education was established by the Ottoman state.[6] By the outbreak of World War I, ninety-eight public schools had been established, of which only three were secondary schools. Approximately one-ninth of the school-age population attended these schools. Alongside the state schools, several different systems operated. Most notably, many towns and villages established *kuttab* schools that concentrated on teaching basic literacy and the Qur'an. In addition, Jewish and Christian schools existed, often with a considerable degree of external support.

The establishment of the British mandate brought no sudden transformation in the educational system, but it did result in several significant but gradual trends. First, the town and village kuttab schools were absorbed into the government system, doubling the number of students under direct government supervision. The step effectively integrated secular and religious education at the primary and secondary levels, a step that has never been reversed. Second, the system was gradually expanded, so that by the end of the mandate, over one-quarter of school-age Arab children were in government schools. The private system also expanded, though slightly more slowly: by the end of the mandate approximately one-sixth of the Arab school-age population attended private Muslim or Christian schools. Third, secondary and postsecondary technical education was expanded, though generally quite modestly. (Indeed, one of the primary purposes of this expansion was simply to produce teachers to staff the primary schools.) Fourth, the steady but slow increase in the system was accomplished while assigning a diminishing share of the state budget to education. In the first three years of the mandate, education absorbed slightly over 6 percent of the budget; in the last three years, the share had dipped well under 5 percent. A final feature of the mandate was the effective construction of separate Jewish and Arab educational systems. The public system was almost exclusively Arab; the Jewish community administered independent school systems.

Palestinians clashed with the mandatory government in the education arena on several fronts. First, the administration of the system lay largely outside Palestinian hands. There were some Palestinian senior officials in the first years of the mandate and in the final decade, but the position of director (the chief educational official in the country) was always British. The extreme centralization of the educational administrative structure increased the importance of such senior positions, leaving Palestinians frustrated at their inability to influence the system. Second, the curriculum drew criticism on nationalist grounds. It is true that there was no attempt to introduce a British curriculum; indeed, mandate officials worked with the preexisting Ottoman curriculum and turned generally to Egypt for modifications. Yet the curriculum for some subjects (especially history and geography) seemed to some Palestinians to be inappropriately oriented toward Europe, and contemporary history was judged as too sensitive to broach in the classroom. Finally, schools proved to be loci of nationalist political action, and students and teachers increasingly participated in strikes and demonstrations.[7]

By the time the mandate ended in 1948, many of the features of the Palestinian educational system lay firmly established: it was increasingly designed to serve the entire population but was starved of the resources to meet that mission; administration was highly centralized; control of the system was politically sensitive, chiefly on nationalist grounds; the curriculum was largely imported and ignored Palestinian national identity; and the public system was supplemented by an extensive private system. None of these features has changed in the subsequent half-century.

Indeed, in some ways the result of the partition of Palestine in 1948 was to accentuate these features of Palestinian education. There were, it is true, important structural changes. The West Bank educational system was fully absorbed by the Jordanian Ministry of Education; the Gaza schools retained some theoretical autonomy but switched completely to the Egyptian curriculum. The UN Relief and Works Agency (UNRWA) established schools in the refugee camps; these followed the curriculum and structure prevailing in the area they functioned. In addition, the Jordanian Ministry of Awqaf administered some schools as well, especially in Jerusalem. The educational system continued to expand in accordance with prevailing practice in Jordan and Egypt. New schools were constructed, making education available to the vast majority of the population. The number of years of schooling available greatly expanded as well: the mandate-era system concentrated on a few years of primary education; the post-1948 systems made availability of primary and secondary education the norm (though UNRWA focused simply on the first nine grades, usually leaving secondary education to the other systems).

This expansion and set of structural changes did not change the other features of the Palestinian educational system. Jordanian and Egyptian control did not mean an infusion of new resources—Egypt's leaders were not interested in having Gaza become a drain on state finances, nor were they in any position to offer Gazans opportunities that they could not offer Egyptians. Residents in the West Bank were probably more fortunate, especially because of the lower proportion of refugees in the population, the greater concentration of educational institutions prior to 1948, and the extensive system of private schools. But joining the West Bank to Jordan hardly offered greater fiscal resources for Palestinian education. To be sure, both Egyptian and Jordanian administration expanded the educational system, but both concentrated on quantity rather than quality. Palestinian national identity received only slightly more expression than it had under the mandate. Students in Gaza studied the Egyptian curriculum, and those in the West Bank followed the Jordanian. While the Palestinians were no longer ignored (indeed, both the Egyptian and Jordanian governments introduced material on the Palestinians), Palestinians themselves were still relatively powerless over such matters. Palestinian students devoted greater attention to Pharaonic Egypt and the Hashemite leadership of the Arab Revolt than to their particular history. Changes did occur, however: the common Arab practice of tracking secondary students into scientific and literary streams was adopted in both the West Bank and Gaza. In one way, the centralization of the system actually increased: both Jordan and Egypt brought their matriculation examination, enforcing a high level of curricular uniformity. And with postsecondary education extremely limited in the West Bank and Gaza, Palestinian students who wished to continue their studies generally did so in Egypt and Jordan.

Thus, the educational structure in the West Bank and Gaza at the time of the Israeli occupation in 1967 exhibited all the features of other educational systems in the Arab world. Moreover, it gave far greater expression to a general Arab identity than to any specifically Palestinian identity. For most Palestinians, the situation represented an improvement: education was more available, and the curriculum and administration of the schools lay in Arab hands. The educational controversies of the mandate period became muted in this atmosphere.

That changed dramatically in 1967 with the Israeli occupation, and every conceivable aspect of Palestinian education became highly contested—though often with few practical changes resulting. As under the mandate, Palestinians claimed increasingly bitterly that their rulers were denying the educational establishment the resources necessary to operate effectively.

Construction of new schools came to a virtual halt.[8] Yet the expectation of universal education created under Jordanian and Egyptian rule continued; the rapidly growing population soon filled existing schools past capacity. By the time that the Palestinian Authority assumed control of the educational system, average class size exceeded thirty-six students.[9] This crowding was not exceptional by the standards of the developing world, but it masked a greater strain placed on teachers and physical facilities: many schools operated on two shifts per day to accommodate the growing number of students; three shifts per day were not uncommon in Gaza. And it was not merely buildings that appeared underfunded: teacher training received drastically reduced support.[10] Newly emerging Palestinian universities did greatly expand the opportunities for teacher training in Palestinian institutions, but no support was available for these efforts from the authorities now governing Palestinians.

As under the mandate, the conflict over education extended to the curriculum. This time, however, it was the Palestinians who resisted any change: for all their problems, the Jordanian and Egyptian curricula were unmistakably Arab. Fearing that any attempt to introduce changes would open up possibilities for Israeli influence, Palestinian educational officials successfully clung to preexisting curricula.[11] Israeli officials did not contest the existing curricula and allowed the matriculation examination to continue. Yet they reviewed textbooks entering from Jordan and Egypt, censoring those they found offensive.[12] Palestinian nationalists denounced this effort, which they claimed was aimed at eliminating any trace of Palestinian nationality from the classroom. Educators objected on additional grounds: the banning of texts (or sections) left some subjects with huge gaps (especially history, literature, and religion); in addition, the process of censorship seemed arbitrary (often depending on the individual personality of the Israeli officer) and slow (delaying new texts at least one year).

Not only did the Israeli occupation resume all the disputes of the mandate period in increasingly bitter form, it also introduced some new ones. Perhaps the most complex issue involved Jerusalem. Immediately after the 1967 war, Israel annexed eastern parts and suburbs of the city, incorporating a substantial Palestinian population. Initially, Israel shifted the curriculum of the East Jerusalem public schools to follow that of its Arab schools, but it abandoned the attempt in 1974 after families deserted the public for the private system. After that point, Jerusalem public schools theoretically fell under the Israeli-controlled municipal government and the Israeli Ministry of Education but were effectively reincorporated into the Jordanian system prevailing elsewhere in the West Bank. Israel did introduce Hebrew-language instruction, beginning in the third grade, but since the subject was not on the Jordanian tawjihi matriculation examination, students and teachers were given little incentive to study the language with enthusiasm. Civics was also added. The return to the Jordanian system was fraught with ambiguities: the Israeli government financed schools, but diplomas were issued in the name of the Jordanian minister of education. One Palestinian village in the new municipal boundaries (Bayt Safafa) had been divided by the 1948 lines. The Israeli half followed the Israeli Arab curriculum; the Jordanian half followed the Jordanian curriculum. After 1967 the two schools were unified but were forced to teach two different curricula. In one important way, neither Israelis nor Palestinians were interested in resolving or even publicizing these ambiguities. Israelis were reluctant to acknowledge their failure to incorporate the East Jerusalem population; Palestinians were not anxious to have the glare of publicity undermine the restoration they had wrested from the Israelis with such difficulty.[13]

The intifada turned Palestinian schools from a metaphoric battleground into a literal one. To be sure, periodic crises had afflicted education earlier in the Israeli occupation. In the first year of the occupation, the exodus of some teachers (especially Egyptian teachers from Gaza) and nationalist boycotts had led to a brief drop in enrollments.[14] After that time, however, students returned to the classroom. Teachers attempted to organize a strike in 1980 (the leaders were dismissed). Yet not until the outbreak of the intifada in 1987 did schools themselves become a sustained theater of confrontation. At that time, schools became centers of political resistance even more than they had at any time under the mandate. Nationalist boycotts combined with Israeli closures to disrupt the regular educational process completely. In the first four years of the intifada, one-third to one-half of school days were lost.[15] A General Union of Palestinian Teachers in the Occupied Territories established itself in Jerusalem in 1990.[16] A popularly organized literacy campaign attempted to fill the gap left by the partial collapse of the educational system.[17]

Thus, by the time that Israel negotiated with the PLO in the early 1990s, schools and education had moved to the center of the nationalist struggle. And the nationalist issue completely dominated the educational agenda as well: Palestinians themselves focused all their educational efforts on wresting control of schools, teachers, students, and curricula from Israeli hands. The Israeli occupation was held responsible for starving the system of resources and forbidding any expression of Palestinian identity.

When Palestinian autonomy was negotiated in 1993 and 1994, PLO negotiators insisted on total control over the educational system. Israeli negotiators put up little resistance. Even as the two sides wrangled over matters as minute as what to call (and how to design) Palestinian travel documents, educational issues proved simple to resolve. Before many other aspects of autonomy were negotiated, the entire educational system for the West Bank and Gaza was delivered to the Palestinian Authority, even in areas where Israel maintained direct security control. Israel quietly tolerated Palestinian penetration of the East Jerusalem educational system, unwilling to develop any alternatives to thinly disguised PA control. The Israeli mayor of Jerusalem did put up some resistance, but as time went on, Israeli contestation of Palestinian control of East Jerusalem schools diminished.[18]

Beginning with the 1994–95 school year, the newly created Palestinian Ministry of Education began to assume authority over Palestinian education. Its first curricular move—consistent with the view that the solution to educational problems all began with removing Israeli control—was simply to restore the Jordanian and Egyptian systems in their entirety. Banned textbooks were restored, republished on the West Bank under the name of the PNA.

The process began with some excessive optimism. One Palestinian educator ascribed all difficulties to the Israeli occupation and stated, "After we have come to know from this the obstacles in the educational process, the treatment becomes easy."[19] Yet Palestinian educational officials realized early that merely transferring control over education from Israel to the PNA would not solve the problems of overcrowded classrooms, ill-equipped schools, and multiple shifts. Officials in the newly created Ministry of Education therefore worked with international donors to identify a list of priorities—yet the amount estimated for school construction reached $230 million, far more than anyone was likely to give.[20] And with the PNA completely dependent on such assistance for virtually all its capital expenditures, domestic funding for school construction was quite limited.[21] The Ministry of Education was subject to severe pressures even for recurrent expenditures: while Palestinian educators had for years called for smaller class size, external donors were very reluctant to assist significantly with the operating budget. Hiring more teachers was unlikely to appeal to those denouncing the PNA civil service as bloated; the World Bank, for instance, lauded the Palestinian educational system for its efficiency and cited a slight decline in the student-teacher ratio (a major goal of Palestinian educators) not as progress but instead as a worrying sign.[22]

Simple resumption of the pre-1967 system not only failed to resolve all problems but also created some new ones. Under Jordanian rule, teachers— as public employees—were barred from forming unions. The Israeli occupation took a similarly dim view of teachers' unions. Yet nationalist logic pushed the PNA in a very different direction: the PLO had encouraged (and funded) an attempt to establish a Palestinian teachers' union in the West Bank (more grassroots but still partisan "coordinating committees" had emerged as well); UNRWA teachers throughout the Palestinian diaspora had also organized and formed a General Union of Palestinian Teachers.[23] Since both organizations operated under PLO sponsorship, the PNA could hardly repudiate them. With the first union based in Jerusalem and the second in Tunis, the PNA worked to contain the rivalry that quickly developed and combine the two. Yet its success in the formal organizational sense did not prevent labor problems; indeed, it deepened them. Many teachers felt that the newly combined union was too beholden to the Palestinian leadership to represent them effectively. A series of wildcat strikes in 1997 and 2000 resulted in the re-emergence of rival "coordinating committees" of teachers demanding formation of a new union (see Chapter 5).

While attempting (generally unsuccessfully) to resolve the fiscal and labor crises associated with the PNA's assumption of control over education, a longer-term process was initiated to create a full and integrated Palestinian curriculum. Writing a new curriculum was an arduous process, and the first fruits of the effort would not enter the Palestinian classroom until September 2000, six years after the PNA assumed responsibility for education. Recognizing that in the mean time there was no specifically Palestinian content in the curriculum, the Ministry of Education quickly composed a set of textbooks for the first six grades; these books were simply to offer some Palestinian content to supplement the Jordanian and Egyptian books while a comprehensive national curriculum was designed.

In one sense, this new series, begun in 1994, *Al-tarbiyya al-wataniyya* (National Education), represents a departure from the history of Palestinian education: the books present themselves as the authoritative voice of a Palestinian state. Yet in another sense, production of the series is best understood as an act of resumption rather than departure. The books treat the Palestinian nation and homeland as continuous entities that date back thousands of years; they ignore any ruptures in Palestinian history (generally treating anything connected with Israel—whether related to war or peace—extremely obliquely if at all). In presenting Palestinian history and nationality as seamless, and in seeking to present the educational process as the transmission of truths and values from one generation to the next, the interim curriculum resembles other Arab curricula. While these books were issued, however, a far more ambitious effort was begun, informed (but only partially) by a daring alternative vision of Palestinian education.

THE LOST CENTURY OF ARAB EDUCATION
AND THE EMERGENCE OF A PROGRESSIVE ALTERNATIVE

In the 1990s, even before the construction of the PNA, an alternative vision of education, concentrating on ideal citizenship and democratic practice, arose within the Palestinian educational community. Deeply critical of existing educational practices, advocates of the new vision have provoked surprisingly little opposition and increasingly dominate public discussions of education. The core of the alternative vision is to recast the question around which the educational system—especially pedagogy but also the curriculum—is based. Rather than asking, "What body of knowledge should students be taught?" newer approaches ask, "What kind of citizen do we want?" The effect is to justify a profound critique not merely of the substance of the existing curriculum but even more of prevailing educational methods. Just as Palestinians faced the prospect of writing a curriculum based on instilling national values, groups arose attempting to leapfrog immediately to fostering individuality and critical thought.[24]

The new educational vision emerged among three distinct (and hardly coordinated) groups. First, some Palestinian intellectuals, generally secular and often on the left, were attracted to educational issues because of their desire to build a more participatory and democratic national culture. Such intellectuals often had a strong interest in educational issues but were not academic specialists in education—nor did all speak respectfully of educational administrators in the emerging Ministry of Education. While nationalism was often their point of entry to educational issues, their focus broadened to democracy, especially after the creation of the PNA. This was the case with Ibrahim Abu Lughod, a Palestinian political scientist with an American Ph.D. who taught for many years at Northwestern University. In the 1972 he, Nabil Sha'th (later a leading Palestinian negotiator), and some other intellectuals called for a greater interest in education and publishing for children.[25] Abu Lughod participated in some discussions of education sponsored by UNESCO. With the founding of the PNA, Abu Lughod became one of the few diaspora intellectuals to return, taking an administrative position at Bir Zayt University. Another political scientist at Bir Zayt with a special interest in human rights and democracy, 'Ali Jarbawi, began to share Abu Lughod's educational interests. Other Palestinian intellectuals brought in different disciplinary perspectives. A group of archaeologists, for instance, began work to train teachers in integrating visits to archaeological sites with their classroom instruction.[26]

A second group of Palestinian educational reformers consisted of educational specialists. They combined the general interests of the intellectuals with specific educational expertise. While most shared general Palestinian nationalist aspirations, it was not nationalist education that interested them. Many received graduate training overseas, especially in American schools of education, and had a professional and international orientation. The idea of a Palestinian-designed curriculum had strong attraction, of course, but their major focus was educational: to turn Palestinians into a community of active and critical learners on the basis of the most recent developments in educational theory.[27] For instance, Liyana Jabir, an educational researcher, sought to educate Palestinian teachers on the "discovery method" (in which the teacher's role is "active and not simply transmittal") and on "cooperative learning," bringing in insights from academic educational literature.[28]

In developing their ideas, these educators not only shared a highly critical view of existing educational practices but also often extended this to a broader and quite trenchant social critique. Already in the first intifada, some educators had begun a reading campaign to compensate for the extended school closings. Munir Fasheh, a specialist in mathematics and science education involved in the reading campaign, expressed an emerging consensus among education specialists, though in unusually harsh terms:

> In my thirty years of experience in various Palestinian educational settings, I have often seen superficial and symbolic improvement that disguises real deterioration underneath: Palestinian students acquire diplomas but no learning abilities; they learn textbook theories but not the ability to construct their own explanations of experiences and phenomena. Schools encourage ready-made solutions and discourage experimentation and innovative ideas. Palestinians build universities that lack good libraries and that impede students' development of the abilities to express, organize, and produce knowledge; and they build structures and organizations that lack community bonding and community spirit. Enacting visible, but often merely symbolic, improvement without deeper and longer lasting change deceives people and blinds them from seeing the opportunities that are being lost, as well as what could and should be done instead. Palestinians need to create alternatives in their minds and in their practice to deal with current challenges and the increasing demands on formal education.[29]

Maher Hashweh, a specialist in science education at Bir Zayt University, developed a similar but more specific critique after studying the attitudes and practices of science teachers in Palestinian schools. Convinced that a constructivist approach not only more accurately reflects scientific development but also can be a basis for science instruction by encouraging active learning and critical thinking, Hashweh found existing practices wanting:

> Firstly, in Palestinian schools knowledge explained by the teacher and found in one official textbook is unquestionable and is to be remembered for future use only. Secondly, the school examination system focuses on the memorisation of information. Thirdly, there is high esteem in the Palestinian society for Western scientific knowledge. This might cause the Palestinian teachers to accept both the scientific knowledge and the empiricist beliefs about its nature which come with it in the same package. Finally, mostly male school teachers are usually unchallenged; although the Palestinian society is probably not as patriarchal as some other Eastern societies, knowledge is still legitimised by the status of the person who has that knowledge.[30]

Even seemingly technical subjects—like mathematics—were not exempt from this critique. Fasheh denounced existing education for treating mathematics as a dead subject, divorced from social reality; he wrote, "this reflects the extent to which we have been conditioned to be passive participants in the teaching process."[31]

The third group developing a vision of educational reform consisted of teachers. The reforming teachers echoed rather than repudiated the dim view of existing pedagogy taken by the first two groups. Complaints about the curriculum and the physical resources made available for education were fairly common among teachers. In the 1980s, often during the extended school closures occasioned by the intifada, some groups of teachers began to meet to discuss techniques and pedagogy. Ramallah proved an active area in this regard, and some schools (such as the Friends School) began to earn reputations as institutions friendly to innovation and reform. While much organization concentrated on political issues (and was connected to political parties), some teachers worked to separate their efforts from broader partisan and political attempts to mobilize the population, feeling that this would distract them from issues related to education. In the early 1990s, some groups took the step of formalizing by forming NGOs (see Chapter 5 on this issue more generally). In 1989, the Tamer Institute was founded in Ramallah; in 1991, al-Mawrid Teacher Development Center was established in the same city.[32] The new organizations took on ambitious projects. For instance, al-Mawrid produced a guide for teaching democracy in the classroom not through abstract political instruction but through the case method, focusing on contexts the students could find immediately applicable to their own lives.[33] The organization also produced a series of guides for teaching local history in various West Bank cities, attempting to help educators integrate the students' immediate environment into the curriculum.

The availability of international funding, especially after 1994, led to new organizations being founded (and some members of existing ones splitting off to form their own organizations). In 1995, some of those involved in al-Mawrid formed a new NGO, the Teacher Creativity Center (TCC), that managed to pursue a critique of current practices and build links to external donors and to the Ministry of Education. Its director criticized existing pedagogy in the Arab world as designed only to transmit information from one generation to the next; such an approach was cast as no longer appropriate. Instead, students had to be taught to become critical and active thinkers. The group began to print a magazine on education; sponsored by local businesses, it was distributed to local teachers. A pamphlet entitled "The Importance of Dialogue in the Classroom" was also distributed. The impetus to form a formal organization came in response to an opportunity for modest funding from the Canada Fund.[34] By 1999, the TCC had developed a mission statement:

> The Teacher Creativity Center (TCC) is a non-governmental, nonprofitable organization established in 1995, by a group of motivated teachers working in different schools in Ramallah, Palestine. TCC aims at developing the concepts of civic education, democracy and human rights at the community level through the educational process; at creating a cadre capable of promoting the growth of a progressive generation that contributes and participates effectively in building a democratic Palestinian civil society, as well as developing the teacher's skills and concepts at all levels in private, government and UNRWA schools in Palestine. Through cooperation and coordination with other institutions, NGO's, and individuals involved in fields like education, civics and democracy as well as other relevant issues in human rights, TCC strongly believes that the efforts and energy spent, will ultimately lead to the promotion of teachers and to their acquirement of the necessary tools and skills to improve their quality of teaching. This in turn will produce a cadre of students capable of thinking for themselves, and participating in the responsibility of building a democratic Palestinian civil society.[35]

The organizers of the TCC had a particular (though hardly exclusive) interest in civic education; they encountered early resistance from their colleagues, fellow teachers who claimed that civic education was meaningless in the oppressive Palestinian political environment. Some charged the TCC with importing "American ideas" and accepting existing political realities. Yet the TCC activists insisted that it was not necessary to wait for the resolution of all political issues before change could take place within the class-room. The current director of the TCC states that teachers became far more receptive after the teachers' strike of 1997; "they then realized how important the rule of law is, how important democracy is."[36] Instead of waiting for democracy to come to Palestine, the educational system had to begin on its own to act in a democratic manner. The current system—based on memorization and examination—supported undemocratic politics in the eyes of such reformers. It needed to be replaced by one that encouraged independent thought and free expression; this would help bring more democracy to the country.[37] The TCC's location in Ramallah—where the Ministry of Education and its Curriculum Development Center are also located—allowed it to form a partnership with education authorities. While the ministry was initially guarded, it began to turn to the TCC in managing workshops on human rights and civic education and on drafts of new textbooks.[38]

Al-Mawrid and the TCC did not stand alone in the educational field. A wealthy Palestinian family with a British-based foundation established the al-Qattan Center for Educational Research in Development in Ramallah in 1998. The al-Qattan Center worked to apply current educational research in a Palestinian setting; it also held workshops for teachers and focus group discussions on pedagogical and curricular matters.

Six NGOs active in the educational field (including Tamer, al-Mawrid, and the TCC) formed and began publishing a bimonthly newsletter on educational issues, *Al-multaqa al-tarbawi*, distributed as an insert in the daily *Al-ayyam*.[39] Authors in the newsletter, many of them teachers, contributed articles on topics like role of the teacher, gender in the curriculum, nonviolence, Christian education, summer camps, and education for children with special needs. The tone of the articles varied, but all expressed an enthusiasm for change and innovation. One article in December 1999 on education in the coming millennium went so far as to issue the harsh and sweeping judgment that the twentieth century was "a lost century for Arab education."[40]

The educational NGOs provided an opportunity for the three groups—intellectuals, educational specialists, and teachers—to work together to ensure that the twenty-first century was not also lost. But the reformers' most important opportunity came almost as soon as the PNA assumed responsibility for education. In 1995, at the beginning of the second school year under its auspices, the PNA established a Curriculum Development Center under the leadership of Ibrahim Abu Lughod, a leading advocate of fundamental educational reform; he was joined by his Bir Zayt colleague, 'Ali Jarbawi. They assembled a committee to evaluate the existing curriculum and propose a new one. The committee consisted of not only specialists in education but also intellectuals with an interest in educational issues; the committee also worked to reach out to teachers. About half of the experts consulted had studied in the United States. The resulting report constitutes perhaps the most stinging and detailed indictment of existing education in Arab countries and the most radical reform proposed by an official body since universal education was introduced.

The final report of the Abu Lughod committee took one year to produce.[41] A thick volume (over six hundred pages in length), the report is often unsettling reading. It is merciless in some of its prose; it is also replete with terminology far more common in conversations about education in the United States than in the Arab world. Abu Lughod himself claims credit for introducing the term *empowerment (tamkin)* into Arabic;[42] the report also refers repeatedly to fostering "critical" and "creative" thought while denouncing "memorization" and treatment of students as "empty vessels."

The Abu Lughod report proposed a comprehensive reformulation of the Palestinian educational system, covering every aspect of classroom education. Perhaps the most daring ideas centered on secondary education: the report advocated the complete abolition of the tawjihi examination in order to free teachers and students from the evidence on memorization and standardization. The enforced tracking of secondary students into literary and scientific tracks (based on examination) would be eliminated as well. Instead, students would be free to choose between an academic and technical track (with considerable overlap between the two). Secondary school students would be allowed an increasing amount of choice among courses as they progressed in their studies.

Even in areas where they settled on recommending only mild reform, the committee showed a willingness to rethink established procedures in fundamental ways. For instance, elimination of the summer vacation was seriously considered, though ultimately rejected. The committee did advocate a new school schedule, however. The school day was to begin earlier, and periods were to be shortened for the lower grades (based on the shorter attention span of younger students) and lengthened for the upper ones. Primary schooling was to start one year earlier, at age five. Some subjects were to be introduced earlier (English, as an international language, was to begin at the first grade). The committee even considered some radical reform of religious education—such as greatly reducing it or switching to an emphasis on comparative religion or ethics rather than religious knowledge. Ultimately religion proved to be too controversial a subject for even the daring Abu Lughod committee to resolve within its year of operation; the committee reported the various ideas but did not endorse any. The report did emphasize a more complex national identity than was traditional by including not only specifically Palestinian and broader Arab and Islamic dimensions but also international elements. With a large and diverse diaspora, and with ambitions to participate in global economic and political affairs, Palestinian children were to learn that their identity encompassed a cosmopolitan, global dimension. As if to underscore this international dimension, the committee studied a large variety of other curricula (including some from the United States, Europe, and even Israel).

Yet for all its willingness to rethink all aspects of education, the most radical aspects of the committee's work lay in two other areas. First, it established a far more open and participatory method for designing the curriculum than had existed in the past. The committee jealously guarded its autonomy from the Ministry of Education and other structures of the PNA. In consulting with teachers, for instance, the committee reached directly to teachers themselves rather than going through the ministry or school bureaucracy.[43] The committee conducted comprehensive surveys of teachers and studied the results, citing them in support of its arguments for radical reform. It also scheduled a series of meetings with teachers. 'Ali Jarbawi goes so far as to claim that most of the committee's ideas came from teachers themselves.[44] The committee sought out other audiences—students, recent graduates, and religious figures—to discuss their impressions and present initial ideas. As it began to draw up its proposals, the committee held a series of "town meetings" (Abu Lughod claims to have introduced the concept to Palestinians) in the West Bank and Gaza.[45] The work—and the prospect of a Palestinian-authored curriculum—generated considerable public interest and excitement.

Second, the committee's report focused far more attention on pedagogy than on curricular content. Implicitly the committee argued that the realization of Palestinian aspirations depended far more on how students were taught then what they were taught. In this respect, for instance, the report denounced two aspects of the current curriculum. First, it treated its subjects as discrete, paying little attention to connections among various fields of knowledge. In their proposal, members of the committee focused on the integration of the curriculum. For instance, the proposal at the primary level suggests:

> Teaching these subjects will be organized in an integrated way so that the teacher will connect the subjects studied during the instructional process. For instance, the teacher of the class should connect mathematics during instruction with the other subjects, like science, history, etc. This will help the students achieve an integrated, unified, and

coordinated view toward the curriculum and toward the experiences of life as a whole. Arithmetic skills, for example, will develop as if they are skills connected with the comprehensive ability of the student to use them in all subjects and real-life situations, and not as if they are isolated behaviors used only in mathematics.[46]

A similar sensibility leads to a second major theme in the report: the need to make education practical and connected to Palestinian reality. The existing curriculum is criticized mercilessly as arid, abstract, and impractical. After presenting the results of a survey of social studies teachers, for instance, the report charges that instruction is "without meaning because it appears as if it is separate from the external world and unconnected to reality."[47] To repair this, the very basis of instruction must change: teachers must lecture far less and engage students in exercises and applications far more.

In their emphasis on practicality and integration, the authors of the report present their argument primarily in terms of rendering Palestinian education useful and accessible for the students. When they add broader social usefulness to this concern for the student, their vision presents an even greater challenge to existing education. Two elements of this new pedagogy appear consistently throughout the Abu Lughod report: first, education must be democratic; second it must foster independent, critical thought. The (largely unspoken) purpose of this revolution in pedagogy goes beyond the needs of individual students to the perceived exigencies of a thoroughly democratic society.

The first innovation, a democratic classroom, is based on a conception of democracy (to be examined more fully below) that is related less to majority rule and more to a model of proper social interaction and decision making. For the reformers, a democratic classroom does not mean that students are to elect their teachers or textbooks, but they are to discuss in an atmosphere of freedom and mutual respect. Teachers should transform themselves from classroom authorities to guides who help students teach themselves and each other. They are encouraged to use a variety of instructional techniques (group projects, experimentation, case studies, field trips) that encourage interaction among the students and between the students and the teacher. Teachers are also enjoined to arrange their classrooms to foster the same kind of interaction.[48] Such an atmosphere is to prevail in all areas of the curriculum—even, for instance, in science and language instruction.

The second of these pedagogical innovations—the emphasis on critical thought—grows similarly out of a harsh view of the current instructional approach in which "the teacher views the learning student as a 'container to be filled.'"[49] The existing curriculum places the teacher at the center of the educational process; its philosophy "relies on the storage of information." This fails to lead to the development of "creative, critical thought"; indeed, the goal of the current curriculum is "not to change but to imitate."[50] In opposition to this "traditional" curriculum, the report focuses its proposed methods "on considering the student the center of the instructional process and on creating students who are lifelong learners."[51] The new curriculum is to

> make manifest *that truth is not absolute or final and that definitive canons do not exist.* Learning cannot take place by giving the students *information* as if it is a collection of *facts* that must be memorized. The curriculum must develop the critical, analytical sense among the students by concentrating on following the scientific method, which focuses fundamentally on *the importance of verification by the accuracy of information and the credibility of sources.* Free, open, unshackled inquiry must take the place of receipt of what the curriculum sets out and arranges. The curriculum must therefore encourage the process of understanding instead of *the development of the ability to memorize . . . .* What is important is not obtaining information but how to use it.
>
> The curriculum must focus as well as *developing independence of thought among the students.* This is what makes the individual able to interact with his environment and surroundings. The individual is the basis of society, and the independence of the individual is the basis of the existence of a vital, active society. (emphasis in original)[52]

This is the essence of the new curriculum—the shift from teacher's authority to student's individuality, from absolute to relative truth, from receiving knowledge to discovering it, from uniformity to pluralism, from constituting a dutiful member of society to fostering an active and freethinking citizen.

Oddly, it is precisely the boldness of this approach that leads to the reticence of the report on the two most controversial subjects the committee had to consider: religion and the history and geography of Palestine. On both subjects, consistency in demanding critical thought and democracy in the classroom would have endangered the proposed reform.

With regard to religion, an emphasis on democratic interaction and critical thought led some committee members in directions that others did not wish to follow. Certainly, changing the emphasis on teaching religious texts as divine revelation would have provoked strong opposition. And the Ministry of Education made clear that it would not be receptive to such a recommendation, fearful of the public response.[53] One ministry official explained: "Of course, there was no question that the curriculum had to include religion. This is wanted by all Palestinians—Muslims and Christians."[54] Thus, for the committee to pursue a change in religious education would have divided the members, embroiled it in a more controversy than it wished to stir up, and ultimately failed. Yet the secularist bias of the committee came through in a subtle manner: the report called for separating religion from history and civics and criticized the overlap between the subjects in the existing curriculum. This approach stood at odds with the same committee's constant call for integration among all other parts of the curriculum.

Palestinian history and geography proved a difficult subject for the same reason. Both Abu Lughod and Jarbawi recalled that they were asked time and again how they were to approach issues such as borders, the Arab-Israeli conflict, the refugee issue, and so on.[55] Once again, they largely avoided such topics; Jarbawi explained that they were concerned that any extended treatment would quickly become the object of debate, obstructing a broader consideration of their proposal.[56] And as with religion, their brief consideration of such issues seemed to be at odds with their general approach. The emphasis on critical thought, free discussion, and the absence of fixed truths gave way to a recommendation that the curriculum simply stick to the facts. The report acknowledges the importance and sensitivity of the issue that it summarizes in the form of the question "What Palestine do we teach?":

> Is it the historical Palestine with all its total geography or the Palestine which is a product of the signed political agreements with Israel? And how should Israel be dealt with? Is it merely a neighbor or a state that is founded on the destruction of most of Palestine?
>
> *This might be the most difficult question but the answer need not be so difficult. The new curriculum must be a Palestinian creation. It must acknowledge the realities of the situation without falsifying historical truths and their repercussions in various dimensions in the context of social science instruction.* (emphasis in original)[57]

This vague emphasis on "realities" left little to contest—or to guide a textbook writer. In a public discussion in 1996, Abu Lughod similarly made the issue of teaching Palestine deceptively simple: "Our approach must be to tell the truth. Everything else follows." Yet in the same meeting, he later added an observation more in keeping with the general ethos of the report—though without abandoning the emphasis on "the facts":

> [T]he history of the Arabs has not really been written. There is no Palestinian history. This is the job of Palestinian academic institutions. Having one book is not enough. We don't want one interpretation—let us rather get the facts at least. Once students are armed with the basic facts, our teaching of how to think will take over.[58]

The unspoken argument is that Palestinians must write their own history but that they cannot until they are willing to do so in the same spirit of open debate and critical inquiry that will guide the curriculum as a whole. That time may not have come. In 2001, Fouad Moughrabi, a colleague of Ibrahim Abu Lughod, was still making the same argument, this time more explicitly by calling for a "revisionist" Palestinian history, mindful that this might disturb accepted nationalist truths:

> Palestinian scholars and historians need to engage in critical self-reflection and historical revisionism so as to produce a more accurate history of their society using rigorous standards of historical research based on available archive material and oral history. By its nature, a revisionist Palestinian history is bound to be oppositional and critical, but the facts as ascertained by objective scholars, including Israeli ones, bear out the Palestinian narrative in its broad lines, so there is no reason not to proceed. Palestinian history as written for school children should not be apologetic, not should it try to accommodate whatever scripts others may wish to impose for political reasons.[59]

Because the effort to write Palestinian history is embryonic at best, and because it would be too controversial to allow students such total freedom in debating such sensitive national issues, the authors of the Abu Lughod report fall back on the "realities" and "facts" that they tried to evict from other parts of the curriculum—hoping that a generation of students trained to engage in critical inquiry rather than uncritical absorption will allow a future reform based not simply on dry presentation of the facts but also on attempts to foster democratic and critical debate.

The irony is that the advocates of democracy in education lost their boldness not so much in the face of such difficult topics as because of fear of public opinion. Religions and nationalist truths were too sensitive to treat in the same critical spirit as pedagogy, classroom leaning, or mathematics education. Those who wished to build a democratic educational system were willing to take up God and Palestine, but they were unwilling to take on the people. Ultimately a very different conception of democracy determined the fate of the radical reform the committee proposed.

AN UNEASY COMPROMISE: WRITING THE FIRST PALESTINIAN NATIONAL CURRICULUM

In 1996, the Abu Lughod committee finished its work, published its report, and returned the matter of curriculum development to the Ministry of Education. Ministry officials immediately saw some causes for concern.

Some were offended by the brashness of the report's tone; others wondered about some of the curricular changes recommended.[60] Yet most of the concerns raised were far more practical: How would the new schedule be implemented without causing chaos? Who would pay for the new textbooks and teacher training? How was the ministry to effect curriculum reform? It was clear to some in the ministry that changes would have to be made before the report could be adopted. The suggested schedule—which varied by grade level—would cause scheduling nightmares because school buildings (and sometimes teachers) were often shared among different levels.[61] Was it really possible to lower the age for entering school to five, and if so, how could the transition be managed? The new textbooks would have to be introduced gradually—while some foreign assistance might be available for the project, most donors preferred to stay away from such a politically sensitive area.

The Ministry of Education decided to formulate its own proposal based on the Abu Lughod committee's work. Unlike the committee, however, the ministry focused not on pedagogy but on practical administrative matters.[62] The ministry adopted many of the suggestions of the Abu Lughod committee—such as the abolition of literary/scientific tracking in secondary school and the introduction of self-selected academic/technical tracks; the introduction of English-language education in the first grade; and the introduction of civic education—while balking at others, such as the abolition of the tawjihi. Outside a few subjects, the Abu Lughod committee had recommended only some minor changes in the time devoted to various subjects; these minor changes were generally incorporated into the Ministry of Education plan. In the eyes of ministry officials, they were transforming the aspirations of the Abu Lughod committee into reality; in the eyes of some educators the ministry was robbing the report of its much of its spirit and focusing only on bureaucratic aspects.[63] And supporters of reform worried that the ministry was using lack of funds as a pretext to ignore parts of the report, even those that would cost little money.

The Ministry of Education finished its plan in 1997. Anxious to imbue it with full political legitimacy, the ministry submitted the plan to the cabinet, which approved it in December of that year. The plan then went to the PLC, which approved it in March 1998. In short, the adoption followed a procedure similar to that for passing a new law. While there was great interest in the idea of a Palestinian-authored curriculum, there was surprisingly little interest in the details. PLC members did show concern but focused almost all their attention on the sensitive nationalist issues. On most other matters (such as religion and budgetary exigencies), they supported the ministry with little discussion. There was greater unease on matters like the geography and history of Palestine, on which the ministry's plan gave little guidance.[64] In the end, the PLC approved the Ministry of Education's plan but underlined the need to work to make sure that sufficient funds were made available and that teachers were appropriately trained. A small number of minor changes were introduced, most with directly political implications (for instance, the phrase describing Palestine as a "peace-loving state" was changed to "a state loving a just peace").[65]

Following that approval, public discussion concerning the curriculum all but disappeared. When the issue has arisen on some rare occasions, the patterns have been similar: nationalist concerns about content are voiced, but the efforts of the Ministry of Education are not questioned. For instance, in December 1999, the PLC Committee on Education and Social Affairs discussed the curriculum in a periodic report; it did little but laud the efforts of the ministry for following the most appropriate and modern methods of curricular development.[66] When the committee's report was presented to the PLC as a whole, some members raised national concerns. One deputy sarcastically remarked (probably on the basis of the *Al-tarbiyya al-wataniyya* series) that "our coast extends from Bayt Hanun to Rafah" (i.e., from the northern to the southern end of the Gaza Strip) and insisted that on border issues and history, the curriculum should not be dictated by Israel. Marwan Kanafani, a deputy heading the Palestinian delegation to a joint committee on incitement established under the Wye Accords, assured his fellow members that Israel had nothing to do with the curriculum and that the joint committee had not even addressed the issue.[67] In short, the message from the PLC to the Ministry of Education was clear: the ministry was free to develop the curriculum as it saw fit. Coverage of Palestinian geography and borders might be reviewed carefully; on all other matters, the ministry had a free hand.

The ministry's first step to move beyond the Abu Lughod report and implement a new curriculum was to constitute a curriculum development team. A permanent Curriculum Development Center (CDC), operating directly under the Ministry of Education, replaced the autonomous (and explicitly temporary) Abu Lughod committee. Curriculum teams were composed to write the various textbooks; the teams were headed by specialists and worked out of the public eye (and largely in isolation from each other, contrary to the emphasis of the Abu Lughod committee on integrating different parts of the curriculum).[68] The teams were to produce a complete set of textbooks for the first and sixth grades to be introduced in September 2000. The following year, the second and seventh grades were to have their new textbooks; the process would continue adding two grades each year until the entire school system switched to the new books. CDC officials felt this schedule was ambitious but feasible. In fact, the effort to write new textbooks was one of the few PNA projects to run precisely on schedule.

Two features of the CDC distinguished it from the process followed (and favored) by the Abu Lughod committee. First, the new CDC consisted of specialists in education and administrators rather than Abu Lughod's broader team of intellectuals and educators; its task was seen as less aspirational and visionary, more administrative and practical and attentive to immediate constraints.[69] Second, the CDC has been far more cautious about wider involvement in the curriculum-writing effort. The current effort is taking place without town meetings and public forums; CDC officials have limited themselves to periodic statements that they are maintaining the original schedule. When the first drafts of the first- and sixth-grade textbooks were finished in December 1999, the CDC refused to allow them to be examined outside the Ministry of Education.[70] In February 2000, the CDC did present the civic education books in a workshop for teachers organized by the Teacher Creativity Center.[71] And outside consultants were brought in, though they did not discuss their work publicly. In the late spring and summer of 2000, as the CDC finalized the first- and sixth-grade textbooks, it held unpublicized workshops with educators but would not allow the drafts to be circulated widely. Its critics feel that the CDC has departed from the injunction of the Abu Lughod committee that "curriculum writers must approach the project as a partnership activity, realizing that they have as much to learn as they do to impart."[72]

To be sure, the ministry's plan mentioned some of the key themes of the Abu Lughod report, such as fostering critical thinking. And Ministry of Education officials do not hesitate to speak of cultivating a respect for democracy and human rights.[73] Other influences are subtler. For instance, the ministry has decided to retitle educational inspectors *(mufattishin*—a position bequeathed by the mandate to both the Israeli and Palestinian school system designed to ensure that schools followed official policies) as supervisors *(mushrifin)*, announcing that they are now no longer to search for violations as much as assist and train.[74]

Inspectors may have been replaced by supervisors, but other hallmarks of centralization continue: the call to abandon the tawjihi was scuttled—not because the examination had defenders but because it was still regarded as a critical tool to maintain uniformity in instruction and curriculum. There is still a single approved textbook, published by the ministry, for every subject in every grade. Indeed, in one respect the degree of centralization is increasing: in the past, Christian students in predominantly Muslim schools were simply excused from religious education; Christian private schools were free to devise their own religious instruction. Now the CDC has convened representatives of the various Christian denominations to write a single textbook series in Christian religion for all Christian students in Palestinian schools.[75] And the Palestinian Ministry of Education still stresses quantity over quality. Indeed, the mission of the ministry seems to augment this aspect of the Palestinian educational system, despite its already heavy burdens. The ministry's plan explicitly sets out as objectives expanding secondary education to include 70 percent of the population and eradicating illiteracy.[76]

Such goals do not prevent the adoption of many elements of the Abu Lughod committee's proposals, but they have led many to greet the report with skepticism. It is true that the progressive educational vision has been influential in many private Palestinian schools (especially those in the more cosmopolitan areas of Jerusalem and Ramallah). Yet in classrooms with forty students or more, in which many teachers feel that most of their time and energy is spent in quieting students and keeping order, the progressive vision seems like a luxury.[77]

Still, the curriculum and textbooks produced by the CDC, beginning with the first and sixth grades in September 2000, showed some unmistakable influence of the progressives. New subjects (such as civic education) were introduced. New exercises and assignments were added that conformed to the pedagogical vision of the groups pressing for innovation and reform. Much of the curriculum showed the signs of unresolved debates or uneasy compromises. For instance, some Palestinian educators had criticized older educational material for reinforcing traditional gender roles. Others insisted that proper Islamic behavior—deemed to include modesty in dress—be inculcated in students. While the two viewpoints were not mutually contradictory, their proponents often regarded each other as adversaries. The outcome in the textbooks was an uneasy compromise with something for everyone. A striking number of Palestinian males were shown preparing food and working in the kitchen. The texts explicitly endorsed women's sporting activity on Islamic grounds (provided they are properly clothed and men are not spectators). Women covered (generally with the *hijab,* in which the face is visible but not hair) coexisted happily in illustrations with those unveiled. In illustrations of religious life, however, even young girls and women at home wore the hijab. And a husband instructed not only his children but also his wife on the duty of prayer.[78]

THE NEW TEXTS: DIVERGENT PEDAGOGIES
IN THE UNPROBLEMATIC STATE OF PALESTINE

The new texts showed signs of contest and controversy.[79] They did this sometimes through using diverse, sometimes almost contradictory, approaches. Arabic language books struck the most strident nationalist tones; civic education books proclaimed liberal values. At other points they betrayed conflict through the topics they avoided. In general, some of the approaches stressed by the progressives coexisted with a far more traditional approach. But in matters characterized by political controversy, the texts sidestepped most controversial issues, portraying Palestine as an un problematic state with a difficult history but a normal present. In some ways, the new texts simply followed the path of the interim 1994 *Al-tarbiyya al-wataniyya* series (the temporary supplementary books introduced to grades 1 through 6 while the new comprehensive national curriculum was prepared). Those interim books had embodied much of what the progressives criticized. Yet the new books showed many of the same features, allowing the reformers some influence but hardly victory.

Transmission of Authority versus Cultivation
of Independent Thought

The *Al-tarbiyya al-wataniyya* books had embodied the feature of modern Arab education that most offended the progressives—the focus on inter-generational transmission of values and authority. The texts not only taught a sense of respect for older generations (though they certainly did so, by examples in the lower grades and by explicit instruction in the upper grades). They went beyond this to create a seamless web of authoritative structures: students were taught to locate themselves with regard to God, nation, family, state, school, and other social institutions (such as sports clubs). Texts sometimes elided effortlessly among these: parental authority affirmed and was based on religious truth; good family life was necessary to cultivate wider social virtues.

The Abu Lughod committee sought radical change in this regard, insisting that students be encouraged to think independently and critically. The curriculum plan introduced by the Ministry of Education defended the older approach, while nodding in the progressives' direction:

> Bringing tradition into life does not mean using it as seclusion or a
> shelter; on the contrary, it means providing the young people with
> principles of understanding their own limits and to what extent they
> can participate in international culture. The role of the curriculum is

deepened to include full and better understanding of tradition and produce a creative thinking ability to preserve and develop it, too.[80]

For the ministry, then, critical thought and individuality had their place, but
the underlying purpose of the curriculum was to transmit and preserve values rather than evaluate or change them. Additionally, the vision pursued
by the CDC and the Ministry of Education restored the centrality of religion in the curriculum. The officially sanctioned plan eschewed the various
reforms reviewed (but not endorsed) by the Abu Lughod committee in favor
of a more conservative approach in which the "intellectual basis" of the
entire curriculum was said to be faith in God.[81] Whereas the Abu Lughod
committee presented Palestinian identity as consisting of three elements
(international, Arab-Islamic, and specifically Palestinian), the Ministry of
Education plan paid far less attention to the international dimension and
designated the Islamic dimension as distinct (rather than combined with the
Arab).[82]

The newer texts issued beginning in 2000 reflected this insistence on
transmission of authority with the acknowledgment of a need to allow independent thinking. In general, the substance of the material stressed the first
dimension (though with decreased enthusiasm compared to the 1994 *Al-
tarbiyya al-wataniyya* series), while the pedagogy encouraged by the new
books made notable forays on the second dimension.

With regard to content, the books reiterated the message of obedience to
parents, connecting it with national and political loyalties. First-grade students were taught in *Islamic Education:*

> I love my mother who bore me, and I obey her.
>
> I love my mother who nursed me, and I obey her.
>
> I love my mother who teaches me, and I obey her.
>
> I love my father who provides for me, and I obey him.
>
> I love my father who teaches me, and I obey him.
>
> I love my mother and my father, and I obey them.[83]

Duty to God and to parents were specifically linked.[84] Sixth graders were
taught that a "society free from crime" depends on family, school, and other
institutions.[85] The books revealed a clear mission of instilling loyalty to
God, homeland, school, and family. Moral lessons intruded on virtually
every subject, sometimes supported by a Qur'anic verse. First graders studying Arabic language were taught a story of an honest boy who returned
some money dropped by a vendor at school; the story was followed with a

Qur'anic verse to memorize and further lessons on the value of cleanliness.[86] Sixth-grade Arabic education began by warning students that the best gift bestowed by God is the mind, but that if it was not used, one would turn toward evil and destruction.[87] A sixth-grade science book used verses from the Qur'an to buttress its teachings on human races and natural forces (such as wind); it adduced a scientific justification for neat and proper behavior (such as sitting up straight).[88] Religion, school, science, and parents all stood in positions of overlapping authority. Even hygiene was linked to religious and family duties.

This message of integrated structures of authority and tradition was only slightly qualified. Occasionally the texts addressed the tension between "imitation" and "creativity" directly: sixth graders were taught as part of their "national education" that imitating a teacher is good but that imitating youth in things "not appropriate for our genuine Arab culture and our traditions and customs" could be bad. Creativity was good when it leads to innovation and progress.[89]

Yet the books made concessions to a far more active pedagogy that qualified much of the stress on authority. Most often, the new attitude was expressed indirectly: the texts made a tremendous effort to engage the student actively and consider practical applications and further thought. The authors of the books peppered their lessons with outside activities, essays, questions for reflection and study, and encouragement of critical thinking. Most lessons began by explaining their purpose to the student in direct language and end with a series of activities. Seventh-grade students, for instance, were told to bring in a newspaper story that had a point of view different from their own; it was also suggested that they bring two articles on the same subject from different newspapers to compare them.[90]

The books made strong efforts to link to local and concrete applications and examples or make the information more accessible. To make the lesson on the prophet Muhammad's life more active, for instance, students were asked to fill in a modern-day identity card for him.[91] In mathematics, students were asked how long it should take to make the 180 kilometer trip from Nablus to Hebron in an automobile averaging 45 kilometers per hour.[92] Most lessons in all subjects started with the local and the familiar and built outwards. First-grade national education, for instance, progressed in the following order: family and house, I and my school, the neighborhood, my town, my homeland. Seventh graders started studying civil society by examining local organizations; they began studying democracy in a family setting (in which women had a voice and differences were settled by dialogue). Far more daringly, the books even pushed the students to engage in critical thought when dealing with difficult and sensitive topics. Sixth-grade students were asked to evaluate the policies used by Mu'awiyya (the fifth caliph and founder of the Umayyad dynasty) in solidifying his authority and building his state; they were then asked to consider the hereditary method for selecting rulers—an assignment that was likely to lead some to question early Muslim and current Arab political practice in some countries.[93] And sixth graders were also asked to confront the situation in which parents instruct their children to do something wrong. (The problem was addressed in a book by Salih, a righteous Muslim who instructed his family on religious matters each day after evening prayers. He explained that children were required to obey their parents except in such circumstances.) This lesson was followed by a discussion of the rights of children in Islam and an invitation for students to give their opinions on some difficult situations (in which a father forbade his son to continue his studies or his daughter to play sports because she was a girl).[94]

The concessions to the progressives were real. Science books claimed to take a constructivist approach, for instance, implicitly undermining the idea that science was a set of discovered truths to be taught. NGOs were lauded for their contribution to Palestinian society—and seventh graders were even told of human rights organizations without mention of the PNA's strained relations with them.[95] The books imparted different messages on gender, many clearly inspired by the progressive desire to question traditional roles. Most of all, the stress on critical thinking and classroom interaction motivated many of the suggested activities. Yet despite the attempt to build a more interactive pedagogy, ultimately the new set of texts did not meet the central mission of the progressive educational vision: the books were still generally based on the idea that they imparted knowledge from a position of authority; they might encourage more active learning, but their encouragement of critical, creative, and independent thought was limited.

National Identity

The earlier *Al-tarbiyya al-wataniyya* series focused exclusively on "national education" by teaching students that the role of the individual citizen was to identify with and contribute to Palestinian society. Indeed, the fifth-grade student was told, upon opening the book, that this was the essential purpose of national education: "Dear male/female student; the chief goal of learning *al-tarbiyya al-wataniyya* is to work to prepare and raise an upright citizen and to strengthen his sense of belonging to his *umma* and his homeland."[96]

The new books actually increased the emphasis on nationalism. Given the opportunity to write a comprehensive curriculum for the first time, the Palestinian educators writing the new books inserted nationalist symbols in every conceivable location and illustration. Every school flew a Palestinian flag, homes had pictures of the Dome of the Rock, classrooms exhibited nationalist slogans on their blackboards, computers displayed Palestinian flags, a school bus carried the name "Palestine School," Jerusalem was mentioned in any possible context, and even children playing soccer wore the jerseys of the Palestinian national team. A grammatical point was illustrated with a quotation from the 1988 declaration of independence. The texts did not merely deliver the message subliminally: they asked children to color the flag, describe their duties toward Jerusalem, and repeat, "I am from Palestine" and "My nationality is Palestinian." In learning calligraphy, second-grade students copied "Jerusalem is in the heart of every Arab."[97] Seventh-grade students graduated to "Beloved Palestine, how can I live far from your peaks and valleys?"[98] The students read nationalist writings when studying Arabic and counted Palestinian flags while studying arithmetic. And students did not merely study English; they learned it from books entitled *English for Palestine*.

The 2000 textbooks propounded a seamless sense of national identity. Religious, territorial, family, and Arab identities were not merely complementary; they were often coterminous to the point that they might be confused. And they were timeless. Palestine was, according to a second-grade text, the "land of fathers and grandfathers." Its first inhabitants were the "Arab Canaanites," who "built a number of cities, including the city of Jerusalem, which they named Yabus."[99] The Arab and Palestinian nations were eternal entities, stretching back to the beginning of history. And the timelessness was not merely ethnic but also territorial: a sixth-grade unit on "The Arabs before Islam" included a map of the Arab world that followed the current borders of Syria and Iraq even while the lessons spoke of Nabatean and other ancient civilizations.[100] Pre-Islamic civilizations in these areas were treated as Arab; students learned that Mesopotamian, Sumerian, Akkadian, Babylonian, Amorite, Assyrian, Chaldean, and Canaanite art were Arab. Seventh graders were told of a Canaanite myth of a bird who flew away from its homeland looking for food but so missed its homeland that it endeavored to return. (Lest the symbolism be too subtle for the students, the book posed the question of whether the story could be applied to those in the Palestinian diaspora.)[101] Ancient Israel was mentioned but not integrated into history in any systematic way; the authors did not seem to know how to explain the ancient presence of Jews in the country.

The timelessness took on unintended ironies when Jerusalem was dealt with. These textbooks, of course, did not originate an anachronistic and often exclusivist nationalism in dealing with Jerusalem; it had been a very strong element in constant references by Israeli politicians since 1967 to Jerusalem as Israel's "eternal and undivided capital." In the Palestinian case, the art text lauded Nebuchadnezzar for ending "the Hebrew occupation of Urusalim."[102] A unit on Jerusalem described it as an Arab city since its founding by the "Arab Canaanites" and claimed that Ibrahim (Abraham) paid the *jizya* (a tax paid by non-Muslims under Muslim rule) to the local king. This text unwittingly undermined its own message, however: descriptions of the walls of Jerusalem used feet and miles, units rarely employed by Palestinians, thus suggesting that the authors relied fairly mechanically on English-language texts in their effort to affirm Jerusalem's Arab nature.[103] And in a more subtle way the text undermined its own message: no part of Jewish West Jerusalem was mentioned, indicating that the textbook authors acknowledged that the Palestinian nature of the city was neither total nor timeless.

The eternal nature of the Arab nation and homeland was presented as harmonious with the Arab identity as Muslim: indeed, national and religious identities were sometimes hard to separate in the texts. This elision from national to state to religious identity sometimes took the form of direct instruction: sixth graders were taught that Islam made defense of the homeland a religious duty and were introduced to a series of concentric circles (family, town, province, state, Islamic world). The same lesson explicitly inculcated that Palestinian, Arab, and Muslim identities were simultaneous and reinforced each other.[104] That message was delivered in less direct ways. "Arab and Islamic history" formed a single topic. The introduction to the sixth-grade text explained: "[I]f the Arabs before Islam were dispersed groups that were not disciplined by any system, they were able to arise by way of the Islamic order, and the Muslim Arabs became leaders in science, culture, and morals."[105] As part of their national education, sixth graders were taught that Islam and the Arabic language unified the Arab homeland (even including Christians who lived together with Muslims under the banner of Islam).[106]

The 2000 textbooks did introduce a new theme into the propagation of national identity: unity, especially among Muslims and Christians. Indeed, the importance of tolerance and unity were stressed almost too insistently: one might suspect that sectarian tensions ran quite strong. Tolerance was described not simply as necessary for national unity but as a religious injunction for both Muslims and Christians, with the practice of the seventh-century Muslim conquerors of Jerusalem held up as a model and precedent.[107] And it was not simply sectarian divisions that worried the

authors: for all the stress on family, students were also instructed that trib-
alism and "familism" were undesirable and un-Islamic.[108]

The Unproblematic State of Palestine

Palestinian identity, sovereignty, borders, and national symbols have not
merely been contested; they have been connected to violent international
conflict. This makes their treatment especially sensitive and difficult for
textbook writers. Remarkably, the 1994 interim *Al-tarbiyya al-wataniyya*
books presented Palestine to the students as neither problematic nor contested in any way. It had all the accoutrements that one would expect a state
to have: citizens, a flag, a declaration of independence, borders, a capital, and
a clear political structure. Indeed, with the well-integrated sense of national
identity characteristic of the series, the existence of these features was presented in the same simple, accessible, and reportorial style in which the
crops of the country or the life of the prophet Muhammad were presented.
The watchwords of the Palestinian national movement—struggle, revolution, and liberation—barely appeared in the texts. Rather, the state of
Palestine appeared as a natural entity, completely unproblematic in all its
aspects. A politically seasoned reader might view the Palestine presented as
the one that Palestinians wish existed. This is accurate but does not go far
enough: the Palestine presented was not merely a wish but also a matter of
national consensus. The *Al-tarbiyya al-wataniyya* series hewed very
closely to aspirations that would unite most Palestinians.

In this regard, the Palestine presented in the newer texts beginning in
2000 was as unproblematic a state as the Palestine of the 1994 books. In
some ways it was even more complete. It continued to have a flag, a system
of national government, local government, and other symbols and accoutrements of statehood. Indeed, some of these could now be described in
more detail: the establishment of the government of the PNA, the election
of the PLC, the resumption of Palestinian control over courts allowed the
texts (especially sixth-grade *National Education*) to describe the state of
Palestine with some accuracy and depth.

The textbooks remained aspirational, and not just in politics. Palestine
was a country with wide and clean streets, spacious houses equipped with
computers and satellite dishes, loving and smiling parents, and loyal, happy,
and polite children. Traffic was orderly and pedestrians crossed only in
crosswalks. On occasion, alternatives were presented but generally as examples of inappropriate or immoral behavior rather than harsh reality.

There were still unacknowledged gaps and silences. Local government
was described as elected; no explanation was given for the fact that no elec-

tions had taken place when the texts were written. Sometimes passing over limitations in silence required artful devices: sixth graders were taught about circles with an illustration of coins. Because the PNA had not yet issued currency, coins from the British mandate era (with "Palestine" written on them in both Hebrew and Arabic) were used.[109] Perhaps the bitterness of the second intifada led to a retreat from this generosity in the 2001 textbooks: this time a mandate-era stamp was illustrated, bearing the word *Palestine* in both English and Arabic, but the Hebrew was erased.[110]

Occasionally the dodges were less artful. A state was defined as "a group of individuals who live in a defined geographic place and submit to a specific political authority." The declaration of Palestinian statehood of 1988 was then discussed, with no mention of the fact that all aspects of statehood for the Palestinians remained contested.[111] The constitution of Palestine presented a particular problem. At the time the books began coming out, the PNA had no constitution. Although the PLC had passed a Basic Law, it did not go into effect until July 2002 (see Chapter 3). The authors of the 2000 book did quote from the draft Basic Law, but they could not pretend that it was operative when they wrote. Yet they still asked the student to find clauses from the "constitution of the State of Palestine," a nonexistent document, to write in their notebooks.[112] By the time the 2001 books were written, the authors of the civic education book decided to turn to the draft constitution for the Palestinian state presented by a PLO committee.[113] The books showed children decorating a neighborhood to prepare for "Independence Day," an occasion yet to be celebrated.[114] First graders were told a cartoon story in which a teacher led a group of schoolchildren from Gaza on board a bus to take a tour of Jerusalem—a trip impossible for Gazan schoolchildren since before the first students to use these books were born.[115] Closures, checkpoints, and identity cards disappeared in a Palestine without impediments or conflict.

Indeed, the symbols of Palestinian nationality and the icons of nationalism were normal and largely peaceful. The slogans and symbols that dominated Palestinian national expression for a generation—return, armed struggle, revolution, the *fida'i*—still barely appeared. It must be noted in passing (see this chapter's appendix for more detail) that those who charge that these textbooks incited hatred of Israel miss this point. By ignoring the problematic aspects of Palestinian national and political life, the books largely avoided mention even of those issues that anger most Palestinians in the post-Oslo period (such as home demolitions, continued detention of prisoners, and settlement expansion). Palestine expressed itself in flags, institutions, and unity. Its heroes were more likely to be literary than political or military. Its history was alluded to in passing but not explored in depth. There were, however, as will be seen soon, some very jarring exceptions in which a far more conflictual and cruel reality intruded on the texts.

Avoidance of Controversy and the Limitations on Unproblematic Palestine

The authors of the 1994 *Al-tarbiyya al-wataniyya* series had presented only the national consensus or those issues on which the Palestinian leadership had staked an unambiguous position. Matters that remained unresolved or that deeply divided Palestinians and could not easily be addressed were thus largely ignored in what might be best characterized as an embarrassed silence. The failure to treat such pressing subjects, then, stemmed neither from political hostility to Israel nor from renunciation of nationalist Palestinian claims but from the desire not to move beyond a clear national consensus or the explicit policy of the leadership. Such an attitude meant that there was no guidance on how to teach Israel, Zionism, or the borders of Palestine. At some points, the texts seemed based on recognition of the fluidity and uncertainty of the present. Sixth graders were not presented with a map of Palestine; instead, a box was left blank with the instructions: "In the neighboring rectangle, sketch a map of Palestine" and its administrative divisions.[116] Leaving critical national issues (including maps) to the discretion of the individual teachers and students was not a product of a sudden burst of decentralization; instead, it was recognition that the national consensus or leadership decisions might overtake any written text. In short, it was timidity rather than uncompromising nationalism that explained the silence.

The 2000 textbooks resembled the 1994 *Al-tarbiyya al-wataniyya* series in their efforts to steer away from sensitive or difficult topics. In explaining the concept of species, one of the new books explained that animals that are not alike cannot "marry" and have children—a rather Victorian presentation. Discussions of sensitive political topics often showed a similar reticence. This was most marked in the matter of the borders and geographical nature of the state of Palestine. The newer books broke some of the silence of the 1994 series and avoided devices like having the students draw their own maps. But they were no more clear.

This was probably most noticeable in the case of maps. If there is any issue that has attracted more international attention, it is the presence of maps in Palestinian textbooks that do not indicate the existence of Israel. But the maps omitted much more than Israel; they also omitted the borders of the Palestinian state. The books included many maps; all presented the ambiguity of the borders of Palestine without addressing the subject directly in the text. Absent any authoritative borders, the books dodged the issue: maps of the entire area of mandate-era Palestine (including Israel) were sometimes historical or topographical so that the drawing of current political boundaries could be avoided. Israel was thus not indicated, but often neither were Jordan, Syria, Lebanon, or Egypt. Other maps clearly did mark off the area as distinct but also marked off the West Bank and Gaza with different colors or dotted lines—without explaining what such indications signified. Sometimes Palestine's provinces were drawn (including only the West Bank and Gaza). On one occasion, Palestinian telephone area codes were indicated on a map that covered only the West Bank and Gaza—no mention was made that these area codes straddled the 1967 borders and were thus shared with Israel. Maps of cities indicated the existence of those within the 1967 borders of Israel with a significant Palestinian population before and after 1948 (Jaffa, Nazareth, Beersheva, Akka, and Haifa), but the significance of these cities was not explained: Were they included because they were the birthplace of many schoolchildren's grandparents or because they still contained Palestinians? No explanation was ever given. And the texts did not help. These cities were mentioned as Palestinian but often in connection with the past (a large picture of Jaffa accompanied a unit devoted to an author from the city of Jaffa who wrote of his leaving the city in 1948; in the background of the picture most of Tel Aviv loomed unexplained in the background). Perhaps the most puzzling map was one of the province of Jenin.[117] It would be difficult to find an area more devoid of Israeli settlements, but there is one, and it was omitted from the map. The area was largely surrounded by the 1967 border of Israel, but neither a border nor anything on the far side of the border was indicated—pre-1967 Israel was simply terra incognita. The books bore the marks of unresolved controversies both among Palestinians and with the neighbors of the emerging Palestinian state.

The same marks of controversy emerged more strongly in the books on Islamic education. The authors relied heavily on the life of the prophet and the history of the early Muslims to explain Islamic history, doctrine, and creed. And that led them to include the relations of the Jews of Medina with the prophet and the early Muslims. The 2000 texts were less timid than their 1994 predecessors in this regard, but they were no less ambiguous. The conflicts between the early Muslims and the Jews were mentioned, and the Jews were held responsible. But the implications for contemporary Palestinian-Israeli relations were less clear: students were instructed that Jews broke early agreements with Muslims but that Muslims were bound to keep agreements as long as the other side observed them as well. The analogy between Islam in the seventh century and the current conflict was made more directly at one point: students were instructed to mention incidents of violence that "our people" had been exposed to from enemies and then were asked how the enemies and occupiers had dealt with the inhabitants of occupied countries. Following this, they were asked how Muslims had dealt with those countries that they won control of—implicitly condemning Israeli and European imperial practices but still holding up tolerance and coexistence as an Islamic norm. The authors of the books on Islamic education were far less reticent than their colleagues writing on history, national education, civic education, and geography to address sensitive issues, but they still seemed to find ambiguity useful.

Yet occasionally more discordant voices broke through. By far the most disconcerting elements in the books appeared when the authors of the Arabic language texts insisted on portraying the tragic realities of Palestinian life. These were not reserved for sixth graders: first-grade children were exposed to some harsh stories. Not all of these were political: in one, a boy was hit by the car and returned to school in a wheelchair (resolving to be more careful crossing the street). In another, a man fell ill and was unable to pay the hospital bill. The story had a happy conclusion only in that he avoided being forced to sell his land when his wife sold all her gold. Other stories and illustrations were more political. In one picture, an Israeli settlement (easily identifiable with its red roofs, fence, and Israeli flag) sat perched on a hilltop overlooking a Palestinian village: no conflict was implied and no explanation was given. In another, a tree was uprooted by a green-colored vehicle (presumably, but not explicitly, belonging to the Israeli army). In a short cartoon story full of despair, a mother in a camp was shown losing all hope when the rain came through her roof. In the story, her neighbors heard the cry of the children and took them away, as the mother expressed the wish that it would have been better to die than to have come to the camp.[118]

Sixth graders were treated to selections only slightly subtler. One unit covered life in an Israeli prison (though it was not identified as Israeli by name). Another was devoted to an author describing his flight from Jaffa in 1948. In his narration, he boarded a boat with his precious book manuscript on Palestinian history, only to see it tossed into the sea. In a poignant and highly symbolic passage, he resolved to overcome the devastation and recreate what he had lost. And perhaps the oddest such unit was a selection concerning Mahatma Gandhi. Gandhi's nonviolence was presented in laudatory terms and compared with the beginning of the Palestinian intifada. But the same unit also included a section of Mahmud Darwish's widely recited poem "Identity Card," expressing far less Gandhian sentiments: "Write down, at the top of the page, I do not hate people. And I do not attack anyone. But I . . . if I am hungry, I eat the flesh of my conqueror. Beware . . . beware . . . of my hunger and of my anger."[119]

The more recent textbooks—those for grades 1, 2, 3, 6, 7, and 8, issued between 2000 and 2002—broke some of the silences of the earlier books, but they still failed to develop any sustained or coherent explanation of the Palestinian present. The issue of borders was not even raised, and the books gave no clear message on the subject. Almost all in-depth descriptions of Palestine focused on the West Bank and Gaza, described in every book as "the two parts of the homeland."[120] Yet other locations did receive passing mention, generally with no explanation. Palestine as a geographical (as opposed to a political) entity clearly included areas such as the Negev in the books. Some cities were mentioned as Palestinian (chiefly Jaffa, Beersheva, and Acre) that fell within the pre-1967 borders of Israel, but these descriptions lacked depth or context and often had an anachronistic quality about them. For instance, in a second-grade text, a family took a trip to Jaffa, smelling lemons and oranges along the way.[121] This, of course, was the Jaffa of the past; current drivers entering the city pass through densely populated suburbs and traffic and are more likely to smell diesel fumes than citrus. And the books still maintained some of the awkward silences of the 1994 books. The textbook authors simply failed to explain the Oslo Accords, Palestinian borders, checkpoints, or many other sensitive issues. Some textbook teams (especially those working on Arabic language) were been far more willing to confront sensitive issues than others, but none found a way to present an authoritative and comprehensive explanation of the recent past or the present of Palestine.

Some elements of an explanation began to emerge, to be sure, but they were notable for their gaps. On areas where a clear national consensus existed among Palestinians, or where the Palestinian leadership had given clear and authoritative declarations of a position, the textbook authors lost all bashfulness. Jerusalem, for instance, was repeatedly described as the capital of Palestine (though its precise borders were not mentioned). The responsibility for the refugee problem was squarely placed on Israeli shoulders, and the right of return was unambiguously affirmed. Indeed, the books issued for the second and seventh grades in 2001 were far stronger in this regard than the first- and sixth-grade books, authored before the September 2000 intifada. Authoritative Palestinian documents (especially the declaration of independence of 1988) were quoted wherever possible, demonstrating the authors' inclination to rely on authoritative texts on sensitive issues wherever possible. The structure of the PLO and the PNA were covered in some detail. There were references to Palestinian prisoners held by Israel and pictures of Israeli bulldozers destroying houses and uprooting olive trees.

Thus, as much as the authors of the 2000 textbooks seemed to wish to avoid some of the gaps of the 1994 series (including references to some of the conflictual and tragic aspects of Palestinian life), they did not do so in any coherent manner. There was no narrative to explain where the camps came from, where Palestine's borders were located, who the occupiers were, or when to turn from Gandhian nonviolence to desperate vengeance. The textbooks spoke with clashing voices. Allowing students to sort through different approaches, think through problems themselves, and balance competing accounts is central to the progressive educational alternative. But that was not what these books encouraged. The tensions were real but unexplained and even unacknowledged. Students were neither asked to weigh the different perspectives nor given the tools to do so. In a sense, these texts (and especially the unexplained illustrations) threw a burden on to the teacher and the student, both of whom could infuse the ambiguities and silences with many different meanings. In one of the rare mentions of Israeli settlements, students were asked to assess their environmental effects. But there was no text or set of resources that showed them how to do so. In one unexplained illustration, soldiers encountered a group of people on the road outside a village. Who were the soldiers and why were they there? Were they expelling the inhabitants, guarding the village, checking identity papers, or distributing supplies after a natural disaster? Students were asked to describe what they saw—forcing them to supply not only the details but also the entire context and meaning.

Like their predecessors, the 2000 books were compelled to fall back on authoritative texts and decisions where they existed and into ambiguity and silence when they did not. The very covers of the books bore this out. At the time that the first books were issued, the Central Committee of the PLO had authorized a delay until 13 September 2000 for a declaration of statehood on the West Bank and Gaza. In what name could the texts—printed over the summer of 2000—be issued? Was there to be a State of Palestine or merely a PNA? Most books avoided this issue by simply bearing the name of the Ministry of Education on the cover. But those books that were issued in two parts (with the second book to be used in the later half of the year) had the second part bear the name of the State of Palestine, in clear anticipation of a declaration of statehood (which did not, in fact, come), based not on vague hope but on the text of an earlier Central Committee decision. Where the

Palestinian leadership had indicated a clear position (on the goal of a Palestinian state, on Jerusalem as its capital), the books were clear. Where the leadership had given the authors no clear direction, they followed none, either by lapsing back into silence or by presenting creative if confusing and sometimes tense ambiguities.

Palestine was to be a normal state, and that often meant passing over some parts of history and the present in silence. Ziad Abu-Zayyad, a Palestinian legislator explained in a roundtable discussion between Palestinian and Israeli activists and educators:

> [W]e are in the process of writing a new curriculum, not because of pressure from Israel or from anybody else, but because we are preparing ourselves to be an independent state, a state that lives under normal conditions, and we want our children to learn in normal conditions and to learn a positive and not a negative national curriculum.[122]

The ability of the authors to avoid sensitive subjects may not last forever: eleventh- and twelfth-grade history books (due out in 2005 and 2006) will have to address Palestinian and Arab history in detail. Initial indications are that the plans are to use official documents and statements as much as possible, but some sustained narrative cannot be avoided.

CONCLUSION: DIFFERING DEMOCRATIC VISIONS

Palestinian education has been a site of contestation for a century. In the Ottoman period and especially under the mandate and the Israeli occupation, Palestinians struggled increasingly bitterly over expressions of nationalist identity. Since the creation of the Palestinian Authority, the nature of contestation has changed: the contending parties are now mostly Palestinian (outside parties, especially some Americans and Israelis, retain an interest in Palestinian education, but it is extremely focused and selective). And with this shift has come another: no longer has contestation over Palestinian education focused almost exclusively on nationalist issues; increasingly it is democracy that is at issue.

Indeed, the current struggle to define the Palestinian curriculum is in its very essence a struggle over the meaning of Palestinian democracy. Advocates of the progressive alternative invoke democracy at every step, yet they do not have a monopoly on the use of the word. The Ministry of Education and the *Al-tarbiyya al-wataniyya* series also make references to democracy. It might at first glance seem that the term *democracy* has been used to mean so many things that it no longer means anything. But while the meaning of *democracy* is general, it is not boundless: in the context of the debate over Palestinian education, the term is used in two very different ways.

The Ministry of Education follows a traditional, procedural definition of democracy. This meaning may seem mechanistic: people elect representatives who design and implement policy. A system is democratic when its decision-making structures are based on the will of the majority. Such a view is more specific than many contemporary uses of the term, but it is very consistent with definitions of democracy that were current throughout the world until quite recently. The Ministry of Education wishes to design a curriculum that is based on the values of the majority and of their elected representatives. The Palestinians have a variety of political structures that can be presented as democratic. Their president, Yasir 'Arafat, was elected both by the population of the West Bank and Gaza and by the Palestinian National Council (an imperfect democratic structure, to be sure, but the only one that represents all Palestinians, including those in the diaspora). The minister of education serves because he was appointed by an elected president and holds the confidence of the PLC, the legislative body elected to represent Palestinians in the West Bank and Gaza. And the PLC reviewed the proposed curriculum and approved it by majority vote. In all these ways, the emerging curriculum is very much a democratic creation.

This definition of democracy, oriented as it is to majoritarianism and governing procedure, has fallen out of favor in public discussions throughout the world in recent years. Increasingly democracy is defined more broadly (and often amorphously) as a collection of social and political practices that range far beyond simple majoritarianism to include a collection of liberal values. Freedom of speech, rule of law, and tolerance of difference are increasingly viewed not simply as consistent with democracy but as part of its essence. This broadening of the meaning of democracy is a historical curiosity because democracy was so long perceived as inimical to many such liberal values. In other words, democracy is increasingly defined as incorporating precisely the features that it used to be seen as undermining.

The broadening of the term *democracy* can be frustrating, especially for political analysis. An analytically useful definition would allow us to discern what is a democracy and what is not, or perhaps how democratic a political system is. The older meaning, focusing on majoritarianism, did precisely that. Yet the newer, broader meaning is less analytically useful. By defining democracy as incorporating so many elements, many of which operate in tension with each other, we no longer can identify a democracy (or the degree of democracy) with much clarity.

Yet it is not the search for analytical clarity that drives the newer, broader definition of democracy. Instead it is driven by normative concerns: What makes us value democracy? What kind of democracy do we want? How can we best maintain it? The shift from an analytic to a normative definition of democracy was partly motivated by events in interwar Europe, in which governments that were explicitly undemocratic proved to be far worse enemies of liberal values than democracies ever were. Yet the shift was visible earlier in some areas; it is interesting to note that the broadening of the definition of democracy took place partly on the ground of educational reform. John Dewey, writing in 1916, explicitly redefined democracy as extending beyond majority rule; for Dewey, democracy combined individualism and common interests in a way that made possible individual and social dynamism; the task of education was to prepare individuals to protect and develop further such a democratic society:

> The devotion of democracy to education is a familiar fact. The superficial explanation is that a government resting upon popular suffrage cannot be successful unless those who elect and who obey their governors are educated. . . . But there is a deeper explanation. A democracy is more than a form of government; it is primarily a mode of associated living, of conjoint communicated experiences. . . .
>
> The widening of the area of shared concerns, and the liberation of a greater diversity of personal capacities which characterize a democracy, are not of course the product of deliberation and conscious effort. On the contrary, they were caused by the development of modes of manufacture and commerce, travel, migration, and intercommunication which flowed from the command of science over natural energy. But after greater individualization on one hand, and a broader community of interest on the other have come into existence, it is a matter of deliberate effort to sustain and extend them. Obviously a society to which stratification into separate classes would be fatal, must see to it that intellectual opportunities are accessible to all on equable and easy terms.[123]

It is such an image of democracy that drives Palestinian educational reformers. A democratic educational system for them is not one that mechanically reflects the decisions of the majority or their elected representatives but one that prepares democratic citizens able to balance and foster the simultaneous development of individual and community. The authors of *Al-tarbiyya al-wataniyya*, officials of the Ministry of Education, and, to a lesser extent, the authors of the 2000 textbooks ask, "What kind of society do we want?" and turn to elected officials and fundamental authoritative expressions of the national will (like the declaration of independence) for answers. The reformers instead ask, "What kind of citizen do we want?" and concentrate on methods to develop independent thinkers capable of contributing to (and taking advantage of) democratic life.

While one American thinker, John Dewey, may have helped forge the link between education and the broader conception of democracy, the vision of the Palestinian reformers resembles more closely the approach of a current American writer on the relationship between democracy and education, Amy Gutmann. Participating in a broader effort to redefine democracy as "deliberative democracy," Gutmann writes against a simply majoritarian definition:

> The ideal of democracy is often said to be collective self-determination. But is there a "collective self" to be determined? Are there not just so many individual selves that must find a fair way of sharing the goods of a society together? It would be dangerous (as critics often charge) to assume that the democratic state constitutes the "collective self" of a society, and that its policies in turn define the best interests of its individual members.
>
> We need no such metaphysical assumption, however, to defend an idea closely related to that of collective self-determination—an ideal of citizens sharing in deliberatively determining the future shape of their society.[124]

More succinctly, Stephen Holmes defines democracy as "government by public discussion, not simply the enforcement of the will of the majority."[125] This view of democracy does not return any of the analytical utility of the strictly majoritarian definition, but it does go beyond merely defining away the difficulties of combining liberalism with democracy. The advocates of "deliberative democracy" claim that their definition presents a democracy that will survive over time and allow for a true melding of the advantages of democracy and liberalism.

Gutmann uses the conception of "deliberative democracy" to develop a democratic theory of education—education in a democracy is to "teach the skills and virtues of democratic deliberation," and it does so while allowing for some democratic control over the educational process that falls short of majoritarianism. Instead, "educational authority is shared among parents, citizens, and professional educators," who themselves deliberate in accordance with liberal principles.[126] "Democratic education is best viewed as a shared trust, of parents, citizens, teachers, and public officials, the precise terms of which are to be democratically decided within the bounds of the principles of nondiscrimination and nonrepression."[127]

None of the Palestinian advocates of the progressive educational alternative cite Gutmann, and probably few (if any) have read her work. Yet their stated goals—and the process by which the Abu Lughod committee designed its proposal—show a remarkably similar spirit and ethos. For these reformers, Palestinian democracy is not merely about enforcing the will of the majority. It is about building a society in which Palestinian citizens deliberate about public policies and social and political values, while retaining a significant zone of personal autonomy. They wish to build an educational system that not only will serve such a society but also is itself a product of it. This goal is ambitious, and, as of this writing, only a few beginning steps have been taken.

Palestinians in the West Bank and Gaza often complain that their political system is undemocratic. There is some truth to the complaint, though according to older conceptions of democracy, much less than is often claimed. If the contest over education is any indication, however, the problem is not simply that Palestinians have not yet built a democracy; the problem is also that they have not agreed how to define it.

APPENDIX: THE INCITEMENT CHARGE

Any treatment of Palestinian education must confront the oft-repeated claims that Palestinian textbooks instill hatred of Israel and Jews. In a sense, this issue is at most tangential to this inquiry, which focuses on internal Palestinian politics and portrays textbooks more as outcomes of domestic struggle than as producers of international conflict. But virtually every discussion in English on Palestinian education repeats the charge that Palestinian textbooks incite students against Jews and Israel. It may therefore come as a surprise that the books authored under the PNA are far more innocuous than this charge implies. What is more remarkable than any statements they make on the subject is their silence—the PNA-authored books often stubbornly avoid treating anything controversial regarding current Palestinian national identity, forcing them into awkward omissions and gaps. The first generation of Palestinian textbooks written in 1994, the *Al-tarbiyya al-wataniyya* books, make no mention of any location as Palestinian outside the territories occupied by Israel in 1967; those books go to some lengths to avoid saying anything about Israel at all, and the few exceptions are hardly pejorative. The second generation—issued beginning in 2000—breaks some of that silence but with neither the consistency nor the stridency that critics of the textbooks allege.

Then where do persistent reports of incitement in Palestinian textbooks come from? Virtually all can be traced back to the work of a single organization, the Center for Monitoring the Impact of Peace (CMIP). The center claims that its purpose is "to encourage a climate of tolerance and mutual respect between peoples and nations, founded on the rejection of violence and the changing of negative stereotypes, as a means to resolving conflicts."[128] Critics charge that the center's real purpose is to launch attacks on the PNA, and the center's own reports suggest such suspicions are well founded.[129] CMIP began operation by issuing its first report in 1998 on Palestinian textbooks, which might best be described as tendentious and highly misleading. When the PNA issued a new series of books for grades 1 and 6 in 2000, the center rushed out a new report that passed over significant changes quite quickly before presenting its allegations of "delegitimization of Israel's existence," implicit "seeking of Israel's destruction," "defamation of Israel," and "encouraging militarism and violence." In contrast to the alacrity with which it studied Palestinian textbooks, CMIP's work on Israeli textbooks proceeded at a far more leisurely pace, taking years rather than months. The report on Israeli books followed a very different method: rather than quoting example after example of offending passages with little historical context or explanation (a method that would have produced a very damning report indeed), the report on Israeli textbooks is nuanced and far more careful. Incendiary quotations are explained, analyzed, and contextualized in the report on Israeli books; they are listed with only brief and sensationalist explanations in the reports on Palestinian books. In short, the center is fair, balanced, and understanding toward Israeli textbooks but tendentious on Palestinian books.

The center's work has been widely circulated: its reports are the source for virtually any quotation in English from the Palestinian curriculum. Indeed, its influence has begun to be felt in policy circles and has informed congressional and presidential statements in the United States, numerous newspaper columns, and—more recently—a decision by some external donors to cut off funds for Palestinian education. Since the center's reports have dominated the public debate with considerable effect and little contestation, it makes some sense to examine them.

While often highly misleading and always unreliable, most of the contents of the center's reports are not wholly fabricated. Clearly false statements are rare, though when they do occur they are far from minor. For instance, the center's first report on Palestinian textbooks, issued in 1998, included the statement that "PA TV is a division of the Palestinian Authority Ministry of Education,"[130] which allowed the report to saddle the Palestinian educational establishment with any statement broadcast on Palestinian television. The statement was false, however. In its second comprehensive report on Palestinian textbooks, issued in 2000, on the new books for the first and sixth grades, the center claimed that "the PA has rejected international calls" to modify books for the other grades.[131] In fact, as will become clear, the plan to replace the textbooks in question was as old as the PNA itself and was proceeding according to a well-published schedule when the center's report was issued. Several lesser errors occur throughout the center's work.

But the real problems with the center's reports lie elsewhere. In particular, three sets of flaws characterize its work (and much of the public debate about Palestinian textbooks more generally). First, the center generally ignores any historical context in a way that renders some of its claims sharply misleading. In its 1998 report, the center adduced numerous incendiary statements about Israel and Jews from books in use in Palestinian schools. Some of the statements quoted were indeed were highly offensive to Jews and sharply anti-Israeli.[132] Yet they came not from books authored by Palestinians but from Egyptian and Jordanian books used in Gaza and the West Bank, respectively.[133] The books were distributed by the PNA, to be sure, but they antedated its establishment. (The center's report does hold the PNA responsible for distributing the Egyptian and Jordanian books and therefore holds Palestinians responsible for the content. Here it displays an odd double standard: it does not note that since 1994, Israel has distributed the same books in East Jerusalem, removing only the cover with the PNA seal. The only books that the Israelis refused to distribute were those authored by the PNA—the *Al-tarbiyya al-wataniyya* series—even though those books were free of the content that Israel objected to. The likely reason for this odd policy is that Palestinian sovereignty—implied by using PNA-authored books—was far more problematic for Israel than anti-Semitism.)

By sharp contrast to the Egyptian and Jordanian books, the 1994 *Al-tarbiyya al-wataniyya* series of supplementary books authored by the PNA verged on blandness. As was discussed in the preceding chapter, they made no mention of any Palestinian area within 1967 boundaries of Israel and indeed went to some length to avoid any controversial matter whatsoever. An organization naming itself for monitoring "the impact of peace" might be expected to compare the older, non-Palestinian books with the newer, Palestinian ones. Indeed, such a task would seem basic to its mission. The center goes beyond failing to live up to its name; its reports consistently obfuscate the distinction between the old and new books. It does not simply fail to note the change; in one of its rare falsehoods, the center claimed that in the 1994 series, Israel does not exist.[134] (The treatment of Palestinian history in those books is extremely brief, but Israel is indeed referred to;

remarkably, the text resorts to awkward phrasing to avoid citing Israel in some negative contexts.) It is difficult to escape the conclusion that the center has been far more interested in criticizing the PNA than in honestly assessing the changes produced in Palestinian education by the Oslo Accords.

The second problem with the center's work is its prosecutorial style. Its reports offer little more than brief themes and then list statement after statement purporting to prove the point. Any evidence that contradicts the center's harsh message, such as maps that clearly draw Palestinian governorates as covering only the West Bank and Gaza, an extended and laudatory treatment of Gandhi's nonviolence, or a tour of Palestinian cities that includes only those under PNA rule, is ignored, obscured, or dismissed. Other evidence is interpreted inaccurately. For instance, a topographical map of Palestine (most likely inserted to avoid treating any sensitive political issues regarding borders) is presented as a denial of Israel's existence. Many of the selections included are presented in a highly tendentious manner: a unit on tolerance is criticized for omitting Jews, while a reading of the entire unit makes perfectly clear that its topic is tolerance within Palestinian society.[135] 'Izz al-Din al-Qassam is mentioned in texts as a Palestinian national hero; the center's 2000 report explains:

> The primary terrorist organization operating against Israel since the signing of the Oslo Accords is the Hamas, whose members terrorized Israeli citizens with suicide attacks, primarily on buses. The terror wing of the group is called the "Az Aldin Al Kassam" squad, named after the terrorist who fought the British and Jews before the establishment of the State of Israel. The new PA schoolbook glorifies Kassam.[136]

In essence, the center provides a context for the mention of al-Qassam that, while accurate, is irrelevant to the text: it deliberately obscures how the text itself presents al-Qassam or how Palestinians would understand a reference to him. Al-Qassam was killed at the beginning of his attempt to organize a rebellion against the British mandate. Subsequent generations of Palestinians have been able to read various dimensions into his short career: for mainstream nationalists, he is a rebel against the British; for Islamists, a warrior for Islam; and for leftists, a mobilizer of the popular classes. To imply that mentioning al-Qassam is an implicit endorsement of suicide attacks and bus bombings is thus based on a hostile, inaccurate, and even dishonest reading—what matters is not whether the texts cite him but how they present him. Palestinian texts mention him only as a martyr in the struggle against British imperialism.[137]

In short, the purpose is clearly to indict the textbooks and the PNA rather than to analyze and understand the content of the books. Were the center to take a similar approach in other countries, including Israel, it could easily find comparable material.[138]

The final and perhaps the largest problem with the center's work lies not simply with the reports themselves but in how they have been read. The center's conclusions may be unsupported by the evidence it presents and undermined by the evidence it overlooks. But it does include some qualifications and elliptical wording that usually prevent its reports from promulgating outright falsehoods. When its reports gain wider circulation, however, the buried qualifications get lost. The center's 2000 report actually admitted that changes had occurred in the Palestinian-authored books but then attempted to undermine its own admission:

> A few changes were noted in the new PA books. The open calls for Israel's destruction found in the previous books are no longer present. However, given the de-legitimization of Israel's existence, together with teachings such as the obligation to defend Islamic land, the seeking of Israel's destruction has merely been shifted from the explicit to the implicit.
>
> Another change is that certain overtly anti-Semitic references defining Jews and Israelis as "treacherous" or "the evil enemy," common in the previous books, are likewise not present. However, given the books' portrayal of Israel as a foreign colony that massacred and expelled Palestinians, the defamation of Israel continues even if the word "enemy" has been removed.[139]

In short, the new books removed the earlier offensive material, but the center acknowledged the change in passing and then immediately denied its significance.

Thus, it is not surprising when public references to the textbooks based on the center's report lose any subtlety and make erroneous claims about the new books. Charles Krauthammer claimed that since the signing of the Oslo Accords, the Palestinians had "intensified the propaganda, the antisemitism, in their pedagogy and in their media" and that while Israel had "assiduously" changed its textbooks to prepare for peace, "on the Palestinian side, the opposite was happening."[140] Rather than being lauded for having removed offensive material, the Palestinians were criticized for introducing it, based on inaccurate rumors or CMIP's reports. In 2001, U.S. Senator John McCain claimed that Palestinians "are teaching their children in textbooks that Israelis have to be destroyed."[141] In 2002, the president of the Middle East Media Research Institute testified before Congress that the

"Nazis would have commended" the new textbooks. Similarly, the Israeli Minister of Education claimed that "like the Nazis," 'Arafat used Palestinian textbooks to cultivate "eliminationist hatred."[142] One *Jerusalem Post* columnist falsely charged: "The incitement to hatred of Jews and the destruction of Israel, which has always been part of the Palestinian school curriculum, was intensified."[143] A spokesperson for Israeli settlers in the West Bank introduced a puzzling charge that would probably have made even the center's staff blush: "We teach our children to respect life, while they teach that if you die with Jewish blood on your hands you go to heaven and are fed with grapes by 15 virgins."[144]

The Palestinian textbooks were such a politically attractive target that even those who were better informed as to their content criticized them. Hillary Clinton, running for the U.S. Senate, criticized Palestinian textbooks in a way that buried her acknowledgment that the new first- and sixth-grade books, authored by the PNA itself, were different: "All future aid to the Palestinian Authority must be contingent on strict compliance with their obligation to change all the textbooks in all grades—not just two at a time."[145] After her election, her comments lost even this subtlety: in June 2001 she joined with her fellow senator from New York, Charles Schumer, in a letter to President George Bush, introducing the false charge (clearly based on a center report): "A book that is required reading for Palestinian six graders actually starts off stating, 'There is no alternative to destroying Israel.'"[146] As the second intifada took on diplomatic as well as violent dimensions, the Israeli government cited textbooks as evidence of Palestinian bad faith and hostile intentions.

With wildly inaccurate charges circulating, it did not take long before the Palestinian textbooks could be used to taint even those who were not associated with them. A former American ambassador to Morocco, claiming expertise on UNRWA, stated that the United Nations funded the textbooks (it did not).[147] The European Union came under steady fire in the press for supporting the books.[148] CMIP actually encouraged European parliamentarians to pressure the European Commission on the matter, even though the EU provided no funding for the books. While some European states did provide funding to the Curriculum Development Center, the EU did not, leading an exasperated spokesman to declare: "The Commission utterly rejects the promotion of intolerance or hatred, as it rejects poor journalism."[149] Such explanations did not stop the campaign from taking a bizarre form: a group of European parliamentarians worked to amend the EU budget to stop the funding (which it did not give in the first place) for books that removed anti-

Semitism from the Palestinian curriculum. They scored a victory of sorts in November 2001 when a rider was added to the EU budget insisting that EU-supported textbooks not contradict basic European values.[150] Because of the drumbeat of pressure over books, the EU finally conducted its own review of the books, which concluded that "allegations against the new textbooks" were "proven unfounded" and that CMIP reports had used quotations out of context and badly translated material, "thus suggesting an anti-Jewish incitement that the books do not contain."[151]

The UN, UNRWA, and EU were not alone: a less successful campaign targeted the United States, where an anonymous organization called Stand with Us urged a letter-writing campaign to "American lawmakers," stating, "I am very concerned that our tax dollars are going directly to finance the hate-filled textbooks that are utilized in every classroom of every Palestinian school."[152] No American funding supported either the new or the old books.

To its credit, after 1999, the Israeli government held back from joining the campaign.[153] But the bitterness of the second intifada made the target too tempting, and in the fall of 2001, Israeli officials began to take the lead in denouncing the Palestinian textbooks. The Israeli Foreign Ministry joined the lobbying campaign in the European parliament. In March 2002, a cabinet minister issued a report resembling the CMIP's work in tone, content, and method.[154] Given the intensity of feeling aroused by Palestinian suicide bombings and a general atmosphere of war, such propagandizing should be no surprise. It took a dangerous form, however, when Israeli military officials apparently began to believe their government's claims. On 23 April 2002, an Israeli intelligence officer justified the extraordinarily destructive takeover of the Ministry of Education (in which computer hard drives were systematically removed, other equipment was destroyed, and examination records were taken) largely in terms of the textbooks.[155] She laid responsibility for the books at the feet of the Canadian government, later forcing an embarrassed Israeli embassy spokesman in Canada to repudiate the charge.[156]

The center's reports were the clear source for most of the charges on the content, whether cited or not. A member of the U.S. Congress wrote to the *New York Times:*

> According to the Center for Monitoring the Impact of Peace, today's sixth-grade Palestinian students are required to read the textbook "Our Country Palestine," which has a banner on the title page of Volume I that reads, "There is no alternative to destroying Israel."[157]

The charge was false, though it was widely repeated and even displayed in an advertising campaign by an organization calling itself (with unintended irony) "Jews for Truth Now." Yet none of the textbooks included such a phrase. The member of Congress and others had read the center's carelessly written report in a careless manner. The original report had actually claimed: "An old book introduced into the PA curriculum is filled with virulent anti-Semitism." It then claims that there is a banner on the title page stating, "There is no alternative to destroying Israel." No textbook included such a phrase. The book *Our Country Palestine* was not a new text but an old geographical guide to Palestine begun in the 1940s and published in some subsequent editions. And those looking for the supposed banner could not find it (nor could I). Certainly the edition available to the textbook authors in Ramallah did not include the phrase.[158] Further, the claim that the book was introduced into the curriculum is highly misleading. Its author's evacuation from Jaffa in 1948 was described, and, at the end of the unit, students were given a suggested activity of looking up the name of their town or village in the book.[159] To leap from this suggested activity to a charge of inculcating virulent anti-Semitism seems curious.

It was not merely journalists and members of Congress who were misled by careless reading of the center's reports. Even sloppy academics were led astray. One wrote of "systematic indoctrination" of "school children in particular" with "vile anti-Semitic and anti-Israeli propaganda," claiming that this was part of a plan by 'Arafat to launch military confrontation with Israel.[160] A scholarly journal published an analysis of Palestinian textbooks that reproduced quotations from the center's reports (without attribution), mistakenly claiming that all the texts came from Palestinian-authored books (whereas most came from the Egyptian and Jordanian books being phased out).[161] An equally groundless, though far more bizarre, analysis of Palestinian textbooks begins with wholesale (though unattributed) borrowings from the center's reports and then adds:

> Public acclaim, a non-ending orgy of sex and all the booze you can drink, constitute a powerful combination of incentives for igniting the imagination and motivation of pubescent youth, aged 12 and up. Along with the emotionally charged scenes of actually stoning Jews and Jewish property, what more is needed to convince them that killing Jews is a worthy and honorable vocation? The PA is certainly preparing a huge army for the future that, socially and psychologically, will be trained to commit unmitigated violence against Israel and the Jewish People on behalf of Islam, the Arabs and Palestine.[162]

The vitriolic and often inaccurate criticisms of Palestinian textbooks should not obscure that those books do treat Israel with a remarkable awkwardness and reticence. And Jews are mentioned primarily in a religious context (connected with the beginning of Islam) and not in a political context. The silence on such issues is more confused and embarrassed than it is hostile, however, as the preceding chapter established.

7　Conclusion

> [A]lthough not sovereign or independent, and indeed although
> bound by myriad restrictions imposed by the agreements with the
> Israelis, the new Palestinian Authority has more power over more
> of its people in more of Palestine than any Palestinian agency has
> had in the twentieth century. With this power has come responsi-
> bility and accountability, which cannot be shirked or shunted off
> onto another actor. In these circumstances, although the Palestinian
> Authority can and undoubtedly will blame others for its failures,
> using the PLO's old scenario of Palestinians facing insuperable odds
> to explain away failures or describe them as triumphs, it is possible
> that for the first time this strategy will not work, and that the
> Palestinian leadership will be held accountable for its actions by
> its own people.
>
> RASHID KHALIDI, *Palestinian Identity: The Construction
> of Modern National Consciousness*

In September 2000, the Palestinian Bar Association approved its bylaws. The process of unifying preexisting organizations had been tortuous, but the step finally allowed lawyers to prepare for elections and the construction of a unified and professionalized body. Palestinian journalists were prepar-ing to hold a meeting to found a new professional association at the end of the same month. Engineers, dentists, and others worked on drafting laws to unite their long-divided professions. Various bodies representing Palestinian teachers agreed to stop their rivalry and consolidate their activities. Accountants held a brief strike in protest of an incident in which security forces had entered their headquarters in Gaza. At the same time, a small committee of experts presented drafts of a new Palestinian constitution to various workshops as it moved toward completion of its work. First-grade and sixth-grade teachers began using a Palestinian-authored curriculum for the first time; they also pondered whether to resume their strike of the pre-vious spring. The PLC moved toward adoption of a framework of civil and criminal laws that would unify the West Bank and Gaza for the first time since the British mandate. The Ministry of Finance worked to prepare the first complete budget in Palestinian history, armed with PNA pledges to end the practice of running a considerable part of its activities off the books.

NGO activists geared up for a new set of proposals to international funders as USAID began its new project and the World Bank renewed its separate effort. A group of NGOs agreed to form a committee to monitor local elections, in the hope that they would be scheduled soon. For most Palestinians active in society and politics, most of September 2000 was a normal month.

Yet as these efforts were underway, the political framework making them possible was collapsing. Negotiations with Israel turned increasingly acrimonious. While many observers interpreted this tension at the time as a positive sign—showing perhaps that both sides were nearing historic concessions—Palestinians of all political stripes in the West Bank and Gaza drew different conclusions. Continued construction in Israeli settlements, an only recently reversed sharp economic decline associated with the Israeli policy of closure, and the continued reality of occupation had led most Palestinians to grow cynical about the negotiations. The efforts described in this book were based largely on an attempt to build Palestine regardless of the outcome of those negotiations. Their successes were notable and real, as were their failures.

Rashid Khalidi, even as he stated that the creation of the PNA resulted in a body that had to accept its share of responsibility, also noted the concern of many Palestinians that if Palestinian autonomy was permanently frozen according to the supposedly interim arrangements of the Oslo Accords, a "misshapen and grotesque creation" would result.[1] By September 2000, many Palestinians feared that this creation was not merely materializing but deeply entrenching itself. And at the end of the month, the limited ability to separate institution building from the relationship with Israel seemed to vanish. Widespread violence throughout the West Bank and Gaza, reimposition of the harshest forms of closure, and fiscal crisis brought on by Israeli refusal to transfer VAT and other tax revenues to the PNA led to a rapid reversion of Palestinian politics to nearly total concentration on nationalist issues. None of the activists described in this book ever believed they could ignore Israel, but many believed that they could render it less relevant to their daily lives and determined not to subordinate all their efforts to the nationalist struggle. Others believed that building autonomous institutions and a strong civil society would actually aid the nationalist cause. In September 2000, the outbreak of the second intifada forced many Palestinians to rethink the logic of their actions.

RETURN TO THE INTIFADA

The return to violent confrontation with Israel deeply affected all of the institutions discussed in this book, but not in easily predictable ways.

And sometimes short-term effects differed profoundly from long-term effects.

The immediate effect of the second intifada was to shift the issues and organizations that mattered in Palestinian politics. Nationalism had hardly disappeared from the Palestinian agenda, but the construction of the PNA after 1993 had allowed other issues to arise, involving not simply whether a Palestinian entity would emerge but how it would be governed. The second intifada initially made such matters seem secondary or even irrelevant: to argue for transparency in governance or better communication between ministries and NGOs seemed out of place while violence was escalating. Institutions that had been submerged for years—most particularly political parties (and especially the local militias and armed groups they sponsored)— suddenly surged forward, taking the initiative in leading Palestinian society in increasingly violent confrontation with Israel. Much of the Palestinian population became spectators as armed groups—based in political parties and movements and sometimes the security services—launched attacks on Israelis and became themselves the object of harsh Israeli counterattacks. While Palestinians blamed Israel for initiating violence in September 2000, within weeks it was clear that whatever the genesis of the intifada, these Palestinian groups were determined to continue it. The Palestinian leadership left itself open to attempts to arrange cease-fires but lacked both the will and the ability to stop enthusiastic activists. From the beginning some Palestinians openly questioned the "militarization" of the intifada. And in late 2001 and 2002, critics of "operations" against civilians in pre-1967 Israel became increasingly vocal. But the militias and groups involved in the intifada refused to heed these calls, and they seemed to have significant pop- ular support. To be sure, almost all non-Islamist Palestinian leaders (includ- ing, for instance, Marwan al-Barghuti, who asserted himself as leading spokesman for the intifada in the West Bank) insisted that their goal was the creation of a Palestinian state in the West Bank and Gaza with Jerusalem as its capital—the same goal that more senior leaders had proclaimed lay behind the Oslo Agreements. But such statements were either not heard in Israel or not believed (partly because they often included reference to the right of Palestinian refugees to return to their homes); and the actions of the militant groups convinced most Israelis that the intifada was predicated on the rejection rather than the acceptance of a two-state solution. (Harsh Israeli countermeasures had a similar effect on Palestinian opinion, leading most to conclude that Israel was not interested in allowing a Palestinian state to emerge.) Israel held not simply the militant groups but the PNA as a whole responsible for the violence, charging that the senior leadership took no action to rein in the groups (which was largely true, though some short-lived attempts were made) or that the PNA leadership was instigating, planning, and executing violent attacks (for which Israeli officials made increasingly strident claims but could adduce little evidence).[2] Thus, Israel increasingly targeted not simply those directly involved in the violence but PNA institutions and, beginning in March 2002, even some civil institutions far removed from the nationalist struggle. The immediate effect was devastating.

As a result of the escalating violence, many of the official and unofficial bodies that had taken prominent roles in Palestinian society and politics between 1993 and 2000 found themselves extremely hampered; even those that could continue felt compelled to change their operations and sometimes their missions. On an official level, many of the quasi-state institutions presented in this book could no longer operate with much effectiveness. Courts could not try civil cases if litigants could not appear; criminal cases depended on the functioning of a police force that was disintegrating. Even some of the alternative legal structures could no longer operate: the legal departments of the governorates, which had emerged as leading agents of mediation, were based in buildings that were the targets of Israeli strikes. The security services, which had played a less formal but equally important role in dispute resolution since the beginning of the PNA, were also targets, especially in 2002. This encouraged many to use other forms of justice (traditional vengeance and mediation) not as supplements to the official system but as alternatives. The Supreme State Security Court, less beholden to notions of due process, turned its vengeful eye toward suspected collaborators. The PLC met occasionally and continued to work on some of the most important pieces of legislation but found itself forced to use videoconferencing for its rare sessions in order to overcome the effects of closure. Its greatest legislative achievement, the Basic Law, was finally endorsed by the president in May 2002, but implementing its provisions remained difficult. The PLO committee charged with drafting a permanent constitution for statehood completed its work out of the limelight, its project seemingly legalistic and even naïve in the midst of the violence. Schools continued operating and the new curriculum was introduced, but the Israeli closure and military campaigns disrupted the educational process. In 2002, a major campaign coincided with the tawjihi test, forcing students to wait until the Israeli army withdrew to finish the most important educational examination of their lives.

Nonofficial bodies in the PNA similarly found themselves disrupted by the violence of the intifada. For some organizations, this meant that ambitious plans had to be shelved and even many existing operations had to be suspended. Younger journalists working to found a new syndicate had to postpone their plans. Lawyers prepared for bar association elections but were told by a court that they could not hold them because the closure made fair balloting impossible. Teachers had a new curriculum, but it proved difficult to get the new textbooks to the schools. Those who had struck for higher salaries in the past now found themselves forced to accept delays as the fiscally strapped PNA struggled to meet its payroll.

For other organizations that had worked to build a normal society, removed from the occupation and conflict with Israel, the eruption of the intifada led them to redirect their efforts. Many of the grassroots organizations that had struggled to operate in the circumstances prevailing from 1993 to 2000 suddenly found that their emphasis on local social service and voluntarism—which had seemed outmoded—was now increasingly needed by a society dealing with intermittent fighting, closure, and economic crisis. NGOs that had worked to professionalize and focus their operations found themselves called upon to return to the days of the first intifada, when they were often the primary providers of a wide range of services. And the insistence of many NGOs on emphasizing non-nationalist issues could not be sustained. The Teacher Creativity Center continued to hold workshops to train teachers, but it also worked to gather one million signatures worldwide to protest Israeli policy and document and publicize the effects of closure on education.[3]

In April 2002, the entire network of PNA and societal institutions came under direct attack. In the wake of a series of suicide bombings, Israel launched a military campaign encompassing most West Bank cities. The proclaimed purpose was to eliminate the infrastructure enabling terrorist attacks, but for whatever reason an extremely wide range of political and civil institutions was targeted. Some, like Palestinian security services, had a clear connection to the ostensible Israeli goal (because of the involvement of some of their personnel in violence against Israeli targets). Others had a less direct but still clear connection (such as Palestinian broadcast media, which found their equipment destroyed, presumably because some could be quite fiery after the onset of the intifada). But the scope of the campaign extended far beyond such targets, with devastating effects for Palestinian institutions. Governmental bodies with no connection with the violence— such as the PLC and the Ministry of Education—were ransacked; many governmental bodies found hard drives and written records confiscated. And NGOs were similarly (but unevenly) affected. Al-Mawrid, a leading educational NGO in Ramallah, had its offices destroyed; the Qattan Center, another NGO, escaped unscathed. The widespread destruction, the confisca-

tion of records, the scale of looting, and the targeting of apparently innocuous organizations convinced many Palestinians that the true purpose of the
campaign was to destroy Palestinian political and social institutions. Yet if
this was the case, the pattern of Israeli action seems quite puzzling (educational test results, for instance, were taken, but the record-keeping areas of
the PLC were ransacked with their contents left behind). The haphazard pattern of destruction suggests that the Israeli goals were far less systematic
than the bitter Palestinian charges implied, though the purpose behind the
destruction remained unclear and the selection of targets obscure (and perhaps arbitrary).[4]

Whatever the purposes, the effect of the campaign, however devastating,
in some ways underscored the resilience of many Palestinian institutions.
This was true in an immediate sense: critical governmental bodies managed
to continue functioning, as did many NGOs. The educational network, probably the most extensive bureaucracy administered by the PNA, continued
functioning and reopened schools as soon as the campaign subsided. Social
service NGOs found themselves increasingly needed as the population of
the targeted cities sought to recover from the campaign. And international
donors stepped in to fill some of the gap. The PNA budget was covered
partly by European and Arab donors; external donors supported NGOs providing basic services to the Palestinian population as well.

Yet the resilience of institutions was demonstrated on a more fundamental level beginning in the following month, when an agenda of reform
suddenly attracted a diverse international and domestic set of supporters.
The issues raised by Palestinians for years—codified most thoroughly in
the Rocard report (see Chapter 1)—suddenly burst to the forefront of Palestinian and even global attention. From a domestic perspective, the intifada
and the Israeli military campaign had starkly illustrated the need for political reform to strengthen Palestinian institutions: existing institutions had
failed to resolve the conflict with Israel through either peaceful or violent
means; they had been unable to protect Palestinians from an extremely
intrusive military campaign; and the reason given for their weakness—that
it was premature to develop permanent institutions in an interim stage—
lost whatever persuasive power it had ever had. Prior to the second intifada,
the reformers' strongest argument had been that it was necessary to build
strong institutions to make the occupation less relevant and enable people to
live normal lives; now they could add another argument for skeptics who
saw the occupation as inescapable: only strong institutions could protect
Palestinian society and manage the struggle with Israel. In May 2002, the
advocates of reform suddenly seemed far less irrelevant, and they took

advantage of their new prominence to argue for a series of political changes in the Palestinian Authority.

Anxious to cast their own positions in terms of the new interest in institutional reform, prominent Palestinian leaders rushed to proclaim their fealty to the cause. Nabil 'Amr, a minister given the task of mediating between the PLC and the executive (and often therefore forced to explain away presidential and ministerial actions), resigned, complaining that the PNA leadership was not seriously pursuing reform. Leaders of the security services and leading ministers joined the calls. At one point, even the head of the military judiciary (itself an object of reformers' ire) spoke of the need for reform in terms of separation of powers and judicial independence.[5] One leading columnist sarcastically commented that since leaders were so solidly behind reform, the Palestinian population must be the true obstacle. He proposed that "the people be dismissed" so that the "the sincere and righteous gentlemen, the enemies of corruption" in the government could remain and hold the people accountable for their failures.[6]

To add to the pressure, the European Union formally and publicly conditioned continued support for the PNA on a series of administrative, legal, and fiscal reforms (many similar to, though less extensive than, those advocated in the 1999 Rocard report).[7] In light of the strange alliance in favor of reforms, some of its erstwhile advocates began to back off.[8]

On 15 May 2002, Yasir 'Arafat responded to the growing domestic and international pressure by convening the PLC to deliver a speech vowing to launch a reform program and hold new elections. While 'Arafat's speech was short on specifics, the PLC asked its political committee to write its own program, which was approved on the day following 'Arafat's speech by the whole body. That program listed all the demands the PLC had made over the years, including approval of the Basic Law, enforcement of existing laws, respect for public freedoms, reduction in the cabinet, fiscal reforms, steps against corruption, limitation of the authority of the provincial governors, and abolition of the State Security Courts.[9]

'Arafat took five significant steps in the next month to demonstrate his new commitment to reform. First, he signed the Law on the Independence of the Judiciary. Second, he endorsed the Basic Law, which had waited five years for his signature. Third, he formed a new cabinet (one minister even inaccurately promised that it would actually meet as a cabinet, abandoning the practice of assembling only a vaguely defined "leadership" group). Fourth, he promised new PLC and presidential elections as well as long-delayed local elections. Fifth, he directed the cabinet to come up with a more comprehensive reform program (which it did, in a very ambitious form resembling the other calls for reform).[10] Each of these steps frustrated the reform mongers as much as it satisfied them, however (in ways more fully explored in the preceding chapters). The judicial law was approved and published, but not before senior judges had lobbied unsuccessfully for delay; even after publication, 'Arafat succumbed to their pressure to prolong the life of the existing Supreme Judicial Council for one additional year. 'Arafat's endorsement of the Basic Law came with changes that, however minor, did not have the PLC's approval. The new cabinet retained many old ministers (including some accused of corruption), and 'Arafat was reluctant to submit it to the PLC for a vote of confidence. The decree establishing the cabinet did not even mention the Basic Law as the source of its authority and included more ministers than were allowed in the draft passed by the PLC.

In the midst of these domestic reform efforts, a major complication was added. On 24 June 2002, U.S. President George Bush went beyond general encouragement of reform to a specific demand that Palestinian reform required "new and different leadership": that is, reform without replacing 'Arafat would not be deemed reform. Palestinian institution building had a new, powerful, but very problematic friend.

Despite its novelty, execution of the U.S. vision of reform was explicitly based on the need for multilateral coordination. In 1994, the initial effort at international assistance for the emerging Palestinian Authority had led to the creation of some donors' forums and working groups, though these tended to draw episodic high-level U.S. attention and had begun to decay in any case. Yet after President Bush's June 2002 speech, such coordination drew higher-level attention as the United States consulted with other global and regional actors, sometimes working through the "Quartet" of the United Nations, Russia, the European Union, and the United States. The EU and some European states had shown more sustained interest and experience in many governance issues, and the United States could be unusually deferential in the deliberations—for instance, in September 2002 a Quartet statement endorsed the European call for early elections despite U.S. suspicions (though in a subsequent Quartet meeting the following December that call was forgotten). And the U.S. vision of reform, though it did introduce some unfamiliar elements, drew largely on themes emerging from Palestinian reform discussions (such as the need for new elections on the national and local levels and legislative empowerment).

The United States, which had led international actors in the view that Palestinian governance was largely a secondary issue and a distraction from the critical issues of peace negotiations and security, came to develop views on a whole host of matters that had seemed arcane just months previously. Other donor states and some Arab states were pulled in to the Quartet's consultations in areas such as Palestinian constitution writing, election timing and procedure, and fiscal reform. These efforts drew an ambivalent Palestinian response. The senior leadership was desperate for international support and therefore willing to cooperate but also concerned that some parties (especially Israel and the United States) defined reform in terms of their replacement. And Palestinians more enthusiastic about reform welcomed the sudden international attention but worried that many of their proposals might be tainted by the association with external actors deemed unfriendly. For instance, the United States in particular showed interest in the introduction of the post of prime minister to the Palestinian political order; Palestinians who had long pressed for such a change (in order to make executive authority both more diffuse and more accountable) continued their efforts but showed some nervousness that they might be seen as promoting an American rather than a Palestinian agenda.

RESUMING RESUMPTION

Two years after the outbreak of the second intifada, the PNA and its institutions still survived, as did many of the institutions and practices developed after 1993. The intifada and the associated crises—which affected all aspects of Palestinian life—did not stop the efforts to resume Arab Palestine. In institutional terms, everything was disrupted but nothing was destroyed. The work of the post-1993 period showed far more staying power than might have been expected. Even in the midst of political violence, those who pursued the various projects to resume Arab Palestine could point to real and lasting accomplishments.

For those who sought to build Palestine by resuming from its past, the years after 1993 had been spent ensuring that Palestinian institutions and practices would build on the legacy of the Palestinian past. And by 2002, they could point to several areas of real success. In the legal and constitutional arenas, the steady usurpation of Palestinian courts and laws in the years after 1967 was not only halted but partially reversed. To be sure, in all these areas Palestinian institutions remained in a state of uncertainty: the legal framework was incomplete and eclectic; the courts were inefficient and sometimes chaotic; and the constitutional framework aspired to resume the most liberal aspirations of the past but remained mired in the most authoritarian legacies. Thus, the task was hardly complete; indeed, it had only begun. The symbols of Palestinian identity—some old, some new—were now openly displayed as if they were emblems of a sovereign state rather than slogans of a revolutionary movement. Palestinian national identity now had firm institutional expression in a whole host of bodies besides the PLO. In a sense, those who viewed Palestinian politics as a struggle for the reemergence of Palestine from its past could point to the second intifada as powerful evidence of the primacy of their project. Between 1993 and 2000, leadership calls to close ranks were regarded by many as cynical maneuvers to use nationalism to silence dissent. With the beginning of the intifada, the demand for national unity could no longer be regarded as a rhetorical trick by those who sought only to impose their vision of the proper path for Palestinians.

The project of resuming Palestine as an Arab entity similarly survived the outbreak of widespread violence in September 2000. It is true that in economic terms, the Palestinian economy remained as closely tied to Israel as it had been prior to the Oslo Accords. The second intifada underscored that message quite painfully, with widespread job loss, depletion of the public treasury, and even the fizzling of an attempt to boycott Israeli products. Yet on other fronts, the turn to Arab links, sources, and models could point to many successes: the comprehensive law codes being passed were largely Egyptian and Jordanian in inspiration, the school curriculum resumed its stress on Arab identity while introducing a strong Palestinian dimension, and professional associations worked to build bodies that were similar to their counterparts in neighboring Arab countries. In some ways, those who sought to affirm the connection of Palestinian institutions with Arab models sought not simply to imitate but also to lead. The new curriculum bore similarities in structure and content to the Egyptian and Jordanian, but it was to be more progressive and democratic. The constitution would follow the framework of republican Arab documents but would correct their oversights and mistakes. NGOs would engage the state not merely as supportive supplicants but also as partners and watchdogs. Palestinian politics would show the broader Arab world brighter alternatives for their own development. The record since 1993 shows that such dreams were probably excessively ambitious, but in some areas (such as legislative drafting or curriculum writing) it could be said that Palestinians not merely borrowed but also improved. Few in the rest of the Arab world took much notice, however, and the second intifada reintroduced the Palestinians to the bitter side of Arab politics: they garnered tremendous sympathy but precious little support.

The second intifada imposed the harshest constraints on those who had worked since 1993 to resume normal political life and make relations with Israel less relevant. For Palestinians in the West Bank and Gaza, after

September 2000 Israel was everywhere. Those who wished to build liberal and democratic institutions and practices could hardly pursue their goals in the same ways in an atmosphere that produced closure, institutional paralysis, and violence. While it may have temporarily stymied most of their efforts, however, it did not deter them from their goals. Indeed, for many of the advocates of political reform, the second intifada provided an occasion to seek a wider social base for their platform of political reform, buttressed now by the argument that national crisis required the sort of unity that only reform could provide. For the first two years of the intifada, they were unable to make much progress under prevailing conditions in which most institutions struggled at best to continue pre-intifada operations. Nevertheless, their project was not forgotten—it received an indirect presidential endorsement when 'Arafat made political reform central to one of his rare public addresses given after the beginning of the second intifada, an address to the PLC on 10 March 2001.[11] By 2002, their project suddenly became the focus of not only domestic but also international attention.

Thus, the period from 1993 to 2000 marked not merely the resumption of Arab Palestine (in the eyes of its proponents) but also its entrenchment. The political pessimism that understandably (even justifiably) prevailed during the second intifada obscured the staying power of some of the pre-2000 accomplishments. Any future efforts to build Palestinian institutions will launch from a very different starting point from that marked by the signing of the first Oslo Agreement in 1993 and the founding of the PNA in 1994. The resumption of Arab Palestine was based on a wishful reading of the past and an optimistic reading of the future. It has been punctuated by failure, violence, and frustration, but it will be difficult to reverse.

Notes

CHAPTER 1: RESUMING ARAB PALESTINE

1. See Council on Foreign Relations, "Strengthening Palestinian Public Institutions— Executive Summary," Independent Task Force Report, Michel Rocard, chairman, Henry Siegman, project director, Yezid Sayigh and Khalil Shikaki, principal authors, June 1999, p. 8, retrieved 22 November 2002 from www.cfr.org/publication.php?id=3184. The full text is "Strengthening Palestinian Public Institutions—Full Report," June 1999, retrieved 22 November 2002 from www.cfr.org/publication.php?id=3185.

2. An English translation of the decree is available from the Palestinian Ministry of Planning and International Cooperation. See "Building the State," retrieved 24 December 2002 from the PNA Web site: www.pna.net/search/TitleDetails.asp?txtDocID=202. The decree refers to Henry Siegman of the Council on Foreign Relations.

3. See, e.g., Nur al-Din al-Faridi, "International Report Advises the Palestinian Authority to Rely on the Principle of the Separation of Powers and Diminish the Competencies of the Presidency," *Al-hayah*, 4 November 1999.

4. For the PNA position paper, see Higher National Committee for Institutional Development, "A Proposed Short Term Action Plan for the Development of Palestinian Public Institutions," 3 November 1999, retrieved 24 December 2002 from the PNA Web site: www.pna.net/search/TitleDetails.asp?txtDocID=55.

5. See Sa'ida Hamad, "Gaza: 'Development Council' Answers the Recommendations of the 'Reform [Committee],' " *Al-hayah*, 13 January 2000; see also Amira Hass, "Chairman Arafat Straightens out His Financial Accounts," *Ha'aretz*, 13 January 2000.

6. See "Economic Policy Framework Progress Report," 31 May 2000, prepared by the Palestinian Authority in collaboration with the staff of the International Monetary Fund.

7. 'Abd al-Karim Dalbah, "Al-Ahmad: The Overlapping of Authorities Is the Chief Problem Confronting the Implementing of the Projects of the Ministries," *Al-ayyam*, 29 February 2000, p. 7.

8. The interview with ʿAbd Rabbuh was published in *Al-ayyam*, 1 May 1999; translated in World News Connection (a subscription-based service) as "Palestinian Culture Minister on Policies," 7 May 1999, FBIS-NES-1999-US06; and published in English as "PA Minister of Culture and Information Yasir ʿAbid Rabbu, Interview," in the *Journal of Palestine Studies* 28 (Summer 1999): 156–59. The security official quoted is Samih Kanʿan; see Hadeel Wahdan, "Above the Law," *Palestine Report* 6 (10 May 2000), retrieved 22 January 2003 from www.palestinereport.org. Kanʿan insisted in a personal interview in Ramallah on 20 July 2000 that Preventive Security had established a firmer sense of mission and pattern of behavior but admitted that other security services were different and that the problems of overlap and competition still existed. Some leading officials have even raised the sensitive issue of the corruption of their colleagues in public. See the comments of Industry Minister Saʿdi al-Krunz in "Minister Critical of Fellow Officials," *Jerusalem Times*, 27 August 1999.

9. David Sewell, "Governance and the Business Environment in the West Bank/Gaza," Working Paper Series No. 23, Social and Economic Group, Middle East and North Africa Region, World Bank, May 2001, retrieved 26 December 2002 from http://lnweb18.worldbank.org/mna/mena.nsf/Attachments/WP+23/$File/WP-23.pdf, p. 25.

10. The topic of Palestinian national identity is highly (and often needlessly) polemicized. Perhaps the most authoritative treatment is Rashid Khalidi's *Palestinian Identity: The Construction of Modern National Consciousness* (New York: Columbia University Press, 1997).

11. For instance, Hillel Frisch's thorough *Countdown to Statehood: Palestinian State Formation in the West Bank and Gaza* (Albany: SUNY Press, 1998) uses the Zionist experience as a benchmark for Palestinian state formation.

12. Khalidi, *Palestinian Identity*, p. 204.

13. An English translation of the statement, "A Cry from the Homeland," can be found in "Palestinian Authority Arrests Four Public Figures," 28 November 1999, retrieved 24 December 2002 from the Web site of LAW (the Palestinian Society for the Protection of Human Rights and the Environment): www.lawsociety.org/Press/press/1999/nov_28.html.

14. "Text of the Statement of the Legislative Council," *Al-quds*, 2 December 1999.

15. The oblique wording of the Paris Protocol on Economic Relations makes the fiscal relationship between Israel and the PNA occasionally difficult to discern, but those provisions were largely implemented until the outbreak of the second intifada. In negotiating the arrangements, Israel was insistent that the West Bank and Gaza be treated as an economic unit with an open border, something the Palestinian negotiators reluctantly accepted, partly because of the dependence of many Palestinian workers on employment in Israel. Having determined open borders, the negotiations then resulted in Palestinian agreement to peg their Value-Added Tax (VAT) rates (as well as some other matters, such as gasoline prices) to those set by Israel. If the Palestinians had not charged

a VAT or had set far lower rates, the open border would have resulted in large-scale smuggling of cheaper Palestinian goods into Israel, which Israel was not willing to accept. And since virtually all goods destined for Palestinian markets pass through entry points controlled by Israel, Israel was to collect the VAT and then pass it on to the PNA. As a result, the PNA lacked fiscal autonomy—but it was able to collect revenues far more easily than most Arab states and to do so while minimizing its public role in tax collection.

16. For instance, for an analysis of Palestinian politics that emphasizes the constricting nature of post-Oslo politics, see Rabab Ibrahim Abdulhadi, "Palestinianness in a Comparative Perspective: Inclusionary Resistance, Exclusionary Citizenship" (Ph.D. diss., Yale University, 2000).

CHAPTER 2: THE LEGAL FRAMEWORK

1. Glenn E. Robinson, "The Politics of Legal Reform in Palestine," *Journal of Palestine Studies* 27 (Autumn 1997): 52.

2. For some examples of such views, see ibid.; Raja Shehadeh, *From Occupation to Interim Accords: Israel and the Palestinian Territories* (London: Kluwer Law International, 1997); and George E. Bisharat, "Peace and the Political Imperative of Legal Reform in Palestine," *Case Western Reserve Journal of International Law* 31 (1999): 253.

3. United Nations, Office of the Special Coordinator in the Occupied Territories, "Rule of Law Development in the West Bank and Gaza Strip: Survey and State of the Development Effort," May 1999, p. 16.

4. The decision creating the courts was issued in February 1995. The next month, Gore met with 'Arafat and publicly announced that he "welcomed the decision to prosecute terrorists." See "New Islamic Fundamentalist Group Threatens 'Every Jew in Palestine,' " *Jerusalem Post*, 26 March 1995.

5. Ben Lynfield, "PNC Speaker Concerned over Weakness of Palestinian Authority's Judiciary," *Jerusalem Post*, 22 June 1999, retrieved 22 January 2003 from www.jpost.com.

6. The legal system in Gaza developed less after 1948 and thus remained closer to its mandatory basis, but it was interpreted and implemented by Egyptian-trained lawyers. The vast majority of Gaza lawyers were trained in Egypt. On the West Bank, annexation by Jordan brought Jordanian law. That law often employed different terminology (especially because of the earlier British influence) but moved steadily in style and substance closer to the Egyptian.

7. I have left the Islamic shari'a court system out of this account. The subject has recently received a comprehensive and thorough treatment by Lynn Welchman in *Beyond the Code: Muslim Family Law and the Shar'i Judiciary in the Palestinian West Bank* (The Hague, the Netherlands: Kluwer Law International, 2000). Also of interest is Fadwa Labadi et al., "Islamic Family Law and the Transition to Palestinian Statehood: Constraints and Opportunities for Legal Reform," retrieved 26 November 2002 from Emory University School of Law Web site: www.law.emory.edu/IFL/cases/Palestine.htm.

8. Modern Palestinian legal history has attracted less attention that that of neighboring states. In George Bisharat's *Palestinian Lawyers and Israeli Rule: Law and Disorder in the West Bank* (Austin: University of Texas Press, 1989), there is a brief but helpful description in chap. 2.

9. See, e.g., Raja Shehadeh, *Occupier's Law: Israel and the West Bank* (Washington, DC: Institute for Palestine Studies, 1988). The most comprehensive treatment is Bisharat's *Palestinian Lawyers.*

10. Law 2 of 1994. The designation of the High Court of Gaza was explicitly temporary, pending its transfer to Jerusalem. Some have argued that the step was implicitly temporary in another way. The law was issued when Jericho was the only West Bank city to fall under PNA rule. In the absence of the law, appeals from the Jericho court would have gone to the court in Ramallah, which the Israelis oversaw. Thus, to assert full Palestinian control, this law routed appeals from Jericho to Gaza. Some have argued that, with the full transfer of the Palestinian courts, law has lost its political basis and therefore should no longer be considered valid. For an example of such a view, see Husayn Abu Hunud, *Mahakim al-'adl al-'ulya al-filiastiniyya* (The Palestinian High Courts of Justice) (Ramallah: Palestinian Independent Commission for Citizens' Rights, 1999), pp. 50–51. When the Israelis withdrew from Ramallah, the West Bank High Court resumed full operation in administrative cases, making the law inoperative. However, in 1999, when the chief justice in Gaza won greater control over the West Bank judiciary, the law was cited.

11. Law 5 of 2001, however, assigned election disputes to the High Court, leaving the status of the election court provided for in earlier legislation uncertain.

12. This process was initiated by Law 2 of 1995 and is examined in more detail below. Repealing some military orders had merely symbolic value. For instance, repealing the jurisdiction of the Israeli military courts had effect only in areas controlled by the PNA—where such courts no longer operated anyway. Israeli military courts continued to exercise some jurisdiction in areas under Israeli security control.

13. Decision 287 of 1995.

14. See, e.g., Robinson, "Politics of Legal Reform," p. 55.

15. Ibid., p. 57. In carrying out research in 1999 and 2000, I heard similar complaints voiced in far less charged terms, probably indicating that the conflict had lessened.

16. USAID, which initially held back from involvement in the legal sector because of such obstacles, decided that the situation had become more favorable by 1999 and resumed activities. A preliminary study, "Feasible Options for Rule of Law Programming," produced by Chemonics International in December 1998, concluded that "the precondition of greater willingness among the West Bank and Gaza legal communities to work together has been met" (p. 15).

17. For an extended coverage of the dispute, see Husam 'Izz al-Din, "The Judges Await 'Rebuilding' of the Judicial Apparatus: A Struggle for Jurisdiction and the Intervention of the Security Agencies Deepens the Deterioration of the Situation," *Al-ayyam*, 8 November 1999.

18. A political and legal analysis of the episode can be found in Abu Hunud, *Mahakim al-ʿadl al-ʿulya*, pp. 54–61.

19. The position was taken by a leading judicial dissident, ʿIsa Abu Sharar, at the time of the 1999 judicial strike. See "Ramallah: The Judges Strike, Protesting the Transfer of Some of Them and Demanding Structural Reforms in the Judicial System," *Al-ayyam*, 12 October 1999.

20. Abu Sharar is quoted on the matter of the petition in ibid.

21. The verdict is partially quoted in the report by LAW, the Palestinian Society for the Protecting of Human Rights and the Environment, Independent Judiciary Unit, "Executive Interference in the Palestinian Judiciary," April 1999, retrieved 2 December 2002 from www.lawsociety.org/Reports/reports/1999/judic.html.

22. I have considered the structure of such bodies in Nathan J. Brown, *The Rule of Law in the Arab World: Courts in Egypt and the Gulf* (New York: Cambridge University Press, 1997).

23. See "The Legislature Passes the Law on the Formation of the Law Courts on the First Reading," *Al-ayyam*, 13 March 2000.

24. For instance, the PLC worked with the Ministry of Justice, not the judiciary, over the judicial budget. See "Budget Committee Holds Two Hearings on the Budgets of the Ministries of Planning and Justice," *Al-ayyam*, 28 December 1999, p. 5.

25. "Al-Haqq Greets the Decision of the President to Release Judge Ghazi ʿAtara," *Al-hayah al-jadida*, 20 September 2001.

26. Decision 29 of 2000. The preamble of the text referred to "the important and essential articles of the Law of the Judicial Authority," presumably referring to the draft passed by the PLC. The decision grants the council "the competencies stipulated in the Law of the Judicial Authority," again presumably referring to the unsigned law.

27. "Al-Agha: The President Grants the Judiciary an Independent Budget," *Al-hayah al-jadida*, 4 June 2000.

28. "ʿArafat in the Opening Session of the Legislative Council: [We Are] Prepared Immediately to Complete the Taba Negotiations," *Al-hayah*, 11 March 2001, p. 3.

29. "The President Approves a Package of Laws Related to the Judiciary and Refers the Law of the Judicial Authority to the Legislature to Amend It," *Al-ayyam*, 10 June 2001.

30. Law 5 of 2001.

31. Requiring the creation of the *mahkamat al-naqd* was hardly the end of the effort to construct it: one year later, the court still had not begun operation.

32. There were provisions for a constitutional court in the unsigned Basic Law and the unsigned Independence of the Judiciary Law. When the Judiciary Law was finally signed in 2002, however, it was still unclear what function a constitutional court would serve without an approved constitution.

33. "Legislature Renews Its Complete Support of the President's Cease Fire

Decision and Demands That World Parliaments Condemn the Scandalous Israeli Violations," *Al-ayyam*, 16 January 2002.

34. "The President Approves the Law of the Independence of the Judiciary," *Al-hayah al-jadida*, 15 May 2002, p. 1.

35. See "President 'Arafat Decides to Add Three Clauses to the Judicial Authority to Guarantee Its Independence," *Al-quds*, 27 May 2002.

36. The annual reports of the Palestinian Independent Commission for Citizens' Rights provide extremely comprehensive and helpful coverage of the court system.

37. Three fairly comprehensive evaluations of the performance and nature of the Palestinian legal system can be found in LAW, "Executive Interference"; USAID, "Request for Proposal on 'Strengthening the Palestinian Legal Profession under the Rule of Law' " (RFP 294–99–013), 1999; and United Nations, "Rule of Law Development." On the caseload of the courts, the most well-grounded empirical study was completed by DPK Consulting, "Analysis of Closed Case Survey of Civil Cases in Four Palestinian Pilot Courts," Rule of Law Project-West Bank and Gaza, USAID Contract Number 294-C.00–99–00–159–00, 2001.

38. One lawyer estimated that the number of lawsuits tripled or quadrupled. Karim Shahada, personal interview, Ramallah, February 2000.

39. The justice minister gave the figure as 210,000. See "Abu Mudayn: The 'Slowness' of the PLC in Legislation Causes Disturbance in Public Performance," *Al-ayyam* 1 March 2000, p. 7.

40. DPK Consulting, "Analysis of Closed Case Survey."

41. This and other examples are given in LAW, "Executive Interference in the Judiciary."

42. I have argued that something similar occurs in Egypt. See Brown, *Rule of Law*, chap. 7.

43. I located the Jericho court with some difficulty because of its unassuming entrance. This opened to an even more modest interior: the ground floor was used to store bicycles; to reach the court itself—a suite of several dark offices stuffed with files and papers—one climbed a narrow staircase.

44. "The Lawyers of Jenin Resume Their Appeals Tomorrow before the Magistrate's Court," *Al-ayyam*, 18 May 1999.

45. "Lawyers of the Governorate of Tulkarem Continue Their Strike," *Al-quds*, 27 November 1999.

46. For an excellent treatment of the Palestinian legal profession in the 1970s and 1980s, see Bisharat, *Palestinian Lawyers*.

47. Personal interview with 'Adnan Abu Layla, deputy chair, Palestinian Bar Association, Ramallah, February 2000.

48. The information in this section is based on conversations with officials in development agencies (including the World Bank and USAID), contractors with these agencies, members of the Palestinian legal community, administrators at Palestinian law schools, and senior Palestinian officials dealing with assistance and with legal issues. Because of the political sensitivities discussed in this sec-

tion (and sometimes because of commercial competition among contractors), many of those I spoke with indicated a preference not to be quoted by name. There are two published comprehensive surveys of donor work in the legal field. These surveys are couched in more diplomatic language than that used by the interviewees, but their conclusions are surprisingly frank and detailed. See USAID, "Request for Proposal," and United Nations, "Rule of Law Development." An excellent and politically sophisticated general work on assistance to the PNA is Rex Brynen's *A Very Political Economy: Peacebuilding and Foreign Aid in the West Bank and Gaza* (Washington, DC: United States Institute of Peace Press, 2000).

49. The initial description of the World Bank's West Bank and Gaza Legal Development Project is available in World Bank, "West Bank and Gaza Legal Development Project." Report No. PIC4646, 1997.

50. USAID, "Request for Proposal," Attachment J.4, p. 43.

51. For a general critique of development assistance in law, see Thomas Carothers, *Aiding Democracy Abroad: The Learning Curve* (Washington, DC: Carnegie Endowment for International Peace, 1999), chap. 7.

52. The phrase was used by Hasan 'Abd al-Rahman, PLO representative in Washington, personal interview, June 1999.

53. See "The Palestinian Minster of Justice Charges Errors in the United Nations Report about the Size of International Aid for His Ministry," *Al-hayah*, 11 June 1999.

54. "Abu Mudayn: The Authority Is Seriously Thinking about Refusing to Receive Aid from Donor States When It Does Not Benefit," *Al-ayyam*, 25 January 2000.

55. See Glenn Robinson, *Building a Palestinian State* (Bloomington: Indiana University Press), pp. 110–16; and Adrien Katherine Wing, "Legal Decision-Making During the Palestinian *Intifada:* Embryonic Self-Rule," *Yale Journal of International Law* 18, no. 1 (1993): 95–153.

56. See the comments of the head of the Bar Association in "Abu Mudayn: The Slowness of Litigation," p. 7.

57. I have written of a similar situation regarding the prosecution of offenses on domestic labor in Kuwait. See Brown, *Rule of Law*, chap. 7.

58. See "Why Is the Role of the Tax Authorities Absent," *Palestinian Human Rights Monitor* 2, no. 5 (1998) (entire issue).

59. Most of the information in this paragraph is based on a personal interview with Samih Kan'an, director of external relations for Palestinian Preventive Security (and former commander of the force in Nablus), Ramallah, July 2000. The role of the security forces in automobile thefts and other crimes is acknowledged by most officials involved on both the Israeli and the Palestinian sides.

60. Most of the information on the governorates is based on an interview with Dr. Arij al-'Awda, the director of the legal affairs department for the Governorate of Ramallah and a visit to the department in March 2000. During my visit, I saw one case conclude and one begin.

61. See Bisharat, *Palestinian Lawyers*, pp. 39–43. See also Hillel Frisch, "Modern Absolutist or Neopatriarchal State Building? Customary Law, Extended Families, and the Palestinian Authority," *International Journal of Middle East Studies* 29 (1997): 341–58. Frisch demonstrates how the PNA actually encouraged the use of customary law, though he seems to regard it as an alternative rather than a supplement to positive law (perhaps because his research was conducted early in PNA history). Frisch's view, however, is shared by many leading Palestinian legal figures who view the PNA's involvement in such matters as distasteful, subverting the regular courts. See "Gaza: Legal Figures Call for the Rule of Law and Elimination of Tribalist Manifestations," *Al-ayyam*, 31 July 2001.

62. The mediator for the Ramallah area insisted—in a personal interview punctuated by numerous cell phone calls from various disputants—that the insistence on compensation is universal in Palestinian society, regardless of education, income level, religion, or place of residence.

63. In general, constitutional thought in the United States and the Arab world differs subtly and significantly in this regard. Americans tend to speak of "checks and balances," accepting some overlap and rivalry among branches of government as inevitable and occasionally even desirable. Legal and constitutional figures in the Arab world generally insist on fuller "separation of powers," concerned that deviation from the principle will lead to executive branch domination.

64. I heard these criticisms repeated by Palestinian legal figures during interviews in 1999 and 2000. See also Hadeel Wahdan, "The Authority of the Law or the Law of the Authority," *Palestine Report* 6 (24 May 2000), retrieved 22 January 2003 from www.palestinereport.org.

65. Personal interview, Dr. Arij al-'Awda, Ramallah, March 2000. In a personal interview, the deputy head of the Bar Association acknowledged that the governorates had been responsive to the insistence of the legal community not to get involved in cases already before the courts.

66. I have examined these issues more generally in Brown, *The Rule of Law*, chap. 8. For an extensive treatment of arbitration in Palestinian law, see Marshall J. Breger and Shelby R. Quast, "International Commercial Arbitration: A Case Study of the Areas under Control of the Palestinian Authority," *Case Western Reserve Journal of International Law* 32 (suppl., 2000): 185–258.

67. Interviews with Jerusalem Chamber of Commerce, May 2000, and Jericho Chamber of Commerce, June 2000. A fairly comprehensive treatment of prevailing business practices can be found in Daniel Kalman, Ra'ed Abdul Hamid, Mohammed Dahleh, Ayesha Qayyum, and Tobias Nybo Rasmussen, *Commercial Contract Enforcement in the Palestinian Territories*, Israel/Palestine Center for Research and Information Commercial Contract Enforcement in the Palestinian Territories Series, no. 5, February 1997.

68. An English translation of the decision is included in LAW, "Military and State Security Courts and the Rule of Law in PA-Controlled Areas," May 1999, retrieved 2 December 2002 from www.lawsociety.org/Reports/reports/1999/statesec.html.

69. Human rights groups—and many Palestinian leaders—denounced the court; the most comprehensive legal analysis of its basis and operation is ibid.

70. Israel had a reciprocal obligation to transfer suspects only if they were not Israeli. The provisions are contained in the Israeli-Palestinian Agreement on the West Bank and the Gaza Strip, 25 September 1995, Annex IV, Protocol Concerning Legal Matters, Article 2, Section 7, Transfer of Suspects and Defendants.

71. In April 2002, a court was convened composed of members of the security services present with Yasir ʿArafat in the Ramallah governorate—then surrounded by Israeli forces. The court quickly convicted those accused of involvement in the assassination of the Israeli minister of tourism, paving the way for a negotiated solution to breaking the blockade without surrendering the accused Palestinians.

72. By 1999, the Israelis had submitted forty-six requests for the transfer of suspects. None received a response. Personal interview with Jean-Claude Niddam, Head of Legal Assistance, Israeli Ministry of Justice, Jerusalem, November 1999. Niddam's office is responsible for legal interactions with the PNA. In 2000, the PNA finally did extradite one suspect, though only because the circumstances of the case removed the usual political inhibitions: the crime involved the rape of a young Israeli Arab in Nazareth. The identity of the victim removed nationalist objections to the transfer of the suspect for trial in Israel.

73. See, e.g., "Minister of Judges Demands the Legislative Council to Maintain the "State Security" Courts!!" *Huquq al-nas*, March 2000, p. 27. The comments came in response to a PLC report, the text of which is included in *Huquq al-nas*.

74. Decision 15 of 1998.

75. ʿArafat issued further instructions to the court to consider economic crimes in June 1999. See "Presidential Decision to Transform Economic Violations to 'State Security,' " *Al-hayah al-jadida*, 1 July 1999.

76. "The State Security Courts" *Huquq al-nas*, January 2000, pp. 44–46.

77. Raja Shehadeh, "The Weight of Legal History: Constraints and Hopes in the Search for a Sovereign Legal Language," in *The Arab-Israeli Accords: Legal Perspectives*, ed. Eugene Cotran, Chibli Mallat, and David Stott (London: Kluwer Law International: 1996).

78. Most of the argument in this section is based on an analysis of Palestinian legislative texts. All are published in the official gazette, *Al-waqaʾiʿ al-filastiniyya*, but I have relied on the collection published by the Ministry of Justice's Diwan al-Fatwa wa-l-Tashriʿ under the World Bank's Legal Development Program in 1999, *Majmuʿat al-tashriʿat al-filastiniyya min ʿamm 1994 hatta nahayat ʿamm 1998* (Collection of Palestinian legislation from 1994 until the end of 1998).

79. See, e.g., "Deputies: The Palestinian People Laid Down the Laws for the Palestinian State . . . and Not for the Interim Stage," *Afaq barlamaniyya* 4 (September 2000): 11–12.

80. Decision 1 of 1994.

81. This decision is actually dated 6 May 1994, whereas Decision 1 of 1994 is dated 20 May 1994. It is likely that the later decision was published first, thus explaining the discrepancy between the dates and the numbers.

82. Law 1 of 1994, dated 24 September 1994.

83. Decision 39 of 1998.

84. The law is dated 18 December 1994 but was numbered Law 2 of 1995.

85. Law 5 of 1995.

86. Personal interview with Ibrahim al-Daghma, director of the Diwan al-Fatwa wa-l-Tashri', Ramallah, September 1999. Al-Daghma, who has been involved in much of the legislative drafting for the PNA, stated that those Israeli military orders in conflict with Palestinian laws are not enforced. The claim is plausible—it would essentially involve demoting Israeli military orders from a status equivalent to a law to that of an administrative order or regulation. While this may indeed be the attitude of Palestinian judges and legal authorities, there is no public record of any decree, law, or directive to such effect.

87. Decision 55 of 1996.

88. Decision 20 of 1998.

89. Law 1 of 2001. The Oslo Accords—with their characteristic delicacy on such matters—required that Israeli shekels be used as a circulating currency and offered only the possibility of negotiating a new Palestinian currency. (Protocol on Economic Relations between the Government of the State of Israel and the PLO, Representing the Palestinian People, Article IV). The use of this formulation in legislation was adopted specifically to allow for the conversion to a Palestinian national currency when one was finally issued. See the comments of 'Abd al-Karim Abu Salah, chair of the PLC Legal Committee, in "The Legislature Passes the Law of Civil Court Fees in Its First Reading," *Al-ayyam*, 17 October 2001.

90. See, e.g., Law 13 of 2002.

91. Presidential Decree 1 of 1996.

92. Law 4 of 2001.

93. Law 5 of 2001.

94. The cabinet decision on banking is Decision 1 of 1997; the decision on traffic accidents is Decision 95 of 1994; the decision on the attorney general is Decision 287 of 1995.

95. For an example of this criticism, see Council on Foreign Relations, "Strengthening Palestinian Public Institutions—Full Report," Independent Task Force Report, Michel Rocard, chairman; Henry Siegman, project director; Yezid Sayigh and Khalil Shikaki, principal authors, June 1999, retrieved 22 November 2002 from www.cfr.org/publication.php?id=3184.

96. The passage comes in the explanatory memorandum attached to the law (Law 13 of 1995). The same law also cites the PLO's basic law and the agreement of the PLO's Executive Committee.

97. Presidential Decree 3 of 1998.

98. Paragraph 106 of Law 4 of 1998.

99. Such phrases recur frequently in legislative enactments but generally

with additional authority and legislative history also being cited. On many occasions, however, the brief phrase quoted here is the sole authority adduced for a legislative enactment. See, e.g., Decision 312 of 1995. There are numerous other examples.

100. There are exceptions, however, when such an argument is made explicitly. In July 2000, I participated in a workshop in Gaza in which I asked one member of the Palestinian judiciary how—in the absence of a clear constitutional framework—it could be determined who could develop law and issue new legislation. He answered without hesitation: "President Abu 'Ammar [Yasir 'Arafat]."

101. Law 13 of 1995.

102. Decree-Law 1 of 1998.

103. E.g., the Egyptian constitution clearly bans torture and bars courts from considering confessions obtained by torture. Persistent reports of torture by the security forces make clear that the ban is violated, but the law is not ignored: torturers obscure their own identity so as to make prosecution for torture (which has been attempted) difficult or impossible, and courts have repeatedly acquitted torture victims. The constitutional ban has hardly eliminated torture, but it has had significant effects.

104. Law 9 of 1995. The law contained strong general language supporting freedom of the press but innumerable potential restrictions. For instance, a periodical could not receive funds from a foreign NGO without permission from the minister of information. Editors were responsible for the content of their publications and could be jailed if they did not print corrections.

105. The most comprehensive report on illegal detentions is Ma'en Id'eis, "Detentions in PNA Controlled Areas (Legality and Application)," LAW report, Jerusalem, May 2000, retrieved 2 December 2002 from www.lawsociety.org/ Reports/reports/2000/padetent.html. For additional detail, there are a variety of reports by the Palestinian Human Rights Monitoring Group, available at www.phrmg.org.

106. In 1997, Fayiz Abu Rahma, the successor to Khalid al-Qidra as attorney general, ordered some detainees released. Some of those released were detained again, and Abu Rahma was transferred to the position of presidential advisor.

107. Those accused on involvement in the death of Yusuf al-Baba were tried, according to the minister of justice, after "the president issued an order to arrest the perpetrators." See the interview with Farih Abu Mudayn, *Majallat al-dirasat al-filastiniyya*, no. 30 (Spring 1997): 49–57.

108. The distinction can be useful but I often find it difficult to make in practice, as I have argued in Brown, *The Rule of Law*.

109. See "The Judges and the Lawyers Appraise the Decision of the President to Appoint 26 New Judges in the *Sulh* Courts," *Al-hayah al-jadida*, 10 January 2002; this article lists several attacks. See also James Bennet, "Palestinian Justice Unravels as Mob Kills 3," *New York Times*, 6 February 2002.

110. This authority was endorsed in Cabinet Decision 1 of 1998.

111. Personal interview, Ibrahim al-Daghma, Ramallah, September 1999.

CHAPTER 3: CONSTITUTING AND RECONSTITUTING PALESTINE

1. I examine the purposes of Arab constitutional documents in Nathan J. Brown, *Constitutions in a Nonconstitutional World: Arab Basic Laws and the Prospects for Accountable Government* (Albany: SUNY University Press, 2002). In addition, I have analyzed the draft Basic Law in Nathan J. Brown, "Constituting Palestine: The Effort to Write a Basic Law for the Palestinian Authority," *Middle East Journal* 54 (Winter 2000): 25–43.

2. Hasan Khadr, "The Visionary, the Shepherd, and the Constitution," *Al-ayyam*, 8 May 2001, retrieved 8 May 2001 from www.al-ayyam.com.

3. See the comments of Muhammad Subayh, Palestinian ambassador to the Arab League, reported in Rasha Saad, "State in the Making," *Al-Ahram Weekly*, 17 June 1999, retrieved 24 December 2002 from weekly.ahram.org.eg/1999/434/re1.htm.

4. Much of this effort has subsequently been forgotten, but the prospect of a Palestinian state after the 1988 declaration of independence and the Oslo Accords led to some renewed interest, especially among Palestinians. Two historical works have been published: Muhammad Khalid al-Az'ar, *Hukumut 'umum filastin* (The All-Palestine Government) (Cairo: Dar al-shuruq, 1998; and Samih Shabib, *Hukumut 'umum filastin* (The All-Palestine Government) (Jerusalem: Al-bayadir, 1988). I have relied on these two books as well as a day-by-day press survey, using *Al-ahram*, *Bayrut*, and *Al-nahar*. In addition, an excellent article based partly on British records tells the story in briefer form: Avi Shlaim, "The Rise and Fall of the All-Palestine Government in Gaza," *Journal of Palestine Studies* 20 (Autumn 1990): 37–53.

5. 'Abd Allah's actions and attitude provoked strong bitterness among some Palestinians, resulting in his assassination. The most comprehensive treatment of this controversial subject is Avi Shlaim, *The Politics of Partition: King Abdullah, the Zionists and Palestine 1921–1951* (New York: Columbia University Press, 1990).

6. The cable, dated 28 September 1948, was sent by Ahmad Hilmi to the UN secretary-general. See "Cablegram Dated 28 September 1948 from the Premier and Acting Foreign Secretary of All-Palestine Government to the Secretary-General Concerning Constitution of All-Palestine Government," retrieved 24 December 2002 from the United Nations Information System on the Question of Palestine (UNISPAL) Web site: http://domino.un.org/unispal.nsf/561c6ee353d740fb8525607d00581829/
62b1867e967323068025648e0041673d!OpenDocument.

7. The text of the declaration, "The New Arab State," was printed in *Al-ahram*, 3 October 1948, p. 1.

8. The constitutional documents from the Egyptian period can be found in Judge Mazen Sisalem, Judge Ishak Muhanna, and Legal Advisor Sulieman El Dahdoh, *The Laws of Palestine*, vol. 27 (Gaza: Matabi' mansur, 1996).

9. See Anis al-Qasim, "'Anasir al-nizam al-dusturi li-l-marhala al-intiqaliyya," in *Al-intikhabat wa-l-nizam al-siyasi al-filastini* (Elections and

the Palestinian political system), ed. Khalil Shikaki [al-Shiqaqi] (Nablus: Center for Palestine Research and Studies, 1995), pp. 22–25.

10. I have treated the Jordanian constitutional tradition in more detail in Brown, *Constitutions in a Nonconstitutional World*, chap. 2.

11. The text of what was called the "Declaration of Independence" was widely circulated; I have relied on the version included in Fathi 'Abd al-Nabi al-Wahidi, *Al-tatawwurat al-dusturiyya fi filastin 1917–1995* (Constitutional developments in Palestine 1917–1995) (Gaza: Matabi' al-hay'a al-khayriyya bi-qita' ghaza, 1996), p. 452.

12. Anis al-Qasem, "The Draft Basic Law for the Palestinian National Authority during the Transitional Period," in *The Arab-Israeli Accords: Legal Perspectives*, ed. Eugene Cotran and Chibli Mallat (London: Kluwer Law International, 1996), p. 101.

13. See Naseer H. Aruri and John J. Carroll, "A New Palestinian Charter," *Journal of Palestine Studies* 23 (Summer 1994): 5–17. Anis al-Qasim, leader of this drafting effort, describes the nature of his work in Gary A. Hengstler, "First Steps toward Justice," *ABA Journal*, February 1994, pp. 52–61. The political context of the work is described briefly but well in Hillel Frisch, *Countdown to Statehood: Palestinian State Formation in the West Bank and Gaza* (Albany: SUNY Press, 1998), pp. 141–42. Another account that includes some textual analysis is Gregory Mahler, *Constitutionalism and Palestinian Constitutional Development* (Jerusalem: Palestinian Academic Society for the Study of International Affairs, 1996).

14. For a critical analysis of the law, see Palestinian Centre for Human Rights, *Critique of the Press Law 1995 Issued by the Palestinian Authority* (Gaza: Mansour Press, 1995).

15. See Anis al-Qasim, "'Anasir al-nizam."

16. I did obtain an unpublished document, entitled "Suggestions Concerning the Draft Basic Law for the Palestinian Council," presented by Palestinian negotiators to Israeli negotiators in Cairo in 1994. If it is an accurate indication of the Palestinian position, the Palestinian delegation got most of what it wanted in the final agreement.

17. Law 13 of 1995.

18. PLC Resolution 8/2/1.

19. Wing set out her views before beginning work on the project in Adrien Katherine Wing, *Democracy, Constitutionalism and the Future State of Palestine* (Jerusalem: Palestinian Academic Society for the Study of International Affairs, 1994).

20. This discussion is based primarily on press coverage, supplemented by interviews with some of the council members and legal experts engaged in the effort to draft the Basic Law. For the public argument between 'Arafat and Abu 'Ala', see *Al-sharq al-awsat*, 31 July–2 August 1996. For other analyses of the draft, see Anthony B. Tirado Chase, *The Palestinian Authority Draft Constitution: Possibilities and Realities in the Search for Alternative Models of State Formation* (Jerusalem: Israel-Palestine Center for Research and Information,

1997); and John Strawson, "Palestine's Basic Law: Constituting New Identities Through Liberating Legal Culture," *Loyola of Los Angeles International and Comparative Law Journal* 20 (March 1998): 411–32. Chase also provides an analysis with special focus on human rights and Islamic elements of the Basic Law in *Islam and Human Rights, Clashing Normative Orders?* (Ph.D. diss., Fletcher School of Law and Diplomacy, 2000), chap. 7.

21. See Brown, *Constitutions in a Nonconstitutional World,* for an elaboration of this theme.

22. Because of the increasingly public nature of the drafting process, earlier drafts were less widely circulated; later drafts were often published in several different outlets and quickly translated into English as well. The first draft was leaked to the Palestinian press in December 1993. The second draft was more widely available; I have relied on the copy published in al-Wahidi, *Al-tatawwurat al-dusturiyya.* The third draft was published in Shikaki, *Al-intikhabat.* An English version was published in Cotran et al., *The Arab-Israeli Accords.* The fourth draft was published in *Palestine Report,* 9 February 1996. A draft produced by Bir Zayt University and al-Haqq is often counted as the fifth draft; it was published by al-Haqq under the title *Al-musawwada al-muqtaraha li-mashru' al-qanun al-asasi al-filastini li al-marhala al-intiqaliyya* (The proposed design for the draft Palestinian Basic Law for the Interim Phase) (Ramallah: Mu'asassat al-Haqq, 1996). The draft produced by the legal committee of the PLC is generally counted as the sixth draft; I have relied on a copy circulated by the committee (provided by Muhammad al-Mirghani, and Egyptian scholar of constitutional law who advised the committee). See the English translation of the final version passed on the third reading by the PLC, "Palestinian Legislative Council, Basic Law Draft Resolution, Third Reading," retrieved 25 November 2002 from the Palestinian Society for the Protection of Human Rights and the Environment (LAW) Web site: www.lawsociety.org/LawsT/Laws/BasicL.pdf.

23. The practice of appointing parliamentarians as ministers has inconsistent effects in Arab politics. In Kuwait, members of parliament press for inclusion of a larger number of MPs in the cabinet as a way of increasing popular influence. In Jordan, the practice has been criticized as fostering a sycophantic attitude among MPs aspiring to a ministerial portfolio. The same criticism emerged in the Palestinian case after a large number of PLC members were included in the cabinet.

24. Demonstrating how well they had learned the lessons from other Arab countries' experience, the final draft of the Basic Law allowed the courts to exercise judicial review over the constitutionality of legislation until a specialized constitutional court had been created. In Kuwait, provisions for a constitutional court lay unfulfilled for a decade, and the Kuwaiti courts refused to assume a right of judicial review.

25. This sort of formula is common in Arab constitutions, though precise provisions vary. In Jordan, the parliament must act positively to overturn a decree; in the Palestinian document, inaction would amount to rejection. How-

ever, the Palestinian Basic Law did not go as far as the Kuwaiti constitution, which not only requires that parliament confirm decrees but declares them invalid *retroactively* if they do not receive parliamentary endorsement.

26. 'Ali Khashan, dean of the faculty of law at Al-Quds University, reported that he made the suggestion but council members found it inappropriate to force the president's hand in such a way. Personal interview, Jerusalem, February 2000.

27. Dalal Salama, personal interview, Ramallah, February 2000.

28. Council members did cast around for some way of forcing the president's hand. Some tried to turn to the council's standing orders, which impose a time limit for the president to respond to the council. Others argued that Jordanian and Egyptian laws still apply (by virtue of the president's first decree) and that in both countries parliamentary legislation becomes effective after a specified period if the president fails to act. In November 1997, the PLC briefly debated a motion to consider the Basic Law in effect because of 'Arafat's inaction. The motion was deflected by an agreement to issue a call for 'Arafat to act within two weeks. That deadline passed unnoticed (see the PLC journal, *Al-majlis al-tashri'i*, January 1998). However, most council members lacked the will to try to impose a constitutional order on such an uncertain basis. While they frequently called for promulgation of the Basic Law, council members accepted that nothing could happen until the president acted.

29. Decision 1 of 1994. See Chapter 2 for a further analysis of this decree.

30. Law 5 of 1995.

31. Law 4 of 1995.

32. The reference to the unnamed legal and constitutional principles came in the preamble to Presidential Decree 3 of 1998, issued to ban incitement; it came in fulfillment of a pledge made by the Palestinians as part of the Wye River Memorandum.

33. Law 13 of 1995.

34. See "The Intifada and the Overlap of Sources of Authority," *Afaq bar-lamaniyya* 4 (December 2000): 4–5.

35. The final statement of the Central Committee meeting was printed in *Al-hayah*, 30 April 1999. The most comprehensive coverage of the decisions taken at the meeting was published in a series of articles in *Al-siyasa al-filastiniyya* 6 (Summer 1999).

36. In 1999 and 2000, I interviewed several members of the committee, some of whom were uncertain if they were even members.

37. See "Final Statement of the Central Committee for the Session Held 2–3 July 2000," *Al-ayyam*, 4 July 2000.

38. I was able to attend one of these workshops held in Ramallah in July 2000. The participants in the workshop included PLC deputies, the Palestinian chief justice, and intellectuals and legal figures. Descriptions of some of the workshops are available from the Web site of the Palestinian Center for Public Survey Research in Ramallah: www.pcpsr.org.

39. Some of this discussion is covered in "The Palestinian Constitution and

the Declaration of a State," *Afaq barlamaniyya* 4 (September 2000): 11–12. See also "Points of View about the Palestinian Constitution," *Afaq barlamaniyya* 4 (December 2000): 2.

40. The statement was issued on 10 September 2000 and posted on the Web site of the PNA: see "Palestine Central Council Postpones Establishment of State," retrieved 30 September 2000 from www.palestine-un.org/news/sept00 .pcc.html.

41. I am grateful to Khalil Shikaki for providing me with a copy. The Palestinian Center for Survey and Policy Research in Ramallah has published an English translation, "Palestinian Draft Constitution," retrieved 24 December 2002 in two parts from www.pcpsr.org/domestic/2001/conste1.html and www .pcpsr.org/domestic/2001/conste2.html. An earlier draft is analyzed by 'Aziz Kayid, *Mashru' al-dustur al-filastini al-mu'aqqat* (The draft temporary Palestinian constitution) (Ramallah: Palestinian Independent Commission for Citizens' Rights, 2000). The only other analysis I am aware of is Asem Khalil, "The Palestinian Constitutional System" (Dissertatio ad Licentiam, Pontifica Universitas Lateranesis, Institutum Utriusque Iurus, 2002). Khalil's dissertation has a very useful discussion of citizenship provisions, a subject fraught with difficulties and ambiguities.

42. Brief attention to the call came after the speaker of the Palestinian National Council, Salim al-Za'nun, issued a document entitled "The Charter of the Organization of National Independence," calling for moving toward statehood, political reform, elections, and a constitution for statehood. The text was printed in *Al-sharq al-awsat*, 2 February 2001.

43. See "Statements by President George Bush and Prime Minister Ariel Sharon following meeting Washington, D.C., May 7, 2002," retrieved 25 November 2002 from the Israel Ministry of Foreign Affairs Web site: www.mfa .gov.il/mfa/go.asp?MFAHoloko.

44. The chief justice himself argued in the July 2000 workshop I attended that only a modest constitutional document was appropriate; a more complete order would be appropriate only later.

45. See, e.g., "Deputies: The Palestinian People Laid Down the Laws for the Palestinian State . . . and Not for the Interim Stage," *Afaq barlamniyya* 4 (September 2000): 11–12.

CHAPTER 4: INVENTING A PARLIAMENT

1. This account is based on the text of the Budget Committee reports and a personal interview with 'Azmi Shu'aybi, Ramallah, November 1999. In addition, I personally attended the two sessions.

2. Dalal Salama, deputy from Nablus, personal interview, al-Bira, 9 February 2000.

3. The most comprehensive and useful published treatment of the PLC by far is David Schenker, *Palestinian Democracy and Governance: An Appraisal of the Legislative Council* (Washington, DC: Washington Institute for Near East

Policy, 2000). Barry Rubin, *The Transformation of Palestinian Politics: From Revolution to State-Building* (Cambridge, MA: Harvard University Press, 1999), chap. 2, has a shorter but still useful treatment of the PLC. An excellent coverage that focuses on the legal aspects is 'Aziz Kayid, *Ishkaliyat al-'alaqa bayna al-sultatayn al-tashri'iyya wa-l-tanfiziyya fi al-sulta al-wataniyya al-filastiniyya* (The problematics of the relationship between the executive and legislative branches in the Palestinian National Authority) (Ramallah: Palestinian Independent Commission for Citizens' Rights, 2000).

4. See Article 1, paragraph 1 of the agreement.

5. The English text uses the Arabic word *ra'ees* rather than *president* out of Israeli concerns that calling the Palestinian leader a president—especially in light of the 1988 Palestinian declaration of independence—would imply recognition of statehood.

6. Again out of an Israeli aversion to using terms associated with states, there is no mention of "ministers" but only "members" of the Executive Authority. See Article 5.

7. Article 4.

8. Article 17, paragraph 3.

9. Ahmad Quray', "Editorial," *Al-majlis al-tashri'i*, no. 1 (1999): 3.

10. This was Law 13 of 1995. The same procedure was followed for Law 16 of 1995, which modified some provisions of the earlier law.

11. Perhaps the most comprehensive report on the early operations of the PLC is "The First Months of the Palestinian Legislative Council," a report by the National Democratic Institute for International Affairs, Washington, D.C., May 1996. This account of the early symbolic controversies draws heavily from that report, especially the memorandum by Susan Benda on the March 21, 1996, PLC session.

12. Presidential Decree 2 of 1996 required the members to swear their oath "before the president of the Council." An English translation of the decree is published by the Jerusalem Media and Communication Center, *The Palestinian Council*, 2d ed. (Jerusalem: JMCC, 1998), pp. 22–23.

13. Benda memo, in National Democratic Institute, "The First Months," p. 7.

14. See United States Agency for International Development (USAID), "Request for Proposal for Assistance to the Palestinian Legislative Council," RFP 294–99–012, Attachment J.3, "Council's Performance Indicators," 14 May 1999. This document contains one of the most comprehensive English-language assessments of the council's operations and performance.

15. PLC Resolution No. 16/3/1, 10 April 1996.

16. PLC Resolution 24/4/1, 8–9 May 1996.

17. See PLC Resolution 86/18/1, 12–22 August 1996.

18. "Interview" (with Rawhi Fatuh), *Al-majlis al-tashri'i*, no. 3 (1998).

19. "Abu Salah: Intention to Prepare Suggested Changes to the Internal Organization of the Legislative Council," *Al-ayyam*, 20 April 2000.

20. The PLC began its transcription service and developed it as part of a USAID project; personal interview with Donna Merrill, Associates in Rural

Development, Ramallah, August 1999. On the PLC's ability to produce information, I was told that a request that I made (regarding a committee report and the wording of a PLC resolution) would have to be directed personally to the Speaker. Repeated requests to multiple offices did not receive a direct response.

21. Articles 51 and 55.

22. I have written of this more generally in Nathan J. Brown, *Constitutions in a Nonconstitutional World: Arab Basic Laws and the Prospects for Accountable Government* (Albany: SUNY Press, 2002), chap. 4.

23. See "Do the Members of Fatah in the Legislative Council Form a Parliamentary Bloc," *Afaq barlamaniyya* 4 (August 2000): 12–13.

24. The text of the decree can be found in "The President Issues a Presidential Decree Extending the Session of the Legislature for Three Additional Months," retrieved 26 January 2003 from the Web site of the Office of the President of the State of Palestine: www.p-p-o.com/DATA/data/2002/6/m8–6-2002-l.htm.

25. The Israeli actions are described in a document entitled "Destruction of Palestinian Public Institutions," by Miftah, a Palestinian NGO; retrieved 24 December 2002 from www.miftah.org/PrinterF.cfm?DocId = 710.

26. Statistics based on those reported in Ahmad Quray', editorial, p. 3, and USAID, "Request for Proposal," Attachment J.3.

27. After working to contain tensions between the PLC and the executive, 'Amr resigned in May 2002, calling for comprehensive reforms in the PNA.

28. See, e.g., the description of the 11–12 May 1999 session in "Session Four," *Al-majlis al-tashri'i*, no. 3 (1999).

29. The text of the report is included in JMCC, *The Palestinian Council*.

30. See the remarks of Jim Saxton, "My Almost-Trip to Israel: The Congressman Excluded from Clinton's Entourage," retrieved December 2, 2002, from Israel Resource Review Web site: http://israelvisit.co.il/BehindTheNews/Dec-15–98.htm#trip. Saxton used the report to claim that it refuted Secretary of State Madeleine Albright's assurances that USAID money was all accounted for. While the PLC did report corruption, Saxton's statement was knowingly false, since no USAID money went to the PNA—partly because of legislative requirements mandated by the U.S. Congress and supported by Saxton.

31. See "October 2, 1997," *Al-majlis al-tashri'i*, January 1998.

32. 'Azmi Shu'aybi, personal interview, Ramallah, November 1999. See the interview with Hasan Khraysha, chair of the Oversight Committee of the PLC, in "Interview," *Al-majlis al-tashri'i*, no. 3 (1999). The requirement that the annual report be submitted to the PLC was included in Law 7 of 1998 concerning the public budget.

33. A list of early PLC resolutions is included in JMCC, *The Palestinian Council*. The council's own *Al-majlis al-tashri'i* contains complete records.

34. USAID, "Request for Proposal," Attachment J.3.

35. I examine this in more detail in Brown, *Constitutions in a Nonconstitutional World*, chap. 4.

36. The press conference was covered in all Palestinian newspapers; a summary also appears in "October 8, 1997," *Al-majlis al-tashri'i,* January 1998.

37. "Quiet Meeting in the Legislature Today as a Result of the Meeting of the President with the Deputies of 'Fatah,' " *Al-ayyam,* 30 December 1997.

38. Even resignation would often fail to result in leaving a ministry. The minister of justice, Farih Abu Mudayn, and the minister of social affairs, Umm Jihad (Intisar al-Wazir), both submitted their resignations in anger over disputes about their ministry's affairs. President 'Arafat never acted on either, and both continued to serve.

39. Law 7 of 1998.

40. PLC Resolution 45/7/1.

41. PLC Resolution 99/21/1.

42. "A Window on the Workings of the PA: An Inside View," *Journal of Palestine Studies* 30 (Autumn 2000): 91.

43. PLC, Budget and Fiscal Affairs Committee, "Report of the Budget and Fiscal Affairs Committee," 1997 Draft General Budget for the Palestinian National Authority, unpublished document, Palestinian Legislative Council, Ramallah.

44. PLC, Budget and Fiscal Affairs Committee, "Report of the Budget and Fiscal Affairs Committee," 1998 Draft General Budget for the Palestinian National Authority, unpublished document, Palestinian Legislative Council, Ramallah.

45. 'Azmi Shu'aybi claims that 'Arafat committed to transfer $45 million to the budget; personal interview, Ramallah, November 1999.

46. See the report of the 5 January session in "Seventeenth Session, Third Round," *Al-majlis al-tashri'i,* no. 2 (1999).

47. See the report of the 18 January and 5 April sessions in "Special Session on the Budget," *Al-majlis al-tashri'i,* no. 2 (1999).

48. Palestinian Legislative Council, Budget and Fiscal Affairs Committee, "Report of the Budget and Fiscal Affairs Committee," 1999 Draft General Budget for the Palestinian National Authority, unpublished document, Palestinian Legislative Council, Ramallah.

49. Much of PNA operating revenues came from the value-added tax levied by Israel on goods; according to the agreements negotiated between Israel and the PLO, these tax revenues would be assigned according to where the good was finally sold. In essence, this meant that Israel collected taxes on good destined for sale to Palestinians in the West Bank and Gaza; Israel was obligated to turn those tax revenues over to the PNA. With the beginning of the second intifada, Israel suspended the revenue transfer, causing acute fiscal crisis.

50. "'Arafat: No One Has the Right to Delay the Rulings of the Judiciary. We Are Prepared to Resume Negotiations Immediately from the Point They Reached at Sharm al-Shaykh and Taba," *Al-hayah al-jadida,* 11 March 2001.

51. PLC Resolution 6/1/518, passed on 10 March 2001.

52. "Al-Zir: We Will Recommend Acceptance of the General Budget, Con-

sidering It an Emergency Budget in the Shadow of the Israeli Aggression," *Al-ayyam*, 2 April 2001.

53. The most complete account of the debate on the budget can be found in "The Legislative Council Approves the General Budget for the National Authority for the Year 2001," *Al-majlis al-tashri'i*, no. 1 (2001), retrieved 26 December 2002 from PLC Web site: www.pal-plc.org/arabic/publications/magazine/y2001/mag1/muazana.pdf. PLC Resolution 6/521/a approved the budget, with the criticisms mentioned.

54. Law 7 of 1998, Article 3.

55. Nina Sovich, "Palestinian Trade Unions," *Journal of Palestine Studies* 29 (Summer 2000): 72–74.

56. Hasan Khraysha, a strident member of the opposition, pushed the legislation when he was chair of the Oversight Committee, but the committee approved the draft even after Khraysha had been stripped of his chairmanship in favor of a member of Fatah. The final committee approval came on 7 May 2000. See "Oversight Committee Approves Draft Law Forbidding Torture of Those Detained and Arrested, Paving the Way for Referring It to the Legislature," *Al-ayyam*, 8 May 2000.

57. The PLC Web site lists the law as having been rejected on 17 May 2000. See "Draft Laws in the Council That Have Been Rejected," retrieved 26 December 2002 from www.pal-plc.org/arabic/laws/lawslist.asp?cat = 9. Despite the saliency of the torture issue, however, the action attracted little attention.

58. The director of the Diwan al-fatwa wa-l-tashri' was supportive of the law. Ibrahim al-Daghma, personal interview, Ramallah, September 1999. The minister of justice called for approval of the law in a PLC session in May 1999. See "Session Four," *Al-majlis al-tashri'i*, no. 3 (1999), description of 11–12 May 1999 session.

59. See, e.g., the comments of PLC member Muhammad Hijazi in "The Legislature Works Hard to Get out the Law on the Independence of the Judiciary," *Al-hayah al-jadida*, 18 August 1999.

60. "The Legislature Passes the Draft Laws of the Judicial Authority and Arbitration and Discusses the Report of the Education Committee about the Situation of the Hospitals," *Al-ayyam*, 4 February 2000.

61. "The Legislature Passes the Law of the Formation of the *Nizami* Courts on the First Reading and Announced the Names of Nine Committees, Waiting for the Decision of the Membership of the Oversight Committee," *Al-ayyam*, 13 March 2000.

62. "The President: It Has Been Decided to Publish the Labor Law in the *Official Gazette* and to Continue Work on Preparing Regulations, Orders, and Laws Related to Its Application and Enforcement," *Al-ayyam*, 2 May 2001.

63. "Minister of Labor Stresses Importance of Promulgating Law of Social Insurance and Formation of Labor Courts," *Al-ayyam*, 14 February 2002, p. 4.

64. "Diwan al-fatwa wa-l-tashri' Submits to Cabinet Draft Amendment to Labor Law," *Al-ayyam*, 25 March 2002.

65. Presidential Decree 1 of 1997.

66. For a critical evaluation of the law, see Joe Baxter and Amy Hawthorne, "Guide for the Planning and Organization of Local Government Elections in the West Bank and Gaza," presented to the Ministry of Local Government and the Supreme Elections Committee of the PNA by the International Foundation for Electoral Systems, January 1998.

67. Law 1 of 1997.

68. This justification was probably sincere, at least in part. While Israel had reluctantly accepted that PLC and PNA presidential elections could include Palestinians in Jerusalem, it never would have accepted elections for municipal governance in East Jerusalem. Proceeding with elections for other Palestinian villages and cities while omitting Jerusalem would have been seen—at least by Palestinians—as a step toward de facto recognition of the Israeli annexation of East Jerusalem.

69. "Session Fifteen," *Al-majlis al-tashri'i*, no. 2 (1999), description of session of 8 December 1998.

70. "The Legislature: The Right of Return of Palestinian Refugees to Their Homes is Sacred," *Al-ayyam*, 16 December 1999.

71. See, e.g., "Quiet Meeting in the Legislature Today as a Result of the Meeting of the President with the Deputies from Fatah," *Al-ayyam*, 30 December 1997.

72. See, e.g., Abu 'Ala''s comments as reported in "West Bank: PA's Quray' on Peace, National Unity, US," *Al-quds*, 21 April 1998, FBIS-NES-98–111.

73. Samar Assad, "Palestinian Health Workers Strike," Associated Press, 23 February 1999.

74. For the favorable World Bank position on the nonsalary provisions of the law, see World Bank, Social and Economic Development Group, Middle East and North Africa Region, *West Bank and Gaza: Strengthening Public Sector Management* (Jerusalem: World Bank West Bank and Gaza Resident Mission, 1999), esp. pp. 9 and 28.

75. See, e.g., "The Legislature Demands Immediate Application of the Law of Civil Service," *Al-hayah al-jadida*, 4 February 2000.

76. The notice was published on 29 February 2000. For a critical analysis, see the press release by LAW, "Protest in Solidarity with Bir Zayt Students Banned, LAW Highly Concerned about Police Chief's Orders," 29 February 2000, retrieved 15 March 2000 from www.lawsociety.org.

77. "The High Court Decided to Cancel the Effectiveness of the Decision to Forbid Organizing Meetings with Permission of the General Director of the Police," *Al-ayyam*, 30 April 2000.

78. Interior Minister Decision 1 of 2000, Issuing the Implementing Regulation for the Law of Public Meetings, No. 12, 1998.

79. Earlier Arab experience showed how influential experienced parliamentarians could be. Arab deputies in the early-twentieth-century Ottoman parliament helped shape constitutional and parliamentary institutions in Syria, Lebanon, Transjordan, and Iraq.

80. On recent Arab parliamentary experience, see Abdo Baaklini, Guilain

Denoeux, and Robert Springborg, *Legislative Politics in the Arab World: The Resurgence of Democratic Institutions* (Boulder, CO: Lynne Reinner, 1999).

81. I have treated this subject more extensively in Brown, *Constitutions in a Nonconstitutional World*, chap. 4.

CHAPTER 5: CIVIL SOCIETY IN THEORY AND PRACTICE

1. Such interdependence has not gone unnoticed in other settings. For a very different set of relationships between state and societal organizations that still display interdependence, see Sheila Carapico, *Civil Society in Yemen: The Political Economy of Activism in Modern Arabia* (New York: Cambridge University Press, 1998).

2. For some of the Palestinian academic writings on civil society, see Ziyad Abu 'Amr, *Al-mujtama' al-madani wa-l-tahawwul al-dimuqrati fi filastin* (Civil society and democratic transformation in Palestine) (Ramallah: Muwatin, 1995); 'Aryan al-Fasid, *Al-bina' al-mu'asasi al-filastini wa-furas al-tahawwul nahwa al-dimuqratiyya* (Palestinian institutional structure and opportunities for transitions to democracy) (Nablus: Center for Palestine Research and Studies, 1999); Mudir Qasis, *Al-tahawwul al-dimuqrati wa-madaniyyat al-mujtama' fi filastin* (Democratic transformation and civility of society in Palestine) (Nablus: Center for Palestinian Research and Studies, 1999); and Walid Salim, *Al-munazzamat al-mujtama'iyya al-tatawwu'iyya wa-l-sulta al-wataniyya al-filastiniyya: nahwa 'alaqa takamuliyya* (Voluntary societal organizations and the Palestinian National Authority: Toward a complementary relationship) (Jerusalem: Muntada abhath al-siyasiyya al-ijtima'iyya wa-l-iqtisadiyya, 1999).

3. Baruch Kimmerling and Joel S. Migdal, *Palestinians: The Making of a People* (Cambridge, MA: Harvard University Press, 1994), p. 247.

4. Robert Putnam, "Bowling Alone," *Journal of Democracy* 6, no. 1 (1995): 67. The concept of social capital gained greatest circulation after Putnam introduced it in his earlier work, *Making Democracy Work: Civic Traditions in Modern Italy* (Princeton, NJ: Princeton University Press, 1993). For a small sample of some reviews of different uses of the concept, see Michael W. Foley and Bob Edwards, "Beyond Tocqueville: Civil Society and Social Capital in Comparative Perspective," *American Behavioral Scientist* 42 (September 1998): 5–20; and Alejandro Portes, "Social Capital: Its Origins and Applications in Modern Sociology," *Annual Review of Sociology* 24 (1998): 1–24.

5. Putnam, "Bowling Alone," p. 66.

6. Only some writers include extended family ties when discussing social capital, but social capital should include them if they encourage expectations of cooperation.

7. I refer here to an image common to many societies of villages representing an authentic and harmonious past. In the Palestinian case, villages are sometimes portrayed as cohesive social units where members cooperated on matters of common concern. For instance, the corvée—remembered in neighboring

Egypt as a harsh government imposition—is described by some Palestinians as a locally organized affair for public improvements benefiting a village population. For an example of such a portrait, see the way the corvée (*'awna* rather than the less favorable *sukkhra*) is described in the PNA schools' textbook authored by the Curriculum Center, *Al-tarbiyya al-wataniyya*, grade 4 (Ramallah: Curriculum Center, 1998), p. 34.

8. Some of those responsible for introducing the concept have displayed ambivalence about its many uses and meanings. See, e.g., Portes, "Social Capital."

9. For a development of this critique, see Margaret Kohn, "Civic Republicanism versus Social Struggle: A Gramscian Approach to Associationalism in Italy," *Political Power and Social Theory* 13 (1999): 201–35.

10. For an exception, see Peter A. Hall, "Social Capital in Britain," *British Journal of Political Science* 29 (1999): 417–61.

11. Philippe C. Schmitter, "Still the Century of Corporatism?" in *The New Corporatism: Social-Political Structures in the Iberian World*, ed. Fredrick B. Pike and Thomas Stritch (Notre Dame, IN: University of Notre Dame Press, 1974), pp. 93–94.

12. Indeed, this problem was noted from the beginning. Alfred Stepan, in *The State and Society: Peru in Comparative Perspective* (Princeton, NJ: Princeton University Press, 1978), insisted that corporatism should be seen not as a historical given but instead as a mode of interest representation imposed, often in response to crisis.

13. See, e.g., Robert Bianchi, *Unruly Corporatism: Associational Life in Twentieth Century Egypt* (New York: Oxford University Press, 1995); and Marsha Pripstein Posusney, *Labor and the State in Egypt* (New York: Columbia University Press, 1997).

14. "Non-Governmental Organizations Form a Committee to Monitor the Local Elections," *Al-ayyam*, 22 September 2000.

15. See, e.g., the comments of Mustafa al-Barghuti in the conference sponsored by the Welfare Association Consortium in *Palestinian Government/NGO Relations: Cooperation and Partnership*, proceedings of the international conference organized by the Welfare Association Consortium in consultation with the World Bank, February 2000, ed. Mohammed K. Shadid and Caroline Qutteneh (Al-Ram: Welfare Association Consortium, 2001), p. 7.

16. See Emile Sahliyeh, *In Search of Leadership: West Bank Politics since 1967* (Washington, DC: Brookings Institution, 1988), chaps. 3 and 4.

17. The most detailed work on the period before and during the intifada is Joost R. Hiltermann, *Beyond the Intifada: Labor and Women's Movements in the Occupied Territories* (Princeton, NJ: Princeton University Press, 1991). The relationship between parties and NGOs during and after the intifada is covered in Rema Hammami, "NGOs: The Professionalization of Politics," *Race and Class* 37, no. 2 (1995): 51–63. Hammami's more recent article is also useful: see "Palestinian NGOs since Oslo: From NGO Politics to Social Movements," *Middle East Report* no. 214 (Spring 2000): 16ff.

18. See George Giacaman, "In the Throes of Oslo: Palestinian Society, Civil

Society, and the Future," in *After Oslo: New Realities, Old Problems*, ed. George Giacaman and Dag Jorund Lonning (London: Pluto Press, 1998).

19. One example of such a common statement was issued in April 2000 by the leftist parties (the Popular Front, the Democratic Front, the People's Party, FIDA (the Palestinian Democratic Union Party), and the Popular Struggle Front. They criticized the overlap between Fatah and the PNA, arguing that the overlap between the party and the Executive Authority augured a kind of totalitarianism. The text of the statement, "Open Letter," was published in *Sawt al-watan*, no. 63 (May 2000): 42. For an example of a statement including Fatah, see the statement by the National and Islamic Forces on the 2000 teachers' strike: "Call for the Authority to Answer the Demands of the Teachers and Begin Applying the Civil Service Law," *Al-ayyam*, 9 March 2000.

20. Al-Barghuti had successfully competed in the PLC elections, but he showed an independent streak, leaning toward the opposition to the PNA leadership. He publicly and sarcastically criticized senior PNA and Fatah figures, claiming that activists from the West Bank and Gaza had been passed over for senior positions. See, e.g., Marwan al-Barghuti, "The Organizational Condition of the Fatah Movement and Its Relationship with the [Palestinian] Authority," in *Ma ba'd al-azma: Al-taghyirat al-bunyawiyya fi al-hayah al-siyasiyya al-filastiniyya, wa-afaq al-'amal* (What is after the crisis: Structural changes in Palestinian political life and horizons of work), proceedings of the Fourth Annual Conference of the Muwatin Foundation, 22–23 September 1998, ed. Muwatin Foundation (Ramallah: Muwatin Foundation, 1999). Al-Barghuti described the current Fatah leadership in contemptuous terms and charged that the movement now simply approved decisions rather than takes them. He charged as well that as long as 'Arafat served as leader, little Palestinian institutional development could take place. When the second intifada erupted in September 2000, al-Barghuti was quickly able to mobilize party activists in the West Bank (especially Ramallah) to confront Israeli positions and quickly gained both national and international prominence. The career of al-Barghuti shows clearly how Palestinian political parties have functioned poorly in normal electoral politics but far more effectively in mobilization for nationalist action.

21. See, e.g., "Ramallah: Demand to Construct an Emergency National Leadership and Unify Efforts to Confront the Threats Represented by the Sharon Government," *Al-ayyam*, 28 March 2001. The attempt had little long-term effect.

22. See "Hani al-Hasan Calls the National and Islamic Forces to Join the Institutions of the Palestinian Liberation Organization," *Al-quds*, 6 January 2002. For an instance of the forum's independence, see "National and Islamic Forces Call on the President Not to Approve the Exile of Any Palestinian," *Al-ayyam*, 8 May 2002. The call came on the eve of 'Arafat's approval of a settlement to the siege of the Church of the Nativity in Bethlehem involving the exile of some of the Palestinians inside.

23. The organization was formed in 1979 by Palestinian Communist Party activists. See Glenn Robinson, *Building a Palestinian State* (Bloomington: Indi-

ana University Press, 1997), pp. 40–41, for a brief summary of the organization's development.

24. Sara Roy, "The Transformation of Islamic NGOs in Palestine," *Middle East Report*, no. 214 (Spring 2000): 24–26.

25. This point is made in Abu 'Amr, *Al-mujtama' al-madani*.

26. Palestinians will sometimes refer to this kind of politics as the "democracy of factions." Ziyad Abu 'Amr attributes the term to George Giacaman. See Abu ' Amr, *Al-mujtama' al-madani*, p. 83ff.

27. The prominence of Palestinian NGOs has led to several detailed studies of their history and activities. See Sophie Claudet, "The Changing Role of Palestinian NGOs since the Establishment of the Palestinian Authority (1994–1996)," prepared for Nigel Roberts of the West Bank/Gaza Unit and Ishac Diwan of the Economic Development Institute, Macroeconomic and Management Policy, World Bank, July 1996; Denis J. Sullivan, "NGOs in Palestine: Agents of Development and Foundation of Civil Society," *Journal of Palestine Studies* 25 (Spring 1996): 93–100; Muhammad Muslih, "Palestinian Civil Society," *Middle East Journal* 47 (Spring 1993): 258–74; Salim, *Al-munazzamat al-mujtama'iyya al-tatawwu'iyya;* and Jamil Hilal and Majdi al-Maliki, *Institutions of Social Support in the West Bank and the Gaza Strip* (Ramallah: Palestinian Institution for Policy and Economic Research (MAS), 1997). Some Palestinian institutions issue periodic reports that cover NGO activities. Two useful examples are Bir Zayt University's Development Studies Program, which produces an annual publication entitled *Human Development Report—Palestine;* it also published a brief study in 1997, "Evaluation of the Role of Non-Governmental Organizations in the Occupied Territories and the Opportunities for Networking among Them in the Framework of the Palestinian Authority." The Arab Thought Forum publishes an annual volume, *Democratic Formation in Palestine,* with extensive coverage of NGO activity. On earlier forms of organization in the Palestinian diaspora, see Laurie Brand, *Palestinians in the Arab World: Institution Building and the Search for State* (New York: Columbia University Press, 1988).

28. The term *state surrogate* in this context is borrowed from Muslih, "Palestinian Civil Society," p. 259.

29. A 1997 survey of 250 organizations in the West Bank and Gaza reported that one-fourth of organizations existing at that time dated back to the period before 1967. While no breakdown was offered, the authors further reported that only a small number of organizations were founded in the years between 1948 and 1967. See Hilal and al-Maliki, *Institutions of Social Support*, p. 23.

30. The most comprehensive treatment of this is Brand, *Palestinians in the Arab World.*

31. See Abu 'Amr, *Al-mujtama' al-madani*, pp. 26–30.

32. Hillel Frisch goes so far as to identify a conscious effort on the part of the PLO to prevent Palestinian institutions and organizations in the West Bank and Gaza not dependent on the external PLO leadership. See *Countdown to State-*

hood: Palestinian State Formation in the West Bank and Gaza (Albany: SUNY Press, 1998).

33. These incidents are recounted in the discussion of PNA relations with civil society in Abu 'Amr, *Al-mujtama' al-madani*, pp. 75–82.

34. Sullivan, "NGOs in Palestine," p. 97; and Hammami, "Palestinian NGOs," p. 17

35. "Editorial," *Palestinian NGO Project Newsletter*, no. 1 (September 1998).

36. The most commonly cited figures describe a drop of $170 to $240 million per year in the early 1990s to $100 to $120 million in 1993, the year of the signing of the Oslo Accords. These figures include both local and international funds and reflect the general crisis of funding rather than the specific effects of the founding of the PNA. By 1995, only $51 million (of $1.462 billion of Palestinian aid) had been pledged by donors to NGOs, though that figure included $36 million for institutions of higher education. This more accurately reflects the sense of crisis among NGOs when the PNA was founded. NGOs did better than this implies, however, since some funds pledged by donors went to NGOs even when not specifically designated for them from the beginning. I have adopted the figures reported in Claudet, "Changing Role of Palestinian NGOs." An extremely thorough and fair treatment of the enormously complex framework of international assistance more generally can be found in Rex Brynen's *A Very Political Economy: Peacebuilding and Foreign Aid in the West Bank and Gaza* (Washington, DC: United Institute of Peace Press, 2000). Controversies over aid to NGOs are discussed on pp. 187–191.

37. United Nations, Office of the Special Coordinator in the Occupied Territories, "Rule of Law Development in the West Bank and Gaza Strip: Survey and State of the Development Effort," May 1999.

38. The three Palestinian dailies, *Al-ayyam, Al-quds,* and *Al-hayah al-jadida,* all covered the charges, and, to a lesser extent, the response of NGOs during June 1999. See also Hadeel Wahdan, "Fighting over Funds," *Palestine Report* 6 (12 April 2000), retrieved 22 January 2003 from www.palestinereport.org. The $100 million figure was almost certainly a gross exaggeration based on a misreading of the report.

39. The minister did achieve some changes in the oversight of the project, but the episode earned the minister some teasing: see "The Empowerment of the Ministry of NGO Affairs," *Al-ayyam,* 26 June 2001. In this case the minister's comments were unusually harsh, but periodic official criticisms of international assistance were common. For instance, in January 2000, more muted charges about aid were leveled by two Palestinian ministers. See "'Asfur: Foreign Sources Are Forbidden to Support Jerusalem and Palestinian Institutions in It for Political Purposes," *Al-ayyam,* 25 January 2000, p. 4; and "Abu Mudayn: The Authority Is Thinking Seriously about Refusing Receipt of Aid from Donor States It Does Not Benefit From," *Al-ayyam,* 25 January 2000, p. 6.

40. For instance, justice minister Frayh Abu Mudayn charged in June 1999 that the organizations had become too political and had invited judges to inter-

national conferences without going through the Ministry of Justice. See "Widening the Circle of Controversy Concerning the Situation of Popular Organizations," *Al-ayyam*, 14 June 1999.

41. See "Abu Mudayn: The Ministry of Justice Is Working on Improving the Law of Popular Organizations," *Al-ayyam*, 26 June 1999.

42. The union actually dates back to 1990, when it split from the Jordanian organization. Muhammad Fahmi al-Shalalda, president of the union, personal interview, Beersheva, October 1999.

43. For a general overview of the network of NGO unions, see Hasan Ladadwa, "The Palestinian National Authority and Non-Governmental Organizations," *Al-siyasa al-filastiniyya* 6 (Summer 1999): 127–43. The Office of National Institutions, created to coordinate the work of friendly, government-sponsored NGOs, was formed by Presidential Decision 15 of 1994, issued on 28 August, 1994—shortly after President 'Arafat's return. It represented an incomplete attempt to establish clear leadership over NGO activity.

44. Mustafa al-Barghuti, at a conference in 2000, reported that NGOs provide 60 percent of health care services and manage 42 percent of the hospitals, 90 percent of the handicap rehabilitation centers, and 100 percent of preschool education. See his remarks in "Mustafa al-Barghuti" in Shadid and Qutteneh, *Palestinian Governmental/NGO Relations*, p. 7.

45. This account of the NGO Law is based on contemporary press accounts (which covered the public debate fairly well), successive drafts of the law, and interviews with NGO activists, most of whom were so forthcoming about behind-the-scenes maneuvering that I prefer to avoid mentioning them by name. I have not cited any of their remarks unless mentioned independently by two sources. There are several good written accounts of the conflict over the law. See Salim, *Al-munazzamat al-mutam'iyya*, part 5; Sullivan, "NGOs in Palestine"; Claudet, "Changing Role of Palestinian NGOs," Annex 5, later updated as "West Bank and Gaza" in the *International Journal of Not-for-Profit Law* 2 (November 1999), retrieved 26 December 2002 from www.icnl.org/journal/vol2iss2/cr_mideast.html#WEST; and Hammami, "Palestinian NGOs since Oslo."

46. See "Widening of the Circle of Controversy Concerning the Situation of Popular Organizations," *Al-ayyam*, 14 June 1999, and "Abu Mudayn: The Ministry of Justice Is Working on Improving the Law of Popular Organizations," *Al-ayyam*, 26 June 1999.

47. The comments were made at the annual conference of the Welfare Association, February 2000. See Shadid and Qutteneh, *Palestinian Governmental/NGO Relations*, p. 8.

48. "Interior Closes Two Institutions in Bethlehem That Did Not Undertake to Bring Their Positions into Conformity," *Al-quds*, 14 May 2001.

49. For an example of such discussion, see the description of the Forum of Social and Economic Policy Research in Palestine, "Voluntary Community Organizations and the Palestinian National Authority: Towards an Integrated Relationship," June 1999, retrieved 2 December 2002 from www.palecon.org/

masdir/policynote2.htm. Similarly, the Development Studies Program at Bir Zayt University attempted to coordinate development strategy. Nader Izzat Said, personal interview, Ramallah, October 1999.

50. See "Shuqayrat: A Meeting between 'al-Qanun' and Officials of the General Intelligence to Solve the Problems between the Two Sides," *Al-ayyam*, 9 March 2000.

51. Claudet, "Changing Role of Palestinian NGOs," Annex 4.

52. "Ramallah: PICCHR Opens a Training Workshop Introducing the Field of Human Rights," *Al-ayyam*, 3 February 2000.

53. On the legal ambiguities regarding 'Asfur's appointment, see "Questions about the Planned Ministry of Popular Work," *Al-risala*, 5 August 1999.

54. Indeed, many NGO leaders speculated that 'Asfur was appointed to the post as a consolation for being dropped from the negotiating team with Israel. Regardless of the truth of this account, NGOs tended to treat 'Asfur, especially at first, as a gift they had never asked for or even wanted.

55. "'Asfur Calls Popular Organizations to Turn the Page on the Crisis and for Integrated Work with Official Institutions," *Al-ayyam*, 3 August 1999.

56. In a personal interview in Ramallah in September 1999, 'Asfur explained that he did not wish to have the office attached to his ministry in any way.

57. For examples of such sessions, see "Ramallah: The Ministry of NGO Affairs Organizes a Workshop to Discuss Its Strategic Vision," *Al-ayyam*, 3 February 2000.

58. The consideration of zakat committees here is restricted to those operating on the West Bank. I was not able to investigate Gazan zakat committees as thoroughly. My impression is that zakat committees in Gaza probably play a more important role than their West Bank counterparts but that they remain less hierarchically organized and some have retained more distance from the PNA.

59. See, e.g., the comments of 'Azmi Bishara in Abu 'Amr, *Al-mujtama' al-madani.*

60. A 2000 poll listed them as second only to universities in popular trust. "Priorities under a Palestinian State," poll conducted by the Development Studies Program, Bir Zayt University, 31 August–2 September 2000, retrieved 18 January 2001 from the Bir Zayt University Web site: http://home.birzeit.edu/dsp/DSPNEW/polls/poll_1/index.html.

61. The information in this paragraph is based on site visits to the Ramallah and Jerusalem committees in April 2000.

62. The Ramallah committee, one of the largest, has five permanent administrative employees; its clinic has twelve additional employees. The Jerusalem committee has only one paid staff member. The Jerusalem committee reports administrative expenditures of NIS 37,263 out of a total of NIS 297,442 collected.

63. Most of the information in this and the next paragraph comes from a personal interview with Muhammad Shadid, the director of the Welfare Association, al-Ram, July 2000. The Web site www.pngo-project.org contains key

documents on the organization's management of the NGO Project. Information on the NGO Project was also obtained in interviews with two World Bank officials, Joe Saba (Jerusalem, February 2000) and Sophie Claudet (Jerusalem, March 2000).

64. The location—in the neighborhood of al-Ram—has become popular for institutions seeking to maintain a presence in both Jerusalem and the Palestinian territories. The Welfare Association has also moved operations to 'Amman. The Geneva office remains, but most work is now done in Jerusalem and 'Amman.

65. Hammami, "Palestinian NGOs since Oslo," p. 17.

66. The conference was extensively covered by the Palestinian dailies, 14–16 February 2000. I am grateful to Muhammad Shadid for providing me with a prepublication copy of the conference proceedings.

67. Most of the information in this paragraph was collected during a site visit to the organization's headquarters in Ramallah in November 1999.

68. See Robinson, *Building a Palestinian State*, pp. 28–31 and chap. 3.

69. Muhammad Fahmi al-Shalalda, union president, personal interview, Beersheva, October 1999.

70. Both the Jordanian government and international NGOs, notably American Near East Refugee Aid (ANERA), assisted in this effort. Interview with Peter Gubser, ANERA president, Washington, DC, June 1999.

71. Claudet reports that half of the charitable societies and fewer than half of the cooperatives were active, however. See Claudet, "Changing Role of Palestinian NGOs."

72. See UNESCO–West Asia and Bir Zeit University, "Evaluation of the Role of NGOs in the Occupied Territories and the Opportunities of Networking among Them in the Framework of the Palestinian Authority," E/ESCWA/SD-WOM/1997/WG.1/5, 22 September 1997, part 3, "The Status of the Organizations Working in the Field of Marketing Agricultural Products."

73. Personal interview with Adnan 'Ubaydat of ANERA, January 2000, Ramallah.

74. See "Call for Formation of a General Cooperative Union," *Al-ayyam*, 15 February 2000, for brief coverage of the status of the draft law.

75. While most grassroots organizations struggled greatly in the new environment, some could be quite entrepreneurial in this regard. One organization I visited seemed to specialize in making garments that appeared to be American-made to meet local preferences; some carried an (undoubtedly unauthorized) Nike logo.

76. The information on the Women and Childcare Society is gathered from a site visit and an interview with the director, Lidiya al-'Araj, in January 2000.

77. Information on the Qalandiya Cooperative was gathered during a site visit and interview with its general manager in November 1999. The cooperative also publishes a small brochure on its operations.

78. The most comprehensive account of Palestinian diaspora organizations is Brand's *Palestinians in the Arab World*. For a general treatment of the problems

caused by the existence of internal and external organizations for the same sector, see "Palestinian Popular Organizations, Internal and External Problematics," *Afaq barlamaniyya* 4 (September 2000): 15–16.

79. Mu'min Basisu and Wa'il al-Dahduh, "Dualism of Syndicate and Official Positions: Healthy Condition or Symptom of Illness," *Sawt al-watan*, no. 63 (May 2000): 7–11.

80. Actually, Israeli censorship still formally operates for the one Palestinian paper published in Jerusalem, *Al-quds*. The other two Palestinian dailies are published in areas outside Israeli control: *Al-hayah al-jadida* in Gaza and *Al-ayyam* in Ramallah. For a general treatment of the role of media under the PNA, see Amal Jamal, "State Formation and the Possibilities of Democracy in Palestine," *Majallat al-dirasat al-filastiniyya*, no. 40 (Autumn 1999): 112–35.

81. Oddly, the connection of both new dailies to the Palestinian leadership offers them some limited independence. To be sure, the PNA has a richly deserved reputation for interfering in the press. It does so not through direct censorship, however, but by a variety of crude and inconsistent methods. Journalists are sometimes arrested, dailies are threatened with interference in distribution or advertising, and broadcast stations are closed without legal justification. For present purposes, it is important to note that such methods, while they constrain journalism, are so inconsistently used that there is still considerable room for journalists to carry out their work.

82. Husam 'Izz al-Din, personal interview, Ramallah, May 2000.

83. See, e.g., "The Elections of the Press Syndicate: The Causes Which Stand in Front of Its Delay . . . or Its Cancellation!!" *Al-risala*, 29 July 1999.

84. For an account of some of the alleged irregularities, see the press release on the subject by the Palestinian Society for Protection of Human Rights and the Environment (LAW), "LAW Contests Legality of Journalists' Union Elections," 3 January 2000, retrieved 2 December 2002 from www.lawsociety.org/Press/Preleases/2000/January/Jan2.html. See also "Building Palestine," in *Palestine Report* 6 (22 December 1999).

85. See, e.g., "Ramallah: Journalists Working in the West Bank Elect a Preparatory Committee for Holding a General Conference for Journalists within Three Months," *Al-ayyam*, 25 February 2000. The information on the alternative unions is based not only on press coverage but also on an interview with Ja'far Sadaqa, a member of the preparatory committee, in Ramallah in May 2000.

86. See "The Preparatory Committee for the Journalists Syndicate Conference Denounces the Meeting with Beilin in Occupied Jerusalem," *Al-ayyam*, 14 September 2000.

87. The willingness of the new group to adopt more public tactics was illustrated in June 2000 when it organized a demonstration against the security services after some private broadcasters were closed. See "Ramallah: Journalists and Those in the Media Demonstrate to Stop the Excesses of the Security Agencies," *Al-ayyam*, 2 June 2000.

88. See the coverage of the conflict in "The Palestinian Journalists Union:

Between the Legitimacy of Na'im and the Plan of Nabil and Hisham," *Al-'awda*, no. 255 (July 2000): 12–18 (quote on p. 12).

89. Na'im al-Tubasi used this precise phrase to refer to the new organization. See "Who Is behind the Fragmentation of the Journalists Corps?" *Al-risala*, 15 June 2000, p. 13.

90. Al-Tubasi gives his views in "The Palestinian Journalists Union," p. 15.

91. On the legal profession under the mandate, see George Bisharat, *Palestinian Lawyers and Israeli Rule: Law and Disorder in the West Bank* (Austin: University of Texas Press, 1989), pp. 24–26; and Husayn Abu Hunud, *Taqrir hawla niqabat al-muhamiyin al-filastiniyin* (Report on the Palestinian Lawyers Syndicate) (Ramallah: Palestinian Independent Commission for Citizens' Rights, 2000), pp. 15–19.

92. On the period between 1948 and 1967, see Bisharat, *Palestinian Lawyers*, pp. 26–29; and Abu Hunud, *Taqrir*, pp. 21–25.

93. The most thorough coverage of the strike is Bisharat, *Palestinian Lawyers*, chap. 9.

94. Abu Hunud, *Taqrir*, pp. 35–36.

95. The information on the bar association since 1997 is based on interviews with Palestinian lawyers and legal officials during 1999 and 2000, personal interview with 'Adnan Abu Layla, member of the interim board of the bar association, press coverage, and review of relevant legislation. Abu Hunud, *Taqrir*, provides a very useful account.

96. Decision 78 of 1997.

97. Decision 2 of 1999.

98. Law 3 of 1999.

99. Law 5 of 1999.

100. Bylaws of the Civil Lawyers Association (Palestinian Bar Association).

101. Much of the information on these syndicates was collected in interviews with the head of the Pharmacists Syndicate, Dr. Nabil 'Udayli, Bayt Hanina, June 2000 (and a follow-up written communication from him, June 2000), and the head of the Dentists Syndicate, Dr. Sa'id al-Tarifi, Bayt Hanina, May 2000. The affairs of all three of the medical syndicates are covered in the Palestinian press.

102. See, e.g., "Demand Not to Deal with the Draft Law Organizing the Medical and Dental Professions," *Al-ayyam*, 12 May 2000, which reports on Doctors Syndicate complaints that a law drafted in the Diwan al-fatwa wa-l-tashri' robbed the syndicate of its proper role.

103. "The Fourth Pharmacy Conference Calls for Organizing the Profession and Stopping the Flooding of the Market with Graduates," *Al-ayyam*, 26 May 2000.

104. Dr. Sa'id al-Tarifi, personal interview, Bayt Hanina, May 2000.

105. See the complaint about charitable organizations providing dental services in Jaafar Sadaqa and Hiyam Hassan, "Dentistry in Palestine: Taking a Bite out of Tooth Decay," *Jerusalem Times*, 18 February 2000. In May 2000, pharmacists organized a strike over a ministerial decision to allow NGO hospitals to

dispense medicine (presumably on an outpatient basis). See "Pharmacists Protest over Allowing Private Pharmacies in Non-Governmental Hospitals to Dispense Medicines to Those Examined in Their Clinics," *Al-ayyam*, 30 May 2000.

106. The Dentists Syndicate notified all members in 1999 that only those registered as specialists with the syndicate could advertise specialized services. The letter to syndicate members is printed in the Dentists Syndicate annual report *(Al-taqrir al-sanawi)* for 1999, pp. 22–24.

107. The information on the Engineers Syndicate comes from a site visit to its offices in Bayt Hanina May 2000, as well as from some of its publications. Particular useful are Ramadan Safi, "The Progression of Palestinian Engineering Bodies," *Al-muhandis al-filastini*, no. 5 (April 2000): 54–59; Sa'd al-Din Kharma, "The Association of Engineers: Gaza Strip and the Movement toward Unifying the Body of Engineers," *Al-muhandis al-filastini*, no. 5 (April 2000): 60–61; Dayf Allah al-Akhras, "The General Union of Palestinian Engineers: Conception—Aspiration—Reality," *Al-muhandis al-filastini*, no. 5 (April 2000): 61–63; and the 1999 annual report of the syndicate, *Niqabat al-muhandisin markaz al-quds: Al-taqrir al-sanawi 1999* (Jerusalem: Engineers Syndicate, Jerusalem Center, 2000).

108. Much of the information on the chambers of commerce is based on site visits to the Jerusalem Chamber (and an interview with its director, 'Azzam Abu Su'ud) in May 2000 and to the Jericho Chamber (and interviews with its manager, Kazim al-Mu'aqqat and its secretary Salmi Hamad) in June 2000.

109. Occasional elections were held by some chambers—e.g., in Jericho in 1972 and 1990.

110. This story is most effectively told in Hiltermann, *Behind the Intifada*.

111. Nina Sovich, "Palestinian Trade Unions," *Journal of Palestine Studies* 29 (Summer 2000): 69.

112. "Al-Natsha: Presidential Decision Freeing Haydar Ibrahim for Union Work," *Al-ayyam*, 27 March 2000.

113. See the report of the Budget Committee of the PLC on the 2000 budget, January 2000, PLC archives, Ramallah.

114. The formation of GUPT is described best by Brand, *Palestinians in the Arab World*, pp. 38–39, 208–10.

115. The information on the origins of GUPTOT is based on a personal interview with Muhammad Suwan, Jerusalem, February 2000.

116. Ibid.

117. This account of the 1997 strike is based primarily on accounts in the Palestinian press. Since the Higher Coordinating Committee claimed that the PNA was circulating inaccurate information to the press, these accounts themselves became an object of dispute. I have tried to include only those uncontested elements of the affair, noting differences where necessary.

118. This account also relies primarily on press accounts, supplemented by interviews with educators. The Palestinian press reported the 2000 strike more

fully, though some of the retaliatory actions taken against strike leaders drew little mention.

119. His comments were not widely noted. They were reported in "Dr. Abu Shari'a: Inflation Necessitates a Raise for Employees," *Al-hayah al-jadida*, 30 June 2000.

120. The draft was taken up by the PLC in March 2001.

121. One example of this phenomenon is the multiplicity of human rights organizations. The Palestinian Human Rights Monitoring Group, the Palestinian Independent Commission for Citizens' Rights, LAW, Al-Haqq, and the Palestinian Center for Human Rights all issued reports that were widely read internationally; many more organizations operated outside the international spotlight. Almost all of these organizations were identified with a particular individual, and rivalries among the leading activists sometimes inhibited cooperation among them.

122. For a general survey of regional patterns, see Assef Bayat, "Activism and Social Development in the Middle East," *International Journal of Middle East Studies* 34 (February 2002): 1–28.

123. "Affirmation of Continuing Resistance and Construction and Implanting the Institutions of Civil Society," *Al-hayah al-jadida*, 27 April 2001.

124. The Bayt Jalla organization's headquarters was on a hill from which some Palestinians fired into Gilo, the Jewish neighborhood on the next hill. This provoked an Israeli response as well as some incursions. Qalandiya was the site of some clashes; more notably it was also the location of the checkpoint controlling access to Jerusalem.

CHAPTER 6: DEMOCRACY, NATIONALISM,
AND CONTESTING THE PALESTINIAN CURRICULUM

1. This view is surprisingly strong in writings on Palestinian textbooks, in which the conflict between Palestinians and Israelis is blamed on the textbooks themselves. For instance, in reviewing the claims of a group charging Palestinians with a hateful curriculum, an Israeli politician charged, "It is no wonder the call to disturbances, riots and violence found attentive ears among the Palestinian youth this week, since they grow up in an atmosphere of anti-Zionism and anti-Semitism." (See the comments of Limor Livnat in Center for Monitoring the Impact of Peace, "CMIP's Newest Report at the Israeli Knesset," retrieved 2 December 2002 from www.edume.org/news/news3.htm.) The incitement issue is treated more fully below; for present purposes it is enough for me to explain that I view textbooks as more effect than cause: the conflict antedates the textbooks in question by several generations.

2. For two particularly useful works, see Samuel Kaplan, "Education and the Politics of National Culture in a Turkish Community, circa 1990" (Ph.D. diss., University of Chicago, 1996); and Gregory Starrett, *Putting Islam to Work: Education, Politics, and the Transformation of Faith* (Berkeley: University of California Press, 1998).

3. Rif'at Sabah, director of Teacher Creativity Center, personal interview in Ramallah, February 2000.

4. See Starrett, *Putting Islam to Work,* for a description of Islamic education in Egyptian schools. For further historical background on the issue in the Ottoman period, see Benjamin C. Fortna, "Islamic Morality in Late Ottoman 'Secular' Schools," *International Journal of Middle East Studies* 32 (2000): 369–93.

5. The issue was raised in discussions between Clinton and 'Arafat (Hasan 'Abd al-Rahman, personal interview, July 1999, Jerusalem). Fifty members of Congress signed a letter to President Clinton in March 1999 denouncing the "anti-Israel brainwashing of the Palestinian children" in "the educational system and media." Clinton responded that real peace requires "a consistent effort to eliminate all instances of incitement in the media and, most importantly, in the textbooks," and that "we are deeply troubled by remaining instances of Palestinian incitement." See the congressional letter and Clinton's response in Center for Monitoring the Impact of Peace, "Senators and Congressmen Condemn PA Schoolbooks," retrieved 2 December 2002 from www.edume.org/news/news2.htm.

6. The most authoritative treatment of Palestinian educational history prior to 1948 is Abdul Latif Tibawi, *Arab Education in Mandatory Palestine: A Study of Three Decades of British Administration* (London: Luzac, 1956). All statistics in this section are taken from Tibawi's comprehensive survey. A very brief history is available from the Palestinian Ministry of Education in the "Education in Palestine Information Sheet," retrieved 18 December 1999 from the PNA Web site: www.pna.net/reports/edu_in_pal.htm.

7. The information in this and the preceding two paragraphs is drawn largely from Tibawi, *Arab Education.*

8. For instance, Ibtisam Abu Duhou, a Palestinian professor of education at the University of Melbourne who worked as a consultant to the Palestinian Authority in 1997, wrote, "No new schools were built during the first 10 years of Occupation and very few have been built since then." See Ibtisam Abu Duhou, "Schools in Palestine under the Occupation and the Palestinian National Authority," *Palestine-Israel Journal* 3 (Winter 1996): 15–16.

9. Palestinian Ministry of Education, "Education in Palestine Information Sheet."

10. According to Munir Jamil Fasheh, the head supervisor of mathematics instruction in the West Bank between 1973 and 1978, "all training courses and workshops for government school teachers have ceased to exist" since 1978. See Munir Jamil Fasheh, "The Reading Campaign Experience within Palestinian Society: Innovative Strategies for Learning and Building Community," *Harvard Educational Review* 65 (Spring 1995): 68.

11. See Muhammad al-Jiddi, "Light on Education in the Gaza Strip in Palestine: Aspirations for the Future" (Arabic), in *Al-ta'lim al-filastini: ta'rikhan, waqi'an wa darurat al-mustaqbal* (Palestinian education: Historically, currently,

and future needs), ed. Ibrahim Abu Lughod and Hamad Husayn (Bir Zayt: Bir Zayt University, 1997), p. 82.

12. By 1992, 103 textbooks had been banned from use. See Andrew Rigby, *Palestinian Education: The Future Challenge* (Jerusalem: Palestinian Academic Society for the Study of International Affairs, 1995), p. 12.

13. The battles over the Jerusalem curriculum have not attracted much public attention for this reason. The most thorough account from an Israeli perspective can be found in Amir S. Cheshin, Bill Hutman, and Avi Melamed, *Separate and Unequal: The Inside Story of Israeli Rule in East Jerusalem* (Cambridge, MA: Harvard University Press, 1999), chap. 6. The information here is drawn from that account and from personal interviews with Wahid Musa, inspector of Israeli government schools in East Jerusalem, Jerusalem, November 1999, and Maher Hashweh, professor of education at Bir Zayt University, Ramallah, August 1999.

14. Al-Jiddi, "Light on Education," p. 78.

15. Rigby, *Palestinian Education,* pp. 15–16.

16. Personal interview, Muhammad Suwan, president, General Union of Palestinian Teachers, Shu'afat, February 2000.

17. Fasheh, "Reading Campaign Experience."

18. The brief Israeli attempt to switch East Jerusalem schools to the Israeli curriculum is described above. After abandoning that attempt, Israel allowed the censored Jordanian books into East Jerusalem. In 1994, East Jerusalem schools began using the Jordanian textbooks republished by the PNA, though Israel attempted to remove any sign that they were approved by the PNA. And the new *Al-tarbiyya al-wataniyya* series was kept out of government schools in Jerusalem because it was wholly authored by the PNA Ministry of Education. In 1997, the mayor announced that he wished to see the East Jerusalem schools switch to the Israeli curriculum (see "Olmert Meets with Palestinian Journalists and Discusses Services," *Al-quds,* 2 July 1997). But no attempt was made. When the new Palestinian textbooks were issued for grades 1 and 6 in 2000, all Palestinian schools in East Jerusalem adopted them.

19. Al-Jiddi, "Light on Education," p. 88.

20. See Palestinian Ministry of Education, "Education in Palestine Information Sheet." The same report also states that $100 million is needed "as capital investment for school construction, rehabilitation and maintenance." No explanation is given for the discrepancy in the two figures. Some funding was forthcoming from donors—e.g., the International Development Agency had funded the construction of ten or eleven schools in Gaza, and Saudi and the Italian funds had led to the construction (or plans for) seventeen schools in the West Bank by 2000. See "Bank Group Operations," *West Bank and Gaza Update,* January 2000, p. 12 (English version), or p. 10 (Arabic version—the figure for schools in Gaza differs in the two versions, presumably because of an editing error).

21. New schools were still constructed. Between the school years beginning in 1995 and 1998, the number of government schools in the West Bank and

Gaza increased from 1,074 (according to Palestinian Ministry of Education, "Education in Palestine Information Sheet") to 1,230 (see "The Central Agency for Statistics Publishes the Fifth Issue of the Educational Statistical Book for the School Year 1998/99," *Al-hayah al-jadida*, 7 July 1999). Yet in 2000 the PNA was calling for the construction of 450 more schools. See "Janin: Celebration Opening al-Zawiya Mixed Primary School," *Al-ayyam* 9 May 2000, p. 3.

22. World Bank, Social and Economic Development Group, Middle East and North Africa Region, *West Bank and Gaza: Strengthening Public Sector Management* (Jerusalem: World Bank West Bank and Gaza Resident Mission, 1999), p. 45. For a more extensive treatment of education by a World Bank official, see Sue Berryman, "Palestinian Education: A Sector Review," *West Bank and Gaza Update*, no. 1 (1999) (entire issue). According to the work of one researcher, it may have been low salaries, however, that led to severe morale problems, at least among male teachers. See Unni Kjus Aahlin, "Palestinian Teachers' Role and the Effect of Their Training in the Construction of a New Education" (paper presented at the annual meeting of the Comparative and International Education Society, San Antonio, TX, March 2000).

23. The information on the West Bank union comes from a personal interview with a founder, Muhammad Suwan, president, General Union of Palestinian Teachers, Shu'afat, February 2000. On the General Union of Palestinian Teachers, see Laurie Brand, *Palestinians in the Arab World: Institution Building and the Search for State* (New York: Columbia University Press, 1988).

24. Unni Kjus Aahlin, a Norwegian educator familiar with Palestinian education, pointed out to me in a personal communication (30 May 2002) that there is a developmental aspect to the balance of tradition and individuality. This makes the reformer's distaste for transmission of values even more notable. Since a Palestinian curriculum had never been written, it is remarkable that many wished the opportunity not simply to instill identity and conformity to national norms but to develop individualism and democracy.

25. Denis As'ad, "The Arab Youth [Publishing] House: A Significant Educational Experiment" (Arabic), *Al-multaqa al-tarbawi*, no. 10 (December 1999).

26. "Ramallah: Tourism and Archaeology Opens a Workshop about the Special Touring Guide for Schools," *Al-ayyam*, 8 September 1999. The same archaeologists produced the first Palestinian-authored English-language travel guide; see Palestinian Association for Cultural Exchange, *PACE Tour Guide of the West Bank and Gaza Strip "Palestine"* (Ramallah: PACE, 1999).

27. For one expression of this orientation, see Zaynab Habash, *Tarshid al-manahij al-madrasiyya fi al-daffa al-gharbiyya wa-qita' ghazza* (Guiding the school curricula in the West Bank and the Gaza Strip) (Jerusalem: n.p., 1996).

28. See Liyana Jabir, "Education by Discovery: The Method of Its Application, Its Advantages, and Its Limitations," and "Cooperative Learning: Its Theoretical Bases, Its Advantages, and Guidance on Its Application" (both in Arabic), unpublished working papers, al-Qattan Center for Educational Research and Development, both undated.

29. Fasheh, "Reading Campaign Experience," p. 68.

30. Maher Z. Hashweh, "Palestinian Science Teachers' Epistemological Beliefs: A Preliminary Survey," *Research in Science Education* 26, no. 1 (1996): 97.

31. Munir Jamil Fasheh, "Is Math in the Classroom Neutral—Or Dead," *For the Learning of Mathematics* 17 (June 1997): 24.

32. Isma'il al-Nujum, director, al-Mawrid Teacher Development Center, personal interview, Ramallah, July 2000; see also Al-Mawrid, *Palestine and Education: The "Teaching Palestine Project"* (Ramallah: Al-Mawrid, 1997).

33. The al-Mawrid guide included a case in which a student acts aggressively toward a teacher; the student is expelled after the teacher threatens to resign, but relatives of the students attempt to mediate the dispute. See Maher Hashweh, *Al-tarbiyya al-dimuqratiyya: Ta'allum wa-ta'lim al-dimuqratiyya min ajl istikhdamiha* (Ramallah: Al-Mawrid, 1999). The unit was used in some local schools, though one school administration found the material too sensitive and pulled out of the project. For an English-language description of the center's work (including the democracy project), see Maher Hashweh and Ismail Njoum, "A Case-Based Approach to Education in Palestine: A Case Study of an Innovative Strategy" (paper presented at the Selmun Seminar, "Innovative Strategies in Meeting Educational Challenges in the Mediterranean," Malta, 13–19 June 1999).

34. Personal interview with Rif'at Sabah, director, Teacher Creativity Center, Ramallah, February 2000.

35. Teacher Creativity Center, "Strategic Plan for 1999–2004," unpublished document.

36. Personal interview with Rif'at Sabah, director, Teacher Creativity Center, Ramallah, February 2000.

37. Rif'at Sabah, "The Curriculum and the Political System," *Al-multaqa al-tarbawi*, no. 9 (October 1999).

38. See "Al-Bira: Opening of the Training Round about the Techniques of Teaching 'Civic Education' in Palestine," *Al-ayyam*, 28 December 1999; and "Evaluation of the Civics Curriculum for the Sixth Grade and Its Role in Changing Negative Social Values," *Al-ayyam*, 11 February 2000.

39. The other NGOs were the Early Childhood Resource Center (Jerusalem), the Educational Information and Coordination Project (Ramallah), the Young Scientists Club (Ramallah), the Tamir Social Education Foundation (Ramallah), and the Consciousness and Participation Foundation (Bethlehem).

40. Salah al-Subani, "The Problems of Arab Education and the Conditions of Maintenance and Progress in the Third Millennium," *Al-multaqa al-tarbawi*, no. 10 (December 1999).

41. Curriculum Development Center, *Al-manhaj al-filastini al-awwal li-l-ta'lim al-'amm: al-khitta al-shamila* (A comprehensive plan for the development of the First Palestinian Curriculum for General Education) (Ramallah: CDC, 1996). I have referred to the group in the text as the Abu Lughod committee rather than its formal name (despite his objection to me, expressed in a personal communication) to distinguish it from the permanent Curriculum

Development Center that was established after the first body of that name had completed its work.

42. Personal interview with Ibrahim Abu Lughod, Ramallah, October 1999.

43. ʿAli Jarbawi, personal interview, Ramallah, January 2000.

44. Ibid.

45. Personal interview with Ibrahim Abu Lughod, Ramallah, October 1999.

46. Curriculum Development Center, *Al-manhaj al-filastini al-awwal*, p. 90.

47. Ibid., p. 449.

48. Ibid., pp. 105–6.

49. Ibid., p. 35.

50. Ibid., pp. 53–54.

51. Ibid., p. 104.

52. Ibid., pp. 455–56.

53. ʿAli Jarbawi, personal interview, Ramallah, January 2000.

54. Khalil Mahshi, Director General, International and Public Relations, Ministry of Education, personal interview, Ramallah, August 1999.

55. Interviews with Ibrahim Abu Lughod, Ramallah, October 1999, and ʿAli Jarbawi, Ramallah, January 2000.

56. ʿAli Jarbawi, personal interview, Ramallah, January 2000.

57. Curriculum Development Center, *Al-manhaj al-filastini al-awwal*, pp. 454–55.

58. Ibrahim Abu Lughod, "Summary," in "Education Strategies and the Future Needs of a Palestinian Curriculum, Roundtable with a Presentation by Dr. Ibrahim Abu Lughod, Head of the Palestinian Curriculum Development Center," 15 August 1996, Palestinian Academic Society for the Study of International Affairs, Jerusalem, retrieved 2 December 2002 from www.passia .org/meetings/96/meet28.htm.

59. Fouad Moughrabi, "The Politics of Palestinian Textbooks," *Journal of Palestine Studies* 31 (Autumn 2001): 15–16. Moughrabi, like Abu Lughod, was a Palestinian-born and American-educated academic. He joined and then succeeded Abu Lughod at the Qattan Center, an educational NGO.

60. Ali Jarbawi, personal interview, Ramallah, January 2000.

61. Khalil Mahshi, personal interview, Ramallah, August 1999.

62. The Ministry of Education proposal was published; see General Administration of Curricula, Palestinian Curriculum Development Center, *First Palestinian Curriculum Plan* (Jerusalem: al-Maʿarif, 1998).

63. There may be some truth to the complaints that the Ministry of Education showed little interest in the spirit of the report—in a visit to the Curriculum Development Center in August 2000, I discovered that officials could locate only one copy of the report after considerable searching.

64. Personal interview with Dalal Salama, member of PLC's Committee on Education and Social Affairs, al-Bira, February 2000.

65. Palestinian Legislative Council, "Report of the Committee on Education

and Social Affairs on Palestinian Curriculum," submitted to PLC and approved, 31 March 1998.

66. Palestinian Legislative Council, "Report of the Committee on Education and Social Affairs," submitted to PLC and approved, 30 December 1999.

67. "The Legislature Approves the Recommendations of the Committee of Education and Religious Affairs," *Al-quds*, 31 December 1999.

68. The coordinator for the sixth-grade team, a specialist in Islamic education, explained that the team for each subject follows the path it sees as appropriate. See Dr. Hamza Zib Mustafa, "The Palestinian Curriculum Is a Glorious Experiment in the History of the Palestinian People," *Al-quds*, 11 September 1999.

69. Khalil Mahshi, personal interview, Ramallah, August 1999.

70. After an article appeared in *Al-hayah* on 28 December 1999 announcing that the drafts were completed, I requested copies. A senior official in the CDC declined, explaining that the minister of education would have to review them personally before they would be released outside the ministry. At the same time, however, the CDC was organizing training sessions for teachers and other education officials based on the new textbooks, indicating that the curriculum was less provisional than was claimed.

71. "Evaluation of the Civics Curriculum for the Sixth Grade and Its Role in Changing Negative Social Values," *Al-ayyam*, 11 February 2000.

72. Curriculum Development Center, *Al-manhaj al-filastini al-awwal*, p. 221.

73. See General Administration of Curricula, *First Palestinian Curriculum Plan*, p. 5. In March 2000, the Ministry of Education directorate for Gaza organized an essay competition for secondary school students on democracy. See *Al-ayyam*, 9 March 2000, p. 4.

74. "Workshops on New Curriculum," *Al-hayah al-jadida*, 19 January 2000.

75. Personal interview with 'Umar Abu al-Humus, deputy director, CDC, Ramallah, August 1999.

76. General Administration of Curricula, *First Palestinian Curriculum Plan*, p. 5.

77. Both Abu Luhgod and Jarbawi reject this argument but acknowledge that they heard it from many teachers. Personal interviews, Ramallah, October 1999 and January 2000.

78. Curriculum Center, *Islamic Education*, grade 6 (Ramallah: Curriculum Center, 2000), part 1, p. 49.

79. Despite the tremendous international controversy surrounding Palestinian textbooks, there are few academic studies on their content. When I first wrote on the subject in 2000, nothing had been published. Since then a few studies have come out. Moughrabi, "Politics of Palestinian Textbooks," 5–19, attempts to shift the terms of the debate from incitement and anti-Semitism to pedagogical and educational criteria. Goetz Nordbruch's *Narrating Palestinian Nationalism: A Study of the New Palestinian Textbooks* (Washington, DC:

Middle East Media Research Institute, 2002) highlights the tension between democratic and nationalist themes in the books. While he sometimes overstates his findings, his research is careful and most of my differences with him are matters of degree. The *Palestine-Israel Journal* published a special issue on "Education in Times of Conflict" (vol. 7, no. 2, 2001). The articles by Ramzi A. Rihan ("The Palestinian Educational Development Plan: Promise for the Future") and Sami Adwan ("Schoolbooks in the Making: From Conflict to Peace") include material on the new books.

80. General Administration of Curricula, *First Palestinian Curriculum Plan*, p. 8.

81. Ibid., p. 7.

82. Ibid., p. 26.

83. Curriculum Center, *Islamic Education*, grade 1, part 1, p. 39.

84. See, e.g., Curriculum Center, *Our Beautiful Language*, grade 6 (Ramallah: Curriculum Center, 2000), part 1, p. 19.

85. Curriculum Center, *Civic Education*, grade 6 (Ramallah: Curriculum Center, 2000), unit 4.

86. Curriculum Center, *Our Beautiful Language*, grade 1 (Ramallah: Curriculum Center, 2000), part 2, unit 6.

87. Curriculum Center, *Our Beautiful Language*, grade 6, part 1, p. 4.

88. Curriculum Center, *General Science*, grade 6, part 1 (Ramallah: Curriculum Center, 2000), pp. 10–11.

89. Curriculum Center, *National Education*, grade 6 (Ramallah: Curriculum Center, 2000), unit 3, the section "Imitation and Creativity."

90. See Curriculum Center, *Civic Education*, grade 7 (Ramallah: Curriculum Center,, 2001), the unit "The Media."

91. Curriculum Center, *Islamic Education*, grade 1 (Ramallah: Curriculum Center, 2000), part 1, p. 57.

92. Curriculum Center, *Mathematics*, grade 7 (Ramallah: Curriculum Center, 2001), p. 135.

93. Curriculum Center, *Arab and Islamic History*, grade 6 (Ramallah: Curriculum Center, 2000), the unit "The Umayyad Caliphate."

94. Curriculum Center, *Islamic Education*, grade 6, pp. 45–61.

95. Curriculum Center, *Civic Education*, grade 7, p. 46, mentions al-Haqq and the Palestinian Independent Commission for Citzens' Rights.

96. Ministry of Education, *Al-tarbiyya al-wataniyya*, grade 5 (Ramallah: Ministry of Education, 1998), p. 2. To clarify which set of texts I am indicating, I refer to the 1994 supplementary series by its Arabic title, *Al-tarbiyya al-wataniyya*. When I refer to the books beginning in 2000 that cover the same subject, I translate the title to *National Education*.

97. Curriculum Center, *Arabic Writing*, grade 2 (Ramallah: Curriculum Center, 2001), p. 22.

98. Curriculum Center, *Arabic Writing*, grade 7 (Ramallah: Curriculum Center, 2001), p. 4.

99. Curriculum Center, *National Education,* grade 2 (Ramallah: Curriculum Center, 2001), part 1, pp. 4–5

100. Curriculum Center, *Arab and Islamic History,* grade 6, unit 1. North African areas are not included. All of mandatory Palestine is included as is Alexandretta, a district transferred from Syria to Turkey under the French mandate, a move still regarded as illegitimate by Syria.

101. Curriculum Center, *National Education,* grade 7 (Ramallah: Curriculum Center, 2001), p. 7.

102. Curriculum Center, *Arts and Crafts,* grade 6 (Ramallah: Curriculum Center, 2000), p. 38. The reference to ending the Hebrew occupation of Jerusalem is striking because it pits the pre-Islamic Arabs against those mentioned in the Qur'an as prophets, undermining (almost certainly unconsciously) the close identification between Arabs and Islam that pervade other textbooks.

103. There is the additional irony, similar to that of the reference to Nebuchadnezzar, of using the word *jizya:* it places Ibrahim, a Muslim prophet, in the position of a non-Muslim and the idol worshipper (as the pre-Muslim Arabs are described) in the position of a Muslim ruler. See Curriculum Center, *Our Beautiful Language,* grade 6, part 22, pp. 20–23.

104. Curriculum Center, *Islamic Education,* grade 6, part 1, pp. 66–69.

105. Curriculum Center, *Arab and Islamic History,* grade 6, introduction, iv.

106. Curriculum Center, *National Education,* grade 6, unit 1, part 1.

107. Ibid., unit 3, section "Tolerance." See also Curriculum Center, *Civic Education,* grade 3 (Ramallah: Curriculum Center, 2002), p. 25.

108. Curriculum Center, *National Education,* grade 6, unit 3, section "Values."

109. This is the only time that Hebrew appears in the texts. Curriculum Center, *Mathematics,* grade 6 (Ramallah: Curriculum Center, 2000), part 2, p. 77. When units of currency are mentioned in the mathematics text, an unspecified *dinar* is mentioned—the name of the prospective Palestinian currency. In reality, prices in the West Bank and Gaza are almost always denominated in Israeli shekels.

110. The stamp is on the cover of Curriculum Center, *National Education,* grade 2.

111. Curriculum Center, *National Education,* grade 6, unit 2, section "The State," p. 29

112. Ibid., unit 2, section "The Constitution."

113. Curriculum Center, *Civic Education,* grade 7, p. 46.

114. Curriculum Center, *National Education,* grade 1, part 2, p. 32.

115. Curriculum Center, *Our Beautiful Language,* grade 1, part 2, unit 7, "Nationalism."

116. Ministry of Education, *Al-tarbiyya al-wataniyya,* grade 6 (Ramallah: Ministry of Education, 1998), p. 20.

117. Curriculum Center, *Principles of Human Geography,* grade 6 (Ramallah: Curriculum Center, 2000), p. 48.

118. All these stories are from Curriculum Center, *Our Beautiful Language,* grade 1, part 2.

119. Curriculum Center, *Our Beautiful Language*, grade 6, part 2, unit "Gandhi," p. 110.

120. The phrase is used in the preface of each book issued in 2000 and 2001.

121. Curriculum Center, *Our Beautiful Language* (2001), grade 2 (Ramallah: Curriculum Center, 2001), pp. 60–61.

122. "Not Only at School: Education, Occupation, Activism and Dialogue: A Round-Table Discussion," *Palestine-Israel Journal* 8, no. 2 (2001): 80.

123. John Dewey, *Democracy and Education* (New York: Free Press, 1916), pp. 87–88.

124. Amy Gutmann, *Democratic Education* (Princeton, NJ: Princeton University Press, 1999), p. 289.

125. Stephen Holmes, "Precommitment and the Paradox of Democracy," in *Constitutionalism and Democracy*, ed. John Elster and Rune Slagstad (New York: Cambridge University Press, 1988), p. 233.

126. Gutmann, *Democratic Education*, p. xiv.

127. Ibid., p. 288.

128. See the center's Web site, www.edume.org.

129. Some critics point to the identity of the center's first director, Itamar Marcus, to support their suspicions. Marcus is an Israeli political activist of the West Bank settlement of Efrat who previously lobbied to keep West Bank aquifers under Israeli control. His work on textbooks led Prime Minister Binyamin Netanyahu to appoint him to a joint committee with the Palestinians on incitement. He also went on to found an organization that searches Palestinian media for anti-Israeli and anti-Jewish statements. CMIP eventually broke its link with Marcus and attempted to disguise his past leadership of the organization. My own critique of CMIP's work focuses on its methods and conclusions, not the personality of its staff. I should note, however, that CMIP's first report after Marcus's departure abandoned the misleading technique of mixing quotations from the non-Palestinian books and the Palestinian books; CMIP also issued a new edition of its first report with some of the earlier errors repaired. Still, in its other material, CMIP continued to mislead its readers: it led a lobbying campaign in the European Parliament to eliminate EU assistance for the new books. CMIP worked hard to conceal the fact that the EU gave no assistance. And it continued to deny the significance of changes in the Palestinian-authored texts.

130. "The Palestinian Authority School Books," retrieved 13 August 1999 from the Web site of the Center for Monitoring the Impact of Peace: www.edume.org.

131. "The New Palestinian Authority School Textbooks—November 2000," retrieved 26 December 2002 from the Web site of the Center for Monitoring the Impact of Peace: www.edume.org/news/nov00.htm.

132. The report's method of listing large number of statements from the books led it to include all sorts of material under the anti-Israel rubric. For instance, any mention of Jerusalem made by a Palestinian character was listed as questioning the Israeli nature of the city. Since Jerusalem was designated as a

matter for final status negotiations, the idea that the Palestinians questioned Israeli annexation should have been unsurprising. What is more surprising—and unremarked in the report—is that all mentions of locations in Jerusalem in the Palestinian-authored books refer only to the Old City and a few Arab neighborhoods. If textbooks are taken as indications of negotiating positions—an implicit assumption of the report—then the Palestinians showed far more willingness to compromise on Jerusalem than Israel.

133. The center's report does include some excerpts from these books, but none can fairly be viewed as hostile to Israel or to Jews. The texts are examined in more detail below.

134. Center for Monitoring the Impact of Peace, "CMIP launched in Congress (September 1998)," retrieved 2 December 2002 from www.edume.org/news/news1.htm.

135. My son attended a Tel Aviv school that celebrated "Tolerance Day," assuring all students that Israelis can be religious or secular, light-skinned or dark-skinned, and Jewish or Arab. Following the center's methodology, such a unit might be lambasted for failing to include Palestinians who do not hold Israeli citizenship and for denying Palestinian identity (by not mentioning it).

136. "The Palestinian Authority School Textbooks for the Year 2000," retrieved 26 December 2002 from the Web site of the Center for Monitoring the Impact of Peace: www.edume.org/reports/3/3.htm.

137. To follow the center's methodology of insisting on giving its own—rather than the textbook's—characterization of historical figures, a similarly unfair report on an American textbook from the late 1930s lauding Abraham Lincoln might be portrayed as carrying a procommunist message because of the role of the Abraham Lincoln Brigade in the Spanish Civil War. Perhaps a less farfetched analogy might be blasting an Israeli textbook that included Yitzhak Shamir for encouraging political assassinations of British and UN officials and massacres of civilians.

138. The center eschews such a prosecutorial approach in its treatment of Israeli textbooks. Were it to be more consistent in its approach, it could easily (and, to some extent, unfairly) smear the efforts of Israeli educators. My own son's experience in a fourth-grade class in Tel Aviv can bear this out. He was given maps that included all the PNA territories in Israel and none that excluded them. (With Israel not having determined its borders or recognized Palestinian sovereignty, this is understandable, but the center hardly approaches Palestinian textbooks with such sympathetic understanding.) A unit on the history of the land included no significant material on the Palestinian population, and the only treatment of Muslims (the Ottomans) was negative. A biblical text (Joshua) was presented that defined the borders promised to the Jews as ambitiously covering much of Jordan and Syria. While the text itself could not be changed, the edition given to my son included notes designed to ensure that the students understood the nature of these borders (the same book was reticent only when dealing with an incident involving a prostitute: the commentary indicated that the word *prostitute*—an unfortunately common playground epithet at my

son's school—really meant "vegetable seller." In short, the edition showed embarrassment when the text mentioned sex but not when it dealt with borders.) Perhaps most shocking, my son was given a song sheet during a unit on the history of the city of Tel Aviv that advocated beating and even the death of Arabs (the song lauded a guard for beating up Arabs and quoted him saying, "Get out of here, 'Abd Allah, you should die, God willing, but just not in Tel Aviv").

My point here is not that Israeli textbooks are racist (my vague impression is that the secular educational establishment has exhibited steadily growing sensitivity over how such matters are to be taught). I only wish to observe that a report using the same selective techniques as the center could easily portray them extremely negatively. (A completely fair account should mention that the offensive verse in the song was not taught to the students in my son's class after my wife and I complained to the teacher, who apologized profusely and expressed extreme embarrassment that she had circulated a song with such words.)

Fuller and more fair-minded treatments of Israeli textbooks are now available in English. See Elie Podeh, *The Arab-Israeli Conflict in Israeli History Textbooks* (Westport, CT: Bergin and Garvey, 2001). Also of interest is Daniel Bar-Tal, "The Arab Image in Hebrew School Books," *Palestine-Israel Journal* 7, no. 2 (2001): 5–18. Ruth Firer, an education specialist at Hebrew University, has worked extensively on this subject. Most of her publications are in Hebrew, but some of her findings are available in English. See, for instance, "Human Rights in History and Civics Textbooks: The Case of Israel," *Curriculum Inquiry* 28 (1998): 195–209. In addition, she has been involved in a joint project with Sami Adwan of Bethlehem University studying Israeli and Palestinian textbooks, the results of which should be published soon by the Georg Eckert Institute for International Textbook Research. A summary of their research was published by *Common Ground News,* 28 March 2002.

For a refreshingly thoughtful and nonpolemical essay on some of the debate over Israeli textbooks, see Anita Shapira, "History as She Is Fraught," *Ha'aretz,* 1 February 2002.

139. "The New Palestinian Authority School Textbooks—November 2000."

140. Without a hint of irony, Krauthammer simultaneously denounced the Israeli changes, favorably citing a book that covered the issue "in rather great and shocking details." See the transcript of remarks delivered at the American Enterprise Institute, "Is the Israeli/Palestinian Peace Process Dead, and If So, What's Next," 6 November 2000, retrieved 2 December 2002 from the American Enterprise Institute Web site: www.aei.org/past_event/conf001106.htm.

141. Interview with John McCain, *Rolling Stone,* 27 September 2001, p. 36.

142. Yigal Carmon, testifying before the U.S. House Committee on International Relations, 18 April 2002; Limor Livnat, "The Victim Has Changed," *Jerusalem Post,* 12 April 2002, retrieved 12 April 2002 from www.jpost.com.

143. Berl Wein, "Illusions," *Jerusalem Post,* 26 October 2000, retrieved 26 October 2000 from www.jpost.com.

144. Christina Lamb, "Intifada: The Next Generation," *Sunday Telegraph*, 15 October 2000, p. 26

145. "Hillary Clinton: Link PA Aid to End to Antisemitism," *Jerusalem Post*, 26 September 2000, retrieved 26 September 2000 from www.jpost.com.

146. For the text of the letter, see "Schumer, Clinton Call for Eradication of Hate Rhetoric by the Palestinian Authority," retrieved 2 December 2002 from Hillary Clinton's Web site: www.senate.gov/~clinton/news/2001/06/2001614111 .html.

147. Ambassador Marc Ginsberg, "Fox Special Report with Brit Hume," 30 April 2002.

148. Gerald Steinberg criticized European assistance and diplomacy for ineffectiveness in 1999, writing that "new Palestinian textbooks dealing with the Arab-Israeli conflict contain the same myths and hostility." (See Gerald M. Steinberg, "The European Union and the Middle East Peace Process," *Jerusalem Letter*, no. 418 (15 November 1999). Steinberg's description of the books published by 1999 is unsupportable even by the tendentious standards of the center.

149. Commission of the European Communities, "Statement on Behalf of Commissioner Patten on Press Reports Regarding Alleged EC Funding for Text Books Used by the Palestinian Authority," press release, 27 April 2001. The statement came after a story in the *European Voice* on the textbook controversy.

150. "EU Money to Be Denied for PA Schoolbooks," *Jerusalem Post*, 2 November 2001.

151. "Palestinian Schoolbooks," press release issued 15 May 2002 in Brussels by the General Secretariat of the Council of the European Union Press Office.

152. The organization's Web site later posted a model letter addressed to "world leaders" asking, "How many Palestinian textbooks need to say: 'there is no alternative to the destruction of Israel' before you question the sincerity of the Palestinian authority?" (retrieved 26 December 2002 from www. standwithus.com/actions/033002asp).There was no textbook that posed such a question.

153. Individual Israeli politicians did raise the issue. Natan Sharansky claimed on the eve of the 2001 elections that 'Arafat "used the Palestinian textbooks to teach the current generation to hate far more than the previous one." See Norman Doidge, "Up against Tyrants," *Jewish World Review*, 6 February 2001.

154. Dani Naveh, "Inciting and Educating Children towards Hate, Anti-Semitism, and Violence in the Palestinian Authority," March 2002, retrieved 2 December 2002 from the Israeli Prime Minister's Office Web site: www.pmo .gov.il/english/nave/hatred.html.

155. See "Briefing by Colonel Miri Eisin, IDF Intelligence Officer," retrieved 26 December 2002 from Israeli Ministry of Foreign Affairs Web site: www.mfa.gov.il/mfa/go.asp?MFAH011x0.

156. "Israel Clears Canada of Funding Palestinian Hatred: Embassy Admits Charges Were Wrong," *Ottawa Citizen*, 25 April 2002.

157. Steve Israel, letter to *New York Times*, 10 June 2001, Section 4, p. 14.

158. Two Palestinians (Khalil Mahshi and Fouad Moughrabi) looked for editions in the public library and the Ministry of Education in Ramallah and found the editions there—the ones that would have been available to the textbook authors—did not contain the banner. I located an edition published in 1991 that also lacked the banner (Mustafa Murad Dabbagh, *Biladuna Filastin*, Kafr Qara': Dar al-Huda, 1991). To date, I am aware of no independent verification of the center's claim for any edition of the work. And the center makes other mistakes: it claims the book is dedicated to "those who are battling for the expulsion of the enemy from our land!" In fact, the dedication is to "those who strove for maintaining the Arabness of Palestine."

159. CMIP insisted that since the sixth-grade textbook referred students to *Biladuna Filastin*, the work in its entirety legitimately should be considered part of the PNA curriculum. In making this claim, it failed to note that students were directed to look up their home, not read the sections including the passages in question. In any case, its standard here was the precise opposite of the one used for Israeli textbooks in which it specifically excluded supplementary but non-textbook material, even if students were to be examined on it on the *bagrut* (the Israeli equivalent of the tawjihi). CMIP's report on Israeli books explicitly excluded "novels that are taught in literature classes and used in the matriculation exams, such as *Hirbat Hiz'a* by Israeli author Yizhar Smilansky, describing a group of Israeli soldiers who torture an Arab during the Independence War of 1948." See Center for Monitoring the Impact of Peace, "Arabs and Palestinians in Israeli Textbooks," 2000, retrieved 2 December 2002 from www.edume.org/reports/5/intro.htm.

160. Efraim Karsh, "Clear-cut Victory," *Jerusalem Post*, 11 March 2002, retrieved 11 March 2002 from www.jpost.com.

161. Raphael Israeli, "Education, Identity, State Building and the Peace Process: Educating Palestinian Children in the Post-Oslo Era," *Terrorism and Political Violence* 12 (Spring 2000): 79–94.

162. Shlomo Sharan, "Israel and the Jews in the Schoolbooks of the Palestinian Authority," in *Israel and a Palestinian State: Zero-Sum Game*, ed. Arieh Stahv (Shaarei Tikva: Ariel Center for Policy Research, 2001), retrieved 26 December 2002 from Israel Behind the News Web site: www.israelbehindthenews.com/Archives/May-16-01.htm#jihad.

CHAPTER 7: CONCLUSION

1. Rashid Khalidi, *Palestinian Identity: The Construction of Modern National Consciousness* (New York: Columbia University Press, 1997), p. 202.

2. In May 2002, an Israeli government team headed by Dani Naveh, minister of parliamentary affairs, produced a report entitled "The Involvement of Arafat, PA Senior Officials and Apparatuses in Terrorism against Israel, Corruption and Crime," based on documents captured during military operations. The report made international headlines because it claimed that such documents

proved that 'Arafat was personally involved in planning and execution of attacks, but it produced no evidence for the charge. It did show what was already fairly well accepted—that parts of 'Arafat's party (Fatah) and members of the security forces were participating in such attacks. Tying them personally to 'Arafat required reading the documents extremely selectively and ignoring strong counterevidence (such as the fact that Marwan al-Barghuti, whose role in groups participating in violence was less open to question, was hardly under 'Arafat's control and indeed spoke contemptuously of 'Arafat in public even before the intifada began). Thus, the more extreme Israeli charges were not supported. But the involvement of members of Fatah and the security forces in terrorism was far clearer.

3. See the advertisement placed by the Teacher Creativity Center in *Al-ayyam,* 15 May 2002.

4. The effects of the April 2002 Israeli military campaign were hotly debated internationally, with most attention focusing on Jenin. However, the destruction of civil and political institutions was best documented in the Ramallah area. Israeli and foreign press accounts covered this sporadically. The most comprehensive document was compiled by a group of Palestinian NGO activists, the Palestinian NGO Emergency Initiative in Jerusalem, and titled "Destruction of Palestinian Non-Governmental Organizations in Ramallah Caused by IDF Forces between March 29 and April 21, 2002," 22 April 2002, retrieved 26 December 2002 from www.pna.gov.ps/new/repintrodo2.pdf. The document seems carefully researched and based on eyewitness accounts.

5. See "Independence of the Judiciary Requires Reconstruction of What the Occupation Destroyed and Stability in the Political Situation," *Al-ayyam,* 19 May 2002.

6. Hasan al-Kashif, "Keeping the Government and Dismissing the People," *Al-hayah al-jadida,* 20 May 2002, retrieved 20 May 2002 from www.alhayat-j.com.

7. See European Commission, "Conditions Attached to the EC's Budgetary Assistance to the Palestinian Authority and the Monitoring by the IMF," 6 May 2002, retrieved 26 December 2002 from European Union Web site: www.eu-oplysningen.dk/evidag/rapid/MEMO_02_90_0_RAPID.

8. In May 2002, one leading intellectual expressed suspicion of American and Israeli talk of reform; he also claimed that Palestinians would have to choose either resistance or reform. See the comments of George Giacaman in "Broad Debate about the Instrument of Reform and Similarity of Opinions Regarding 'Suicide Operations,' " *Al-ayyam,* 19 May 2002. Even some 'Arafat opponents opposed elections as unsuitable because of the continuing struggle and external pressure. See, e.g., the comments of Haydar 'Abd al-Shafi, "Abdul-Shafi Demands Delay in Reform," *Jerusalem Times,* 23 May 2002.

9. An English translation of the report was published as "The Complete Text of the PLC's 'Reform Charter' Presented to President Arafat" in the *Jerusalem Times* on 23 May 2002.

10. This reform program, which became known as the "One Hundred Day

Plan," was published by WAFA, the Palestinian News Agency, on 26 June 2002, after its presentation by Sa'ib 'Urayqat, the minister of local government. Retrieved 1 July 2002 from www.wafa.pna.net.

11. The speech was widely covered in the Palestinian press. On the connection between the second intifada and the calls for political reform more generally, see Rema Hammami and Jamil Hilal, "An Uprising at a Crossroads," *Middle East Report*, no. 219 (Summer 2001): 2–7, 41.

Bibliography

INTERVIEWS

'Abd al-Rahman, Hasan (PLO representative in Washington), personal interviews, Washington, June 1999, and Jerusalem, July 1999.

'Abd al-Shafi, Haydar (PLC member), Gaza, February 1997.

'Amad, Farida (president, In'ash al-usra Society), Ramallah, November 1999.

'Asfur, Hasan, (Minister for Non-Governmental Organizations), Ramallah, September 1999.

'Atiya Abu Mur (World Bank, Ministry of Justice), Ramallah, September 1999.

'Izz al-Din, Husam (*Al-ayyam* newspaper), Ramallah, May 2000.

'Ubaydat, 'Adnan (ANERA), Jerusalem, January 2000.

'Udayli, Nabil (Pharmacists Syndicate), Jerusalem, June 2000.

Abu 'Awad, Husni (director, Zakat Committee, Ramallah), April 2000.

Abu al-Humus, 'Umar, (deputy director, Curriculum Development Center, Ministry of Education), Ramallah, August 1999.

Abu Layla, 'Adnan (deputy chair, Palestinian Bar Association), Ramallah, February 2000.

Abu Lughod, Ibrahim (Al-Qattan Center), Ramallah, October 1999.

Abu Su'ud, 'Azzam (director, Arab Chamber of Commerce and Industry, Jerusalem), Jerusalem, May 2000.

Anabtawi, Nabil (general manager, *In'ash al-usra* society), Ramallah, November 1999.

Ansara, Khalil (attorney), Ramallah, September 1999.

Al-'Araj, Lidiya (Women and Childcare Society), Bayt Jalla, January 2000.

Al-'Awda, Arij (Department of Legal Affairs, Ramallah Governorate), Ramallah, March 2000.

Al-Bakri, Bahjat Rabi' (member, Zakat Committee, Jerusalem), April 2000.

Claudet, Sophie (World Bank), Jerusalem, March 2000.

Daffron, Sandra (DPK, Palestinian Rule of Law Project), Ramallah, July 2000.

Al-Daghma, Ibrahim (director, Diwan al-fatwa wa-l-tashri'), Ramallah, September 1999.

Delaney, Kim (United States Agency for International Development), Tel Aviv, July 1999.

Faraj, Sahar (Qalandia Women's Cooperative Society), Qalandia, November 1999.

Gabai, Yoram (former director-general of the Treasury, Israel), Tel Aviv, May 2000.

Garber, Larry (United States Agency for International Development), Washington, DC, June 1999.

George, Chris (Associates in Rural Development), Jerusalem, July 1999.

Gubser, Peter (ANERA), Washington, DC, June 1999.

Hamad, Salmi (general secretary, Jericho Chamber of Commerce), Jericho, June 2000.

Hashweh, Maher (professor of education, Bir Zayt University), Ramallah, August 1999.

Jarbawi, 'Ali (Palestinian Independent Commission for Citizens' Rights), Ramallah, January 2000.

Kan'an, Samih (director of external relations for Palestinian Preventive Security), Ramallah, July 2000.

Kelly, Ellen (United States Agency for International Development), Arlington, Virginia, December 2001.

Al-Khalidi, Ahmad Mubarak (Al-Najah University and Palestinian Legislative Council Parliamentary Research Unit), Nablus and Ramallah, February 1997, August 1999, December 1999.

Khashan, 'Ali (dean of the faculty of law at Al-Quds University), Jerusalem, February 2000, December 2001.

Mahshi, Khalil (director general, International and Public Relations, Ministry of Education), Ramallah, August 1999.

Mansur, Camille (Bir Zayt University), Bir Zayt, February 1997, February 2000.

Merrill, Donna (Associates in Rural Development), Ramallah, August 1999.

Al-Mu'aqqat, Kazim (manager, Jericho Chamber of Commerce), Jericho, June 2000.

Musa, Wahid (Ministry of Education, Israel), Jerusalem, November 1999.

Niddam, Jean-Claude Niddam (head of Legal Assistance, Ministry of Justice), Jerusalem, November 1999.

Al-Nashashibi, Shukri (attorney), Ramallah, August 1999.

Al-Nujum, Isma'il (director, Al-Mawrid Teacher Development Center), Ramallah, July 2000.

Al-Qadi, Amina (Arab Women's Union), Jerusalem, January 2000.

Sa'id, Nadir 'Izzat (Bir Zayt University), Ramallah, October 1999.

Saba, Joseph (World Bank), Jerusalem, February 2000.

Sabah, Rif'at (director, Teacher Creativity Center), Ramallah, February 2000.

Sadaqa, Ja'far (*Al-ayyam* newspaper), Ramallah, May 2000.

Safi, Ramadan (director for public relations, Engineers Syndicate), Jerusalem, May 2000.

Salama, Dalal (member of PLC's Committee on Education and Social Affairs), al-Bira, February 2000.

Schultz, Keith (Associates in Rural Development), Ramallah, August 1999.
Shadid, Muhammad (Welfare Association), Jerusalem, July 2000, November 2001.
Shakir, Minawwir (Jericho Women's Benevolent Society), Jericho, November 1999.
Al-Shalalda, Muhammad Fahmi (president of the General Palestinian Union of Charitable Societies), Beersheva, October 1999.
Shihada, Karim (attorney), Ramallah, February 2000.
Shu'aybi, 'Azmi (PLC member), November 1999.
Shumal, Shawkat (Beit Jala Olive Cooperative), Bayt Jalla, February 2000.
Sourani, Raji (Palestinian Center for Human Rights), Gaza, February 1997.
Suwan, Muhammad (president, General Union of Palestinian Teachers), Shu'afat, February 2000.
Al-Tarifi, Sa'id (Dentists Syndicate), Jerusalem, May 2000.
Yasir, Haytham (*Al-ayyam* newspaper), Ramallah, May 2000.
Al-Za'im, Sharhabil (attorney), Gaza, February 1997.

UNPUBLISHED DOCUMENTS

Aahlin, Unni Kjus. "Challenges Ahead: Strengthening the School as the Arena for Effective Learning and as Transmitter of Palestinian Values." Paper presented at the Ministry of Education, 20 October 2001.
——. "Palestinian Teachers' Role and the Effect of Their Training in the Construction of a New Education." Paper presented at the annual meeting of the Comparative and International Education Society, San Antonio, TX, March 2000.
——. "A Study on the Construction of Palestinian Education and the Teacher's Role and Professional Development." Qattan Center for Educational Research and Development, January 2001.
Abdulhadi, Rabab Ibrahim Abdulhadi. "Palestinianness in a Comparative Perspective: Inclusionary Resistance, Exclusionary Citizenship." Ph.D. diss., Yale University, 2000.
Baxter, Joe, and Amy Hawthorne. "Guide for the Planning and Organization of Local Government Elections in the West Bank and Gaza." Presented to the Ministry of Local Government and the Supreme Elections Committee of the PNA by the International Foundation for Electoral Systems, January 1998.
Chase, Anthony B. Tirado. "Islam and Human Rights, Clashing Normative Orders?" Ph.D. diss., Fletcher School of Law and Diplomacy, 2000.
Chemonics International. "Feasible Options for Rule of Law Programming." December 1998.
Claudet, Sophie. "The Changing Role of Palestinian NGOs since the Establishment of the Palestinian Authority (1994–1996)." Prepared for Nigel Roberts of the West Bank/Gaza Unit and Ishac Diwan of the Economic Development Institute, Macroeconomic and Management Policy, World Bank, July 1996.

Council on Foreign Relations. "Strengthening Palestinian Public Institutions—Full Report." Independent Task Force Report, Michel Rocard, chairman; Henry Siegman, project director; Yezid Sayigh and Khalil Shikaki, principal authors, June 1999. Retrieved 22 November 2002, from www.cfr.org publication.php?id=3184.

Dawr al-Muʿallim/a fi al-difaʿ ʿan huquq al-insan (The role of the teacher in defending human rights). Proceedings of an international conference held by the Teacher Creativity Center, Ramallah, March 2001. Ramallah: Teacher Creativity Center, 2001.

DPK Consulting, Inc. "Analysis of Closed Case Survey of Civil Cases in Four Palestinian Pilot Courts." Rule of Law Project—West Bank and Gaza, USAID Contract Number 294-C.00–99–00–159–00, 2001.

Hashweh, Maher, and Ismail Njoum. "A Case-Based Approach to Education in Palestine: A Case Study of an Innovative Strategy." Paper presented at the Selmun Seminar, "Innovative Strategies in Meeting Educational Challenges in the Mediterranean," Malta, 13–19 June 1999.

Idʿeis, Maʿen. "Detentions in PNA Controlled Areas (Legality and Application)." LAW society report, Jerusalem, May 2000, retrieved 2 December 2002 from www.lawsociety.org/Reports/reports/2000/padetent.html.

Jabir, Liyana. "Cooperative Learning: Its Theoretical Bases, Its Advantages, and Guidance on Its Application" (in Arabic). Unpublished working paper, Al-Qattan Center for Educational Research and Development.

———. "Education by Discovery: The Method of Its Application, Its Advantages, and Its Limitations" (in Arabic). Unpublished working paper, Al-Qattan Center for Educational Research and Development.

Kaplan, Samuel. "Education and the Politics of National Culture in a Turkish Community, circa 1990." Ph.D. diss., University of Chicago, 1996.

Khalil, Asem. "The Palestinian Constitutional System." Dissertatio ad Licentiam, Pontifica Universitas Lateranesis, Institutum Utriusqe Iurus, 2002.

Labadi, Fadwa, Penny Johnson, Rema Hammami, and Lynn Welchman. "Islamic Family Law and the Transition to Palestinian Statehood: Constraints and Opportunities for Legal Reform." Retrieved 26 November 2002 from Emory University School of Law Web site: www.law.emory.edu/IFL/cases/Palestine.htm.

National Democratic Institute for International Affairs. "The First Months of the Palestinian Legislative Council." Washington, D.C., May 1996.

Naveh, Dani. "Inciting and Educating Children towards Hate, Anti-Semitism, and Violence in the Palestinian Authority." March 2002, retrieved 2 December 2002, from Israeli Prime Minister's Office Web site: www.pmo.gov.il/english/nave/hatred.html.

Palestinian Legislative Council. File on the Basic Law (collection of documents and correspondence regarding the draft Basic Law for the Palestinian National Authority). 1994–1998. Archives of the Office of the Speaker, Ramallah.

———. Budget and Fiscal Affairs Committee. "Report of the Budget and Fiscal

Affairs Committee," 1997 Draft General Budget for the Palestinian National Authority. Unpublished document, Palestinian Legislative Council, Ramallah.

———. Budget and Fiscal Affairs Committee. "Report of the Budget and Fiscal Affairs Committee," 1998 Draft General Budget for the Palestinian National Authority. Unpublished document, Palestinian Legislative Council, Ramallah.

———. Budget and Fiscal Affairs Committee. "Report of the Budget and Fiscal Affairs Committee," 1999 Draft General Budget for the National Authority. Unpublished document, Palestinian Legislative Council, Ramallah.

———. Budget and Fiscal Affairs Committee. "Report of the Budget and Fiscal Affairs Committee," 2000 Draft General Budget for the National Authority. Unpublished document, Palestinian Legislative Council, Ramallah.

———. "Report of the Committee on Education and Social Affairs," 31 March 1998 and 30 December 1999.

Palestinian Society for Protection of Human Rights and the Environment (LAW). "Military and State Security Courts and the Rule of Law in PA-Controlled Areas." May 1999, retrieved 2 December 2002, from www.lawsociety.org/Reports/reports/1999/statesec.html.

———. Independent Judiciary Unit. "Executive Interference in the Judiciary." April 1999, retrieved 2 December 2002, from www.lawsociety.org/Reports/reports/1999/judic.html.

UNESCO-West Asia and Bir Zeit University. "Evaluation of the Role of NGOs in the Occupied Territories and the Opportunities of Networking among Them in the Framework of the Palestinian Authority." E/ESCWA/SD-WOM/1997/WG.1/5, 22 September 1997.

United Nations, Office of the Special Coordinator in the Occupied Territories. "Rule of Law Development in the West Bank and Gaza Strip: Survey and State of the Development Effort." May 1999.

United States Agency for International Development. "Request for Proposal on 'Strengthening the Palestinian Legal Profession under the Rule of Law'." RFP 294–99–013, 1999.

———. "Request for Proposal for Assistance to the Palestinian Legislative Council." RFP 294–99–012, 1999.

World Bank. "West Bank and Gaza Legal Development Project." Report No. PIC4646, 1997.

PERIODICALS

Afaq barlamaniyya (Ramallah), 1999–2002.
Al-ahram (Cairo), 1948–1949.
Al-Ahram Weekly (Cairo), 1998–2002.
Al-ayyam (Ramallah), 1996–2002.
Bayrut (Beirut), 1948–1949.
Ha'artez (Tel Aviv), 1997–2002.
Al-hayah al-jadida (Ramallah), 1996–2002.
Huquq al-nas (Jerusalem), 1999–2001.

Jerusalem Post (Jerusalem), 1994–2002.

Jerusalem Times (Jerusalem), 1996–2002.

Majallat al-dirasat al-filastiniyya (Beirut), 1998–2001.

Majallat al-qanun wa-l-qada' (Gaza), 2000–2001.

Al-majlis al-tashri'i (Ramallah), 1998–2002.

Al-muhandis al-filastini (Jerusalem), 1999–2000.

Al-nahar (Beirut), 1948–1949.

New York Times (New York), 1996–2002.

Palestine Report (Jerusalem), 1996–2002.

Palestinian NGO Project Newsletter (Jerusalem), 1998–2001.

Al-quds (Jerusalem), 1996–2002.

Al-risala (Gaza), 1999–2000.

Al-sharq al-awsat (London), 1996–2002.

Al-waqa'i' al-filastiniyya (Gaza; online version available at http://lawcenter
.birzeit.edu/arabic/pg), 1994–2002.

West Bank and Gaza Update (World Bank publication, Jerusalem), 1998–2001.

BOOKS AND ARTICLES

Abbas, Mahmoud (Abu Mazen). *Through Secret Channels.* Reading, MA: Gar-
net, 1995.

Abu 'Amr, Ziyad. *Al-mujtama' al-madani wa-l-tahawwul al-dimuqrati fi
filastin* (Civil society and democratic transformation in Palestine). Ramallah:
Muwatin Foundation, 1995.

Abu Duhou, Ibtisam. "Schools in Palestine under the Occupation and the Palestinian National Authority." *Palestine-Israel Journal* 3 (Winter 1996): 15–20.

Abu Hunud, Husayn. *Mahakim al-'adl al-'ulya al-filiastiniyya* (The Palestinian
High Courts of Justice). Ramallah: Palestinian Independent Commission for
Citizens' Rights, 1999.

———. *Taqrir hawla niqabat al-muhamiyin al-filastiniyin* (Report on the
Palestinian Lawyers' Syndicate). Ramallah: Palestinian Independent Commission for Citizens' Rights, 2000.

Abu Lughod, Ibrahim, and Hamad Husayn, eds. *Al-ta'lim al-filastini: Ta'rikhan,
waqi'an wa darurat al-mustaqbal* (Palestinian education: Historically, currently, and future needs). Bir Zayt: Bir Zayt University, 1997.

Adwan, Sami. "Schoolbooks in the Making: From Conflict to Peace." *Palestine-
Israel Journal* 7, no. 2 (2001): 57–69.

Arab Thought Forum. *Democratic Formation in Palestine* (annual volume).
Jerusalem: Arab Thought Forum, 1996–2000.

Aruri, Naseer H., and John J. Carroll. "A New Palestinian Charter." *Journal of
Palestine Studies* 23 (Summer 1994): 5–17.

As'ad, Denis. "The Arab Youth [Publishing] House: A Significant Educational
Experiment" (Arabic). *Al-multaqa al-tarbawi,* no. 10 (December 1999).

Aweiss, Salem. "Educating for Peace: Visions and Reality." *Palestine-Israel Journal* 7, no. 2 (2001): 41–45.

Al-Az'ar, Muhammad Khalid. *Hukumut 'umum filastin* (The All-Palestine Government). Cairo: Dar al-shuruq, 1998.

Baaklini, Abdo, Guilain Denoeux, and Robert Springborg. *Legislative Politics in the Arab World: The Resurgence of Democratic Institutions.* Boulder, CO: Lynne Reinner, 1999.

Bar-Tal, Daniel. "The Arab Image in Hebrew School Books." *Palestine-Israel Journal* 7, no. 2 (2001): 5–18.

Basisu, Mu'min, and Wa'il al-Dahduh. "Dualism of Syndicate and Official Positions: Healthy Condition or Symptom of Illness." *Sawt al-watan,* no. 63 (May 2000): 7–11.

Bayat, Asef. "Activism and Social Development in the Middle East." *International Journal of Middle East Studies* 34 (February 2002): 1–28.

Bianchi, Robert. *Unruly Corporatism: Associational Life in Twentieth Century Egypt.* New York: Oxford University Press, 1995.

Bir Zayt University, Development Studies Program. *Human Development Report—Palestine.* Ramallah: Bir Zeit University, 1999.

Bisharat, George E. *Palestinian Lawyers and Israeli Rule: Law and Disorder in the West Bank.* Austin: University of Texas Press, 1989.

———. "Peace and the Political Imperative of Legal Reform in Palestine." *Case Western Reserve Journal of International Law* 31 (1999): 253–92.

Brand, Laurie. *Palestinians in the Arab World: Institution Building and the Search for State.* New York: Columbia University Press, 1988.

Breger, Marshall J., and Shelby R. Quast. "International Commercial Arbitration: A Case Study of the Areas under Control of the Palestinian Authority." *Case Western Reserve Journal of International Law* 32, suppl. (2000): 185–258.

Brown, Nathan J. "Constituting Palestine: The Effort to Write a Basic Law for the Palestinian Authority." *Middle East Journal* 54 (Winter 2000): 25–43.

———. *Constitutions in a Nonconstitutional World: Arab Basic Laws and the Prospects for Accountable Government.* Albany: SUNY Press, 2002.

———. *The Rule of Law in the Arab World: Courts in Egypt and the Gulf.* New York: Cambridge University Press, 1997.

Brynen, Rex. *A Very Political Economy: Peacebuilding and Foreign Aid in the West Bank and Gaza.* Washington, DC: United Institute of Peace Press, 2000.

Carapico, Sheila. *Civil Society in Yemen: The Political Economy of Activism in Modern Arabia.* New York: Cambridge University Press, 1998.

Carey, Roane, ed. *The New Intifada.* London: Verso, 2001.

Carothers, Thomas. *Aiding Democracy Abroad: The Learning Curve.* Washington, DC: Carnegie Endowment for International Peace, 1999.

Chase, Anthony B. Tirado. *The Palestinian Authority Draft Constitution: Possibilities and Realities in the Search for Alternative Models of State Formation.* Jerusalem: Israel/Palestine Center for Research and Information, 1997.

Cheshin, Amir S., Bill Hutman, and Avi Melamed. *Separate and Unequal: The Inside Story of Israeli Rule in East Jerusalem.* Cambridge, MA: Harvard University Press, 1999.

Cotran, Eugene, and Chibli Mallat, eds. *The Arab-Israeli Accords: Legal Perspectives.* London: Kluwer Law International: 1996.

Curriculum Development Center. *Al-manhaj al-filastini al-awwal li-l-ta'lim al-'amm: Al-khitta al-shamila* (A comprehensive plan for the development of the first Palestinian curriculum for general education). Ramallah: CDC, 1996.

Dabbagh, Mustafa Murad. *Biladuna Filastin.* Kafr Qara': Dar al-Huda, 1991.

Dentists Syndicate. *Al-taqrir al-sanawi* (Annual report). Jerusalem: Dentists Syndicate, 1999.

Dewey, John. *Democracy and Education.* New York: Free Press, 1916.

Elster, John, and Rune Slagstad, eds. *Constitutionalism and Democracy.* New York: Cambridge University Press, 1988).

Engineers Syndicate. *Al-taqrir al-sanawi* (Annual report). Jerusalem: Engineers Syndicate, 1999.

Farsoun, Samih K. *Palestine and the Palestinians.* Boulder, CO: Westview Press, 1997.

Fasheh, Munir Jamil. "Is Math in the Classroom Neutral—or Dead." *For the Learning of Mathematics* 17 (June 1997): 24–27.

———. "The Reading Campaign Experience within Palestinian Society: Innovative Strategies for Learning and Building Community." *Harvard Educational Review* 65 (Spring 1995): 66–92.

Al-Fasid, 'Aryan. *Al-bina' al-mu'asasi al-filastini wa-furas al-tahawwul nahwa al-dimuqratiyya* (Palestinian institutional structure and opportunities for transitions to democracy). Nablus: Center for Palestine Research and Studies, 1999.

Firer, Ruth. "Human Rights in History and Civics Textbooks: The Case of Israel." *Curriculum Inquiry* 28 (1998): 195–209.

Foley, Michael W., and Bob Edwards. "Beyond Tocqueville: Civil Society and Social Capital in Comparative Perspective." *American Behavioral Scientist* 42 (September 1998): 5–20.

Fortna, Benjamin C. "Islamic Morality in Late Ottoman 'Secular' Schools." *International Journal of Middle East Studies* 32 (2000): 369–93.

Freire, Paulo. *Pedagogy of Freedom: Ethics, Democracy, and Civic Courage.* Lanham, MD: Rowman and Littlefield, 1998.

Frisch, Hillel. *Countdown to Statehood: Palestinian State Formation in the West Bank and Gaza.* Albany: SUNY Press, 1998.

———. "Modern Absolutist or Neopatriarchal State Building? Customary Law, Extended Families, and the Palestinian Authority." *International Journal of Middle East Studies* 29 (1997): 341–58.

Giacaman, George, and Dag Jorund Lonning, eds. *After Oslo: New Realities, Old Problems.* London: Pluto Press, 1998.

Gutmann, Amy. *Democratic Education.* Princeton, NJ: Princeton University Press, 1999.

Habash, Zaynab. *Tarshid al-manahij al-madrasiyya fi al-daffa al-gharbiyya wa-qita' ghazza* (Guiding the school curricula in the West Bank and the Gaza Strip). Jerusalem: n.p., 1996.

Hall, Peter A. "Social Capital in Britain." *British Journal of Political Science* 29 (1999): 417–61.

Hammami, Rema. "NGOs: The Professionalization of Politics." *Race and Class* 37, no. 2 (1995): 51–63.

——. "Palestinian NGOs since Oslo: From NGO Politics to Social Movements." *Middle East Report*, no. 214 (Spring 2000): 16ff.

Hammami, Rema, and Jamil Hilal. "An Uprising at a Crossroads." *Middle East Report*, no. 219 (Summer 2001): 2ff.

Haniyya, Akram. "Camp David Papers." *Al-ayyam*, 8 August 2000.

Hashweh, Maher E. "Palestinian Science Teachers' Epistemological Beliefs: A Preliminary Survey." *Research in Science Education* 26, no. 1 (1996): 89–102.

Hengstler, Gary A. "First Steps toward Justice." *ABA Journal*, February 1994, pp. 52–61.

Hilal, Jamil, and Majdi al-Maliki. *Institutions of Social Support in the West Bank and the Gaza Strip*. Ramallah: Palestinian Institution for Policy and Economic Research (MAS), 1997.

Hiltermann, Joost R. *Beyond the Intifada: Labor and Women's Movements in the Occupied Territories*. Princeton, NJ: Princeton University Press, 1991.

Hroub, Khaled. *Hamas: Political Thought and Practice*. Washington, DC: Institute for Palestine Studies, 2000.

Israeli, Raphael. "Education, Identity, State Building and the Peace Process: Educating Palestinian Children in the Post-Oslo Era." *Terrorism and Political Violence* 12 (Spring 2000): 79–94.

Jamal, Amal. "State Formation and the Possibilities of Democracy in Palestine." *Majallat al-dirasat al-filastiniyya*, no. 40 (Autumn 1999): 112–35.

Jerusalem Media and Communication Center. *The Palestinian Council*. 2d ed. Jerusalem: JMCC, 1998.

Kalman, Daniel, Ra'ed Abdul Hamid, Mohammed Dahleh, Ayesha Qayyum, and Tobias Nybo Rasmussen. *Commercial Contract Enforcement in the Palestinian Territories*. Commercial Contract Enforcement in the Palestinian Territories Series, no. 5. Jerusalem: Israel/Palestine Center for Research and Information, February 1997.

Kayid, 'Aziz. *Ishkaliyat al-'alaqa bayna al-sultatayn al-tashri'iyya wa-l-tanfiziyya fi al-sulta al-wataniyya al-filastiniyya* (The problematics of the relationship between the executive and legislative branches in the Palestinian National Authority). Ramallah: Palestinian Independent Commission for Citizens' Rights, 2000.

Khalidi, Rashid. *Palestinian Identity: The Construction of Modern National Consciousness*. New York: Columbia University Press, 1997.

Al-Khazarji, 'Abd al-Salam, and Radiya Husayn al-Khazarji. *Al-siyasa al-tarbawiyya fi al-watan al-'arabi* (Educational policy in the Arab world). 'Amman: Dar al-shuruq, 2000.

Kimmerling, Baruch, and Joel S. Migdal. *Palestinians: The Making of a People.* Cambridge, MA: Harvard University Press, 1994.

Kohn, Margaret. "Civic Republicanism versus Social Struggle: A Gramscian Approach to Associationalism in Italy." *Political Power and Social Theory* 13 (1999): 201–35.

Ladadwa, Hasan. "The Palestinian National Authority and Non-Governmental Organizations." *Al-siyasa al-filastiniyya* 6 (Summer 1999): 127–43.

Mahler, Gregory. *Constitutionalism and Palestinian Constitutional Development.* Jerusalem: Palestinian Academic Society for the Study of International Affairs, 1996.

Al-Mawrid. *Palestine and Education: The "Teaching Palestine Project."* Ramallah: Al-Mawrid, 1997.

Ministry of Education. General Administration of Curricula (Palestinian Curriculum Development Center). *First Palestinian Curriculum Plan.* Jerusalem: al-Ma'arif, 1998.

Ministry of Justice, Diwan al-fatwa wa-l-tashri'. *Majmu'at al-tashri'at al-filastiniyya min 'amm 1994 hatta nahayat 'amm 1998* (Collection of Palestinian legislation from 1994 until the end of 1998). Gaza: Ministry of Justice, 2000.

Moughrabi, Fouad. "The Politics of Palestinian Textbooks." *Journal of Palestine Studies* 31 (Autumn 2001): 5–19.

Mu'asassat al-Haqq. *Al-musawwada al-muqtaraha li-mashru' al-qanun al-asasi al-filastini li al-marhala al-intiqaliyya* (The proposed design for the draft Palestinian Basic Law for the interim phase). Ramallah: Mu'asassat al-Haqq, 1996.

Muslih, Muhammad. "Palestinian Civil Society." *Middle East Journal* 47 (1993): 258–74.

Muwatin Foundation, ed. *Ma ba'd al-azma: Al-taghyirat al-bunyawiyya fi al-hayah al-siyasiyya al-filastiniyya, wa-afaq al-'amal* (What is after the crisis: Structural changes in Palestinian political life and horizons of work). Proceedings of the Fourth Annual Conference of the Muwatin Foundation, 22–23 September 1998. Ramallah: Muwatin Foundation, 1999.

Nordbruch, Goetz. *Narrating Palestinian Nationalism: A Study of the New Palestinian Textbooks.* Washington, DC: Middle East Media Research Institute, 2002.

"Not Only at School: Education, Occupation, Activism and Dialogue: A Round-Table Discussion." *Palestine-Israel Journal* 8, no. 2 (2001): 70–84.

Palestinian Association for Cultural Exchange. *PACE Tour Guide of the West Bank and Gaza Strip "Palestine."* Ramallah: PACE, 1999.

Palestinian Centre for Human Rights. *Critique of the Press Law 1995 Issued by the Palestinian Authority.* Gaza: Mansour Press, 1995.

Palestinian Independent Commission for Citizen's Rights. *Annual Report.* Ramallah: PICCR, 1996–2001.

———. *Mashru' al-dustur al-filastini al-mu'aqqat* (The Draft Temporary Palestinian Constitution). Ramallah: PICCR, 2000.

"The Palestinian Journalists Union: Between the Legitimacy of Na'im and the Plan of Nabil and Hisham." *Al-'awda*, no. 255 (July 2000): 12–18.

Pike, Fredrick B., and Thomas Stritch, eds. *The New Corporatism: Social-Political Structures in the Iberian World*. Notre Dame, IN: University of Notre Dame Press, 1974.

Podeh, Elie. *The Arab-Israeli Conflict in Israeli History Textbooks*. Westport, CT: Bergin and Garvey, 2001.

———. "History and Memory in the Israeli Educational System: The Portrayal of the Arab-Israeli Conflict in History Textbooks (1948–2000)." *History and Memory* 12, no. 1 (2000): 65–100.

Portes, Alejandro. "Social Capital: Its Origins and Applications in Modern Sociology." *Annual Review of Sociology* 24 (1998): 1–24.

Posusney, Marsha Pripstein. *Labor and the State in Egypt*. New York: Columbia University Press, 1997.

Putnam, Robert. "Bowling Alone." *Journal of Democracy* 6, no. 1 (1995): 65–78.

———. *Making Democracy Work: Civic Traditions in Modern Italy*. Princeton, NJ: Princeton University Press, 1993.

Qasis, Mudir. *Al-tahawwul al-dimuqrati wa-madaniyyat al-mujtama' fi filastin* (Democratic transformation and civility of society in Palestine). Nablus: Center for Palestinian Research and Studies, 1999.

Rigby, Andrew. *Palestinian Education: The Future Challenge*. Jerusalem: Palestinian Academic Society for the Study of International Affairs, 1995.

Rihan, Ramzi. "The Palestinian Educational Development Plan: Promise for the Future." *Palestine-Israel Journal* 7, no. 2 (2001): 19–33.

Robinson, Glenn E. *Building a Palestinian State*. Bloomington: Indiana University Press, 1997.

———. "The Politics of Legal Reform in Palestine." *Journal of Palestine Studies* 27 (Autumn 1997): 52.

Roy, Sara. "Civil Society in the Gaza Strip: Obstacles to Social Reconstruction." In *Civil Society in the Middle East*, ed. Augustus Richard Norton. Leiden, the Netherlands: E. J. Brill, 1996.

———. "The Transformation of Islamic NGOs in Palestine," *Middle East Report*, no. 214 (Spring 2000): 24–26.

Rubin, Barry. *The Transformation of Palestinian Politics: from Revolution to State-Building*. Cambridge, MA: Harvard University Press, 1999.

Sabah, Rif'at. "The Curriculum and the Political System." *Al-multaqa al-tarbawi*, no. 9 (October 1999).

Sahliyeh, Emile. *In Search of Leadership: West Bank Politics since 1967*. Washington, DC: Brookings Institution, 1988.

Salim, Walid. *Al-munazzamat al-mujtama'iyya al-tatawwu'iyya wa-l-sulta al-wataniyya al-filastiniyya: nahwa 'alaqa takamuliyya* (Voluntary societal organizations and the Palestinian National Authority: Toward a complementary relationship). Jerusalem: Muntada abhath al-siyasiyya al-ijtima'iyya wa-l-iqtisadiyya, 1999.

Savir, Uri. *The Process*. New York: Random House, 1998.

Sayigh, Yezid. *Armed Struggle and the Search for State: The Palestinian National Movement, 1949–1993.* New York: Oxford University Press, 1999.

Schenker, David. *Palestinian Democracy and Governance: An Appraisal of the Legislative Council.* Washington, DC: Washington Institute for Near East Policy, 2000.

Shabib, Samih. *Hukumut 'umum filastin* (The All-Palestine Government). Jerusalem: Al-bayadir, 1988.

Shadid, Mohammed K., and Caroline Qutteneh, eds. *Palestinian Government/NGO Relations: Cooperation and Partnership.* Proceedings of the international conference organized by the Welfare Association Consortium in consultation with the World Bank, February 2000. Al-Ram: Welfare Association Consortium, 2001.

Shehadeh, Raja. *From Occupation to Interim Accords: Israel and the Palestinian Territories.* London: Kluwer Law International, 1997.

———. *Occupier's Law: Israel and the West Bank.* Washington, DC: Institute for Palestine Studies, 1988.

Shemesh, Moshe. *The Palestinian Entity 1959–1974: Arab Politics and the PLO.* 2d rev. ed. London: Frank Cass, 1996.

Shikaki [al-Shiqaqi], Khalil, ed. *Al-intikhabat wa-l-nizam al-siyasi al-filastini* (Elections and the Palestinian political system). Nablus: Center for Palestine Research and Studies, 1995.

Shlaim, Avi. *The Politics of Partition: King Abdullah, the Zionists and Palestine 1921–1951.* New York: Columbia University Press, 1990.

———. "The Rise and Fall of the All-Palestine Government in Gaza." *Journal of Palestine Studies* 20 (Autumn 1990): 37–53.

Shu'aybi, 'Azmi. "A Window on the Workings of the PA: An Inside View." *Journal of Palestine Studies* 30 (Autumn 2000): 88–97.

Sisalem, Judge Mazen, Judge Ishak Muhanna, and Legal Advisor Sulieman El Dahdoh. *The Laws of Palestine.* Vol. 27. Gaza: Matabi' mansur, 1996.

Sovich, Nina. "Palestinian Trade Unions." *Journal of Palestine Studies* 29 (Summer 2000): 69–74.

Stahv, Arieh. *Israel and a Palestinian State: Zero-Sum Game.* Shaarei Tikva: Ariel Center for Policy Research, 2001.

Starrett, Gregory. *Putting Islam to Work: Education, Politics, and the Transformation of Faith.* Berkeley: University of California Press, 1998.

Stepan, Alfred. *The State and Society: Peru in Comparative Perspective.* Princeton, NJ: Princeton University Press, 1978.

Strawson, John. "Palestine's Basic Law: Constituting New Identities through Liberating Legal Culture." *Loyala of Los Angeles International and Comparative Law Journal* 20 (March 1998): 411–32.

Al-Subani, Salah. "The Problems of Arab Education and the Conditions of Maintenance and Progress in the Third Millennium." *Al-multaqa al-tarbawi,* no. 10 (December 1999).

Sullivan, Denis J. "NGOs in Palestine: Agents of Development and Foundation of Civil Society." *Journal of Palestine Studies* 25 (Spring 1996): 93–100.

Tibawi, Abdul Latif. *Arab Education in Mandatory Palestine: A Study of Three Decades of British Administration.* London: Luzac, 1956.

Trouillot, Michel-Rolph. *Silencing the Past: Power and the Production of History.* Boston: Beacon, 1995.

Velloso de Santisteban, Agustin. "Palestinian Education: A National Education against All Odds." *International Journal of Educational Development* 22 (2002): 145–54.

———. "Peace and Human Rights Education in the Middle East: Comparing Jewish and Palestinian Experiences." *International Review of Education* 44 (1998): 357–78.

———. "Women, Society and Education in Palestine." *International Review of Education* 42 (1996): 524–30.

Al-Wahidi, Fathi 'Abd al-Nabi. *Al-tatawwurat al-dusturiyya fi filastin 1917– 1995* (Constitutional developments in Palestine 1917–1995). Gaza: Matabi' al-hay'a al-khayriyya bi-qita' ghaza, 1996.

Welchman, Lynn. *Beyond the Code: Muslim Family Law and the Shar'i Judiciary in the Palestinian West Bank.* The Hague, the Netherlands: Kluwer Law International, 2000.

"Why Is the Role of the Tax Authorities Absent." *Palestinian Human Rights Monitor* 2 (August 1998), entire issue.

Wing, Adrien Katherine. *Democracy, Constitutionalism and the Future State of Palestine.* Jerusalem: Palestinian Academic Society for the Study of International Affairs, 1994.

———. "Legal Decision-Making during the Palestinian *Intifada:* Embryonic Self-Rule." *Yale Journal of International Law* 18, no. 1 (1993): 95–153.

World Bank, Social and Economic Development Group, Middle East and North Africa Region. *West Bank and Gaza: Strengthening Public Sector Management.* Jerusalem: World Bank West Bank and Gaza Resident Mission, 1999.

Index

Compositor:	BookMatters
Text:	10/13 Aldus
Display:	Aldus
Printer and Binder:	Maple-Vail Manufacturing Group